My Neighbor, My Enemy

Justice and Community in the Aft

M000204140

My Neighbor, My Enemy tackles a crucial and highly topical issue – how do countries rebuild after ethnic cleansing and genocide? And what role do trials and tribunals play in social reconstruction and reconciliation? By talking with people in Rwanda and the former Yugoslavia and carrying out extensive surveys, the authors explore what people think about their past and the future. Their conclusions controversially suggest that international or local trials may have little relevance to reconciliation in post-war countries. Communities understand justice far more broadly than it is defined by the international community, and the relationship of trauma to a desire for trials is not clear-cut. The authors offer an ecological model of social reconstruction and conclude that coordinated multi-systemic strategies must be implemented if social repair is to occur. Finally, the authors suggest that while trials are essential to combat impunity and punish the guilty, their strengths and limitations must be acknowledged.

ERIC STOVER is Director of the Human Rights Center at the University of California, Berkeley, USA, and Adjunct Professor in the School of Public Health there. He has served as an "Expert on Mission" to the International Criminal Tribunal for the former Yugoslavia and the International Criminal Tribunal for Rwanda. In the early 1990s, he conducted research on the medical and social consequences of land mines in Cambodia and other post-war countries. His findings helped launch the International Campaign to Ban Land Mines, which received the Nobel Prize in 1997. His books include *The Breaking of Bodies and Minds: Torture, psychiatric abuse, and the health professions* (with Elena O. Nightingale); *Witnesses from the Grave: The stories bones tell* (with Christopher Joyce); *The Graves: Srebrenica and Vukovar* (with photographer Gilles Peress); and *A Village Destroyed: May 14, 1999, war crimes in Kosovo* (with Fred Abrahams and Gilles Peress). His forthcoming book, *The Witnesses: War crimes and the promise of justice in The Hague*, will be published in 2005.

HARVEY WEINSTEIN is Associate Director of the Human Rights Center at the University of California, Berkeley, USA and Clinical Professor in the School of Public Health there. He has worked in the countries of the former Yugoslavia for more than five years, primarily in Bosnia and Herzegovina and in Croatia, and was co-principal investigator on a MacArthur Foundation project titled "Communities in Crisis: Justice, Accountability, and Social Reconstruction in Rwanda and the former Yugoslavia" and a Hewlett Foundation grant titled "Intrastate Conflict and Social Reconstruction." He was also principal investigator and directed the Forced Migration and Health Project funded by the Refugee Health Program of the State of California. Currently, he is co-principal investigator on a project funded by the United States Institute of Peace to assist in the development of a curriculum in history for Rwanda.

My Neighbor, My Enemy

Justice and Community in the Aftermath of Mass Atrocity

Edited by

Eric Stover

and

Harvey M. Weinstein

CAMBRIDGE
UNIVERSITY PRESS

CAMBRIDGE UNIVERSITY PRESS
Cambridge, New York, Melbourne, Madrid, Cape Town, Singapore, São Paulo

Cambridge University Press
The Edinburgh Building, Cambridge CB2 2RU, UK

Published in the United States of America by Cambridge University Press, New York

www.cambridge.org
Information on this title: www.cambridge.org/9780521834957

© Cambridge University Press 2004

First published 2004

A catalogue record for this publication is available from the British Library

Library of Congress Cataloguing in Publication data
My neighbor, my enemy : justice and community in the aftermath of mass
atrocity / edited by Eric Stover, Harvey M. Weinstein.
    p.   cm.
Includes bibliographical references and index.
ISBN 0-521-83495-3 (hb) – ISBN 0-521-54264-2 (pb)
1. War crimes.   2. Genocide.   3. International criminal courts.   4. Reparations.
5. Retribution.   6. Social justice.   I. Stover, Eric.   II. Weinstein, Harvey M.
K5301.M9   2004
341.6′9 – dc22   2004047285

ISBN-13 978-0-521-83495-7 hardback
ISBN-10 0-521-83495-3 hardback

ISBN-13 978-0-521-54264-7 paperback
ISBN-10 0-521-54264-2 paperback

Transferred to digital printing 2006

For the families of the missing

Contents

Part II   Social reconstruction and justice

Part III   Survivors and justice

Contents

Contributors

Editors

ERIC STOVER is Director of the Human Rights Center and Adjunct Professor of Public Health at the University of California, Berkeley, USA.

HARVEY M. WEINSTEIN is Associate Director of the Human Rights Center and Clinical Professor of Public Health at the University of California, Berkeley, USA.

Contributors

DINO ABAZOVIC is a member of the Faculty of Political Sciences and Director of the Center for Human Rights at the University of Sarajevo, Bosnia and Herzegovina.

DEAN AJDUKOVIC is Professor of Psychology and Director of the Postgraduate Psychology Program at the University of Zagreb, Croatia.

MIKLOS BIRO is Professor of Psychology at the University of Novi Sad, Serbia and Montenegro.

PAMELA BLOTNER is Assistant Professor of Visual and Performing Arts at the University of San Francisco, USA.

DINKA CORKALO is Assistant Professor in the Department of Psychology, Faculty of Philosophy at the University of Zagreb, Croatia.

ALISON DES FORGES is a consultant to Human Rights Watch, New York, USA.

DINO DJIPA is Research Director of Prism Research in Sarajevo, Bosnia and Herzegovina.

ARIEL DORFMAN is a Chilean expatriate writer whose books have been translated into more than forty languages and whose plays have been performed in over one hundred countries. His latest book is *Other Septembers, Many Americas: Selected provocations, 1980–2004.*

LAUREL E. FLETCHER is Acting Clinical Professor of Law in the Boalt Hall School of Law and Director of the Globalization Project of the Human Rights Center at the University of California, Berkeley, USA.

SARAH WARSHAUER FREEDMAN is Professor of Education and Research Fellow of the Human Rights Center at the University of California, Berkeley, USA.

JODI HALPERN is Assistant Professor of Bioethics in the School of Public Health at the University of California, Berkeley, USA.

DÉO KAMBANDA is Professor of Education at the National University of Rwanda, Butare, Rwanda.

URUSARO ALICE KAREKEZI is Director of Justice Projects for the Center for Conflict Management at the National University of Rwanda, Butare, Rwanda.

BRONWYN LEEBAW is Assistant Professor in the Department of Political Science at the University of California, Riverside, USA.

NAOMI LEVY is a graduate student in the Department of Political Science at the University of California, Berkeley, USA.

TIMOTHY LONGMAN is Associate Professor of Political Science and African Studies at Vassar College and a Research Fellow of the Human Rights Center at the University of California, Berkeley, USA.

PETAR MILIN is an assistant in the Department of Psychology at the University of Novi Sad, Serbia and Montenegro and Research Fellow, Laboratory for Experimental Psychology at the University of Belgrade, Serbia and Montenegro.

INNOCENT MUGISHA is a lecturer in the Faculty of Education and Director of the Distance Learning Program at the National University of Rwanda, Butare, Rwanda.

EVODE MUKAMA is a lecturer in the Faculty of Education at the National University of Rwanda, Butare, Rwanda.

IMMACULÉE MUKASHEMA is a lecturer in the Faculty of Education at the National University of Rwanda, Butare, Rwanda.

JEAN MUTABARUKA is a lecturer in the Faculty of Education at the National University of Rwanda, Butare, Rwanda.

BETH MUTAMBA is a researcher with the Center for Conflict Management at the National University of Rwanda, Butare, Rwanda.

ALPHONSE NSHIMIYIMANA is a researcher with the Center for Conflict Management at the National University of Rwanda, Butare, Rwanda.

PHUONG PHAM is Adjunct Assistant Professor at the Payson Center for International Development and Technology Transfer at Tulane University and a Research Fellow of the Human Rights Center at the University of California, Berkeley, USA.

NAOMI ROHT-ARRIAZA is Professor of Law at the University of California, Hastings College of Law.

THÉONÈSTE RUTAGENGWA is National Coordinator for the Center for Non-Violent Communication in Kigali, Rwanda.

BETH LEWIS SAMUELSON is a graduate student in the School of Education at the University of California, Berkeley, USA.

RACHEL SHIGEKANE is Senior Program Officer at the Human Rights Center and a lecturer in Peace and Conflict Studies at the University of California, Berkeley, USA.

Foreword

It is comforting to watch the trials afterwards.

After the bombs and the machetes. After the war of brother against brother and neighbor against neighbor. After the torn bodies and the burnt-out villages. After the faces of grief and the faces of those who are so beyond grief they cannot speak and cannot cry. After the children blown up or hacked to death. After the rubble and the fires.

After all of this and too much more, so much more than anybody should be expected to witness, let alone live, yes, it is comforting to hear about, see from time to time, the trial of the man, some of the men, held responsible for any one of these outrages against humanity.

Comforting to watch the accusations, the evidence, the witnesses.

Justice is being done, punishment will be meted out, a balance has been redressed to a universe gone mad.

I am one of those who has been consoled and moved by those exemplary rituals of the law during which violators of human rights are forced to accept and obey the rules, the very civilized behavior, they have so pitilessly flouted. I have been among those who proclaim how urgent and necessary such proceedings are for the well-being of our wounded humanity. Important for the victims, instructive for the victimizers, healthy for the community that was damaged, and deeply satisfying for those who watched from far away and could do nothing to stop the horror. I have celebrated tribunals and judgments and truth commissions, the attempts to establish an official version of what went wrong so that everyone in a divided nation can agree on the past and perhaps come together to build a different future. I have felt that it is imperative, after a trauma, to find ways to decipher and perhaps tell the story embedded in the pain. I have murmured to myself the hope that this is how humans mitigate fear, purge its effects, send a warning message to other perpetrators that they will not be safe.

And yet, crucial as these efforts to deal with the unspeakable may be, beneath my enthusiasm there has always lurked the suspicion that such performances of justice are not enough, that they do not answer by themselves, cannot answer, the really hard questions left in the wake of destructive conflicts inside nations.

It is the singular merit of this book that it asks those questions, does not flinch from examining up close, brutally up close, the aftermath of genocide and ethnic cleansing, the dilemmas that flood societies that have gone through those chaotic and ravaging events. How can survivors coexist with those who killed their most beloved kin? How can trust be restored to a community where our best friends betrayed us, refused us refuge? Can the needs of an international war crimes tribunal for forensic evidence be reconciled with the needs of families desperate to identify and bury their butchered relatives? Indeed, can reconciliation ever be truly achieved in a society where the perpetrators deny their crimes? How is the damage repaired? Through money? Through symbolic and moral acts? Person by person or collectively? By providing education to the children of the dead or providing resources to the group that was injured? And can the ruined fabric that once held a society together ever be sewn together again? How to change the obdurate conditions that led to these conflicts in the first place, how to insure they will not recur? Can a different form of common identity, forged in tolerance and not in detestation, be built by former enemies who are now again neighbors? Are there ways in which trials and legal proceedings can be understood not as the ultimate solution to every horror that consumed that landscape but as part of an on-going quest for long-term peace? Are there alternative systems of restorative justice which more efficiently integrate the vast and still-fearful community, taking into account the customs and traditions of its own members? And how to involve the victims in the definition of what is to be done, how to avoid imposing upon them formulas from afar and from above, how to make them true participants in the rebuilding of their lives?

The many authors of this book, in their essays, reports and meditations, dare to put these and many other searing questions to the inhabitants of the former Yugoslavia and Rwanda, two of the most maliciously infamous zones of our contemporary humanity, and rather than offer gratifying answers, afford readers a view from the ground up, allowing the people who continue to live in those places to express the extraordinary complexity of lives that are strangely hopeful in the midst of so much desolation. As attention is lavished in this book on the survivors of mass terror themselves, we come to realize that it is in the shadow of the demolished mosques and the blighted fields that the predicament of these men and women can be truly illuminated, and that if these inhabitants of terror and faith are interrogated from the ground up with respect and open-mindedness, then creative responses – artistic, judicial, economic, educational, psychological – can be discovered and implemented.

From the ground up. If I have repeated these words, there is a reason, and more than one. First, because those words hint at the basic philosophy that has animated the editors of this remarkable volume – the confidence that those who have been most hurt have the best idea of how to mend the destruction, and that it is on the ground therefore, in the field so to speak, that solutions, no matter how tentative, will be found. But also, *from the ground up*, because I sense a secret pattern weaving in and out of the voices collected in *My Neighbor, My Enemy*. Not only the certainty that we can learn from the extreme savagery inflicted by one human on another, one group on another. Not only the conviction that we must not lie about the immense difficulties arising from those atrocities – we cannot let ourselves grow comfortable with easy explanations that do not address the underlying causes of the catastrophe. But *from the ground up* primarily because the protagonists of this tragedy – and those who possess the courage to listen to them – understand that there is no other way of honoring the murdered dead, those who are under the ground, below the earth, demanding to be heard, demanding that we build a world where people die peacefully in their beds when their time has come, surrounded by the friends of yesterday and the neighbors of tomorrow. The fundamental message of this book: there is no other way of bringing back the dead than to tell the truth.

ARIEL DORFMAN

Acknowledgments

This book is the culmination of more than four years of investigation by ten research teams in four countries, speaking six different languages and representing nine different disciplines. It is a tribute to our researchers that each one put ethnic and cultural differences aside and made concerted efforts to reach beyond the narrowness of a disciplinary perspective in order to engage with colleagues to understand the complexities of social reconstruction. As editors, we would be remiss if we did not recognize the enormous strength it took to surmount these barriers. Despite the uneasy ups and downs of negotiations and compromise, our researchers are a model of collaboration across cultures and conflict.

To all of our participants who survived ethnic cleansing and genocide and who live daily with the consequences of the horrors, we express our gratitude for the countless hours you gave us, for the time you spent in answering survey questions, for putting up at times with our naiveté, and for helping us understand the resilience of the human spirit. Thank you for sharing your stories, your tears, your hopes, and your courage.

These studies could not have been completed without the generous financial and moral support of the John D. and Catherine T. MacArthur Foundation and Mary Page, the director of the Program on Global Challenges; the William and Flora Hewlett Foundation and Melanie Greenberg, then director of the Conflict Resolution Program; and The Sandler Family Foundation which has supported the vision and direction of the Human Rights Center at the University of California, Berkeley from its inception. A grant from the Rockefeller Foundation allowed us to bring all the researchers and relevant others together in July, 2003 at the Villa Serbelloni in Bellagio, Italy for a conference titled "Justice in the Balance: Rebuilding Communities in the Aftermath of Genocide and Ethnic Cleansing." The chapters for this book were developed at that meeting. The Villa provided the perfect setting to stand back and assess what we had learned while Lake Como and the gardens provided the calming atmosphere that promoted collaboration and intellectual risk-taking. We are grateful to all of those who attended, challenged our thinking and encouraged us to keep to the task of making sense of the mounds of data we had collected.

There are so many individuals and organizations whose efforts made our work easier and who led us in critical directions of inquiry. In the Balkans, none of our work could have been done without the generous assistance of Senada Kreso. Her understanding of cultures and her incredible abilities at organizing, interpreting, and translating, along with her ability to pick up the phone and arrange meetings with just about anyone, made her an unbelievable asset to the work. Her passion for Bosnia sensitized us in ways that have deeply affected our understanding of that beautiful land. Laurie Lola Vollen, Doug Ford and their colleagues at Physicians for Human Rights in Tuzla helped us to begin our journey in 1998 and provided administrative support (and a place to stay) as we made our way around the Balkans. In Sarajevo, we were helped immensely by the staff of the Center for Human Rights at the University of Sarajevo, and especially its former director, Ermin Sarajlija and librarian Sasa Madacki. The Center's Aida Mehicevic was a fabulous "fixer." To Mirsada Muzur at Prism Research, thanks for encouraging Dino to become involved and for tempering Bosnian irony with Australian sunshine. In Zagreb, the Society for Psychological Assistance staff was unfailingly helpful in hosting meetings and arranging contacts in Zagreb and in Vukovar. We have been very fortunate to work with several organizations that facilitated the research, including the Humanitarian Center for Integration and Tolerance in Novi Sad, Serbia, and Montenegro; the Center for Peace, Non-Violence, and Human Rights in Osjiek, Croatia, and especially Branka Kaselj and Snjezana Kovacevic; the Helsinki Committee and the Human Rights Center in Mostar, Bosnia and Herzegovina; the SMRRI Group in Serbia and Montenegro; and the Helsinki Committee in Belgrade. In each country, we found organizations that were committed to peace and human rights and who fearlessly pursued that objective despite pressure to conform to nationalist ideologies. We feel honored to have had the opportunity to work with them.

So many people smoothed our way as fixers and interpreters. The stories they heard were not always easy or pleasant but they carried out their roles with courage and dignity. Among these, we especially thank Biserka Belicza from Zagreb whose effusive humor should be bottled and sold, and Lejla Efendic from Sarajevo who took on additional duties as a researcher when she re-interviewed several witnesses who had testified at the International Criminal Tribunal for the former Yugoslavia (ICTY).

Finally, we thank those in official positions in international institutions who consented not only to meet but also who expressed their opinions directly and honestly. From the Office of the High Representative (OHR) in Bosnia and Herzegovina, we received support and information that provided context and a larger dimension to what we heard in the towns and villages we visited. We especially thank Peter Bach, then (OHR) legal advisor, and the political offices at the OHR office in Mostar for their briefings and perspectives. At the ICTY, we received overwhelming support from current and present staff of the Office of the Registrar and the Office of the Prosecutor. We especially thank Graham Blewitt, Danielle Cailloux, David Tolbert, Wendy Lobwein, Monica Naslund, Caitriona Palmer, Brenda Hollis, Alexandra Milenovic, Daniel Saxton, John Hocking, Liam McDowell, Sam Muller (now with the International Criminal Court), and Refik Hodzic. Judge Nevanthem Pillay, formerly with the International Criminal Tribunal for Rwanda (ICTR) and now a judge with the International Criminal Court, was always thoughtful in answering our questions and open to discussing our critiques of the ICTR's work.

In Rwanda, we were fortunate to work with the Center for Conflict Management at the National University of Rwanda in Butare. Through their endeavors and contacts, we were able to meet with many in government who were helpful in granting permissions for our work and in facilitating its progress. We want to single out Beatrice Buyoga whose administrative capacities made dealing with bureaucracy so much easier. The faculty at the Center assisted us greatly in finding student-assistants to help us carry out the survey and to translate the questionnaire results. The Faculty of Education at the University also was instrumental in selecting students to work with us in the school interviews and focus groups and assisting in the translations of the transcripts. Our work could not have been completed without the support of the Ministry of Education, which allowed us to work in the schools and to ask hard questions.

At home, little would have been accomplished without the untiring efforts of Liza Jimenez, the administrative assistant for the Human Rights Center. With her unfailing sense of humor and "can-do" attitude, she has made it possible for us to work across countries with minimal hassle. She has injected a little "salsa" into our daily lives and has made the University procedures much easier to deal with. We owe her a great deal. Our Berkeley colleague David Cohen and our friend and editor Jonathan Cobb provided thoughtful comments on some of the chapter drafts.

The writing of the book was supported by writing residencies awarded to Eric Stover by the Ucross Foundation and the East–West Center and to Harvey Weinstein by Blue Mountain Center. It is a luxury indeed to have the unfettered opportunity to write, especially when surrounded by the beauty of flowers, woods, blue sky, water, and stimulating colleagues.

So many people have contributed to the studies and to this book. Professor Marita Eastmond of the University of Gothenburg, Sweden whose anthropological eye helped broaden our understanding of communities, and scores of graduate students whose critical perspectives always make one pause, especially Bronwyn Leebaw, now at the University of California, Riverside; Emily Shaw; Naomi Levy; Beth Lewis Samuelson; Damir Arnaut; Daska Babcock-Halaholo; Kerstin Carlson; Anne Mahle; Edisa Pestek; Gordan Radic; Tamara Todorovic; Hannah Scholl; Khanh Bui; and Suman Paranjape. As Victor Peskin has worked on his dissertation about the *ad hoc* international tribunals, he provided us with astute insights, as did Craig Pollak as he developed his master's thesis on the burial of the dead from Srebrenica. We are grateful to Gilles Peress, whose powerful photographs grace the cover of this book. We also want to thank Ariel Dorfman, whose experiences with the terror of repression in Chile color the moving preface that he contributed.

Our wives gave us unflagging support in the preparation of this book. Rhona Weinstein has been a colleague, advisor, and muse to Harvey throughout this project. Her sage and sometimes pithy comments have kept him on track, and her unwavering belief in him has always been a great source of strength. The long distance, and his sometimes being in unknown places, has been stressful, but she has always seen the larger picture, and in that sense has contributed much to the project and to the people of these countries. During this project, when Harvey became gravely ill, it was Rhona who kept him going. This book is in great part a reflection of her determination to hang on, to not let go, and there are not enough expressions of gratitude that can encompass his appreciation. Eric and his wife, Pamela Blotner, also a contributor to this volume, conducted research together in Croatia and Bosnia and Herzegovina. Pamela's wit, intelligence, and love of people and art make her a wonderful traveling partner, friend, and soulmate.

Finally, the editors must acknowledge each other. Put two strong-willed perfectionists together and that can spell disaster. That has not been the case here. The collaboration has been fruitful, occasionally joyful, and a privilege for both of us. Hopefully, this book, the product of four years of intense discussion and debate, will translate into policies and practices that make the rebuilding of divided societies a more thoughtful and deliberate process.

Introduction: conflict, justice and reclamation

Harvey M. Weinstein and Eric Stover

Truth is the cornerstone of the rule of law, and it will point towards individuals, not peoples, as perpetrators of war crimes. And it is only the truth that can cleanse the ethnic and religious hatreds and begin the healing process.[1]

Madeleine Albright, 1993

While there are various means to achieve an historic record of abuses after a war, the most authoritative rendering is possible only through the crucible of a trial that accords full due process.[2]

Michael Scharf, 1997

We are forced to live together . . . Because of that we are all pretending to be nice and to love each other. But, it is known that I hate them and they hate me. It will be like that forever.

Mostar resident, 2001

I don't understand this word "reconciliation." I can't reconcile with people, even if they are in prison . . . If a person comes to ask my forgiveness, I will pardon him after he has resuscitated the members of my family that he killed!

Genocide survivor, Rwanda, 2002[3]

Since the fall of the Berlin Wall in 1989, the world has experienced an upsurge of intrastate wars rooted in ethnic and religious differences. From the highlands of Central America to the islands of South-east Asia, whole societies have been torn asunder by violence so virulent and fierce it has turned community against community, neighbor against neighbor. Nowhere has the physical and human toll of such violence been more evident than in Rwanda and the former Yugoslavia, where more than a million people died in the early 1990s. These wars were not clashes between cultures or civilizations, nor were they the result of ancient ethnic or tribal hatreds. They were fabricated wars, forged out of the raw opportunism of political extremists who inculcated and exploited paranoia and nationalist myths to stoke the fires of ethnic hatred.

When the fighting ended, these countries faced the daunting task of rebuilding their blasted homes and institutions and mending a social fabric frayed by distrust and betrayal. In a human landscape disfigured by loss and mass displacement, they have had to decide how to confront the past: how much should they remember? How much should they forget? What should they teach their children? What should they do with the leaders who orchestrated the violence? The underlings who carried it out? The bystanders who did nothing to stop it? Where should they draw the boundary between enough justice to destroy impunity and punishment so harsh that it becomes revenge? And how can they reunite communities where thousands of people have been raped, maimed, and tortured by their fellow citizens? In this book, we look at how former enemies learn to live together.

In the summer of 1998, we spent a month traveling to villages and towns throughout Bosnia and Herzegovina, Croatia, and Serbia. Although it was not our first visit to the region, it was the first in which we asked people to tell us about justice. We spoke with refugees and politicians, teachers and priests, writers and laborers, the young and the old. The encounter we remember most vividly was a meeting one warm evening with a group of Bosnian Muslim women on a hilltop outside of Sarajevo who surrounded us and demanded "the truth" about their lost men. The women were refugees from Srebrenica, the enclave seized in July 1995 by Serb forces, who killed over 7,000 boys and men. When we asked the women what justice meant to them, an elderly woman, dressed in the traditional Muslim dimjie with a kerchief over her head, stood up and grabbed a young boy standing by her side. Placing him in front of her, she demanded: "Do you see this boy? He is my grandson. And I will teach him to remember and to hate. I will teach him to kill!" For this sad woman, justice meant vengeance – direct and unhampered by due process or morality.[4]

This book examines the lives of members of different ethnic groups in Rwanda and the former Yugoslavia who were once neighbors and who, in only a matter of weeks and months, turned against one another. Now at peace, they must get on with their lives, find jobs, send their children to school, rebuild their homes, shop, and if possible, find meaning in a ruined landscape where those who tortured and those who survived see each other daily or are asked to work together to achieve a life worth living. It is an excruciatingly difficult transition to make, given the bitterness and loss that is wrapped like a shroud around their lives. Some will make it, but many – like the elderly refugee outside of Sarajevo – never will.

In 1999, with the assistance of the John D. and Catherine T. MacArthur Foundation, we assembled a multi-disciplinary team of researchers – psychologists, epidemiologists, lawyers, anthropologists, public health specialists, political scientists, educators, artists, and human rights activists – from five countries to find an answer to one of the most pressing moral dilemmas of our time: how do societies torn apart by war and mass atrocity pursue justice for past crimes and, at the same time, rebuild their shattered communities? We particularly wanted to know what effect the international community's preoccupation with criminal trials of suspected war criminals was having on the process of rebuilding after war. Was punishment important? For whom? Did it matter if trials took place in another country? Did they help or hinder reconciliation?

For four years, our research teams traveled throughout Bosnia and Herzegovina, Croatia, Yugoslavia, and Rwanda meeting and interviewing a wide range of people. Some researchers spent months at a time observing daily life as it unfolded in selected cities and towns. Others observed exhumations of mass graves and then tracked down and interviewed witnesses who had testified against the alleged perpetrators. Still others administered population-based surveys to explore attitudes about justice, identity, collective memory, and reconciliation. In particular, we wanted to look at the associations of justice, accountability, social reconstruction, and reconciliation. We were interested in the multiple levels of societal repair – from individual to family to neighborhood to society.

Our field research was informed by a wide range of theories, including those developed by anthropologists and social psychologists to understand identity, ethnicity, and culture, and by political scientists and legal scholars to examine nationhood, the rule of law, and principles of justice. The relationship of geography and environment to memories of home raised questions about attachment to place and the collective memory of geographically rooted groups. The psychology literature provided us with a framework for understanding group processes and the nature of stereotyping. The study of trauma opened up the debate on the expression of traumatic experience, reflecting discipline disagreements on the importance of biology or social suffering.

Many assumptions about the effects that justice has on individuals and societies have gone unexamined and unchallenged far too long. Some of the most frequently repeated, and those that we perhaps most wish to be true, are due careful scrutiny. Consider this statement by Antonio Cassese, an Italian jurist and the first president of the International Criminal Tribunal for the former Yugoslavia (ICTY), who summarizes the theoretical arguments of how justice reportedly contributes to peace and reconciliation:

Trials establish individual responsibility over collective assignation of guilt, i.e., they establish that not all Germans were responsible for the Holocaust, nor all Turks for the Armenian genocide, nor all Serbs, Muslims, Croats, or Hutus, but individual perpetrators – although, of course, there may be a great number of perpetrators; justice dissipates the call for revenge, because when the Court metes out to the perpetrator his just deserts, then the victims' calls for retribution are met; by dint of dispensation of justice, victims are prepared to be reconciled with their erstwhile tormentors, because they know that the latter have now paid for their crimes; a fully reliable record is established of atrocities so that future generations can remember and be made fully cognizant of what happened.

Like Cassese, many other astute writers and political leaders have extolled the virtues of criminal trials but seldom are such assertions grounded in empirical data. Indeed, a primary weakness of writings on justice in the aftermath of war and political violence is the paucity of objective evidence to substantiate claims about how well criminal trials or other accountability mechanisms achieve the goals ascribed to them. Jennifer Widner, in her analysis of the role African courts have played in post-conflict transitions, writes: "Because the language of the rule of law is now so much in vogue, observers too often tend to assume that courts can easily promote peace and democratic change in post-conflict regimes, without looking closely at the grounds for such optimism."[5]

By imposing a "legal order" on what is often the irrational (power-driven though it may be), the international community seeks to use criminal trials to contain and to deter violence, and to discover the truth about specific events and to punish those responsible. Yet truth, in the eyes of those most affected by collective violence, often lies not in the facts themselves but in their moral interpretation, and how facts are interpreted is often manipulated and distorted by the very people who initiated the violence.

Justice, like beauty, is in the eye of the beholder and can be interpreted in a variety of ways. For many of our informants, justice meant having a job and an income; for others, it was returning to the home they had lost; still others saw justice as the ability to forget the past and move on with their lives. For some, justice was testifying at a trial against the soldiers and paramilitaries who had murdered their families and destroyed their homes. For others, justice had to be exacted by revenge. Some said justice could only take place once their neighbors looked them directly in the eye and apologized for betraying them. Still others said it was finally learning the truth about their missing relatives and receiving their bodies for proper burial.

Over the past ten years, a number of international observers have drawn a close connection between the process of justice (defined here as trials) and reconciliation (a term loosely used to mean people re-forming prior connections, both instrumental and affective, across ethnic, racial, or religious lines). This inferred relationship has come to occupy center stage in post-conflict societies. Diplomats in particular have supported the assumption that reconciliation is a legitimate objective of international criminal trials. Reconciliation, we suggest, is a murky concept with multiple meanings. Although reconciliation is a lofty and worthwhile goal, our studies have led us to question the validity of this vague assertion, the narrow perspectives of each of the disciplines that study or work with societies after mass violence, and the lack of attention to the opinions and wishes of those whose lives have been so destroyed. Perhaps Mahmood Mamdani best expresses the limitations of a narrow perspective when he writes: "To manage the tension between reconciliation and justice creatively, do we not need to think of reconciliation as not just political but also social, and justice as not just criminal and individual, but also social and systemic?"[6]

In our view, the pursuit of criminal justice, as important as it is, should not be held up as some kind of panacea for righting past wrongs or as a "magic bullet" for "healing" victims and war-torn societies. Nor should it be viewed as an isolated ahistoric phenomenon removed from the realm of politics and everyday life. "To show that justice has its practical and ideological limitations is not to slight it," writes the American legal scholar Judith Sklar. "The entire aim is rather to account for the difficulties which the morality of justice faces in a morally pluralistic world and to help it recognize its real place in it – not above the political world but in its very midst."[7]

This book has three goals. The first is to move debates and discussions about justice beyond mere wishful thinking, to unhinge it from high-blown assumptions and assertions, and to ground it in the everyday life of those who should be most affected by it. The second is to demonstrate through empirical studies how ethnic hatred, whether newly created through the manipulation of power or a legacy of colonial oppression, can affect the rebuilding of post-war countries. The final goal is to provide the international community with an ecological model of social reconstruction that can be applied to assist post-conflict societies where ethnic identification was a salient dimension of the violence. Here we define social reconstruction as a process that reaffirms and develops a society and its institutions based on shared values and human rights. It is a process that includes a broad range of programmatic interventions, such as security, freedom of movement, access to accurate and unbiased information, the rule of law, justice, education for democracy, economic development, cross-ethnic engagement, that work together and at multiple levels of society – the individual, neighborhood, community, and state – to address the factors that led to the conflict.

This book adds to the existing literature on transitional justice and social violence[8] an empirical perspective of justice and social reconstruction gained from multiple methods of inquiry applied in the field. We believe that the use of qualitative field methods in conjunction with well-controlled quantitative survey research can illuminate the experiences of survivors of war and mass atrocity and offer new ways of responding to social suffering.

Given the immensity of the task before us, we had to make choices about what to examine in our research. Some of those decisions were based on the expertise in the research group; others arose from the realization that we had neither the time nor funds to study all of the factors that were contributing to social reconstruction in Rwanda and the former Yugoslavia. By employing extensive field research, we were able to observe the nuances of physical and social change – the building of a new school, the return of refugees. Yet we were unable to examine the role of religion[9] or women or pop culture in the process of societal transformation. While we looked at attitudes and beliefs about justice, ethnicity, reconciliation, and poverty, we did not study the media in detail or the contribution of economic factors.[10] Such limitations notwithstanding, we feel our findings will help illuminate the interplay of justice and social processes in communities still divided by war and mass atrocity.

Communities in crisis

Ashutosh Varshney, in his thoughtful examination of ethnic violence in India, suggests that "until we study ethnic peace, we will not be able to have a good theory of ethnic conflict . . . Despite rising violence, many communities in the world still manage their interethnic tensions without taking violent steps."[11] Unlike Vashney's, our field studies did not include communities of ethnic peace, largely because the totality of the genocide and collective violence in Rwanda and the former Yugoslavia left few communities directly or indirectly untouched by the violence.

In the former Yugoslavia we focused on three towns: Mostar, Vukovar, and Prijedor. We chose these towns because they had experienced intense physical destruction and widespread ethnic conflict and expulsions, and because ethnic tensions continued to color the lives of the inhabitants. The reader may find a detailed account of the specific events that engulfed each of these towns in several sources.[12]

Mostar

Mostar is a city of some 70,000 people settled along the banks of the Neretva River in western Bosnia and Herzegovina. At the narrowest point of the river, the Turkish Sultan built a bridge – a single broad span of white cobalt – in the late 1500s. Known as the Stari Most, the bridge – and Mostar itself – came to symbolize the very idea of Bosnia and Herzegovina, a place where Catholic, Orthodox, and Muslim peoples lived distinctively, but together in mutual tolerance. Prior to the latest war, the population of the city was ethnically diverse – 31 percent were Croat (Roman Catholic); 33 percent Bosniak (Muslim); 17 percent Serb; and 19 percent were described as "others."[13]

In the early 1990s, two ethnic wars devastated Mostar, resulting in the deaths of about 4,000 people. The first war pitted the Bosnian Serbs against the allied Bosnian Croats and Muslims, and lasted until 1992. It was followed by another, even more destructive assault by the Croats on the Muslim community, which lasted three years and forced thousands of Bosniaks to flee to other parts of the country. On November 9, 1993 (four years to the day after the tearing down of the Berlin Wall), a missile launched from a Bosnian Croat artillery position ripped through the arch of the Stari Most, and it collapsed into the river below.[14] Today, Mostar is a divided city – Bosniaks live mostly on the east bank of the Neretva River, with some close to its west bank; Croats live primarily on the west bank; and Serbs on the outskirts. Eighty percent of city residents are newcomers. A number of former residents have moved back to the city, but many have chosen to sell their flats and homes to those from the other side rather than live among neighbors who are not of their own ethnicity. Although there is movement back and forth across the river, it is primarily one-way, Bosniaks crossing to the Croat side to shop. It is a city where the two largest national groups rarely socialize, workplaces are minimally integrated, and schools are separated by ethnicity. In microcosm, Mostar epitomizes the difficulties faced by the Federation of Bosnia and Herzegovina, where a Croat minority, aroused by nationalist and even criminal leaders, agitates for a separate Croat entity, similar to that granted the Bosnian Serbs within the state of Bosnia and Herzegovina. A focus on Mostar allowed us to study the evolving relationships of the Bosniak and Croat communities who, while formally in a Federation, remain separated and at cold peace.

Vukovar

Vukovar is a city of 32,000 people nestled on the banks of the Danube in the eastern Slavonia region of Croatia along its border with what is now Serbia and Montenegro. Prior to the onset of the war in 1991, the countryside surrounding Vukovar was a rich farming and wine-producing region, part of the northern "bread basket" of Yugoslavia. The most important industrial plant in Vukovar was the Borovo Company, a rubber and shoe factory, employing some 20,000 people. By the 1980s, Vukovar had developed into one of the economic centers of eastern Croatia.

On June 25, 1991, both Croatia and Slovenia declared their independence from Yugoslavia, unilaterally making the first changes to the international borders of Europe since Yalta. On the same day, the Yugoslav federal government ordered the Yugoslav People's Army (JNA), whose officers were mostly Serbian, to subdue the breakaway republics. Vukovar, lying eighty miles north-west of the Serbian capital of Belgrade, took the brunt of the attack. During the ensuing three-month siege, some 700,000 missiles rained down on the city, killing and displacing thousands of people and causing the destruction of most of the city's buildings. While nationalist Croat provocations had made life very difficult for the Serb population in the months leading up to the war, few were prepared for the virtually total destruction of the city.

Serbs controlled Vukovar from 1991 until 1995. Most of the native Croat population fled or was expelled, leaving the Serbs to rebuild their churches and their homes. The signing of the Erdut Agreement in 1995 allowed the United Nations to offer protection under a transitional administration. The United Nations Transitional Administration for Eastern Slavonia, or UNTAES, under the American general Jacques Klein, paved the way for the return of Croat residents while assuring the preservation of minority rights and protections for the Serb population.

As Croats returned to Vukovar and the surrounding villages in the late 1990s, the nationalist government led by the Croatian Democratic Union, or HDZ, assisted them in rebuilding their homes. However, little was done until 2003 to repair the city's inner core. Many residents, Serb and Croat alike, believe the HDZ made a deliberate decision to leave the signs of war untouched as a punishment to the Serb community. Meanwhile, shortly before his departure General Klein brokered a controversial agreement that led to the segregation of schools and classrooms based on ethnicity. Over the past ten years, a mass exodus of Serbs to Yugoslavia or third countries, along with Croat returns, has shifted the pre-war demographics. Today, some 50,000 Serbs out of a pre-war population of some 70,000 remain in Vukovar and the surrounding region, with about 12,000 in the town itself.[15] The situation in Vukovar afforded us the opportunity to look at changing relationships between Serbs and Croats.

Prijedor

Prijedor is a city of 35,000 people, rising to well over 100,000 with the surrounding villages, in the north-west of the Republika Srpska, the Bosnian Serb entity of the state of Bosnia and Herzegovina. Like Vukovar, Prijedor was prosperous before the war, boasting a mix of mining, industry, and agriculture. Prior to the war, the city's population was roughly

42.5 percent Serb and 44 percent Muslim and, as elsewhere in the former Yugoslavia, interethnic relations had been harmonious since the end of the Second World War.

In April 1992, Bosnian Serb residents took control of Prijedor and the surrounding villages, destroying the Catholic church and all of the mosques. Over the next two months, arrests, torture, rape, and expulsions became the fate of the city's Muslim population. British journalist Ed Vuillamy made Prijedor famous in the summer of 1992 when he discovered the existence of Serb-run concentration camps in Omarska, Keraterm, and Trnopolje. Images of starving men behind barbed wire mobilized world opinion against the Serbs and ensured Prijedor's place in the annals of inhumanity. Although there are no reliable data, a local non-governmental group estimates that 3,227 people died in the city and surrounding countryside during the war. By early 2000, 650 sets of remains had been recovered from mass graves around the city, of which 464 were eventually identified.[16] Between 2001 and 2003, some 15,000 Bosniaks returned to the Prijedor area, primarily to the village of Kozarac, where new homes, mosques, and shops have emerged, allowing us the opportunity to examine the relationships between Bosniaks and their Serb neighbors.

Rwandan communities

The demography of Rwanda, which is one of the most densely populated countries in the world, is vastly different from the former Yugoslavia. A small, very hilly country, most of its population works in agriculture. There are two principal ethnic groups, the Hutu (about 84 percent) and Tutsi (15 percent), who live intermixed on hillsides and in villages and towns throughout the country.[17] A third group, the Twa, comprise about 1 percent of the population and were originally forest dwellers, now primarily laborers. During the genocide, they were both victims and killers.

Our studies in Rwanda focused on four communes selected to represent geographic diversity, level of urbanization, varied experiences of the genocide and subsequent war, and degree of interaction with the International Criminal Tribunal for Rwanda. At the time of the genocide, 1994, Rwanda was divided into 11 prefectures, and each prefecture was divided into communes, making a total of 154 communes throughout the country. The communes were further divided into sectors and then into cells.

The four communes under study were **Ngoma** (commonly known as Butare town) and **Mabanza**, located in the south and central regions, respectively, of Rwanda; and **Buyoga** and **Mutura** in the north and north-east region, respectively. Ngoma is the second largest urban center in Rwanda, while the other three communes are rural. In Mutura, massacres of Tutsi began in 1991. Ngoma has a large number of Tutsi survivors, as well as a large number of Tutsi returnees who had been exiled for years in Uganda, Congo, and Burundi. The genocide occurred in only three out of thirteen sectors of Buyoga, since the other sectors were in the Rwandan Patriotic Front's (RPF) zone of control; however, there are numerous reports of civilian massacres by the RPF during the war. Buyoga, Ngoma, and Mutura all experienced revenge killings following the RPF's rise to power, and they saw large numbers of people flee across the border, where many of them experienced illness, violence, and other traumatic experiences. In contrast, Mabanza was under French control for several months, which resulted in a lower incidence of Tutsi deaths and revenge attacks by the RPF and its supporters.

While we cannot generalize our findings to the whole of Bosnia and Herzegovina, Croatia and Rwanda, our cities were chosen to represent the diversity of exposure to violence as well as the difficulties inherent in reclaiming life while dwelling among former enemies.

The pursuit of justice

"Justice," wrote the American legal scholar Edmond N. Cahn in 1949, "is unwilling to be captured in a formula. Nevertheless, it somehow remains a word of magic evocations."[18] The notion that justice somehow possesses "miracle-working powers" is not a new idea, nor is it one that is likely to go away. The human desire to "right wrongs" is as old as recorded history. We pursue justice because we wish to be vindicated and, more importantly, to have what we have lost returned. Yet it seldom is.

The pursuit of justice after war and political violence can take many forms, including criminal and civil trials, truth commissions, lustration programs, and reparations. Some nations, like Brazil, have tried to forget crimes by passing amnesty laws.[19] Others, like Chile and South Africa, have created truth commissions to gather the stories of victims, the truth about what happened, and at whose hands. Still others, like the former states of Czechoslovakia and East Germany, have introduced lustration programs to purge abusive officials from positions in government and the private sector. A few countries, like Argentina, have placed their leaders on trial for past human rights abuses. Most of the time, successor governments create these mechanisms without seeking the opinions of the populace.

Failing to intervene to stop the carnage in Rwanda and the former Yugoslavia, the international community established the International

Criminal Tribunal for the former Yugoslavia in 1993, and a similar tribunal for Rwanda the following year (see Chapters 1 and 2). The architects of these tribunals placed primary responsibility for the prosecution of war crimes in the hands of international authorities that would be free from local influences. In effect, they created institutions that by definition were geographically and, to a certain extent, linguistically remote from the regions of conflict. Kept apart from the vicissitudes of post-war reconstruction, the Rwandan and Yugoslav Tribunals were to conduct trials of suspected war criminals based on the presentation and debate of facts pertaining to specific events.

The reality is that these tribunals have limited mandates and resources, restricted powers of subpoena, and no authority to make arrests. With such limitations, they can never come close to meting out justice to all war criminals, let alone serve as a beacon for reconciliation in countries torn apart by ethnic cleansing and genocide. Even the idea that they will individualize guilt and thus differentiate between the criminal leaders of a nation and their deceived populations is fraught with ambiguity.

Individuals need some form of justice to acknowledge the wrongs done to them, just as societies need it to establish boundaries by which individuals can be held responsible for their behavior toward their fellow citizens. Yet, as we argue in this volume, justice is most effective when it works in consort with other processes of social reconstruction and reflects the needs and wishes of those most affected by violence. This is perhaps the greatest lesson that has emerged since the international community began its experiment in international criminal justice over ten years ago.

How then do we connect institutional mechanisms of justice with the myriad processes of social repair as communities emerge from the ashes of genocide and other forms of mass violence?

Contrary to the admonitions of many observers that the logic of horrific events can never be understood, or that the analysis of them somehow demeans the memory of the dead, it is imperative that we understand the psychological, social, and political processes that push individuals and societies beyond the pale. To do this, we must apply theories of social identity, social categorization, stereotyping, collective memory, and community to map the dynamics of societal breakdown. As we have examined these issues across countries and cultures, we have become aware that while some universal mechanisms underlie the phenomena of ethnic violence, we also must pay particular attention to context. Most importantly, the views and opinions of those most affected by mass violence must be solicited and given serious consideration. Finally, instead of paying lip-service to the limitations of justice, we must recognize its strengths by clarifying what its objectives are, and, in operational terms, how it can be grounded in local traditions and practices, and thus contribute to the rebuilding of community life. Armed with such knowledge, we can then decide what form(s) justice should take.

Justice is a process – often a contentious one – that can evolve into different forms over time. Consider Rwanda, where national and international trials have been accompanied by an alternative system – gacaca – a form of community justice where prisoners are brought before lay judges elected from the village populations and trained briefly in a system of dispensing justice (see Chapters 2 and 3). Undoubtedly, these community-based courts will be judged against the standards of international criminal justice and are likely to be found wanting. Yet what is lost in these appraisals is what Drumbl[20] calls "globulitarianism" – the phenomenon by which justice is defined primarily by western conceptions of trial process, whether it be common law or civil law, and not by what may be more reasonable for a specific culture or tradition.

Ultimately, for many in the international community, what appears critical is not what makes sense to the people most affected by mass violence but whether the form of justice mirrors that of the developed world – what Mani[21] calls "legal justice." This, in turn, raises the question of the objectives of criminal trials: are they primarily to extend the jurisdiction of international humanitarian law and forge new legal ground? Or to punish and separate individuals from the collective that initiated the violence? Or are they intended to deter future violence? Ultimately, to determine the contribution that justice can make to survivors of mass violence, we need to understand what justice means to them and acknowledge what trials can reasonably be expected to accomplish. Perhaps the deputy minister of justice in Rwanda was right when he said, "What you end up with in a post-genocide society is not justice . . . perhaps we should think of another word for it."[22]

Finally, we must dispense with the trope that justice can be "healing."[23] Madeleine Albright and others have alluded to trials and truth commissions almost as a form of national therapy for individuals and societies beset with the psychiatric syndrome of post-traumatic stress disorder. Trials as national ritual or performance[24] are conceptualized as critical to reconciliation because the catharsis of truth-telling, along with the inscribing of national memories, will lead to a decrease in suffering and a renewed commitment to reconciliation. At the individual level, analogies to the psychodynamic model of psychotherapy suggest that emotional abreaction (that is, the reliving of traumatic events with the release of pent-up emotions) will somehow "heal" survivors.[25] They will leave the witness stand and, in the best evangelical model, walk unaided to a new and better life. An implicit assumption is made that, after a sufficient number of survivors have testified, a collective release will occur and that a society will be healed.

The idea of cathartic treatment dates to the mid-1890s when investigators discovered that symptoms of hysteria, a vaguely defined and highly controversial disorder at best, "could be alleviated when the traumatic memories, as well as the intense feelings that accompanied them, were recovered and put into words."[26] Today, psychotherapists take a critical view of the compelling fantasy of a fast, cathartic cure. Some note that an "injudicious catharsis," even in the safety of a therapeutic session, let alone a public trial, may have profoundly negative effects. They also caution against premature catharsis and indicate that a context must be established in which overwhelming memories can be contained and explored over time. While catharsis may have a short-term benefit for some, healing is a long-term process that involves significantly more than emotional abreaction and testifying at a trial.

The complexities of reconciliation

Reconciliation – like justice – is an ambiguous term. Yet it is often touted as a desirable and a necessary step toward a lasting peace. The *Oxford English Dictionary* defines "reconcile" as "to bring (a person) again into friendly relations . . . after an estrangement . . . To bring back into concord, to reunite (persons or things) in harmony."[27] In the context of war and political violence, reconciliation has been described as "developing a mutual conciliatory accommodation between antagonistic or formerly antagonistic persons or groups."[28] True reconciliation, writes Tina Rosenberg, is achieved when the citizens of a country, including those who have in the past illegally abused power, "are ready to live a normal life in a normal country."[29]

Yet what do such abstract notions as "mutual conciliatory accommodation" or "a normal life in a normal country" mean to a woman who has been held captive and repeatedly raped by members of a paramilitary gang who were once her classmates? Or to a child who watched his neighbors slaughter his entire family? And what does it take for such survivors to reach a point where they are willing or even able to consider reconciliation?

It is often argued that trials and truth commissions promote reconciliation by forcing societies emerging from war or periods of political violence to "come to terms" with the past, achieve "closure" and stability, and rebuild a new system of governance based on democratic principles.[30] Truth commissions, it is said, work toward these ends through the process of "restorative justice," which is defined as societal healing of damages resulting from past crimes. Restorative justice focuses on victims and perpetrators and tries to restore their dignity not through recrimination but by "mediation and dialogue" so as "to generate the space for expressions of approbation, remorse, and pardon, as well as the resolution of conflicts."[31] The best-known example of the restorative approach has been the work of the South African Truth and Reconciliation Commission, which over a period of five years held public hearings where both victims and perpetrators told horrific details of past crimes.

Proponents of criminal trials believe prosecutions promote reconciliation through the process of "retributive justice." The retributive approach views justice as largely a means of *taming* vengeance (but not necessarily *excising* it) by transferring the responsibility for apportioning blame and punishment from victims to a court that acts according to the rule of law. Retributive justice, it is said, promotes reconciliation by holding *individuals* accountable for past crimes, not entire groups or communities, and thus reducing the desire to exact revenge against entire groups. By establishing individual guilt in the immediate aftermath of war and ethnic cleansing, it is theorized that retributive justice helps dispel the notion of collective blame for war crimes and acts of genocide.

This somewhat simplistic but attractive concept of justice illustrates the intense need of humanity to seek parsimonious explanations for complex phenomena. Although the rule of law can lend order to anarchy or chaos through the establishment of norms that regulate behavior, it does not necessarily provide all of the critical components that are needed to promote reconciliation. This is because international law and its institutions are not designed to focus on the social and psychological processes that guide how people form attachments in groups and communities. The law cannot, nor should it, determine what the elements of trust are that help individuals and communities build social networks that may lead to "harmony." Nor should it try to overcome the power of ethnic or other identifications. The law has neither the knowledge nor the tools to take on such complex processes.

Social reconstruction and reclamation

During the course of our research, we frequently asked ourselves whether the term "reconciliation," fraught as it is with religious overtones and overused as a way of promoting concepts of justice, actually hindered our understanding of the mechanisms of social repair in post-war countries. In the end, we decided that the terms "social reconstruction," defined earlier, and "reclamation" better captured these processes. Funk and Wagnall's *New Standard Dictionary* of the English Language (1938) defines reclamation as "The act or process of reclaiming in any sense; restoration, as to ownership, cultivation, or a moral life." *The Oxford English Dictionary* (1961) offers three definitions: the action of calling or bringing back from wrongdoing; the action of reclaiming from barbarism; and the making (of land) fit for cultivation. Contained in these definitions – the rejection of wrongdoing, the restoration of ownership (in its broadest sense), and the making the land safe for cultivation – lie the strategies for social reconstruction.

In the following chapters, most authors opted to use the more common terminology of "reconciliation." As editors, we have accepted this designation but have chosen in this introductory essay to reframe the concept by introducing the notion of "reclamation" as the most appropriate description of the processes of post-war social repair as we have seen them unfold. Although we have no empirically validated view of what the process of reclamation may involve, we suggest that it must incorporate the elements of identity, culture, memory, and history.

In the 1950s, the psychologist Erik Erikson[32] conceptualized individual identity as the enduring sense of self as seen by others and oneself over a lifetime. His work was path-breaking in that identity was defined in a social context. Since then, social psychologists have expanded Erikson's concept to embrace and theorize about social identity, the processes by which groups form, and how individuals within these groups interact with one another. Muzafer Sherif[33] noted, for example, that patterns of competition and collaboration might be explained by examining how group members share resources.[34] The relationship between group processes and individual identity became the focus of research with the elaboration of social identity theory.

In effect, social identity theory postulates that each of us has a core identity and a social identity, what Henri Tajfel[35] defines as "that part of the individual's self-concept which derives from his knowledge of his membership of a social group (or groups) together with the value and emotional significance attached to that membership." Through interactions with others, we develop an understanding, a schema, of where we belong, a process of categorization that provides meaning. John Turner has termed this "self-categorization theory." A final critical component lies in the process of social comparison to affirm positive self-concept. Tajfel, in a series of experiments, demonstrated the phenomena of in-group favoritism and out-group hostility. By identifying within a social group, we tend to see our group in a favorable light (and, consequently, ourselves), while other groups are seen as inferior. Turner and his colleagues[36] have suggested this is the basic element of ethnocentrism. One very critical consequence of this process is that people, once identified with a group, always choose to increase their economic gain in relation to the out-group rather than choosing a greater absolute benefit that would also reduce the relative gap between the groups.[37] Implicit in these experiments is the notion that community-building can only take place once disparate groups find an alternative identity that unites them, so that the benefits of collaboration outweigh those of competitive advantage.

Although it is not the purpose of this book to search for explanations of why multi-ethnic societies descend into collective violence, it is critical to look at those factors that may overcome difference and lead to reconciliation. For example, Stuart Kaufman[38] focuses on the myths and symbols that help to define ethnicity. Building on the earlier work of Murray Edelman[39] and Anthony Smith,[40] he describes the "myth-symbol complex," a "web of myths and related symbols that collectively define what it means to be a [member of specific group]." Kaufman suggests that ethnic violence arises when a constellation of three factors operate – myths that justify war, fear of annihilation, and opportunity for action. His thinking is similar to that of David Horowitz, who in his book *The Deadly Ethnic Riot*[41] suggests that four factors contribute to the initiation of such a riot – a hostile relationship between these groups ("myth-symbol"), a response to events that mobilize action ("opportunity"), justification (a combination of the first two or "annihilation"), and an assessment that impunity is possible. If these are the mechanisms that trigger ethnic cleansing or genocide, how can they be countered in the processes of reconciliation, and where does justice play its part?

Yugoslav Communist leaders under Tito were well aware of the dangers of myth-symbol complexes. As anthropologist Jack Eller writes,[42] Tito's slogan of "brotherhood and unity" was designed to counter the schisms of the earlier attempts at unification by instituting change based on a well-developed ideology. He quotes Slovenian Communist Edward Kardelj:

The growth of universal culture depends on the consciousness of a universal community or the common interests of all peoples of all languages. And that consciousness will develop parallel with the development of the means of production with the new forms of the social division of labor, with the progress of socialist societal relations . . . we are also speaking of the amalgamation of nations in a universal community.

And yet it did not work. Aleksandr Pavkovic[43] points out that no common national identity encompassing a majority of the population ever emerged in the former Yugoslavia. Is it possible then to find some commonality that will promote the collaboration of diverse groups toward a common goal?

Mark Ross[44] describes the phenomena of psychocultural interpretations and dramas that underlie ethnic conflict. Through an analysis of parades in Ulster, he avers that a deeper understanding of how to approach the resolution of these conflicts is possible. Joanne Nagel, in a discussion of ethnicity and culture, emphasizes that ethnicity is not static, that it is "fluid, situational, volitional and dynamic."[45] "Ethnicity," she writes, "is the product of actions undertaken by ethnic groups as they shape and reshape their self-definition and culture; however, ethnicity is also constructed by external social, economic, and political processes and actors as they shape and reshape ethnic categories and definitions." This suggests a need to think broadly about society-building, and to recognize that legal interventions, while important in their own right, play only a part in reconciliation if one of the goals is to prevent the recurrence of mass violence.

Such considerations lead us to question whether there can be reclamation or promotion of a unifying identity without a historical fiction or myth that is adhered to across groups. Can such a myth emerge out of the ashes of genocide? If the answer is yes, can it be incorporated into state-building, and if so, who generates the myth? John Gillis[46] writes:

the notion of identity depends on the idea of memory, and vice versa. The core meaning of any individual or group identity, namely a sense of sameness over time and space, is sustained by remembering; and what is remembered is defined by the assumed identity. That identities and memories change over time tends to be obscured by the fact that we too often refer to both as if they had the status of material objects – memory as something that is to be retrieved; identity as something that can be lost as well as found . . . memories and identities are not fixed things, but representations or constructions of reality, subjective rather than objective phenomena.

While Gillis is correct about the possibility of shifts in identity, some aspects of identity such as race (even if mixed race), parental origin, place of birth, or childhood experience are immutable. What might be amenable to such shifts is the construct of social identity – to which group do you belong? Where are your loyalties? Whom do you despise? If social identities can be changed, perhaps under the influence of an overarching set of beliefs, they might be harnessed in the process of reclamation.

Robert Putnam writes in his seminal book *Bowling Alone*:[47] "[I]t is important to ask how the positive consequences of social capital – mutual support, cooperation, trust, institutional effectiveness – can be maximized and the negative manifestations – sectarianism, ethnocentrism, corruption – minimized." Putnam refers to two kinds of social capital as critical to the development of a healthy community – "bridging social capital" which focuses across groups and which may "generate broader identities and reciprocity" and "bonding social capital" that focuses on building solidarity within groups.

And so, at a group level, reconciliation involves the reconfiguring of identity, the revisiting of prior social roles, the search for common identifications, agreement about unifying memories if not myths, and the development of collaborative relationships that allow for difference. At the individual level, reconciliation may mean personal reconnection with friends and acquaintances from a former life – a reconnection that raises questions about trust, forgiveness, and attachments in a very intimate way. Societal development necessitates the construction of networks that promote collaboration across social groups. Our task then is to determine whether judicial processes enhance or detract from reclamation, or whether they are even relevant. Further, we ask how the pursuit of justice, more broadly defined, might contribute to this end.

The ecological paradigm of social reconstruction

Much of the thinking about community-rebuilding in post-war societies is devoid of a research framework grounded in the social and behavioral sciences. The ecological paradigm that underlies our research examines the complex interactions that societies manifest while searching for stability and peace over time. The paradigm emerges from the studies of developmental psychologist Urie Bronfenbrenner[48] and community psychologists Seymour Sarason[49] and James Kelly,[50] among others. They argue that strategic interventions or planned change in any one part of a system affect all parts in reverberating pathways. Thus, legal interventions have economic consequences; conflict resolution exercises affect the health status of communities; educational reforms have implications for democratic decision-making.

We would add that a basic tenet of social reconstruction or reclamation is the need for post-war communities to define and take ownership of the processes of justice and reconciliation. Johan Galtung[51] challenges us to consider how this may occur:

That there is a selfish, competitive strain in individuals and nations alike, and that this may express itself in the direct violence released through offensive weaponry and violence . . . all this we know. But under other conditions the opposite comes out, altruism rather than egotism, cooperation rather than conflict and competition. Our task is to understand those conditions.

In other words, a certain degree of conflict arising from class, ethnicity, age, and racial differences exists in all diverse communities. And so the real issue is not one of conflict resolution but of conflict management, particularly at the community level. Yet this notion is rarely articulated in global studies of mass violence. For example, although the 1997 Carnegie Commission Report[52] on "Preventing Deadly Conflict" focuses on diplomatic and multi-lateral interventions, the opinions and beliefs of the people affected most by mass violence are nowhere to be found. The IDEA handbook[53] does a better job at considering the multiple options for bringing various societal groups to the table but does not directly address the question of on-going community involvement.

Laurie Nathan of the Center for Conflict Resolution at the University of Cape Town challenges this macro-level approach to prevention. He notes that approaches that rely on "dispute resolution" may lead to a fragile peace but, in doing so, they fail to make basic structural changes that are essential to long-term peace-building, such as the protection of human rights and the promotion of tolerance and pluralism.[54] Nathan argues that the international community often exaggerates its ability to contribute to stability and a durable peace:

Peacemaking and peace building are not sustainable unless their form and content are shaped by local actors. While individuals and groups locked in conflict are obviously concerned about physical and economic security, they also crave respect, acknowledgment, and affirmation. They want to be involved in decisions which affect their lives, and they resent being treated as the object of some other body's plans.[55]

The concept of local initiative grows out of theory developed in several fields, such as social and community psychology, where empowerment theory has emerged as a critical area of inquiry. Empowerment (an admittedly overused term) is defined as "an intentional, ongoing process centered in the local community, involving mutual respect, critical reflection, caring and group participation, through which people lacking an equal share of valued resources gain greater access to and control over those resources."[56] The key words are participation, control, and critical reflection; analysis and intervention occur at the individual, organizational, and community levels. Public health research examines the contribution of social support, social networks, and control[57] to the well-being and health of communities. From the field of education, Paolo Friere's concept of "conscientization" of the poor in Latin America led to a process of action research that engaged communities in a critical analysis of the causes of their powerlessness and poverty. Adopted by social scientists around the world, participatory action research brings outside researchers to communities where they join with local participants to ask questions, discover answers, and make changes that benefit their lives.[58] Everyone becomes a learner; control of the research is shared; there is a commitment to constructive action leading to self-efficacy and empowerment.[59] From the field of economics, recent conceptions of social capital provide additional insights into the contributions of trust and community cohesion to the well-being of societies.[60] Finally, Kimberly Maynard[61] combines an individual and community perspective in her hypothesized five phases of psychosocial recovery from civil war: safety, communalization and bereavement, trust, personal and social morality, and democratic discourse.

An ecological approach to social change considers all the players and social institutions. Action is taken when the outline of the field is clear and the ramifications of any step for other components of the system can be anticipated. By working at all levels, ownership can be claimed widely and the impetus for change is shared. These issues are even more critical in post-conflict societies where external interventions, such as trials or development schemes or democratization, may be perceived as being imposed by outsiders and not of intrinsic worth.

Organization of the book

The book's contributors applied a wide range of research methods to the study of justice and social reconstruction in Rwanda and the former Yugoslavia. Qualitative approaches included the use of focus groups, key informant interviews, ethnographic studies of conflicted communities, and archival analysis. Quantitative approaches included random, house-to-house surveys to examine, among other things, attitudinal questions about beliefs in justice, trials, ethnic differences, and social repair. While the research teams asked similar questions in both Rwanda and the former Yugoslavia, they were sensitive and responsive to cultural and language differences. In some cases, standardized scales were used to assess the complex relationship between psychosocial stressors and beliefs in reconciliation. Finally, a variety of empirical methods were used at both the population and individual level to explore the nature of betrayal and empathy in determining an individual's commitment to social reconstruction.

The book is divided into three parts. Part 1 examines the legal structures that dispense justice – international tribunals and courts, domestic courts, and alternative domestic legal processes. The authors in Part 1 suggest that judicial mechanisms (be they the traditional ones or new locally constructed alternatives) contribute far less to the social reconstruction of post-conflict societies than was previously assumed. Part 2 explores how communities in Rwanda and the former Yugoslavia view the effects of war and mass violence, see their former enemies, and have used schools to solidify old social identities or create new ones. The authors suggest that community ownership and beliefs in a larger conception of justice can be synthesized to build identities based not on hate but on tolerance. However, before conflicted communities can build a coherent sense of the past they must recognize the futility of violence and acknowledge the role that perpetrators, victims, and bystanders played in it. The authors also suggest that the creation of what Rajeev Bhargava[62] calls a "minimally decent society" is possible after war and mass atrocity. Finally, Part 3 examines the interpersonal effects of war on survivors, and the individual and social barriers that hinder reconciliation. It also explores how individuals in divided communities can overcome their sense of betrayal and loss of trust and, over time, develop an empathic understanding of the pain and loss suffered by former friends and neighbors from the opposing group. This book is intended to help bridge the gap between theory and practice, bring a new empirical perspective to the study of social violence and transitional justice in post-war settings, and broaden both the definition and operational aspects of justice so as to ground it in the daily lives of survivors and their communities. Taken together, the chapters of this volume illustrate the difficulties of rebuilding post-war societies. They also suggest that we must move beyond formulaic approaches like "democratization" and "tribunals" and "truth commissions" and "conflict resolution" if we are to help bring about real social reconstruction and reclamation. Instead, we must develop interventions that focus on multiple levels of a society, attend to the psychological and social aspects of the law, and engage survivors of mass violence as active agents – and not merely auxiliaries – in the processes of social reconstruction after war and mass atrocity.

NOTES

1. Madeleine Albright (1993). Quoted in Payam Akhavan, "Justice in The Hague, Peace in the Former Yugoslavia? A Commentary on the United Nations War Crimes Tribunal." *Human Rights Quarterly* 20 (1998).
2. Michael P. Scharf (1997). Quoted in Mark A. Drumbl, "Punishment, Postgenocide: From Guilt to Shame to Civis in Rwanda." *New York University Law Review* 75 (2000): 12–90.
3. Some quotations in this volume translated from local languages have been edited for grammar and clarity.
4. Eric Stover and Gilles Peress, *The Graves: Srebrenica and Vukovar* (Zurich: SCALO, 2001).
5. Jennifer Widner, "Courts and Democracy in Postconflict Transitions: A Social Scientist's Perspective on the African Case," *American Journal of International Law* 95:1 (2001): 64–75.

6. Mahmood Mamdani, "When Does Reconciliation Turn into a Denial of Justice?" In A. Samatav, ed. *Sam Molutshungu Memorial Lectures* (Pretoria: HSRC Publishers, 1998), 1–22.

7. Judith H. Sklar, *Legalism* (Cambridge, Mass.: Harvard University Press, 1964), 122–123.

8. On transitional justice, see Neil Kritz, ed. *Transitional Justice: How Emerging Democracies Reckon with Former Regimes*, vols. I–III (Washington, D.C.: United States Institute of Peace Press, 1995), Naomi Roht-Arriaza, ed. *Impunity and Human Rights in International Law and Practice* (New York: Oxford University Press, 1995), Gary Jonathan Bass, *Stay the Hand of Vengeance: The Politics of War Crimes Tribunals* (Princeton, N.J.: Princeton University Press, 2001), Priscilla B. Hayner, *Unspeakable Truths. Confronting State Terror and Atrocity. How Truth Commissions Around the World are Challenging the Past and Shaping the Future* (New York: Routledge, 2001). On memory, see Benedict Anderson, *Imagined Communities: Reflections on the Origins and Spread of Nationalism* (London: Verso, 1983), Paul Connerton, *How Societies Remember* (Cambridge: Cambridge University Press, 1989), Maurice Halbwachs, *On Collective Memory* (Chicago: University of Chicago Press, 1992). On social psychology, see Henri Tajfel, *Human Groups and Social Categories* (Cambridge: Cambridge University Press, 1981), Henri Tajfel, ed. *Social Identity and Intergroup Relations* (Cambridge: Cambridge University Press, 1982), Russell Spears et al., *The Social Psychology of Stereotyping and Group Life* (Oxford: Blackwell Publishers Ltd, 1997). On reconciliation, see John Paul Lederach, *Building Peace: Sustainable Reconciliation in Divided Societies* (Washington, D.C.: United States Institute of Peace Press, 1997) and Andrew Rigby, *Justice and Reconciliation: After the Violence* (Boulder: Lynne Rienner Publishers Inc., 2001).

9. Michael A. Sells, *The Bridge Betrayed: Religion and Genocide in Bosnia* (Berkeley: University of California Press, 1996).

10. We spent considerable time researching the economies of the cities we studied. However, although whole country and some regional data were available, we were hampered by the paucity of economic data available at the local level.

11. Ashutosh Varshney, *Ethnic Conflict and Civil Life: Hindus and Muslims in India* (New Haven, Conn.: Yale University Press, 2002), 6.

12. On Mostar, see Sumantra Bose, *Bosnia After Dayton: Nationalist Partition and International Intervention* (Oxford: Oxford University Press, 2002), 95–148. On Prijedor, see Anthony Oberschall, "The Manipulation of Ethnicity: From Ethnic Cooperation to Violence and War in Yugoslavia," *Ethnic and Racial Studies* 23:6 (2000): 982–1001. On Vukovar, see Stover and Peress, *The Graves*. Many books describe the war and its effects; see, for example, Peter Maas, *Love Thy Neighbor: A Story of War* (New York: Knopf, 1995), Laura Silber and Allan Little, *Yugoslavia: Death of a Nation* (London: Penguin Books, 1997), and Chuck Sudetic, *Blood and Vengeance* (New York: Norton, 1998).

13. In this book, we will use the terminology that reflects current reality. The state of Bosnia and Herzegovina is made up of three constituent peoples – the Muslim majority (now called Bosniaks), the Croat minority (who follow

the Roman Catholic faith), and the Serb minority (who follow the Eastern Orthodox faith). These peoples are called "national groups." Prior to
the 1992–95 war, mixing of these peoples was widespread, although some
regions were home to larger numbers of a specific group. War has led to much
internal displacement. In the former Yugoslavia, the common language was
Serbo-Croatian with regional variations. Today, the languages are Bosnian,
Croatian, and Serbian, and while each group understands the others, new
or ancient words are being introduced that serve to widen the gap between
these languages and ensure their uniqueness.

14. See Silber and Little, *Yugoslavia: Death of a Nation*, 291–296.
15. Statistics are available from the Ambassador of France to Croatia at
    www.amb-croatie.fr/croatia/population.
16. Oberschall, "The Manipulation of Ethnicity."
17. Authoritative references on the history of the Rwandan genocide are found in
    Gerard Prunier, *The Rwanda Crisis* (New York: Columbia University Press,
    1995) and Alison Des Forges, *Leave None to Tell the Story: Genocide in Rwanda*
    (New York: Human Rights Watch, 1999).
18. Edmond N. Cahn, *The Sense of Injustice* (NewYork: New York Press, 1949),
    13.
19. For a comprehensive review of the various institutional mechanisms of justice
    and accountability, see Aryeh Neier, *War Crimes: Brutality, Genocide, Terror,
    and the Struggle for Justice* (New York: Times Books/Random House, 1998),
    Martha Minow, *Between Vengeance and Forgiveness: Facing History after Geno-
    cide and Mass Violence* (Boston: Beacon Press, 1998), and Hayner, *Unspeak-
    able Truths.*
20. Mark A. Drumbl, "Punishment, Postgenocide: From Guilt to Shame to *Civis*
    in Rwanda," *New York University Law Review* 75: 5 (November 2000): 1312–
    1322.
21. Rama Mani, *Beyond Retribution: Seeking Justice in the Shadows of War* (Cam-
    bridge: Polity Press, 2002), 6.
22. Elizabeth Neuffer, *The Key to My Neighbor's House: Seeking Justice in Bosnia
    and Rwanda* (New York: Picador, 2001), 259.
23. Kirsten Campbell, "The Trauma of Justice." Presented at the *Human Frailty:
    Rights, Ethics and the Search for Global Justice* Conference, University of the
    West of England. Campbell presents a cogent review of this issue and con-
    cludes that "Justice cannot be understood as the suturing of trauma. It
    requires a fundamental change to the social order which made possible the
    original trauma of crimes against humanity. In this sense, justice remains the
    event yet to come."
24. Mark Osiel, *Mass Atrocity, Collective Memory and the Law* (New Brunswick
    and London: Transaction Publishers, 1997) and Martha Minow, *Between
    Vengeance and Forgiveness.*
25. The banners of the South African Truth and Reconciliation Commission
    proclaimed that "Revealing is Healing." See Brandon Hamber, "Does the
    Truth Heal? A Psychological Perspective on Political Strategies for Dealing
    with the Legacy of Political Violence." In Nigel Biggar, ed. *Burying the
    Past: Making Peace and Doing Justice After Civil Conflict* (Washington, D.C.:
    Georgetown University Press, 2001), 131–148.

26. See Judith Herman, *Trauma and Recovery* (New York: Basic Books, 1992), 12.
27. "Reconcile," *The Oxford English Dictionary*, 2nd edn., vol. XIII (Oxford: Clarendon Press, 1989), 352–353.
28. Louis Kriesberg, "Paths to Varieties of Inter-Communal Reconciliation." Paper presented at the Seventh General Conference of the International Peace Research Association, Durban, South Africa, 1998.
29. Tina Rosenberg, "Latin America." In Alex Boraine, Janet Levy, and Ronel Scheffer, eds. *Dealing with the Past: Truth and Reconciliation in South Africa* (Capetown: Institute for Democracy in South Africa, 1994), 67.
30. See, for example, Priscilla B. Hayner, *Unspeakable Truths*, 154–169; Naomi Roht-Arriaza, "The Need for Moral Reconstruction in the Wake of Past Human Rights Violations: An Interview with Jose Zalaquett." In Carla Hesse and Robert Post, eds. *Human Rights in Political Transitions: Gettysburg to Bosnia* (New York: Zone Books, 1999), 195–213.
31. Bronwyn Anne Leebaw, *Judging the Past: Truth, Justice, and Reconciliation from Nuremberg to South Africa*, PhD dissertation, 2002, University of California, Berkeley, 8.
32. Erik Erikson, *Childhood and Society* (Harmondsworth: Penguin Books, 1967). Also see Erik Erikson, *Identity and the Life Cycle* (New York: Norton, 1980) and "Identity and the Life Cycle: Selected Papers," *Psychological Issues* 1:1 (1959).
33. Muzafer Sherif, *Group Conflict and Cooperation: Their Social Psychology* (London: Routledge and Kegan Paul, 1966).
34. This was elaborated as realistic group conflict theory and social exchange theory.
35. Henri Tajfel, *Human Groups and Social Categories* (Cambridge: Cambridge University Press, 1981), 251.
36. John C. Turner, Michael A. Hogg, Penelope J. Oakes, Stephen D. Reicher, and Margaret S. Wetherell, *Rediscovering the Social Group: A Self-Categorization Theory* (Oxford: Blackwell, 1987).
37. John C. Turner, Rupert J. Brown, and Henri Tafjel, "Social Comparison and Group Interest in In-group Favoritism," *European Journal of Social Psychology* 9 (1979): 187–204.
38. Stuart J. Kaufman, *Modern Hatreds: The Symbolic Politics of Ethnic War* (Ithaca: Cornell University Press, 2001).
39. Murray Edelman, *Politics as Symbolic Action: Mass Arousal and Quiescence* (New York: Academic Press, 1971).
40. Anthony Smith, *The Ethnic Origin of Nations* (Oxford: Basil Blackwell, 1986).
41. David Horowitz, *The Deadly Ethnic Riot* (Berkeley: University of California Press, 2001), 524.
42. Jack David Eller, *From Culture to Ethnicity to Conflict: An Anthropological Perspective on International Ethnic Conflict* (Ann Arbor: University of Michigan Press, 1999), 278.
43. Aleksandr Pavkovic, "Yugoslavism: A National Identity That Failed?" In Leslie Holmes and Philomena Murray, eds. *Citizenship and Identity in Europe* (Brookfield: Ashgate,1999).

44. Mark Howard Ross, "Psychocultural Interpretations and Dramas: Identity Dynamics in Ethnic Conflict," *Political Psychology* 22:1 (2001): 157–177.
45. Joanne Nagel, "Constructing Identity: Creating and Recreating Ethnic Identity and Culture," *Social Problems* 41:1 (1994): 152–176.
46. John R. Gillis, "Memory and Identity: The History of a Relationship." In John R. Gillis, ed. *Commemorations: The Politics of National Identity* (Princeton, N.J.: Princeton University Press, 1994), 3.
47. Robert D. Putnam, *Bowling Alone: The Collapse and Revival of the American Community* (New York: Simon and Schuster, 2001), 22.
48. Urie Bronfenbrenner, *The Ecology of Human Development* (Cambridge: Cambridge University Press, 1977).
49. Seymour B. Sarason, "The Ecological Approach." In Seymour B. Sarason, *Revisiting "The Culture of the School and the Problem of Change"* (New York: Teachers College Press, 1974).
50. James G. Kelly, "Toward an Ecological Conception of Preventive Interventions." In Jerry W. Carter, Jr., ed. *Research Contributions from Psychology to Community Mental Health* (New York: Behavioral Publications, 1968), 75–99.
51. Johan Galtung, "Appreciation in Universal House of Justice." In *To the Peoples of the World: A Baha'i Statement on Peace* (Ottawa: The Association for Baha'i Studies, 1986), 85–86.
52. "Preventing Deadly Conflict." *Carnegie Commission on Preventing Deadly Conflict* (New York: Carnegie Corporation, 1997).
53. Peter Harris and Ben Reilly, eds. *Democracy and Deep-Rooted Conflict: Options for Negotiators* (Stockholm: International IDEA, 1998).
54. Laurie Nathan, "Crisis Resolution and Conflict Management in Africa." Paper presented at the *Consultation on the Nexus Between Economic Management and the Restoration of Social Capital in Southern Africa*, World Bank and Centre for Conflict Resolution, 1999.
55. Ibid.
56. Cornell Empowerment Group, 1989.
57. Lisa F. Berkman, "Assessing the Physical Health Effects of Social Networks and Social Support," *Annual Review of Public Health* 5 (1984): 413–432. Also see S. Leonard Syme, "Control and Health: A Personal Perspective," in Andrew Steptoe and Ad Appels, eds. *Stress, Personal Control, and Health* (New York: John Wiley & Sons in association with the Commission of the European Communities, 1989).
58. Richard A. Couto, "Participatory Research: Methodology and Critique," *Clinical Sociology Review/1987* (1987): 83–90.
59. L. David Brown, "People-Centered Development and Participatory Research," *Harvard Educational Review* 55:1 (1985): 69–75. The beneficial effects of asserting oneself and making decisions about the future were seen in an earlier study from our project where Bosniaks displaced in Bosnia were compared with those who had chosen to emigrate to the United States. See Harvey M. Weinstein et al., "Rethinking Displacement: Bosnians Uprooted in Bosnia and California." In Julienne G. Lipson and Lucia Ann McSpadden,

eds. *Selected Papers on Refugees and Immigrants*, vol. VII (Fairfax, Va.: American Anthropological Association, 1999).

60. Ishiro Kawachi et al., "Social Capital, Income Inequality, and Mortality," *American Journal of Public Health* 87 (1997): 1491–1498.

61. Kimberly A. Maynard, "Rebuilding Community: Psychosocial Healing, Reintegration, and Reconciliation at the Grassroots Level." In Krishna Kumar, ed. *Rebuilding Societies After Civil War: Critical Roles for International Assistance* (Boulder/London: Lynne Rienner, 1997), 203–226.

62. Rajeev Bhargava, "Restoring Decency to Barbaric Societies." In Robert I. Rotberg and Dennis Thompson, eds. *Truth v. Justice: The Morality of Truth Commissions* (Princeton, N.J.: Princeton University Press, 2000), 45–67.

Part I

Institutional approaches to justice

The Yugoslav and Rwandan Tribunals and the establishment of the International Criminal Court have spawned a growing body of research and debate among legal scholars, political theorists, and social scientists about the efficacy of international criminal tribunals and their objectives. A primary weakness of writings on justice after war and mass atrocity is the paucity of objective evidence to substantiate claims about how well criminal trials achieve the goals ascribed to them. Insufficient attention has been paid to the effects, both positive and negative, that tribunals have had on post-war societies.

The authors in Part 1 examine several judicial and non-judicial responses to mass atrocity, particularly in the former Yugoslavia and Rwanda, and describe how these mechanisms have affected survivors. In Chapter 1, Laurel Fletcher and Harvey Weinstein trace the formation of the International Criminal Tribunal for the former Yugoslavia (ICTY) and the international community's aspirations for what it could accomplish in Bosnia and Herzegovina. Based on interviews with Bosnian judges and prosecutors, the authors argue that international tribunals would have greater legitimacy in local communities if they worked in tandem with, and not in isolation from, national judiciaries. They suggest that international tribunals must develop mechanisms to educate local populations not only about their mandates, methods, rules, and procedures but also about the larger questions of bystander involvement and the role of beneficiaries.

In Chapter 2, Alison Des Forges and Timothy Longman examine a wide range of judicial responses to the 1994 genocide in Rwanda, including trials of suspected *génocidaires* before the Rwandan courts; the International Criminal Tribunal for Rwanda (ICTR) in Arusha, Tanzania; and Swiss and Belgian courts. The authors find little evidence that these trials have contributed significantly to the process of reconciliation. Many Rwandans, they argue, are unaware of the ICTR trials, let alone the less publicized prosecutions in Switzerland and Belgium, and they remain suspicious of the national courts that often use their powers to intimidate government critics and opponents.

In Chapter 3, Alice Karekezi and her colleagues describe gacaca, the innovative system of village-based courts created to try lower-level genocide suspects not being tried before the ICTR and national courts. After intensive observation of three local-level courts, Karekezi and colleagues look at the strengths and limitations of gacaca as it has evolved in its early stages. While supportive of the process, they raise serious questions about the training of judges, the participation of communities, the quality of the evidence, and the effects of social pressure. The authors offer a series of recommendations to improve this indigenous approach to justice while recognizing both its creativity and its challenges.

In Chapter 4, Eric Stover and Rachel Shigekane examine the tension that has emerged between the humanitarian needs of families of the missing and the evidentiary needs and limitations of international war crimes tribunals. The authors argue that, above all else, the families of the missing have a desperate need to recover the remains of their loved ones. This powerful exigency overrides whatever desires they have for justice, leading to a clash of expectations when international tribunals lack the resources and political will to undertake forensic investigations aimed at identifying all of the dead.

Eric Stover goes on in Chapter 5 to present the findings of a study of victims and witnesses who testified for the prosecution at the ICTY. For many, merely being in the courtroom with the accused while he was under guard helped restore their confidence in the order of things. Although these witnesses supported war crimes trials in general, most were ambivalent about whether justice had been rendered. Stover argues for more attention to ensuring witnesses a respectful and dignified experience and to supporting those who may face recriminations once they return home.

In Chapter 6, the final chapter of Part 1, Naomi Roht-Arriaza explores the implications of providing reparations to survivors of mass atrocity, especially in the context of poor countries where there may be many victims and multiple claims on scarce resources. She concludes that reparations may be the most tangible and visible expression of both acknowledgment and change in the aftermath of massive human rights abuses, and in that sense, an important contributor to social reconstruction and reconciliation.

1   A world unto itself? The application of international justice in the former Yugoslavia

Laurel E. Fletcher and Harvey M. Weinstein

In the summer of 1992, the contrast between images of emaciated, half-naked Bosniak[1] men, baking behind barbed wire under a relentless sun at the Serb-controlled Omarska prison camp in north/central Bosnia and Herzegovina (BiH), and photographs of well-dressed, well-fed diplomats speaking with reporters outside the United Nations (UN) in New York about the Balkan conflict could not have been more stark. Yet the link between the powerless and powerful became palpable and assumed a distinct legal form when the UN Security Council created the International Criminal Tribunal for the former Yugoslavia (ICTY) in May 1993. Its formation would be critical for those immediately affected by the war and serve as a harbinger of politics in the post-Cold War world. In fact, its creation turned out to be a watershed event that has altered dramatically the landscape of post-conflict interventions.

As demonstrated by the proliferation of war crimes tribunals and other institutional responses to war crimes in Rwanda, Sierra Leone, East Timor, and Kosovo, the question is no longer whether there should be accountability for mass violence, but what form it should take. There has been much debate about the relative merits of trials, truth commissions, or other forms of reckoning such as lustration (the wholesale firing from government positions of those who served under a repressive regime). Those who study how countries might best confront the human rights abuses of a prior regime propose an array of options, yet the events of the last decade suggest that trials, with international involvement, are the preferred response.

The international community's emphasis on criminal prosecutions has led to considerable achievements in the legal and institutional development of international criminal justice. However, there are important lessons to be learned from the challenges, successes, and failures of the ICTY. These lessons can be applied beyond the Balkans to the International Criminal Court, as well as to other international-local courts established in diverse countries and cultures.

In this chapter, we focus on the relationship between the political and social dimensions of the ICTY and its image, efficacy, and long-term impact in BiH and the Balkan region from three perspectives. First, we look at the expectations of the ICTY and argue that many diplomats, the media, and supporters of the court sought to expand its legal mandate beyond the goal of prosecuting alleged perpetrators of war crimes. They wanted the court to achieve a larger, more ill-defined, and unrealistic objective of promoting reconciliation among warring groups. These aspirations raise the provocative question of whether trials can promote reconciliation.

Second, we argue that attempts to link the ICTY to this broader social project, without the political will and infrastructure to support it, undermine the important contributions that international trials can make to post-conflict societies. For example, the ICTY has no formal mechanism through which it maintains a direct relationship to the Bosnian judicial system or to other important legal and social institutions in the country. As a result, the tribunal's public image has suffered and its legitimacy has been compromised. This loss of credibility suggests that without links between the ICTY and the process of national reconstruction these trials might become nothing more than a theoretical exercise in developing international humanitarian law. We argue that perceptions of international courts are critical. These tribunals must be seen as legitimate by those on whose behalf they operate in order for their work to be accepted within affected societies.

Finally, the ICTY has not been directly involved with the larger task of preparing national courts in BiH to undertake domestic prosecutions of suspected war criminals. One premise of international tribunals is that prosecutions of key leaders are essential for a country that has experienced mass violence to begin the process of rebuilding its society. We argue that, given the limited number of international trials and the need to establish robust rule of law in post-war countries, the domestic judicial system assumes a vital importance. Consequently, the synchronization of these two systems of justice becomes critical, so that they work in tandem rather than at cross-purposes.

In this chapter, we examine some of the factors that contributed to the gap between the international community's aspirations for justice and how its application was perceived by those most affected by the violence in the former Yugoslavia First, we look at the relationship of the origins of the ICTY and increased UN responsibility for war crimes prosecutions, and the expectations by tribunal supporters of the ICTY's contribution to reconciliation. Next, we examine the impact of the court's structure on attitudes toward the ICTY by legal professionals within Bosnia.

In particular, the tribunal location, staff, and the "Rules of the Road" program – the process by which Bosnian authorities seek approval from the ICTY before issuing national war crimes indictments – increase the court's vulnerability to de-legitimization as a result of the geographic and legal distance between the court and national judicial systems. Finally, we turn our attention to the institutional relationship between the tribunal and the national judiciary, and its implications for establishing a judicial system in BiH capable of conducting war crimes trials. Before developing the central arguments of this chapter, however, we provide a brief description of the scope and substance of the study that informs our analysis.

Our ideas emerge out of data collected from a survey of Bosnian legal professionals that we conducted in 1999. Because little attention had been paid to understanding the views of those within BiH charged with national administration of justice for war crimes, we conducted an interview study of judges and prosecutors in the country. The survey data provide a perspective on the ICTY, national war crimes trials, and the relationship of justice to social reconstruction from those occupying an important site for transmission and incorporation of the lessons from the ICTY into the legal, political, and social culture of BiH. In particular, the data point to the challenges of applying the experience of the international court to developing the local judiciary. Also the study illustrates the difficulties in inculcating respect for international humanitarian and human rights law among those who engaged in or who supported the violence. In framing our concerns, we draw as well on other sources of data, such as UN documents, memoranda from the ICTY, interviews, and surveys conducted in the Balkans. These will be presented in detail in the chapters of this volume. Based on the experience in the former Yugoslavia (FY), we identify several aspects regarding the relation of international trials to the countries affected by them to promote the contribution of international justice to post-war societies.

Background to the ICTY and questions of its legitimacy

The establishment of the ICTY was a historic event. For the first time since the end of the Second World War, an international court would try individuals accused of the most egregious violations of international humanitarian law. For some fifty years, no international mechanism had existed to hold perpetrators of war crimes criminally accountable for their deeds. In the absence of such a mechanism, international humanitarian law had restrained war to the extent that states and combatants perceived it in their interests to do so. Supporters of the ICTY hoped that the court would rekindle the principles of Nuremberg by holding Balkan war criminals *individually* accountable. They hoped the tribunal would build political momentum to establish a permanent international criminal court, an idea that had been discussed for decades.

Yet the formation and the structure of the tribunal created vulnerabilities that left it open to attacks on its legitimacy from many individuals in the Balkans. For example, regulations devised for the ICTY specifically excluded nationals of the war-affected states from holding legal positions at the court. This decision, understandable though it was to avoid accusations of bias, had negative ramifications. The exclusion of nationals contributed to feelings on the part of some groups in the former Yugoslavia of being abused by the international legal community. Their lack of participation also contributed to a feeling among Bosnian Croats and Bosnian Serbs that the work of the tribunal did not reflect their concerns, and therefore they could not claim any ownership in the judicial process. Another effect of this rule was that those who prosecuted and judged were not citizens of the same country as the accused, nor did they necessarily share the culture or traditions of the alleged perpetrators. This fact alone contributed to misunderstandings and distortions that were used by those opposed to the ICTY. This problem subsequently has been addressed in other countries through the development of hybrid or national courts with international advisors.

The ICTY gave rise to a new generation of legal scholars devoted to the study, exploration, and intellectual inquiry of international criminal law. However, many in the former Yugoslavia did not embrace wholeheartedly the work of the tribunal. Particularly, many within the Bosnian Serb and Bosnian Croat communities perceived its work to be biased and unfair, usually to their own national group. Some noted that it was not the perpetrators from the great powers that were in the dock. The accused came from the Balkan countries – states with relatively weak international political clout. While at first glance this seems reasonable, it became fodder for accusations that the ICTY was a political court and incapable of rendering impartial justice.

These perceptions of the ICTY exposed the fact that, despite the explicit expectation that the court would contribute to peace in the region, the architects of this new court gave little thought to how it would relate to those most affected by the carnage. Given the challenges to build an institution in the midst of war, perhaps this oversight is not surprising. However, it is critical that we begin to understand the untoward effects of establishing international institutions that directly affect people in their own communities. For example, the tribunal's lack of attention to the political and social processes and consequences of its work in BiH threatened the legitimacy of the court in the eyes of the society it was trying to help.

Moreover, the absence of mandated institutional links between the tribunal and those institutions working toward the broader goals of social reconstruction in the former Yugoslavia meant that, from the perspective of those living in the region, the ICTY was a world unto itself. The tribunal was removed physically, culturally, and politically from those who would live most intimately with its success or failure. International justice and national social reconstruction occupied separate spheres, with unfortunate effect. By 1998, the then President of the ICTY, Justice Gabrielle Kirk McDonald, discovered a "crisis in confidence" of the tribunal within Bosnia and undertook efforts to address it. What contributed to this crisis and, more immediately, what can be done to avoid similar mishaps in the future? We designed our study to shed light on these important questions.

The study[2]

We conducted an interview study during the summer of 1999 of a representative sample of thirty-two judges and prosecutors with primary or appellate jurisdiction for national war crimes trials. The samples were drawn from three areas of BiH – the Bosniak-majority area of the Federation, the Republika Srpska (majority Bosnian Serb), and the Bosnian Croat majority area around the city of Mostar. We developed a semi-structured questionnaire, consisting of forty-five items, to solicit information on the following topics: demographics; the role of the judge/prosecutor and courtroom process in BiH; the domestic effects of the ICTY, including perceptions of its practices; common legal definitions in international law; opinions about domestic war crimes trials; attitudes toward the international community; and hopes for the future.

The principal findings indicated that although all participants supported the concept of accountability for those who commit war crimes, their views were modified by national identity as well as identification of their group as "victims." Further, almost all Bosnian Serb and Croat participants expressed concern that the ICTY was a "political" organization, where "political" meant "biased and incapable of providing fair trials." There was a striking lack of understanding by most of the participants of the procedures and work of the tribunal and its blend of common and civil law procedures, selection of cases, issuing of indictments, evidentiary rules, and the length of detention and trials. Although all desired more information with legal content, they perceived their sporadic contact with the ICTY as a sign of disrespect. Further, their contact with international lawyers working to monitor domestic trials and to train local judges was seen as condescending, ignorant, and disrespectful.

The Bosnian legal professionals, in 150 hours of transcribed interviews, expressed six areas of concern: *professionalism*, reflected in the participants' emphasis on high standards and the strict application of legal rules to a case; *justice*, as evidenced by their adherence to the principles of justice; application of the law; support for the *western European legal tradition*; concerns about *corruption* and decline in professional standards; anger about the corrosive effects of *politics* on the judicial system and the threats to an independent judiciary; and finally, their concerns that *international lawyers* acted in Bosnia in ways that reflected little understanding of civil law or any appreciation for Bosnian legal professionals' support of an independent judiciary.

In this chapter, we amplify the results of this investigation to address a critical gap in the effectiveness of an international tribunal – its linkage to the domestic judiciary and its ability to adjudicate national war crimes trials.

The ICTY: aspirations and realities

Justice may have different meanings for world leaders, scholars, human rights activists, and those living in communities emerging from mass violence. The worldwide upsurge of sectarian violence that occurred after the fall of the Berlin Wall raised serious questions about international responsibilities to quell the bloodshed and to achieve peace. One response of the international community has been to strengthen the application of international criminal law. Indeed, the statute of the ICTY frames international prosecutions as a way to achieve peace and stability in the region. Our study suggests that the particular model for justice that the ICTY implements may be too narrow to fulfill this broader political aspiration. To reach these broader goals, additional interventions are necessary to complement the work of criminal tribunals.

Political strategist Rama Mani identifies three forms of justice – rectificatory, legal, and distributive – that can emerge in post-war societies.[3] Rectificatory justice, she argues, is "minimalist" and focuses on redressing specific wrongs. International commitment to criminal trials is retributive – punishing violators of international humanitarian law. Legal and distributive justice are "maximalist" and seek to achieve broader goals. Legal justice is directed at the rebuilding of a judicial system, while distributive justice addresses power relationships and access to opportunity. While the ICTY is pursuing rectificatory justice in the former Yugoslavia, non-governmental organizations (NGOs) and some multi-lateral organizations labor to provide legal justice; their focus is to rebuild the national judicial system and to repair the basic infrastructure. Legal justice includes providing resources, improving judicial and prosecutorial quality, and monitoring trials for compliance with the rules of due process. However, in the case of BiH, the rectificatory justice goals of the ICTY are not sufficiently integrated with the legal and distributive justice efforts of the Office of the High Representative (OHR) and other international and NGOs. Furthermore, those organizations addressing judicial reform do not incorporate into their efforts the broad meaning of justice that addresses the larger questions of power. Thus, international programs to rebuild the BiH judicial system do not explicitly address the underlying processes, like nationalist extremism, that led to the ethnic cleansing or genocide.

The lack of coordination and its focused mandate have adversely affected public perceptions of the ICTY and its ability to play a central role in post-conflict social reconstruction. Ultimately, the absence of an integrated approach becomes a question of resolving conflicting goals and expectations between those working within the tribunal to promote its strict legal mandate and the ambitions of those inside and outside of the Balkans who see the work of the tribunal as part of a more expansive vision for social reconstruction. To understand how this gap developed, we turn now to the confluence of forces that created the court.

Origins of the ICTY

The Balkan conflict was the first post-Cold War crisis to test UN political resolve to end large-scale violations of international humanitarian law and human rights abuses. After years of acquiescence to mass atrocities, diplomats at the UN resurrected Nuremberg as a model for responding to ethnic cleansing and genocide in the FY. Why at that moment was there a renewed and reinvigorated international mandate to uphold international humanitarian law?

First, the war had spun out of control. Hundreds of thousands of refugees were streaming out of the Balkans; photographs in the media daily revealed the horrors of ethnic cleansing; reports of thousands of rapes of Muslim women in Bosnia evoked powerful responses, particularly from women in the West; the destruction of holy places was widespread and devastating. Diplomacy seemed to falter and the leaders of these atrocities appeared invincible. The creation of the ICTY has been attributed to such factors as guilt on the part of the western nations that allowed ethnic cleansing to occur; as a sop to those who could not tolerate the escalation of human rights abuses but did not want to initiate military action; and as a triumph of liberal thinking over those devoted to realpolitik who were concerned more with stability than with rectifying terrible wrongs.

Of particular interest is the fact that one impetus for the ICTY came as the result of a field mission undertaken by six UN ambassadors to the killing fields of BiH, underscoring the importance of witnessing in motivating redress. During their mission, which was proposed by Pakistan and led by Ambassador Diego Arria of Venezuela, what these diplomats saw in the Bosnian towns of Srebrenica and Bihac – the burning of homes and the charred bodies, the terror of refugees, and the wanton devastation – had a lasting impact. Ambassador Arria speaks of the camaraderie that fast developed among the members of the delegation as their reactions to the horror drew them together as witnesses to ethnic cleansing.[4] Not only were the diplomats outraged by what they observed, they pushed the UN Security Council to take action. Members of the smaller and historically non-aligned countries believed that more had to be done to protect the nascent countries of the FY – after all, if inaction became politically acceptable in the post-Cold War era, small, non-aligned countries could expect the same treatment. While there was much ambivalence within the UN regarding the creation of an international tribunal, Nuremberg became the "common denominator" – perpetrators had to be held accountable.

Aspirations for the ICTY ran high. Security Council records are replete with discussion of the need to punish those guilty of war crimes in order to bring justice to the victims, to pave the way for the truth about atrocities to emerge, and to deter would-be war criminals from initiating similar acts. Ambassador Arria recalls that the UN debates did not consider reconciliation as a direct outgrowth of the ICTY. The primary objectives of the tribunal were the punishment of war criminals and restoration of peace and security. Yet the record of debate at the Security Council suggests that the seeds for another goal for the court – that of promoting reconciliation – were planted at its inception. For example, the Hungarian Ambassador to the UN stated during the Security Council debate before the vote to create the court:

The way the international community deals with questions relating to the events in the former Yugoslavia will leave a profound mark on the future of that part of Europe, and beyond. It will make either easier or more painful, or even impossible, the healing of the psychological wounds the conflict has inflicted upon peoples who for centuries have lived together in harmony and good-neighbourliness, regardless of what we may hear today from certain parties to the conflict.[5]

In the words of the Ambassador, we hear what soon emerged as a secondary goal of many who supported the establishment of the tribunal – "healing psychological wounds." Ultimately, the goal of reconciliation became associated with these trials for many supporters in and outside of BiH.

Linking the ICTY mandate and social reconstruction

Tribunal architects hoped the court would create an unassailable historical record of the war capable of engendering contrition among supporters of war criminals.[6] In addition, they hoped to facilitate acceptance of bystanders in communities victimized by the violence. However, in the early years, the ICTY had neither the necessary financial and political resources nor the inclination to take up this larger mandate. Indeed, the tribunal struggled to establish its legitimacy and overcome criticism that it was a "'fig leaf' of the international community established to hide its shame for inaction in the former Yugoslavia."[7] The court defined its mandate narrowly, leaving to others the task of drawing the links between its work and rebuilding social relations within communities in the region. Moreover, as the tribunal began trying cases and handing down verdicts, little, if any, effort was put into facilitating public discussion within the Balkans regarding the relationship of the tribunal's work to social reconstruction. Neither international nor local NGOs saw this important step as central to their mandate. This lacuna contributed to some of the sources of misunderstanding regarding the ICTY and further weakened the court's role in BiH.

Although some supporters hoped the tribunal would contribute to social reconstruction, an explicit mandate to do so and the mechanisms to achieve this aim were not included in its statute or rules (the mandate of the subsequent International Criminal Tribunal for Rwanda [ICTR] explicitly included that goal). The UN resolutions creating the ICTY make no mention of the need to build foundations for social reconstruction in the former Yugoslavia, including consolidation of a national, shared history of the war; the creation of domestic legal institutions that promote and respect strict adherence to the protection of human rights; and democratic institutions capable of guaranteeing individual rights and freedoms. Indeed, it is difficult to imagine that an international criminal court could have achieved these far broader goals.

The legal professionals we interviewed held divergent views about the relationship of the tribunal to social reconstruction. Bosniak participants adhered most closely to the view that the ICTY would promote social reconstruction. They saw the tribunal as an important vehicle for acknowledging the status of Bosniaks as victims of Bosnian Serb and Bosnian Croat aggression and of their fraternal sponsors, Serbia and Croatia. Bosniak judges and prosecutors also viewed the eventual punishment of major accused war criminals such as Slobodan Milosevic and Radovan Karadzic as contributing to social reconstruction. Bosnian Serb participants held decidedly mixed views about the relevance of the tribunal to rebuilding their country. Even those who should have had a professional interest in the ICTY expressed ambivalence about its work. As one Bosnian Serb judge observed: "When someone wants to forgive somebody, he'll do it without a court."[8] Others expressed the opinion that the ICTY was irrelevant to social reconstruction: "The ICTY is not significant for the life of those people here," one participant remarked.[9] Another shared the opinion of several Bosnian Croat legal professionals that economic development, rather than legal accountability, was most critical to promote social reconstruction. Many Bosnian Croat participants echoed the view of their Bosniak counterparts that the ICTY played an important role in stimulating public discussion about the events of the war, which they felt could help improve social harmony.

The study points to the lack of consensus among Bosnian legal professionals regarding the contribution of international criminal trials to reconciliation. It also suggests that the link between international accountability and social reconstruction is not axiomatic. In the case of Bosnia, national politics and the politics of post-war nationalism colored the views of legal professionals toward the tribunal and will require further interventions to secure their support, as a group, for the court.

The structure of the ICTY and its image in the Bosnian legal community

Establishment of the *ad hoc* tribunals implies a new, critical role for the UN in implementing rectificatory justice. The shift toward a legal framework that holds individuals criminally responsible for war crimes reflects the ascendance of the liberal perspective in international relations.

Two traditions underlie foreign policy. The first, the realist perspective, focuses on state security and holds that the nature of governance of a state is irrelevant so long as power remains balanced. The second, the liberal or idealist perspective, promotes democracy, human rights, and individual freedom based upon the assumption that democratic countries promote stability and peace. By framing the debate in post-conflict BiH in human rights terms, those subscribing to the liberal perspective clashed with, but ultimately triumphed over, the strategy of realist diplomats who courted such leaders as former Serbian President Milosevic and Bosnian Serb leader Karadzic to broker a peace agreement. Since the conclusion of the war, the perceived necessity for post-conflict accountability has become accepted widely by the major powers. Yet if international criminal accountability has quickly become the norm for post-conflict countries, it has brought new and unforeseen challenges. With this endorsement, the UN and a wider circle of international tribunal supporters have become invested with establishing the legitimacy of these legal mechanisms. However, this leads us to ask what makes the tribunal legitimate, and to whom.

International scholars, diplomats, and human rights advocates may measure the court's success by its ability to fill its courtrooms with defendants, promulgate evidentiary and procedural rules, and deliver well-reasoned opinions that update and apply international criminal laws to contemporary conflicts. Those living in post-conflict BiH may judge the tribunal according to different criteria, however. For example, the findings of our study suggest that membership of a national group was the most important factor in determining attitudes toward the ICTY. Thus, Bosniaks, almost universally seen as the principal victims of the war, were most supportive of the ICTY. Bosnian Serbs, usually seen as the aggressors in the conflict, held the most negative attitudes; and Bosnian Croats were somewhere in between. Each group sought from the court confirmation of its status as "victim."

This divergence of views prompted a UN commission of experts examining the impact of the ICTY in BiH to observe in November 1999: "It is likely that, except for a very small fraction of the populations of the former Yugoslavia and elsewhere, there is large-scale, if not total, lack of knowledge regarding the international humanitarian laws enforced by the ICTY."[10] A year earlier, ICTY President Justice Gabrielle Kirk McDonald had taken seriously the emerging gap between The Hague and community perceptions in the region. She directed the ICTY to initiate an outreach program that would link the tribunal to communities in the former Yugoslavia. After a weak beginning, the outreach program, to its credit, has made considerable strides. It has begun programs to educate legal professionals and those in the larger community such as high school students, about the work of the tribunal.

Given the lack of past examples of models to inform the public about the accomplishments of international criminal tribunals, it is not surprising that the implementers of this important process struggled to establish appropriate mechanisms. However, its work has been hampered by the unwillingness of countries to provide it with adequate financial resources.

This stinginess reflects the lack of importance given to the problem by those countries that support the ICTY. Moreover, while the international media have given considerable attention to the ICTY's achievements and shortcomings, it has, for the most part, failed to report in any depth on how the Bosnian people view the tribunal's work. The UN, by creating the ICTY, entered into a relationship with post-conflict communities. This relationship needs to be nurtured. An important finding from our studies is that the structure of the court and its interaction with post-conflict communities exert a profound impact on how these communities perceive the work of an international court. In turn, these perceptions may negatively affect the ability of the court to fulfill the social and political aspects of its mission.

"Victor's justice" and the politics of the tribunal

Although proponents of the ICTY hailed the court as a neutral arbiter of Balkan war atrocities, many of those living in the region did not perceive the tribunal as being above politics. Paradoxically, as the Office of the Prosecutor (OTP) became more successful in obtaining the arrest of accused war criminals in the period 1996–98, criticism of the ICTY became more vocal within BiH. In its early years of operation, the tribunal did not devote attention to how it was perceived in BiH. Outright political distortions by nationalist politicians and rumors about the work of the court circulated in the press, particularly in Bosnian Serb and Bosnian Croat areas. These reports served to undermine its credibility and legitimacy within the region.

For example, most Bosnian Serb participants in our study alleged that the tribunal was politically biased against them, basing their view on misinformation that the ICTY had indicted only Serbs. Meanwhile, Bosnian Croat legal professionals felt rebuked by the lack of indictments in connection with the 1991 Serb attack on Dubrovnik and the Bosniak expulsion of Bosnian Croats from central Bosnia in the early years of the war. A few Bosniak participants viewed the court as a cynical gesture from the West, which prosecuted "small fish" while the intellectual masterminds of the carnage remained in positions of power.

Most Bosnian Serb and many Bosnian Croat participants viewed the ICTY as a contemporary form of "victor's justice" imposed on them by the international community. However, virtually all Bosniak participants welcomed the imposition, acknowledging that only an international authority could fairly adjudicate war crimes trials. One Bosnian Serb legal professional stated: "[The ICTY] is too artificial a court and it is under the jurisdiction of powerful societies. There is no justice in that court."

Participants distinguished between political prejudice in judicial decisions and the political dimensions of the ICTY as an institution created by a world body. These legal professionals correctly understood that a political process within the Security Council led to the creation of the court and the appointment of judges and a prosecutor. Unfortunately, supporters of the ICTY are less candid about these aspects.

International tribunals are inherently political in terms of how they are established, their policies and priorities, their relationship to the large multi-lateral organizations and to the police or military units that will arrest the indicted. As the debate regarding the adoption of the ICTY statute makes clear, a goal for the tribunal was to punish those most responsible for atrocities. This objective clearly is a judicial mandate with a forthright political mission to arrest and try the military and political leaders who directed ethnic cleansing. Bosnian Serb and Bosnian Croat legal professionals did not understand the indictments of members of their national group as a natural consequence of the court's mission. They felt the court was singling out their national group for responsibility for atrocities rather than acknowledging them as victims. We believe that more proactive outreach by the ICTY to judges in BiH to explain this "political" aspect of the mission might have helped diminish the sense among Bosnian Serb and Bosnian Croat legal professionals that the court was an illegitimate instrument of the great powers.

The international community, Bosnian legal professionals, and the ICTY

Particular aspects of the court's structure and operation contributed to political resistance to the ICTY by Bosnian legal professionals. For example, as we have noted, the exclusion of nationals of the region from legal positions in the ICTY may have helped to avoid charges of bias against the court, but it meant that those who prosecuted and judged were foreigners. This and other aspects of the court's structure unintentionally reinforced negative attitudes of Bosnian legal professionals toward the international community.

One source of ill-will on the part of the Bosnian legal professionals was the "Rules of the Road" program. The OTP reviewed evidence from BiH authorities under international standards before Bosnian law enforcement could arrest suspected war criminals for trial in a Bosnian courtroom. This vetting process exacerbated rather than reduced tensions between the international and national judicial systems.

According to one NGO representative involved in the program, the OTP viewed the "Rules of the Road" program as an intrusion into their work. Staff resented the additional workload, which the international community had mandated they undertake but for which they had not committed financing.[11] As a result, files from BiH sat in The Hague, unopened. Although the international agreement creating the review process was signed in February 1996, it was not until three years later that the tribunal established a review procedure. Bosnian judges were not informed of these institutional constraints and began sending cases to the ICTY after the agreement was signed. By mid-2002, several years after the OTP finally had its system in place, there was a backlog of some 500 cases. We saw the negative ramifications of this delay reflected in our study.[12]

The attitudes toward the tribunal of the Bosnian judges and lawyers we interviewed need to be considered in the broader context of their interactions with the international community. While legal professionals agreed that the active involvement of the international community was necessary to maintain the peace and rebuild BiH – particularly the judicial system – many felt diminished by representatives of the international community with whom they came in contact. Participants across national groups reported that they perceived that the international community saw them as intellectual inferiors who were ignorant of the relevant law. They, in turn, viewed representatives of the international legal community as ignorant of domestic Bosnian law, its traditions, and the legal institutions in BiH.

In 1999, Elizabeth Rehn, the Special Rapporteur for the UN in BiH, stated that the Bosnian judicial system was corrupt.[13] And the OHR pushed legal reform. Study participants expressed concern about Rehn's allegations. Many alluded to colleagues taking bribes and the lack of training of those entering the profession, but they also felt that remarks from high-level UN officials undermined respect for the Bosnian judicial system. Participants felt that such accusations tarnished the entire profession and gave insufficient praise to those judges and prosecutors who were struggling, in the face of inadequate salaries and resources, to discharge their duties with professionalism. Although the ICTY had no direct role in OHR policy, Bosnian judges' perceptions of the tribunal and its work were colored by their reactions to OHR policies.

Here the focus on legal justice and structural reform affected how legal professionals perceived the rectificatory functions of the ICTY. There was no mechanism to inform the ICTY of this unintended consequence of international legal assistance. Nor did the ICTY have in place any tools, such as regular face-to-face meetings between tribunal judges and staff and Bosnian legal professionals, to address problems as they developed. The Outreach Program currently works to address these and other misunderstandings, and should help to improve and maintain a more positive image of the court within the region.

The ICTY and the rule of law in BiH

The divergence between the aspirations of many ICTY supporters that these trials would enable the devastated countries to move on and the more skeptical perceptions of Bosnian legal professionals raised for us the provocative question of why there appeared to be a gap between the idealized goals of international justice and the views of many Bosnians that such a tribunal was irrelevant. Was the failure of the ICTY to establish its importance to post-war social reconstruction in BiH the result of flawed implementation, flawed design, differing expectations, or a reflection of the limitations of international justice? And, from a normative perspective, what should be the long-range interests of the international community *vis-à-vis* the ICTY? Should it be to create a robust enforcement institution of international criminal law? Or should it be to meet the needs of victims and all citizens by helping to create a domestic judicial system capable of delivering justice? We suggest that the tribunal must succeed not only in delivering rectificatory justice but also in taking the opportunity to help establish domestic legal justice.

The OHR's failure to incorporate the rectification process into its reformation of the national judicial system in BiH has important ramifications. It has meant that international law has thrived while change in the domestic legal processes has been slow. Moreover, legal reform has been hampered by great resentment from local and national governments dominated by nationalist political parties. Furthermore, the legacy of the political history of the country that centered power in the hands of the Communist elite – or those with connections to the Party – has led to on-going problems with corruption and injustice. Our study points to the need for international trials not only to conduct trials but to support the development of parallel teaching and rehabilitative structures addressed to domestic audiences. In this manner, international trials might contribute to achieving justice in its broadest sense. However, this potential has remained largely untapped.

The drama of a controversial trial is the stuff of many Hollywood films. Is there a role, then, for public education in the context of international criminal trials? These tribunals are established to prosecute the most serious international crimes – crimes considered so horrible that they are viewed as crimes against all. We suggest that this value is so important that the pedagogical nature of these trials is a critical dimension of their success or failure. Establishing a historical record, contributing to the collective memory of a society, and securing public support for the scrupulous application of the rule of law might create a social legacy that could strengthen communities against any resurgence of support for the political forces that led to the conflict in the first instance. In other words, society must be aware of the nature and retributive consequences of international trials in order to repudiate the leaders and policies that led to the aggression.

These trials support the underlying societal objective of conferring shame on a much larger body of people – bystanders and the lesser involved. International criminal trials have the effect of stigmatizing groups despite the emphasis on individualizing guilt. Therefore, public pedagogy condemns the political movement or policies for which the defendant is the symbol. Yet our study revealed that trials alone cannot establish an incontrovertible record. Each national group reinterpreted the "facts" according to the views held by that group. If one measure of the success of these trials is society's ability to internalize these lessons and to remember the horrors of the conflict, then educating the public is critical. We want to clarify here that we do not suggest trials should be used as moral theater. Rather we suggest that the process and outcome of trials can be used in ways to counteract the passivity and acquiescence of the population that led to the violence.

Whose obligation is it to carry out this educative function? Clearly, it cannot be that of the court. The court has an obligation to inform and to assure that the population it serves understands the nature of the process and the events as they transpire (as exemplified by the work of the ICTY's Outreach Program). Yet it must fall to a parallel structure, perhaps through a multi-lateral organization, to attend to the moral lessons that emerge from these trials. We suggest that the obligation of the court in this process would be to provide information and cooperate with that organization to facilitate community education.

Two important implications arise from our perspective on public pedagogy: (1) the relationship between a tribunal and the local populace is a critical dimension of its success and (2) the domestic legal system must be influenced by the international one for effective war crimes trials to take place in the country where the crimes occurred. Without these ties to those most affected by human rights abuses, history may well judge the ICTY a success in expanding the reach of international humanitarian law but a failure in promoting the growth and development of a domestic legal system that meets international standards. Unfortunately, to date, these implications largely have escaped attention.

Although it can be argued that fundamentalist or nationalist perspectives are always difficult to influence, the lack of attention to public pedagogy as an outgrowth of the work of the tribunal was evident in our study. Bosnian legal professionals were reluctant to acknowledge that war crimes had been committed in their name and to repudiate the leaders and policies that had led to the war. Across national lines, the interview subjects voiced their belief in universal criminal accountability for perpetrators of war crimes. Yet when asked who was responsible for the war, with few exceptions only the Bosniak participants – whose national group was internationally recognized as the primary victim of aggression – named individual political leaders. Generally, Bosnian Croat and Bosnian Serb legal professionals either were unable to attribute the war to any specific cause or were unable to identify political leaders of their national group – beyond the presidents of Serbia, Croatia, and Bosnia – as directing the violence.

With each national group self-identifying as victims, one dimension of the educative function of the ICTY could have been to pierce the denial about atrocities and for bystanders to acknowledge the crimes committed in their name. The ease with which legal professionals dismissed the trial record suggests that this education would have been critical not only for the general public but also for those trained in the law. Sadly, our study suggests that nationalist perspectives distort the basic principles of legal education. Greater effort is needed by the international community to promote acceptance by domestic judges and prosecutors of the ICTY record about the war and its consequences. This effort should be a high priority if local courts are to assume an expanded role in prosecuting war criminals. A countervailing and accurate presentation of the work of the tribunal becomes more urgent where nationalist politics and media distort the record of the ICTY, intimidate Bosnian legal professionals, and undermine the independence of the judiciary. This educative effort requires cross-fertilization between rectificatory justice and legal justice.

Distributive justice

The aftermath of the war in BiH saw the collapse of a well-entrenched system of power based in the institutions erected by the Communist system. The rising tide of nationalism that reached a tipping point in 1989–1990 and led to the bloody conflict reflected many factors, including economic disparity, a struggle for wealth, power, and influence, and greed. Communist party officials reinvented themselves as nationalist politicians and succeeded in acquiring control over state assets.[14] A criminal class emerged from war-profiteering and introduced new social, economic, and political distortions in the country. While nationalist parties presented themselves as the protectors of their own, many people on all sides who survived the war felt powerless to influence the future of their country as they observed the corruption and scandals that followed in the wake of the Dayton Accords.

Against this backdrop, many Bosnian legal professionals felt increasingly powerless and devalued both as citizens and as professionals. Their situation reflected, in microcosm, the power imbalances that were rife throughout post-war Bosnian society: loss of status, economic insecurity, displacement from their homes, threats to their lives, and political interference with their professional obligations. The attitude of the judges toward the ICTY was influenced not only by nationalism but also by their own experiences living in a country emerging from war and plagued by on-going disarray. The international community must address the anger and lack of efficacy of BiH legal professionals if it hopes that judges and prosecutors will support the tribunal. As with other citizens of the country, attention to issues of social justice that affect them must be considered part and parcel of the strategies put into place to secure the rule of law and social justice.

Conclusions

For Mani's three dimensions of justice to be effective, each component needs to reinforce and build upon the other. Given the political exigencies of post-war BiH, prosecutions of the highest-ranking war criminals will need to be held under the aegis of the international community. Yet a strong rule-of-law system will be delivered not from The Hague but by the national courts of Bosnia and Herzegovina. The ICTY and national judicial officers have much to offer to each other. On a practical level, by prosecuting the "big fish" the tribunal can remove those responsible for past horrors from the reach of contemporary power structures. ICTY judgments build a body of international norms that national courts can apply. BiH judges can use international law to build a legal regime that establishes the respect for human rights necessary to rebuild democratic societies.

For the work of international tribunals to gain traction within the countries where the fighting took place, the cooperation of national judicial systems must be secured. The sheer numbers of potential defendants make national courts the primary force for prosecutions. Judges and prosecutors must have a clear understanding of international law and its administration to enable them to amplify the intended effects of international criminal trials. Furthermore, trials cannot be fair and effective without a court system supported by trained personnel and adequate resources to carry out its function. Finally, judges do not operate in a vacuum: the broader issues of equity and access must be attended to as well.

The longevity and viability of systems of international criminal justice and the emergence of the rule of law in countries emerging from mass violence will depend in large part on the ability of these judicial institutions to work in tandem, not in isolation. With purposeful interactions, these institutions can create synergies that help the rule of law take firm root within national soil.

NOTES

1. The term "Bosniak" emerged during the 1992–1995 war in Bosnia and Herzegovina to differentiate those who followed the Muslim faith and traditions from those who were Roman Catholic (Croats) and Orthodox (Serb).The term "Bosnian" refers to all citizens of the state of Bosnia and Herzegovina.
2. The Human Rights Center and the International Human Rights Law Clinic, University of California, Berkeley, and the Center for Human Rights, University of Sarajevo, "Justice, Accountability and Social Reconstruction: An Interview Study of Bosnian Judges and Prosecutors," *Berkeley Journal of International Law* 18 (1999): 102.
3. Rama Mani, "The Rule of Law or the Rule of Might? Restoring Legal Justice in the Aftermath of Conflict." In M. Pugh, ed. *Regeneration of War-Torn Societies* (London: Macmillan Press Ltd., 2000).
4. Ambassador Diego Arria, telephone conversation with Laurel Fletcher and Harvey Weinstein, 17 December 2002.
5. Virginia Morris and Michael P. Scharf, *A Documentary History and Analysis.* Vol. II of *An Insider's Guide to the International Criminal Tribunal for the Former Yugoslavia* (Irving-on-Hudson, N.Y.: Transnational Publishers, 1995), 171.
6. Madeleine Albright (1993). Quoted in Payam Akhavan, "Justice in The Hague, Peace in the Former Yugoslavia? A Commentary on the United Nations War Crimes Tribunal." *Human Rights Quarterly* 20 (1998): 765.
7. Richard J. Goldstone, *For Humanity: Reflections of a War Crimes Investigator* (New Haven and London: Yale University Press, 2000), 77.
8. The Human Rights Center, *Justice, Accountability, and Social Reconstruction.*
9. Ibid., 132.
10. *Report of the Expert Group to Conduct a Review of the Effective Operation and Functioning of the International Criminal Tribunal for the Former Yugoslavia and the International Criminal Tribunal for Rwanda,* A/54/634, 22 Nov. 1999, at para. 97.
11. Mark S. Ellis, "Bringing Justice to an Embattled Region – Creating and Implementing the 'Rules of the Road' for Bosnia-Herzegovina," *Berkeley Journal of International Law* 17 (1999): 1, 8, 19.
12. International Criminal Tribunal for the former Yugoslavia, "Report on the Judicial Status of the International Criminal Tribunal for the former

Yugoslavia and the Prospects for Referring Certain Cases to National Courts," 2002. (Unpublished.)

13. Available at Radio Free Europe/Radio Liberty website on World Wide Web at http://www.rferl.org/newsline/1999/07/260799.html.

14. Susan L. Woodward, *Balkan Tragedy: Chaos and Dissolution After the Cold War* (Washington, D.C.: The Brookings Institution, 1995), 15–17.

2   Legal responses to genocide in Rwanda

Alison Des Forges and Timothy Longman

In the aftermath of the 1994 Rwandan genocide, both the international community and the government of Rwanda have placed substantial emphasis on the prosecution of alleged perpetrators, in part because they hope that justice will promote social reconstruction. With trials at the International Criminal Tribunal for Rwanda (ICTR) based in Arusha, Tanzania, in national courts in Belgium and Switzerland, in classical courts in Rwanda, and in an innovative, local judicial system, gacaca, the Rwandan genocide has received greater judicial attention than any other case of mass atrocity in recent history. Because of the military defeat of the regime that carried out the genocide and the willingness of many countries to support judicial processes, a very substantial number of the alleged perpetrators have been apprehended and are awaiting trial. Hence, Rwanda might provide an excellent case for determining whether trials do in fact contribute to reconciliation.

Yet each of the judicial initiatives has been beset with problems, and the contribution of the sum of their activities to reconciliation remains unclear. Both international and domestic prosecutions have focused exclusively on the genocide, while war crimes and crimes against humanity allegedly perpetrated by some power-holders in the post-genocide regime have been ignored, compromising the appearance of fairness in judicial processes. The Arusha Tribunal has remained detached from Rwandan society, focusing more on legal processes and contributions to international law than on its potential impact within Rwanda. Domestic prosecutions, meanwhile, have been politicized. Even gacaca, which is being promoted as a community-based initiative that will support reconciliation more effectively than classical justice, remains one-sided and closely controlled by the government (see Karekezi et al., Chapter 3 in this volume). Although stopping impunity and building the rule of law remain essential for Rwandan society to unify and avoid future violence, it remains unclear whether prosecutions as they are now being carried out will contribute to this process, or how they will do so.

Genocide and its aftermath

From April to mid-July 1994, a group of ruthless political leaders bent on holding power launched a genocide against the Tutsi, a minority people who composed some 10 percent of the population of Rwanda. Within hours after a missile brought down the plane carrying the presidents of Rwanda and Burundi on the night of April 6, 1994, government and military officials set in motion a long-planned program to eliminate political rivals to the president and his supporters. The Presidential Guard, elite army troops, and trained civilian militia began to hunt down opposition politicians and civil society activists. They also targeted Tutsi civilians who for years had been accused of serving as "accomplices" to the largely Tutsi Rwandan Patriotic Front (RPF), a guerilla force that began making war on the Rwandan government in 1990. In principle the war had been settled by the Arusha Accords signed in August 1993, but radicals on both sides continued to prepare for a resumption of violence. With the shooting-down of the president's plane and the beginning of killings of civilians, the RPF resumed the armed struggle. Over the following several weeks, government officials, soldiers and police, political leaders, and militia members attacked Tutsi and, to a lesser extent, members of the majority Hutu ethnic group who opposed the new authorities and their genocidal program. By the time the RPF had defeated the government and driven it from the country in July, at least 500,000 people had been slain.[1]

The slaughter in Rwanda constituted genocide,[2] as the organizers intended to eliminate the Tutsi group, if at all possible, or if not, then to eliminate the maximum number. Although often portrayed as a spontaneous mass slaughter by machete-wielding peasants, the genocide was, in fact, both highly planned and remarkably modern in its organization, making extensive use of the administrative structure of the state. Organizers used the radio to order people throughout the country to hunt down Tutsi and to kill them or hand them over to the authorities for elimination. One radio propagandist promised a day when children would have to look at pictures in books to know what Tutsi looked like, because all would be gone from Rwanda.[3] Using the administrative structure of the state, the leaders of the genocide mobilized a substantial portion of the population, seeking to involve the largest number of people possible in what they came to call a "program of civilian self-defense."

In contrast to many other "administrative massacres,"[4] the Rwandan genocide involved a far larger percentage of the population, yet the emphasis of some authors on popular participation fails to take account of the varieties of participation, as well as the extent of official pressure needed to obtain such a high level of mobilization.[5] For a great number of people, involvement often constituted nothing more than passing on information to the authorities or to the militia, for example about where Tutsi were hiding. The organizers of the genocide depicted themselves as the legitimate authorities in charge of the country, a claim that was strengthened by the conduct of other governments, the United Nations (UN), and the Organization of African Unity (OAU), all of which treated the genocidal leaders as the government of Rwanda. Representatives of this government were received in Paris and Cairo, and its delegates continued to sit at the table of the UN Security Council where, by chance, Rwanda was a non-permanent member, and to take their places at the OAU summit meeting held during the genocide. Speaking with this mantle of apparent legitimacy, Rwandan officials warned the population that it must act to defend itself against the RPF and Tutsi civilians, even neighbors, who were secretly working to assure RPF victory and death to the Hutu. Officials and soldiers placed substantial pressure on people to demonstrate at least nominal support for the killing. Hutu who rejected the propaganda about Tutsi and who chose not to participate in the genocide were subjected to reproach on the radio and in public meetings, humiliation, fines, imprisonment, and even death.[6] But whether people participated under duress or willingly, they constitute tens of thousands of people, a number that has complicated efforts at rendering justice for the genocide.

International refusal to recognize the genocide was wrong, both morally and legally. When the killing began, evidence of preparations for mass slaughter had been available to the UN and the United States, France, and Belgium for several months. In addition, a UN peacekeeping force in Rwanda to facilitate implementation of the Arusha Accords was reduced from 1,700 to a few hundred soldiers because none of the major international players wanted to risk resources – financial or human – to protect Rwandan civilians from the slaughter.[7] The silence of the international community and its refusal to intervene cleared the way for the Rwandan authorities to expand the killing beyond the capital to the center and the south of the country. By the time international leaders had acknowledged that genocide was taking place, it was too late.[8] The international community intervened only after the RPF victory had driven millions of mostly Hutu refugees into neighboring Tanzania and Congo (then Zaire).[9]

The International Criminal Tribunal for Rwanda

Even during the genocide, international actors began to talk of the need for justice, an idea that was fed by their sense of guilt. The fact that the

International Criminal Tribunal for the former Yugoslavia (ICTY) was already in existence made the creation of a tribunal an obvious route to administer justice for the Rwandan genocide. Further, since the crimes in Rwanda were so much more blatant and grievous and large in scale than those committed in the former Yugoslavia, failure to create a mechanism comparable to the ICTY would almost certainly have led to accusations of racism. Following the same procedures as those used in the creation of the Hague Tribunal, the UN Secretary General appointed a human rights fact-finding team in August 1994, which found evidence of grave violations of international law, including genocide.[10] Based on these findings, the Security Council adopted Resolution 955 on November 8, 1994, to establish an international tribunal to prosecute "persons responsible for genocide and other serious violations of international humanitarian law committed in the territory of Rwanda and Rwandan citizens responsible for genocide and other such violations committed in the territory of neighboring states, between 1 January 1994 and 31 December 1994."[11]

The resolution creating the ICTR mandated two purposes for the tribunal. First, the Security Council determined that the crimes committed in Rwanda "constitute a threat to international peace and security" and "that the establishment of an international tribunal . . . will contribute to ensuring that such violations are halted and effectively redressed."[12] By holding trials, the international community would make clear that, whatever the intentions of individual states, the world community of states would not allow the authors of such gross violations of human rights to go unpunished. Second, the resolution called upon the ICTR to help bring peace and reconciliation to Rwanda.[13] This mandate differs from that of the ICTY, where the contributions to peace and reconciliation were discussed in Security Council debates but not specifically included in the resolution that established the tribunal.[14]

Having created the ICTR, the Security Council did little to ensure its successful operation. The tribunal was made an organ of the UN, whose bureaucracy was not only heavy and slow-moving but also unfamiliar with the demands of judicial operations. The UN failed initially to give the tribunal a regular appropriation and obliged it to function on the basis of short-term allocations, which meant that it could hire staff on three-month contracts only. As a result, the tribunal had trouble attracting candidates to work under such demanding conditions in a country still recovering from war. Recruitment followed UN procedures, meaning they were lengthy but not necessarily suited to choosing the most appropriate candidate. Posts often took more than a year to fill, and many candidates were hired, even for posts of great responsibility, without ever being interviewed. Many prosecutors came from academia or human rights organizations with little or no experience of criminal prosecutions. Similarly, investigators, drawn largely from police forces from around the world, had no experience of investigating crimes of such magnitude. Virtually none of the tribunal's staff, at least in the early years, knew anything about the history and culture of Rwanda.[15]

At the start, the prosecutor's office, which was originally housed in a devastated hotel that was being converted into an office structure, had no logistical and material support. Staff often lacked basic supplies such as pencils and paper, let alone typewriters or computers. They lacked vehicles to go to massacre sites or to travel to interview witnesses. These problems persisted largely because the ICTR had no powerful advocate on the Security Council or UN Secretariat.[16]

As a result of financial and personnel problems, the initial prosecution efforts were weak and disorganized. Investigators and prosecutors relied too much on witnesses identified by the Rwandan government and organizations of genocide survivors. Most of these witnesses were victims or their family members. They could describe attacks, and name some of the assailants, but they possessed no direct information about the organizers of the attacks. Yet it was the organizers, those most responsible for the genocide, who were supposed to be the target of ICTR prosecutions. Other than witness testimony, investigators made no systematic effort to gather documentary and forensic evidence linking alleged suspects to specific crimes.

Not only was evidence poorly presented in many individual cases, but also the office of the prosecutor lacked an overall prosecution strategy. Before the prosecution had fully launched its own investigations in Rwanda, governments that had already arrested suspects, but that did not want to prosecute them, had delivered them into ICTR custody. In its initial arrests, the tribunal paid insufficient attention to the hierarchy of leaders of the genocide and brought in suspects who had played relatively minor roles in it. This meant that resources intended for the "big fish" were squandered on less notorious suspects. Ultimately, because the office of the prosecutor had no overall view of the genocide, it prosecuted lower-level perpetrators without regard to using the record of their criminal activities to implicate more important figures.[17]

The quality of ICTR judges has also created problems. The tribunal is an amalgamation of civil and common law, and trial chamber judges, of whom there are three on each panel, come from both legal traditions. Some judges are former academics or government officials who have no experience of managing a courtroom. Elected by the UN General Assembly, the judges often appear to pay more attention to political concerns than to experience or competence in judicial matters. At one point the tribunal lacked enough candidates to proceed to the election of new judges, and the deadline for the naming of candidates had to be extended. Moreover, the tribunal has no program to train judges in courtroom management. In the course of trials, judges often interpret the Rules of Evidence and Procedure in different ways according their background, resulting in debates that consume a great deal of time and slow proceedings.

For the first years of the ICTR's operation, the judges worked on a very relaxed schedule, ordinarily four or four and a half days a week, often for only five hours a day. They took long vacations two or three times a year. As a result, even relatively minor trials commonly dragged on for months or even years.[18] Only in 2003, with the election of a new president for the tribunal, did the pace begin to pick up. Second, and more seriously, poor courtroom management often created degrading situations for witnesses. In the most notorious case, a defense attorney was allowed to ask a rape victim inappropriate and demeaning questions. At one point in the questioning, all three judges began laughing. They were amused, apparently, by the clumsiness of the questioning by the defense counsel, who was not experienced in cross-examination. Their laughter was widely interpreted, however, as insulting and humiliating to the witness. Such careless treatment of witnesses contributed to a refusal on the part of the two major survivors' organizations to cooperate with the ICTR.[19]

Finally, the Registry, which is responsible for the administration and logistics of the ICTR, consumes a disproportionate share of the tribunal's resources. In 1997, the UN Office for Internal Oversight Services criticized the Registry for corruption and inefficiency.[20] A year later, one of the judges publicly complained: "We have struggled against a corrupt and incompetent administration. The administration has provided far more obstacles than services to the bench."[21] Power struggles between the Registry and the other two branches of the ICTR, the Prosecution and the Chambers, have also undermined the effectiveness of the tribunal.[22]

Although the ICTR was created to satisfy the needs of the people of Rwanda for justice, the government of Rwanda has treated it with hostility. In the immediate aftermath of the genocide, the Rwandan government asked the UN to consider forming a tribunal but then, displeased with some aspects of the final Security Council resolution, cast the sole dissenting vote against the tribunal's formation.[23] In the nine years since, relations between the ICTR and the government of Rwanda have remained cool. The reasons for this division are in part ideological: Rwanda objects to the fact that the ICTR has primacy over Rwandan courts, is located in Tanzania rather than Rwanda, and excludes the death penalty as a punishment. Further, the Rwandan government has objected to corruption, inefficiency, and slowness on the part of the ICTR. It has used criticism of the tribunal for political purposes, to gain international sympathy, and to encourage increased international assistance.

The Rwandan government has also hindered the tribunal's investigation of crimes allegedly committed by RPF soldiers. In defeating the genocidal government, and in violation of international humanitarian law, RPF soldiers reportedly killed thousands of civilians.[24] The ICTR mandate authorizes the tribunal to prosecute such violations, which are known as war crimes and crimes against humanity. When the chief prosecutor announced in 2002 that she had launched investigations of several high-ranking RPF officers for such crimes, the Rwandan government responded by imposing new travel restrictions on Rwandans, making it impossible for some witnesses to leave Rwanda and travel to Arusha to testify in court. As a result, the ICTR had to suspend three trials in June 2002 for lack of witnesses. The chief prosecutor immediately took the matter to the Security Council, which delayed taking any action until December, and then only reminded Rwanda of its obligations to cooperate with the tribunal under Chapter VII of the UN Charter. In August 2003, the Security Council voted to divide the post of chief prosecutor, creating separate prosecutors for the ICTR and ICTY. While this was promoted as a means to improve the operations of the ICTR, some observers worried that it was more a means of appeasing the Rwandan government by removing Chief Prosecutor Carla Del Ponte at a time when she seemed to be moving toward issuing indictments against RPF officials.[25] With the Security Council pressing the ICTR to bring its prosecutions to a swift conclusion, no RPF soldiers have yet been indicted or brought to trial, raising doubts as to whether anyone from the RPF will ever face prosecution in an international court for crimes committed during 1994. This prosecution of accused from only one party to the Rwandan war has naturally given the impression to some people that the tribunal is working in the interest of one side only. The International Crisis Group (ICG) asserted that "the victims of the crimes of the RPF denounce [the ICTR] as an instrument of the Kigali regime, seeing the ICTR as a symbol of victor's justice."[26]

Whatever its limitations, the ICTR has made contributions to international justice and to establishing accountability for the suffering of many Rwandan people.[27] By late 2003, the tribunal had passed judgment on seventeen defendants, one of whom was acquitted. Another fifty suspects were in detention. Many of those prosecuted by the ICTR represent the persons most responsible for the Rwandan genocide, including the former prime minister and other members of his government, high-ranking military officers, political leaders, and administrative officials. In the first case decided, Jean-Paul Akayesu, the former burgomaster of Taba commune, was found guilty of genocide, the first time such a condemnation had ever been pronounced in an international court. The court also convicted him of rape, ruling that rape was used as a tool of the genocide.[28] The genocide conviction in late 2003 of three figures within the media in Rwanda was also a significant and historic application of international law.[29] ICTR prosecutions helped to isolate past authorities allegedly responsible for the genocide and thus prevented them from establishing a legitimate opposition in exile.[30]

The tribunal's contributions to reconciliation within Rwanda, however, are less clear. As noted in Chapter 10 of this volume, one of the reasons the ICTR has had such a limited impact in Rwanda is due to the fact that most Rwandans have little knowledge of the tribunal's work. In a survey we conducted in February 2002 in four Rwandan communities, 87.2 percent of respondents claimed that they were either not well informed or not at all informed about the tribunal.[31] The tribunal devotes only a very small portion of its budget to publicizing its work, leaving the task instead to organizations such as Internews, an American-based non-governmental organization that has covered the trials and set up programs to help bring this information to Rwanda. In 2002 the ICTR opened a center in the capital, Kigali, to disseminate information about the tribunal. Attractive to a tiny part of the urban elite, the center offers little to the majority of Rwandans, who are illiterate and live in rural areas.

The ICTR suffers from several inherent structural problems that also limit its ability to contribute to the process of reconciliation in Rwanda. In our qualitative research, we found that many Rwandans felt that the work of the ICTR was far removed from their daily lives. Respondents complained that the trials were held far away from Rwanda and were organized using western-style judicial practices that place a heavy emphasis on procedure and have little concern for community interests. As such, the trials have been better vehicles for establishing international law than for contributing to the process of rebuilding Rwandan society. Respondents complained that the tribunal offers survivors of the genocide no formal role other than as witnesses. The fact that many witnesses have felt poorly treated by the ICTR has contributed to negative attitudes toward the tribunal. Many respondents saw the adversarial legal approach applied in the ICTR as foreign to traditional Rwandan methods of conflict resolution, in which communities would come together and determine the nature of events and the punishments and reparations needed to reestablish social equilibrium. Although the majority of the population is not hostile to the ICTR (in contrast to the impression commonly given by the government), people tend to see it as an activity of the international community conducted primarily for its own benefit, with little relevance to processes of reconciliation in Rwanda.

Third-party national prosecutions

The creation of the ICTR and its predecessor has added weight to international human rights treaties and has inspired moves to expand the enforcement of human rights law in national jurisdictions. Since many countries are unwilling to try their former national leaders for alleged violations of human rights or international humanitarian law, often formally or informally granting amnesty in hopes that ignoring past violence will promote reconciliation, victims have turned increasingly to other countries to press their cases. The arrest of former Chilean dictator Augusto Pinochet in 1998 in the United Kingdom on a Spanish warrant for crimes he allegedly committed in Chile[32] inspired moves to arrest other national leaders accused of human rights abuses, including Henry Kissinger and Ariel Sharon.

In the aftermath of the Rwandan genocide, several countries have arrested and tried genocide suspects on their territory. To date, two such trials have taken place. In a 1999 trial before a military tribunal in Switzerland, a Rwandan burgomaster was found guilty of violating the Geneva conventions that require civilians to be treated humanely during wars. He was not charged with genocide because at that time Switzerland had no statute against genocide. He was sentenced to life in prison, a punishment that was reduced on appeal to twenty years, and is currently serving his sentence in Switzerland.

The second trial took place in Belgium, where the crime of genocide had been incorporated into the domestic penal code in an extremely broad fashion in an attempt to make the universal prescriptions against genocide and crimes against humanity real and effective.[33] The Belgian case was initiated by a complaint filed by victims of the genocide with the prosecutor. In the civil legal system, plaintiffs are permitted to play a role in the trial. They were represented by their own lawyers, who helped bring evidence against the accused. This importance of the complainant, true also for Rwandan courts, has no parallel in the ICTR, where victims are limited to serving only as witnesses.

The Belgian case came to trial in 2001 with four Rwandans – two nuns, a professor of physics at the National University of Rwanda, and a businessman – facing a jury comprised of ordinary Belgian citizens chosen at random. The jurors appeared to take seriously their responsibility to pass judgment upon Rwandans who were accused of committing genocide against fellow Rwandans outside Belgian territory. They found the four accused guilty of genocide and sentenced them to jail terms varying from twelve to twenty years. The trial demonstrated the first realization of the concept of universal jurisdiction, which holds that courts everywhere have a duty to investigate and adjudicate grievous crimes, such as genocide and crimes against humanity, because they offend all humankind.

Judicial processes in Rwanda

The overwhelming majority of those accused of participating in the genocide will be tried in Rwandan courts. When the current government took power in 1994, it considered judicial action against those allegedly responsible for the genocide to be an essential element of social reconstruction. Over the past ten years, the government has devoted considerable money and energy to criminal prosecution of alleged perpetrators, although over time the judicial strategies employed by the regime have shifted. While some cases continue to advance slowly through the classic judicial system, the government has sought to speed up criminal prosecution by transferring most cases to local, popularly elected, non-professional courts known as gacaca.

After taking power in July 1994, the RPF began to arrest large numbers of people suspected of participating in the genocide. As the RPF closed camps for the internally displaced in south-western Rwanda in 1995 and refugee camps in Congo (then Zaire) in 1996, thousands more were arrested, bringing the total number in detention to well over 100,000. The capacity of the legal system to deal with these detainees, however, was severely limited. The war and genocide had devastated the judiciary, with most judges, lawyers, and other judicial officers dead or in exile, and the physical infrastructure of the justice system in shambles. Both the Rwandan government and the international community invested heavily in the revitalization of the court system, training new judges and lawyers and rebuilding offices and courts, but trials were slow to begin.[34]

One issue that slowed the judicial process was the lack of a legal basis for trying individuals on crimes of genocide. Although Rwanda was a signatory of the Genocide Convention, the crime had never been incorporated into Rwandan law. As a result, the government spent several years writing a law to treat genocide suspects, which was eventually adopted on August 30, 1996, and commonly known as the Organic Law. The law created special courts, including a special chamber of the Supreme Court, to try suspects accused of participating in the genocide. The law divides crimes into four categories of offender. Category 1 includes: the leaders of the genocide; those who planned, organized, and supervised the killing from the national to the local level; and those who killed with particular cruelty. (The law was later amended to make rape a Category 1 crime.) Category 2 includes people who killed or intended to kill under the orders or direction of others. Category 3 includes those who caused serious bodily injury, while Category 4 includes individuals who committed property crimes. According to the Organic Law, all but those found guilty of Category 1 crimes may receive a reduced sentence in exchange for confession and implication of others.[35]

Even after the law[36] was adopted, the Rwandan government delayed beginning trials, perhaps fearing the political consequences of releasing large numbers of those falsely accused,[37] which would anger their base of support among the Tutsi minority, or finding large numbers guilty, which could alienate the Hutu majority. The first genocide trials did not begin until December 1996, and they advanced very slowly. From 1997 through June 2002, 7,211 persons were tried, of whom 1,386 were acquitted. The rate of acquittal rose from 22 percent in 2001 to 27 percent in 2002, while the number condemned to the death penalty fell from 8.4 percent in 2001 to 3.8 percent in 2002. In 2001 and 2002, the pace of the trials slowed as the judicial system turned its attention to implementing the new judicial initiative, gacaca. By early 2003 some 100,000 people were languishing in prison, many of whom had never been formally charged.

The Rwandan government has criticized the international community for investing more money in the ICTR than in rebuilding the judicial system in Rwanda. In an interview with one of the authors, Rwanda's attorney general said that if money invested in the ICTR was "intended to promote rule of law in Rwanda – they're not getting their money's worth." He compared the amount that the United States Agency for International Development (USAID) was planning to invest in gacaca each year – less than $1 million – with the $5 million the United States had offered as a reward for information leading to the arrest of a genocide suspect indicted by the ICTR. "It seems like a public relations effort," he said. "They did nothing to stop the genocide, so now they want to appear to be standing up for Rwandans."[38] A number of legal experts and political analysts have echoed these sentiments, arguing that rebuilding Rwanda's domestic judicial system should have been given priority over supporting the ICTR.[39] Law professor Jose Alvarez, for example, argues that

While international tribunals need to be kept as an option of last resort, good faith domestic prosecutions that encourage civil dissensus may better preserve collective memory and promote the mollification of victims, the accountability of perpetrators, the national (and even international) rule of law, and national reconciliation.[40]

Many other observers, however, have raised concerns over whether national prosecutions have in fact been carried out in "good faith."[41] Trials in Rwanda have taken place in an atmosphere of authoritarian rule and continuing violence, and some critics have charged that prosecutions have been influenced by political considerations. Although after it assumed power the RPF created a "Government of National Unity," with positions in the various ministries distributed among the RPF and other political parties, and including both Hutu and Tutsi from throughout the country, many observers believe that real power remained in the hands of a limited group closely associated with RPF leader Paul Kagame (who later became president) and his inner circle of former Tutsi refugees from Uganda. The ICG has called the political situation in Rwanda "the façade of pluralism."[42] Since the RPF took power, civil society and the press have been tightly controlled, and politically motivated arrests and assassinations have remained common.[43] The Rwandan Patriotic Army (RPA), the armed wing of the RPF that became Rwanda's national army after its victory, used extensive force to establish its authority over society through massacres of civilians, usually portrayed as "revenge killings," and arbitrary executions.[44] In late 1996, the RPA invaded Congo in large part to close the refugee camps that the RPF perceived as a continuing threat to Rwandan national security. Thousands of Rwandan refugees died in the bombardment of camps or were shot by the RPA as they fled into the forests.[45] In 1997–1998, the RPA again used extensive violence within Rwanda to quell an insurgency in Rwanda's north-western border region with Congo.[46] The government began a program of forced resettlement, compelling people to leave their dispersed homes and to settle in *imidugudu*, government-sponsored villages where they would ostensibly have better access to services but in reality could be more carefully monitored and controlled.[47]

Against this backdrop, many observers, both inside and outside Rwanda, believe the trials of genocide suspects have been unduly influenced by political considerations.[48] Military and government officials have harassed and intimidated prosecutors and other judicial officials, and have pressured some of them into arresting and, in some cases, convicting individuals on the basis of flimsy evidence. Arbitrary arrests have particularly targeted Hutu, especially if they were perceived to be opponents of the new regime. In the initial trials of genocide suspects, the defendants had few rights, with no legal representation and limited access to their case files, even though they faced capital charges. Military and government officials regularly sought to influence the outcome of trials. On April 24, 1998, despite international condemnation, the government executed by firing squad twenty-two individuals convicted of genocide crimes. The executions were carried out in several stadiums around the country before large crowds of spectators, emphasizing the political purposes of implementing the sentence in this way.[49]

The problems plaguing Rwanda's judicial system have arisen not simply from the physical limitations presented by the destruction of the judiciary and the finite resources available for rebuilding but also from the politicization of the judiciary. As discussed further in Chapter 8 in this volume, prosecutions have been undertaken as part of the RPF's political and ideological agenda, which holds that Rwandans were basically one people before the advent of colonialism, that hostility between the Hutu and Tutsi has resulted from a colonial experience gone wrong, and that appropriate political action can erase the animosity between the groups. This political action has included memorialization and commemoration of the genocide, general public information in numerous required public meetings, political re-education in "solidarity camps," and a refashioning of national identity symbolized in a new national anthem, flag, and seal, and the reorganization of the political structure. Within this ideology, trials serve to emphasize the destructive nature of ethnic violence in Rwanda and the role of the RPF in bringing order and rule of law to the country.

While the Rwandan government's effort to reshape Rwandan political culture to eliminate divisiveness has been widely lauded, other political motivations have influenced the government's political program and undermined the government's ability to unify the country. As Longman and Rutagengwa argue in Chapter 8, the RPF leaders have a strong sense of their own moral rectitude and great certainty of their right to rule, and they have been willing to use brutal force to maintain their power. The regime has frequently invoked the genocide to deflect responsibility for its own human rights abuses, claiming that protecting against future genocide requires extraordinary means, a position which leaders of many other governments, shamed by their own failures during the genocide, have been willing to accept. The regime has shown no interest in a truth and reconciliation commission that might expose misconduct on all sides but, instead, has pursued a one-sided justice process.[50] Trials of genocide suspects – and a pointed avoidance of substantial legal cases against RPA soldiers or others who have engaged in abuses – have sought to shape public perception to recognize the moral failings of many Hutu leaders while raising the moral standing of the current national leadership. The courts have also been used extensively to intimidate potential critics and opponents of the regime. Initially, potential opponents were arrested under genocide charges, but more recently they have been charged with fostering ethnic hatreds and divisions, as in the notable case of former president Pasteur Bizimungu, who was arrested in 2001 after trying to form an opposition political party.[51]

Given this politicization of the judiciary, it is not at all clear that investing more in the Rwandan justice system would have promoted the rule of law and encouraged reconciliation in the country. Over time, however, the political strategies of the RPF have shifted, and the performance of the judiciary, at least in treating genocide cases, has improved. The regime has sought to broaden its popular appeal by substantially reducing its use of violence (at least within Rwanda) and holding elections as part of a major decentralization program. It has also recognized that keeping a large number of genocide suspects in prison has become a political liability. The major impetus for developing gacaca as a new judicial strategy came out of a desire to speed up trials of genocide suspects, but it also was driven by discontent with the social impact of the classic judicial approach, with its adversarial nature. As discussed in Chapter 3 in this volume, the gacaca initiative grew out of a series of broad-based meetings organized by President Bizimungu at his residence, Village Urugwiro, in 1998 and 1999. The Village Urugwiro meetings, reminiscent of national conferences held a decade earlier in a number of African countries, brought together several hundred government, business, academic, civil society, and religious leaders to strategize for the country's future. Out of these discussions came a proposal to adapt Rwanda's traditional dispute resolution mechanism, gacaca, to help expedite the prosecution of genocide suspects, to ease their reintegration into the community, and to encourage communities to confront their own involvement in the genocide.[52] While the potential of gacaca to promote reconciliation has been widely lauded,[53] the fact that gacaca remains highly directed by the central government, despite its decentralized structure, and that RPF crimes are strictly excluded from consideration is likely to limit gacaca's impact.

Conclusions

Whether the pursuit of justice is really promoting social reconstruction and reconciliation in Rwanda remains to be determined. Both the international community and the Rwandan government have placed great faith in prosecutions as a means of fighting impunity and promoting the rule of law, but a variety of problems has limited the potential positive impact of the trials. The ICTR has been beset by severe problems that have slowed its progress. Even its accomplishments, however, are having little impact within Rwanda because its work is almost unknown in the country.[54] Domestic trials have been politicized and many Rwandans view them as one-sided, which compromises their ability to promote the rule of law.[55] The one-sided nature of gacaca is likely also to compromise its contribution to reconciliation.

Yet holding accountable those who carried out atrocities remains an important step in the social reconstruction of Rwanda. The failure to hold any individuals accountable for violence perpetrated in the past – in massacres in the early 1960s and 1990–1993 – clearly created an environment where genocide was possible. Yet trials are not a panacea. They must be integrated into a broader program of social reconstruction. Trials will be most effective if they are carried out by a regime that is regarded as legitimate – a representative regime chosen through free democratic elections. The political reforms implemented in recent years, however, have sought to constrain democratic freedoms, because the regime fears that democracy can too easily be distorted through ethnic manipulation. Recent elections that the regime promoted as a "transition to democracy" involved considerable intimidation and manipulation, severely compromising the new government's claim to legitimacy.[56] In this context, it is not clear whether prosecutions, particularly one-sided prosecutions, will serve more to unify or divide the Rwandan population.

NOTES

1. Alison Des Forges, *Leave None to Tell the Story: Genocide in Rwanda* (New York: Human Rights Watch, 1999). See also Gerard Prunier, *The Rwanda Crisis* (New York: Columbia University Press, 1995); Timothy Longman, "Rwanda: Chaos from Above." In Leonardo Villalon and Phil Huxtable, eds. *Critical Juncture: The African State in Transition* (Boulder: Lynne Rienner, 1997); and Timothy Longman, "Democracy and Disorder: Violence and Political Reform in Rwanda." In David Gardinier and John Clark, eds. *Political Reform in Francophone Africa* (Boulder: Westview Press, 1996).
2. The Convention on the Prevention and Punishment of the Crime of Genocide (United Nations General Assembly Resolution 260 A (III), approved December 9, 1948, entering into force January 12, 1951) defines genocide as "acts committed with intent to destroy, in whole or in part, a national, ethnical, racial, or religious group, as such."
3. The genocide received important support particularly from Radio Télévision des Milles Collines (RTLM), a quasi-private radio station set up by extremist Hutu with close ties to the highest levels of state power. On the role of the media in the genocide, see this publication from London-based Article 19, *Broadcasting Genocide: Censorship, Propaganda, and State-Sponsored Violence in Rwanda 1990–1994*, London: Article 19, 1996; and Jean-Pierre Chrétien, ed. *Rwanda: Les Médias du Génocide* (Paris: Karthala, 1995).
4. This term from Mark Osiel, *Mass Atrocity, Collective Memory, and the Law* (New Brunswick: Transaction Publishers, 1997).

5. See, for example, Phillip Gourevitch, *We Wish to Inform You that Tomorrow We Will Be Killed with our Families: Stories from Rwanda* (New York: Farrar, Straus, and Giroux, 1998), and Mahmood Mamdani, *When Victims Become Killers: Colonialism, Nativism, and the Genocide in Rwanda* (Princeton: Princeton University Press, 2001).

6. The actual number of moderate Hutu killed for resisting the genocide is difficult to determine. Clearly, many Hutu were targeted in the initial wave of violence in Kigali, but as the violence spread into the countryside, the focus on Tutsi became more pronounced. Nevertheless, in many communities, a few moderate Hutu were killed in the initial violence as a lesson to others, as demonstrated by the example of Nyakizu in Des Forges, *Leave None to Tell the Story*, 352–431.

7. On the role of the UN, see Michael Barnett, *Eyewitness to a Genocide: The United Nations and Rwanda* (Ithaca: Cornell University Press, 2002). Barnett was on leave from his academic position at the time of the genocide working for the UN. See also United Nations, *The United Nations and Rwanda, 1993–1996* (New York: United Nations Department of Public Information, 1996).

8. For a general discussion of the failure of the international community, see Des Forges, *Leave None to Tell the Story*, 595–691. Samantha Power, *A Problem from Hell: America and the Age of Genocide* (New York: Basic Books, 2002), 328–389 provides an excellent account of the United States' failure in the face of the Rwandan genocide.

9. On the international humanitarian intervention following the genocide, see Des Forges, *Leave None to Tell the Story*, 595–691, and Alan J. Kuperman, *The Limits of Humanitarian Intervention: Genocide in Rwanda* (Washington: Brookings Institution, 2001).

10. Payam Akhavan, "The International Criminal Tribunal for Rwanda: The Politics and Pragmatics of Punishment," *The American Journal of International Law* 90 (1996): 501–510; Lawyers' Committee for Human Rights, "Prosecuting Genocide in Rwanda: A Lawyers' Committee Report on the ICTR and National Trials" (Washington: Lawyers' Committee for Human Rights, July 1997), 3–4.

11. United Nations Security Council, "Resolution 955," S/RES/955 (1994).

12. Ibid.

13. The preamble to the resolution states: "Convinced that in the particular circumstances of Rwanda, the prosecution of persons responsible for genocide and other above-mentioned violations of international law would enable this aim [bringing effective justice] to be achieved and would contribute to the process of reconciliation and to the restoration and maintenance of peace," UN Security Council, "Resolution 955."

14. On the creation and organization of the ICTR, see Akhavan, "The International Criminal Tribunal for Rwanda," and Lawyers' Committee for Human Rights, "Prosecuting Genocide in Rwanda."

15. Frequent personal observation at the ICTR, 1995–2003, by Alison Des Forges; on the problems of staff competence, see Lawyers' Committee for Human Rights, "Prosecuting Genocide in Rwanda," and International Crisis Group (ICG), "International Criminal Tribunal for Rwanda:

Justice Delayed" (Nairobi, Arusha, and Brussels: International Crisis Group, June 7, 2001), 11–12. Criticism of the prosecution has come even from the bench. Shortly after the completion of the first case in 1998, Judge Lennart Aspegren criticized the prosecution staff, saying: "In general, they all have very little or no experience with criminal trials." Joakim Goksr, "Fresh Trouble as Judge Curses Rwanda Tribunal," *The Monitor*, May 2, 1998.

16. Lawyers' Committee for Human Rights, "Prosecuting Genocide in Rwanda," section VI, A and B.

17. The lack of a prosecutorial strategy is well developed by the ICG, "Justice Delayed," 12–13; ICG, "Tribunal Pénal International pour le Rwanda: le Compte à Rebours" (Nairobi and Brussels: International Crisis Group, August 1, 2002), 7–8.

18. See ICG, "Justice Delayed," and ICG, "Compte à Rebours."

19. Julia Crawford, "Rwanda Tribunal Witnesses Unhappy with Their Treatment," *Hirondelle News Agency*, May 29, 2001.

20. Lawyers' Committee for Human Rights, "Prosecuting Genocide in Rwanda," section IV, C and D.

21. Goksr, "Fresh Trouble."

22. ICG, "Justice Delayed," 12.

23. Gerald Gahima, "Re-establishing the Rule of Law and Encouraging Good Governance." Paper presented at the 55th Annual DPI/NGO Conference, New York, September 9, 2002; Government of Rwanda, "The Position of the Government of the Republic of Rwanda on the International Criminal Tribunal for Rwanda (ICTR)," *Website of the Rwandan Embassy to the United States*, available on World Wide Web at http://www.rwandemb.org/prosecution/position.htm; Victor Peskin, "International Justice and Domestic Rebuilding: An Analysis of the Role of the International Criminal Tribunal for Rwanda," *The Journal of Humanitarian Assistance*, May 20, 2000, available on World Wide Web at http://www.jha.ac/greatlakes/b003.htm.

24. Cf. Prunier, *The Rwanda Crisis*, 356–389; Des Forges, *Leave None to Tell the Story*, 692–735; Amnesty International, "Rwanda: Reports of Killings and Abductions by the Rwandese Patriotic Army, April–August 1994" (London: Amnesty International, October 20, 1994).

25. Fears that the ICTR was being manipulated for political purposes led four leading human rights groups to issue a joint statement warning that "in attempting to improve the efficiency of the Prosecutor's office, the Security Council must ensure that changes do not undermine the independence and impartiality of the ICTR, including in prosecuting charges of war crimes and crimes against humanity against members of the Rwandan Patriotic Army (RPA)." Human Rights Watch, "Leading Rights Groups Urge Security Council to Ensure Management Reforms do not Undermine Rwanda Tribunal" (New York: Human Rights Watch, August 7, 2003).

26. ICG, "Justice Delayed," iii; see also Human Rights Watch, "Rwanda: Deliver Justice for Victims of Both Sides" (New York: Human Rights Watch, August 12, 2002).

27. For an overview of the tribunal's early work, see Brenda Sue Thornton, "The International Criminal Tribunal for Rwanda: A Report from the Field," *Journal of International Affairs* 52: 2 (1999): 639.

28. ICG, "Justice Delayed," 3–5.

29. "ICTR Prosecutor Says This Week's Judgements Are Historic," *Hirondelle News Agency*, December 3, 2003.

30. Payam Akhavan, "The Contribution of the International Criminal Tribunal for Rwanda," *Duke Journal of Comparative and International Law* 7: 2 (spring 1997): 325–348.

31. For more discussion of public perceptions of the ICTR, see Timothy Longman, Phuong Pham, and Harvey Weinstein, "Rwandan Attitudes Toward the International Criminal Tribunal for Rwanda," forthcoming.

32. Ariel Dorfman, *Exorcising Terror: The Incredible Unending Trial of General Augusto Pinochet* (New York: Seven Stories Press, 2002); Diana Woodhouse, ed. *The Pinochet Case: A Legal and Constitutional Analysis* (Oxford: Hart, 2000).

33. Under heavy US pressure, Belgium repealed this law in July 2003, but it is still possible to bring charges of genocide against accused persons under certain circumstances. Jean-Pierre Stroobants, "La Belgique Abroge la Loi de Compétence Universelle," *Le Monde*, July 15, 2003; Benedicte Vaes, "Adieu à la Loi de Compétence Universelle," *Le Soir*, July 14, 2003.

34. Lawyers' Committee for Human Rights, "Prosecuting Genocide in Rwanda."

35. Jean-Paul Biramvu, "Justice et Lutte contre l'Impunité au Rwanda: La Poursuite des Crimes de Génocide et des Crimes contre l'Humanité," in Charles de Lespinay and Emile Mworoha, eds. *Construire l'Etat de Droit* (Paris: Agence Intergouvernementale de la Francophonie, 1997); Lawyers' Committee for Human Rights, "Prosecuting Genocide in Rwanda."

36. In an interview in Kigali, August 27, 2002, Attorney General Gerald Gahima estimated the overall number of acquittals at 25%. Human Rights Watch, *World Report 2002* (New York: Human Rights Watch, 2003).

37. Particularly in the first year or so after the genocide, many people were arrested under apparently false charges. Since the large numbers of accused and the lack of judicial personnel made it impossible to investigate prior to arrest, merely charging someone with genocide crimes was sufficient to have them imprisoned indefinitely. Hence, false accusations were used to settle scores, exact vengeance, or for political purposes.

38. Interview by author with Gerald Gahima.

39. Philip Gourevitch has been particularly supportive of the RPF-dominated government and dismissive of the ICTR. See Philip Gourevitch, *We Wish to Inform You*, 251–255. See also Jose E. Alvarez, "Crimes of States/Crimes of Hate: Lessons from Rwanda," *The Yale Journal of International Law* 24 (summer 1999): 365–483, and Madeline H. Morris, "The Trials of Concurrent Jurisdiction: The Case of Rwanda," *Duke Journal of Comparative and International Law* 7: 2 (spring 1997): 349–374.

40. Alvarez, "Crimes of States/Crimes of Hate," 482.

41. Cf. ICG, "Justice Delayed"; Lawyers' Committee for Human Rights, "Prosecuting Genocide in Rwanda."

42. This claim was asserted by a number of the people we interviewed. It is also strongly supported by the ICG, "Rwanda at the End of Transition: A Necessary Political Liberalisation" (Brussels: ICG, November 2002), 10–11. A detailed list of who is in power is presented in Appendix E of the ICG report. A similar analysis about the actual concentration of power is presented in the annual review of Rwandan politics in the publication by the Center for Central African Studies at the University of Antwerp, Stefaan Marysse and Filip Reyntjens, eds. *L'Afrique des Grands Lacs Annuaire* (Paris: l'Harmattan, 1997–2002).
43. ICG, "End of Transition," 11–16.
44. Des Forges, *Leave None to Tell the Story*, 692–735; Alison Des Forges and Eric Gillet, "Rwanda: The Crisis Continues" (New York: Human Rights Watch and Paris: FIDH, April 1995).
45. Timothy Longman and Alison Des Forges, "Attacked by All Sides: Civilians and the War in Eastern Zaire" (New York: Human Rights Watch and Paris: FIDH, March 1997); Filip Reyntjens, *La Guerre des Grands Lacs: Alliances Mouvantes et Conflits Extraterritoriaux en Afrique Centrale* (Paris: l'Harmattan, 1999).
46. Filip Reyntjens, "Talking or Fighting? Political Evolution in Rwanda and Burundi, 1998–1999" (Uppsala: Nordiska Afrikainstitutet, 1999); Amnesty International, *Rwanda: The Hidden Violence: Disappearances and killings continue* (London: Amnesty International, 1998).
47. Human Rights Watch, "Uprooting the Rural Poor in Rwanda" (New York: Human Rights Watch, May 2001).
48. Cf. Ligue des Droits de la Personne dans la Région des Grands Lacs (LDGL), *Entre la Violence Impunie et la Misère: Rapport sur la Situation des Droits de l'Homme: Burundi, RDC et Rwanda* (Kigali: LDGL, 2002), 144–154; Centre de Documentation et d'Information sur les Procès de Génocide (CDIPG), *Quatre Ans de Procès de Génocide: Quelle Base pour les "Juridictions Gacaca?"* (Kigali: LIPODHOR), 36–38; Lawyers' Committee for Human Rights, "Prosecuting Genocide in Rwanda."
49. CDIPG, *Quatre Ans de Procès de Génocide*, 19–54; Lawyers' Committee for Human Rights, "Prosecuting Genocide in Rwanda."
50. On the need for a truth and reconciliation commission, see Jeremy Sarkin, "The Necessity and Challenges of Establishing a Truth and Reconciliation Commission in Rwanda," *Human Rights Quarterly* 21: 3 (1999): 767–823; Mark A. Drumbl, "Punishment, Postgenocide: From Guilt to Shame to Civis in Rwanda," *New York University Law Review* 75: 5 (November 2000): 1221–1326.
51. ICG, "End of Transition," 11–12.
52. Alice Karekezi, "Juridictions Gacaca: Lutte contre l'Impunité et Promotion de la Réconciliation Nationale," *Cahiers du Centre de Gestion des Conflits* 3 (May 2001): 9–96.
53. See, for example, Helena Cobban, "The Legacies of Collective Violence: The Rwandan Genocide and the Limits of Law," *Boston Review* 7: 2 (April/May 2001), available on World Wide Web at http://www.bostonreview.net/BR27.2/cobban.html; Drumbl, "Punishment, Postgenocide."

54. See survey results in Chapter 10.
55. Cf. LDGL, *Entre la Violence Impunie et la Misère: Rapport sur la situation des droits de l'homme: Burundi, RDC et Rwanda* (LDGL, 2002), 153–154; Lawyers' Committee for Human Rights, "Prosecuting Genocide in Rwanda." In our survey, Hutu respondents overwhelmingly supported the idea of including alleged crimes by the RPF in both the ICTR and gacaca trials.
56. Amnesty International, "Rwanda: Run up to Elections Marred by Intimidation and Harassment" (London: Amnesty International, August 22, 2003); ICG, "End of Transition."

3   Localizing justice: gacaca courts in post-genocide Rwanda

Urusaro Alice Karekezi, Alphonse Nshimiyimana, and Beth Mutamba

One day in June 2002, Donatilla Iyankulije, a 27-year-old farmer with no more than a ninth grade education, found herself in the extraordinary position of presiding over a ceremony attended not only by the public but by numerous provincial and national officials, and members of the national and international press. Iyankulije, who lived in the Gishamvu Sector[1] of southern Rwanda, assumed this important public role because she had been chosen as president of a local gacaca court, a new grassroots legal mechanism adopted by the Rwandan government to respond to the legacies of the country's 1994 genocide. The government had selected Gishamvu Sector as one of twelve sectors in the country in which to test the gacaca system, and as president of the gacaca court in one of Gishamvu's three cells, it fell to Iyankulije to preside over one of the inaugural sessions of the gacaca courts held across the country that day.

The Rwandan government's decision to implement gacaca grew out of extensive national-level discussions over the country's future in the late 1990s, in which it was determined that citizen participation in the search for justice would be critical, not only for the manifestation of the truth about what happened in the genocide, but also to the creation of a conducive environment for the reconciliation of Rwandans. Modeled after a traditional Rwandan dispute resolution mechanism but adapted to modern legal sensibilities, gacaca was envisioned as a vast program that would involve a large part of the population either as judges or witnesses.[2] In popular elections held throughout Rwanda in October 2001, Iyankulije was among the 250,000 Rwandans chosen by their fellow citizens to serve as judges known as Inyangamugayo. She then was selected by her fellow Inyangamugayo judges as president of the gacaca court in her cell. After pressure from international scholars, activists, and legal practitioners, the government of Rwanda revised its initial plan and decided to implement gacaca gradually, beginning in one sector in each of Rwanda's twelve provinces, then expanding in November 2002 to one sector in each of the country's districts. Since Gishamvu was the sector chosen to test gacaca in Butare Province, Iyankulije assumed the burden of overseeing the implementation of one of the first experiments in this new, local-level justice mechanism and helping to determine the shape of gacaca courts in the rest of the country.

This chapter provides a local-level analysis of the implementation of gacaca based on the observation of the three cells in Gishamvu Sector of Nyakizu District in Butare Province. A team of fourteen researchers with the Center for Conflict Management at the National University of Rwanda, under the direction of Urusaro Alice Karekezi,[3] undertook the research. The research was conducted over a twenty-month period, beginning with the election of gacaca judges in 2001 and continuing through the first year of the operation of gacaca in Gishamvu.

The emergence of gacaca courts

The genocide and crimes against humanity committed in Rwanda involved atrocities never previously encountered in world history, notably in the immense number of victims in so short a time, the cruelty of the means employed, the extent of popular participation in the crimes, the systematic use of sexual violence, and the destructive consequences for all levels of Rwandan society. Since the end of the genocide of 1994, the new Rwandan government has made the struggle against impunity and the promotion of national reconciliation central to its political program.

Any study of the question of justice in Rwanda must take into account two factors: the emergence of cyclical ethnic violence organized and executed by the apparatus of the state since independence, and the flagrant absence of an institutional response to this generalized violence. Acts of genocide against the Tutsi population began in Rwanda in 1959 and continued into the 1960s. The Rwandan government amnestied itself for its involvement in the violence, and sought to legitimate the violence through two powerful mechanisms – the teaching of a falsified history and popular songs. The construction of the image of the Hutu as the victim of the Tutsi, autochthony, and the virtue of numbers all served progressively to legitimize violence that was essentially political and to establish mutual distrust between groups. Rwandan society became filled with fear, hatred, and violence, which created deep social ruptures and supported a culture of impunity. Thus, despite a relative calm, observers of Rwandan social life noted a progressive criminalization of the population, reaching its paroxysm with the genocide of 1994. The attack by the Rwandan Patriotic Front (RPF) on October 1, 1990 not only relit the genocidal flame in the heart of Rwandan society but also increased it tenfold. On the eve of the genocide, repeated massacres and the absence of a reaction from the state created a foundation for popular mobilization for the genocide, which led to approximately 800,000 victims;[4] thousands of survivors of sexual violence and mutilation; orphans; the forced migration of a large portion of the population; and the detention of more than 100,000 individuals suspected of participation.

Following the 1994 genocide, the new Rwandan government undertook the struggle to fight impunity and promote national reconciliation. This vast enterprise has included judicial responses and non-judicial strategies, such as the public condemnation of the genocide, commemoration, the suppression of the mention of ethnicity on identity cards, the suppression of the teaching of history, the creation of a government of national unity, and the creation of national commissions envisioned by the Arusha Accords of 1993. As part of its program to fight impunity and encourage reconciliation, the government has rebuilt the judicial system and employed judicial means to hold responsible those who committed genocide and crimes against humanity from 1990 to 1994.

As discussed in this volume by Des Forges and Longman in Chapter 2, both the international community and the Rwandan government established courts to try those suspected of participation in the genocide. The decision to develop gacaca courts emerged in a series of "meetings of reflection" to discuss the country's future organized by then-President Pasteur Bizimungu at the presidential residence, Village Urugwiro. At these meetings, which took place from May 1998 to March 1999 and included leaders of government, business, and civil society, the idea of turning to the traditional Rwandan institution for conflict management, gacaca, was proposed as a means to bring forth the truth about what happened, and to create a climate propitious for coexistence in Rwanda. Supporters of the proposal argued that the classical judicial system was limited in its ability to face the complexity and the extent of the problems presented by the genocide. Detractors saw gacaca as a disguised amnesty and feared that it would render the genocide banal. In the end, the decision moved beyond the realm of simple legal considerations, as reflected in comments by the Minister of Defense: "The problem of justice . . . is not a simple problem of texts and courts. It concerns finding an intermediary way between classical justice, the reconstitution of the social fabric, and the prevention of another tragedy, another genocide."[5]

After debate and revisions, the Transitional National Assembly (TNA) adopted a law on October 12, 2000 establishing gacaca courts to try all but the most serious crimes related to the genocide. Despite certain innovations that provide opportunities for social reconstruction, the new law seems to have not entirely taken into account the different obstacles that gacaca courts would face. The new law presented challenges that risked rendering its application difficult.

After the adoption of the law, the government undertook a vast public education campaign, which culminated in the election of judges on October 4, 2001. The elections were deemed successful both by the government and by outside observers,[6] but the implementation of gacaca stalled somewhat, as observers expressed concern over the magnitude of the project and the specifics of how gacaca would be carried out. Training of Inyangamugayo judges took place in March and April 2001, but the government ultimately decided to begin the gacaca trials with a pilot phase. On June 19, 2002, gacaca trials began in only one sector in each of Rwanda's twelve provinces, for a total of eighty pilot cell-level tribunals in the twelve sectors. Four months later, an evaluation by the commission overseeing gacaca concluded that the initial pilot was successful. On November 25, 2002, the program was expanded to encompass one sector in each of Rwanda's districts, for a total of 600, an event that was described as "the large opening" of gacaca. The gacaca initiative was expanded to the entire country in early 2004.

Each gacaca court functions at its own pace, but they all follow a set pattern. The first phase involves a general assembly of the community that focuses on determining how the massacres in the community took place and drawing up lists of suspects in public sessions. In the second phase, which is not held in public, the judges classify the accused into one of four categories as provided for in the organic law on gacaca. In the third phase of gacaca, trials are held in the appropriate court. Category 4 crimes (property crimes) are treated by cell-level gacaca courts; Category 3 crimes (those involving bodily injury) are treated by sector-level gacaca courts; and Category 2 crimes (killing or intending to kill under the direction or orders of others) are treated by district-level gacaca courts. Classical courts continue to try Category 1 crimes, the most serious offenses, including organizing the genocide, participating in killing with particular fervor, and rape.

Those who have adopted and implemented gacaca regard it as a means of encouraging reconciliation. These specialized courts were created in part to accelerate the trials of some 100,000 genocide suspects languishing in Rwanda's prisons, some having already spent more than seven years without trial. The gacaca law also sought to individualize responsibility for the genocide, in the spirit of both Nuremberg[7] and truth commissions instituted in the aftermath of human rights violations elsewhere, especially South Africa.[8] The TNA linked gacaca's search for truth with reconciliation. The gacaca law declares: "The work of testifying is a moral obligation: no one has the right to *derober* ("to conceal, hide"), whatever the cause. Above all, all the inhabitants must relate the facts that happened in their district and furnish proofs." Yet how much this new strategy will actually contribute to reconciliation remains unclear. In studying a particular community in depth over an extended period of time, we hoped to gain a better understanding not only of how gacaca courts function but also their potential for contributing to reconciliation.

Gacaca as a hybrid system

In implementing the gacaca courts, the Rwandan government has reinvented a tradition to serve goals that are both utilitarian and symbolic. Inspired by the model of participation that characterizes traditional gacaca, the resolution of litigation linked to the genocide has been, in a way, delegated to the population. A "participative" justice has been created, fusing different systems of justice. The innovative character of gacaca lies in its mixture of judicial systems and of retributive and restorative justice.

Traditional gacaca is a mechanism for resolving disputes at the local level that has been practiced since before colonial rule and has continued into the post-genocide era. The procedure for gacaca is simple. The plaintiff or victim of an infraction addresses himself to the councilor of a sector. On a fixed day of the week, the councilor calls together the concerned parties, the witnesses, and members of the committee of the cell. After hearing debates, a solution is proposed by the people present. If the decision is not accepted by the parties, they can then address another authority, such as the canton tribunal (a judicial division) or the prosecutor's office.[9]

Traditional gacaca has been concerned essentially with incidents resulting from the fact that people in Rwanda live in close proximity to one another. Its purview has been limited to legal affairs of mild seriousness such as quarrels in a bar, insults, and brawls. Most of the litigation takes place between members of a family or among close neighbors. Gacaca has responded to problems that the official courts categorize as civil affairs, using reimbursement or compensation and accompanying them with a formal, public reconciliation.[10]

Traditional gacaca is an "informal" mechanism for conflict resolution that exists at the margins of the state. Such informal judicial institutions are characterized by direct links between the parties, litigation considered as a community problem more than an individual problem, a trial centered on the victim, social pressure rather than coercion as the principal motivator, a flexible and informal procedure, voluntary participation, and decisions achieved through mutual agreement between the parties and the community, with the restoration of social harmony as the principal goal.[11] Yet as Filip Reyntjens points out, gacaca as practiced in post-independence Rwanda was not fully informal, because it involved the intervention of local authorities to whom the state assigned the responsibility of resolving conflicts that occur at the local level.[12]

In adopting the law for gacaca in 2001, the Rwandan government assigned new responsibilities for the population. The new system that was created is official, since it is created by law, and there are several important differences from traditional gacaca. In some respects, the new gacaca courts have adopted characteristics of formal justice: the trials are no longer voluntary but coercive under the authority of the state, the sanctions are punitive, the gravity of the crimes treated is much greater, the parties concerned are not always present (victims who have been killed, displaced people), there are a variety of fixed rules to follow, and there is an attempt to create an impartial tribunal.[13] Yet the new gacaca courts retain certain characteristics of traditional gacaca. They remain local in character and emphasis is placed on social restoration, with a system of commutation of punishments to works for the public good and a role for reparations, popular participation, simplification of the procedures, the important role played by social pressure, and the absence of professional judicial participation.

The gacaca courts are thus inspired both by the formal judicial system and the informal system. Their innovative character rests in the judicial syncretism that they incarnate and the plurality of their objectives. Yet this clash between formal and informal justice is sometimes difficult to reconcile.

Some observers have been troubled by the degree to which gacaca abandons the classical retributive mode of justice. Retributive justice is characterized by punishment of the guilty, representation of the community by the state, a secondary role for victims, and an adversarial approach in trials.[14] For example, the prosecutor for the Court of Appeals of Nyabisindu told us that he felt that the state was too disengaged from the gacaca process. According to his perspective, the state should reserve the right to present case files at the time of trial. The removal of the state from penal justice removes the element of coercion necessary for the proper functioning of the courts. Paradoxically, the removal of the state from the process risks compromising the motivation for popular participation.

In contrast, some observers worry that gacaca is too punitive and does not sufficiently address the needs of the communities for reconciliation. The model of "restorative" justice emphasizes reparations for the wrongs done to the victim and community, includes an essential role for victims, and strives to create dialogue and negotiation between the parties.[15] Jennifer Balint worries that the gacaca court process puts too much emphasis on punishing people within the local community:

An approach which locates responsibility purely at the local individual level will freeze identities. In the context of Rwanda, the Hutu will remain killer and the Tutsi victim. In the Rwandan national legal proceedings, there is no process at the official level which might allow for an explanation other than the Hutu perpetration of violence against Tutsi victims. There is no room for an explanation of the political dimension to the genocide or its parameters.[16]

The research project and site

Since 1991, the Center for Conflict Management (CCM) at the National University of Rwanda has conducted extensive research on the implementation of a system of gacaca courts, even before the adoption of the gacaca law. The CCM sponsored a colloquium on gacaca courts in March 2000 in Kigali that produced a multi-dimensional and interdisciplinary analysis of the proposed courts.[17] In June 2000, the CCM, in conjunction with the Center for Communication Programs at The Johns Hopkins University, conducted a national-level survey as well as focus group discussions and in-depth interviews on the perceptions of the Rwandan population about gacaca courts.[18] CCM researchers have also carried out an ongoing collection and analysis of documents related to gacaca, and have studied the decision to implement gacaca courts.

The current research project builds on the previous research by focusing on a particular community where gacaca was implemented during the first pilot phase. The research, which is on-going, has been driven by an interest in hearing the voices of Rwandans who themselves experienced the trauma of genocide and war. By studying gacaca intensively at the local level, we hoped to gain an understanding of how well the objectives of the national and international leaders who shaped the gacaca courts coincide with the interests of the Rwandan population. We also hoped to gain a better understanding of how well gacaca is managing the competing models of formal and informal justice, and the competing visions of retributive and restorative justice.

The principal activity undertaken in this project was the observation of the implementation of gacaca at the local level in Gishamvu Sector. Gishamvu is among the sectors of the current Nyakizu District, which before the administrative reform of March 2001 was the seat of Gishamvu Commune. It is divided into three cells – Muboni, Busoro, and Gishamvu. At the time of the 1994 genocide, Gishamvu, although a rural sector, boasted a substantial infrastructure. Gishamvu lies to the south of the city of Butare, on the main paved road running from Butare into Burundi. In addition to the offices of the commune, Gishamvu held the offices of the Sub-Prefecture of Busoro and was home to the Nyumba parish of the Catholic Church, convents for the Bernardine and

Benebikira sisters, and the commercial center of Nyumba. Gishamvu bordered Nyakibanda, where the Catholic Seminary of Nyakibanda was located. During the genocide, both Nyumba Parish and Nyakibanda Seminary served as places of refuge for Tutsi, and ultimately became massacre sites.

The observation of gacaca in Gishamvu Sector began with the election of gacaca judges in October 2001 and continued throughout the period leading up to gacaca's initial implementation in June 2002. CCM researchers have attended gacaca sessions in Gishamvu on a weekly basis, taking notes and monitoring the activities of the courts. In addition, we have conducted interviews with representatives of governmental institutions involved in the preparation of gacaca courts in Gishamvu and have held a workshop with civil society organizations and government officials working with gacaca in Gishamvu. The CCM also filmed some gacaca activities, particularly the presentation of prisoners to the public and the release of confessed prisoners in Butare Province.

Gacaca courts in Gishamvu

Preparations for gacaca

The residents of Gishamvu were initially suspicious of the intentions behind the selection of their sector as one of only twelve sectors in which to implement the pilot phase of gacaca. At the time, the coordinator for the sector, Gérard Rutazibwa, told us: "The choice of our sector created a lot of apprehension within the local population, and we had to organize information meetings to reassure them." The coordinator explained that the sector had been chosen because it included a large number of prisoners who had confessed and also because it had an available office where case files and other records could be safely kept. At the same time, when the decision to begin gacaca in this location was made, Gishamvu had no people outside of prison who had confessed.

The public information meetings helped to establish a good base for launching gacaca in Gishamvu. At the meetings, the residents had the opportunity to pose questions on a range of issues. These included:
• the rights of Inyangamugayo judges to give testimony
• the neutrality of Inyangamugayo judges when dealing with persons close to them and the possibility for them to bring testimony in support of them
• doubts about the integrity of those elected to be judges
• the fear of becoming a target of testimonies

- confusion over the new administrative units
- the case of those who were killed in the cell but who are not identified
- the case of people killed in an area and reparations for them.

The day for gacaca court sessions in each cell was also decided at this meeting, with Muboni meeting on Mondays, Busoro on Wednesdays, and Gishamvu on Thursdays. Even though provincial and district authorities attended and observed the meetings, the local gacaca judges were in charge and fielded all of the questions. We found that this erasure of the authorities and the giving of responsibility to the local population was an important pedagogical tactic that helped to stimulate those who act in gacaca to begin their activities.

Following these meetings, initial concerns gave way to optimism, as reflected in interviews with a number of inhabitants. Jean-Baptiste Nsengiymuva, a single 22-year-old farmer, found that "gacaca is a favor given by the Rwandan state . . . It will permit the dissipation of suspicions between the survivors and those who have their families in prison, because the truth will finally have its day." Innocent Mpakaniye, a 38-year-old farmer, felt that the community was well prepared to begin gacaca because "the population has always participated in grand numbers at the meetings consecrated to providing information about gacaca, and those who participated in these training sessions demonstrated good will to pass on the information to others."

The population of Gishamvu expressed hope that gacaca would bring justice not only for the victims of the genocide but also for the accused. People hoped that exposing the truth would help to re-establish a climate of trust, because in the absence of justice and truth, relations between different categories of the population were given to prejudice and were handicapped by mutual suspicions. In addition, the information campaign and educational sessions seemed to have clarified for the population the purposes of gacaca; however, our impression was that on-going public education about gacaca would continue to be necessary as the program was being implemented.

The role of local people in gacaca

Meetings for all three cell-level gacaca courts took place in the courtyard behind the office of Gishamvu Sector. This location is sufficiently large that the entire general assembly and observers can be seated on the grass facing the bench, and this position facilitates communication between groups. The fact that sitting on the lawn recalled traditional gacaca courts did not go unremarked, since the very name gacaca literally means "small lawn." Traditional gacaca courts were held on small grassy areas where

Table 3.1

Cell	Adult Population	Average Participation	Percentage Participating
Busoro	150	111	74.0%
Gishamvu	345	142	41.15%
Muboni	187	119	63.63%

the participants deliberated over the facts of the problem brought before them.

Although the location of the gacaca meetings in Gishamvu had the advantage of allowing easy communication, the exposure to the sun and rain presented certain disadvantages. When it rains, meetings are cancelled, but even sunny days pose problems, especially for participants who do not have umbrellas or other forms of shelter from the sun. Some people have sought shelter under the porches of homes built along the perimeter of the meeting ground, but this puts them far from the other participants in the meetings. This fact has created tension between these people and the judges, who have had to regularly call on people to rejoin the group. Those seeking shade have frequently resisted for some time before giving in to the requests to return to the main lawn. This behavior raises questions about the spirit with which these people are participating in the meetings and what can be expected from them.

The ability of gacaca to accomplish its goals of bringing justice, revealing the truth about the genocide, and contributing to reconciliation absolutely necessitates the strong participation of members of the local communities. For gacaca to succeed, the general population must furnish information and testify about the guilt or innocence of the accused. Under the coordination of the president of each court, the Inyangamugayo judges are asked to conduct the meetings in a manner that will maximize the collection of information on the genocide and on the accused. The meetings of the general assembly are intended to gather the entire adult population (those aged 18 years or older) in each cell, with the gacaca law setting a quorum of 100 for each cell, regardless of its population. In Gishamvu, the adult population of the three cells varies widely, with Busoro having only 150 adults and Muboni 187, while Gishamvu counts 345 adults, making quorum much easier to reach. A quorum of fifteen out of the nineteen judges per cell is also required for the general assembly sessions to take place.

Table 3.1 provides the average attendance at the gacaca general assembly sections in each cell in Gishamvu Sector. One important aspect to note has been the extensive participation of women. For example, women have constituted on average 60 percent of the participants in the general assembly in Gishamvu cell. Although the assemblies have generally been able to reach quorum, tardiness has been a major problem, creating pronounced delays. In its first meeting, each of the gacaca courts set 10am as the hour to begin all future meetings; in practice this hour has rarely been respected. Until the month of August 2002, the delay in starting meetings was minimal, with meetings starting on average at 10.30am. By the month of November, the delay in the arrival of community members had grown more and more substantial, with quorum not reached in some cases until 12.45pm. On average, in November 2002, the meetings began at 11.40am in Busoro, 11.30 in Muboni, and 11.55 in Gishamvu.

Regarding the important aspect of the involvement of the population in providing testimonies and other general information, our observations have been rather discouraging, especially in establishing lists of the accused. This task was almost completely abandoned to the survivors, who sometimes complained about the silence and the lack of willingness among their neighbors to cooperate by confessing to crimes or even simply supporting the testimony of the survivors. In the end, no confessions for participation in the massacres were registered within the general population; the only confessions were limited to a few who admitted having participated in minor crimes, such as pillaging or manning the barricades.

The presidents of the gacaca courts consistently denounced the silence within the general population. Often they read the lists of accused without reaction from the assembly, even though those listed were the neighbors, friends, and brothers and sisters of those who attended the meetings. People reacted only when they were personally implicated, in order to insist that they were innocent. Sometimes intense "duels" broke out between a survivor who accused someone of participation and the accused who defended himself vehemently and even appeared threatening. The survivors were thus discouraged by the fact that they were the only ones to bring testimonies and charges before the public, sometimes under the denigration of others. It seemed to us that the sentiment of not wanting to attract enemies (kutiteranya) prevailed within the general population.

Nevertheless, we noted the important acceptance of culpability in the massacres on the part of prisoners. Those in detention who had confessed their crimes had the opportunity to bring their testimony to the assembly. Each prisoner addressed the assembly in a similar fashion which became almost formulaic. First, they recognized that the genocide had taken place and expressed their regret. Then they continued by revealing their own implication in great detail. Finally, they concluded with asking forgiveness.

The role of the Inyangamugayo judges in gacaca

The important role that women are playing in gacaca is not limited to their attendance at the general assemblies but can also be seen in the conduct of meetings. Two of the three presidents of the cell-level gacaca courts are women – those in Gishamvu and Busoro. According to the law establishing gacaca, the president of each court is charged with organizing and directing the meetings. The president also names a secretary and delegates responsibilities to other members of the court. Based on our observation, we find that the three presidents have carried out important work and have, on the whole, taken on the greatest responsibilities. Beyond doubt, their leadership, engagement, and sense of responsibility have helped convince the population of the importance of the process. Through their regular presence and their scrupulous respect for rules and procedures (regarding the functioning of meetings, consensus for decisions, etc) they have inspired others to be more effective in their own participation. These presidents, more than the other actors, have made a contribution to ensuring that gacaca reaches its goals.

Besides the presidents, only the secretaries and vice-presidents (in the case of the absence of the presidents) have taken an active role in the conduct of meetings. The secretaries record all the information furnished at the meetings. We are concerned, however, about the quality of these records, even though these notes constitute an important source of data on the way in which the genocide took place. A few instances have already fed our concerns, notably that when questions have been raised that require referring to notes taken at previous meetings, it has proved difficult at times for the secretary to find the requested information, and in some cases the secretaries have insisted that they need more time to peruse their notes. Once the notes have been found, their public reading has confirmed our concerns over their quality. However, the deficiencies that we highlight should not cast doubt on the vital importance of the role that the secretaries have played; information has been recorded, and the secretaries have generally been able to locate whatever information has been requested.

If the role of the presidents and secretaries has on the whole been satisfactory, the conduct of the other Inyangamugayo judges has been less impressive. The theatrical term "walk-on" or "extra" could be applied to most of the other judges, who have generally demonstrated passivity during the meetings. For the work of the gacaca courts to achieve the expected results, the judges must play the role of a catalyst, inspiring the rest of the population to become involved. Unfortunately, most judges have done little more than fill out the required quorum by attending the meetings regularly, and in certain cases they have contributed to the delay or even cancellation of meetings by failing to show up or arriving late. At times it has been necessary to search for them in their homes in order to achieve a quorum. The statistics on judicial attendance are striking: we have noted a mean of 14 out of 19 for Muboni, 16 out of 19 for Busoro, and 15.5 out of 19 for Gishamvu. The bench in Gishamvu was full, with all 19 judges, only once – January 9, 2003.

The highest level of education among the judges in all three cells is three years of secondary school. When we raised this relatively limited level of education as a concern, we were told that the judges elected with more education became part of the higher levels of gacaca courts. The decision to move all of the more educated into sector, district, and provincial courts shows a lack of foresight, because the essential and most important work is being carried out by the cell-level gacaca courts, which have the challenging tasks of drawing up the lists of the damages and loss of life experienced during the genocide, determining those accused of participation, and categorizing their crimes.

The role of the prosecutor's office in supporting the trials has also been problematic. In preparing the lists of the accused, the panels of judges have depended not simply on testimony in the general assemblies but also on case files drawn up by the office of the prosecutor. While these files have provided some valuable information, they have also produced conflicts because of omissions and errors that they contain. Some examples include the following:

- The incomplete identification of individuals. This has led to confusion and sometimes a lack of reaction on the part of the population.
- Some people have been mentioned as witnesses who claimed before the assembly that they had never been to the prosecutor's office, had never been questioned, and had no useful information.
- Some individuals were accused of participating in the genocide, but the dossier gave no details about the nature of their participation.
- Some dossiers accused individuals of participating in the genocide, but there were no witnesses against them in the dossier.

These and other problems with the dossiers produced heated discussions in some meetings, with accusations of kidnapping after the genocide and allegations of a conspiracy of people who denounce others.

Conclusion

Our observations in Gishamvu reveal a dissonance between gacaca courts in theory and in practice. First, limits to the process of inquiry have created substantial and material imperfections in the establishment of lists. The difficulty of obtaining complete information on the number and identity of the dead at Nyumba Church is an example. These limitations arise from the small population of survivors who are available to testify, the demographic changes in communities following the displacement of the population during and after the genocide, and psychosocial factors related to the climate of distrust and division.

A second problem is that while social pressure is expected to be an important motivator for justice, speaking in public carries heavy consequences. The social stakes are high. Each revelation about the whereabouts of a mass grave or the facts about a rape can have profound evidentiary consequences, including the dissimulation or disappearance of proof. For better or worse, the truth becomes an outcome of negotiation between the actors. Truth in gacaca is both relative and social, and is therefore distinguished from theoretical judicial truth based on an inquiry by an impartial third party.

The authority of gacaca judges is based on the respect that they can inspire in the community and is critical to realizing the objectives of each meeting. Yet the election of judges on the basis of the criterion of integrity as specified in the law is not a guarantee of the effective execution of their powers. The judges need to invoke their authority to inspire greater popular participation in the general assemblies, but since this authority is based on their ability to command respect, the outcome remains problematic.

Our observations do not raise particular concerns over due process in the conduct of trials, as the gacaca courts have been effective in following the procedures set down in the law. Yet the effective functioning of gacaca trials will ultimately depend on extensive popular participation, and there are concerns on this account. The Rwandan government has not simply delegated judicial power to the population but has decentralized justice in a fashion that leaves a large margin of flexibility to the population. Popular participation does not in itself corrupt justice, but the quality of that participation does matter. The problem of participation should not be understood simply as a consequence of the reduced governmental role in delivering justice but also as a result of a society torn apart by genocide. Ironically, the lack of popular participation that is due in part to a divided social climate may limit the ability of the gacaca process to rebuild social ties.

Finally, our observations of the pilot phase of gacaca lead us to a few practical recommendations. First, it is important to assure the quality of the recording and conservation of information presented in the gacaca meetings. Second, additional training of the judges is needed and additional education of the population should occur to help clarify their roles and responsibilities. Third, it is imperative to ask prosecutors' offices to assure the quality of the case files they submit to gacaca courts, so that they do not contain errors. Fourth, greater consideration must be given to appropriate locations for gacaca meetings so that meeting conditions do not detract from participation. Finally, a broader section of the population must be called upon to participate actively in the meetings, including civil servants, business people, and other political and social figures in the community. The meetings that we have observed have been attended overwhelmingly by common farmers with limited education and limited experience in public affairs.

NOTES

1. Until 2001, Rwanda was divided into twelve prefectures, each divided into communes, sectors, and cells. The 2001 reforms changed the name of the regional units to "provinces," with few changes to their territorial limits, while the 154 communes were consolidated into 106 districts. The political organization of the districts remained in flux throughout the period of our research.

2. On the decision to implement gacaca, see Alice Karekezi, "Juridictions Gacaca: Lutte contre l'Impunité et Promotion de la Réconciliation Nationale," *Cahiers du Centre de Gestion des Conflits* 3 (May 2001): 9–96.

3. The interdisciplinary research team consisted of Urusaro Alice Karekezi, lead researcher, lawyer and criminologist; Tamasha Mpysis-Mkimbo, political scientist; Alphonse Nshimiyimana, educational psychologist; Beth Mutamba, journalist; Krisjon Rae-Olson, a student of anthropology at the University of California, Berkeley; Yolaine Williams, a student of law at McGill University; Déo Mbonyikebe, sociologist; Angeline Rutazana, Lydia Assayag, Florence Mukarugema, Judith Mulekeyisoni, and Frank Kayitare, lawyers; Kennedy Muyangeyo and Jean-Paul Dushimemungu, journalists.

4. While the exact number of victims of genocidal violence is unclear, estimates range from half a million to over 800,000.

5. *Le Verdict* 1, April 15, 1999. (*Le Verdict* is published by LIPRODHOR.)

6. Human Rights Watch, "Rwanda: Elections May Speed Genocide Trials" (New York: Human Rights Watch, October 4, 2001).

7. Madeline H. Morris, "The Trials of Concurrent Jurisdiction: The Case of Rwanda," *Duke Journal of Comparative and International Law* 7 (1997): 349–374.

8. See Priscilla B. Hayner, *Unspeakable Truths: Confronting State Terror and Atrocity* (New York: Routledge, 2001) and Martha Minow, *Between Vengeance and Forgiveness: Facing History after Genocide and Mass Violence* (Boston: Beacon Press, 1998).

9. Filip Reyntjens, "La *Gacaca* ou la Justice du Gazon au Rwanda," *Politique Africaine* 40 (December 1990): 31–41.

10. Ibid.: 35–36.

11. J. Stevens, *Traditional and Informal Justice Systems and Access to Justice in Sub-Saharan Africa* (Paris: Penal Reform International, 2000), 15.
12. Reyntjens, "La *Gacaca*," 39.
13. Stevens, "Traditional and Informal Justice Systems," 131.
14. K. Daly, "Revisiting the Relationship Between Retributive and Restorative Justice." In H. Strang and J. Braithwaite, eds. *Restorative Justice: Philosophy and Practice* (Burlington: Ashgate, 2000), 36.
15. Ibid.
16. J. Balint, "Law's Constitutive Possibilities: Reconstruction and Reconciliation in the Wake of Genocide and State Crime." In E.C. Christodoulidis and S. Veitch, eds. *Lethe's Law: Justice, Law and Ethics in Reconciliation* (Oxford: Hart Publishing, 2001), 141.
17. The results of this colloquium were published in "Les Juridictions Gacaca et les Processus de Réconciliation Nationale," *Cahiers du Centre de Gestion des Conflits* 3 (May 2001).
18. S. Gabisirege and S. Babalola, "Perceptions about the Gacaca Law in Rwanda: Evidence from a Multi-Method Study," *Special Publication No. 19* (Baltimore: Johns Hopkins University School of Public Health, Center for Communication Programs, 2001).

4 Exhumation of mass graves: balancing legal and humanitarian needs

Eric Stover and Rachel Shigekane

History counts its skeletons in round numbers.
A thousand and one remain a thousand as though the one never existed.[1]
Wislawa Szymborska

Over the past ten years, a growing tension has emerged between the humanitarian needs of families of the missing and the evidentiary needs and limitations of international war crimes tribunals in the aftermath of mass killings.[2] On the one side are families who wish to know the fate of their missing relatives and, if they have died, to receive their remains. In their work exhuming mass graves in thirty-one countries, Argentine forensic anthropologists Mimi Doretti and Luis Fondebrider have found that "families have a desperate need to recover the remains so that they may properly bury them and close – if only partially – the circle of uncertainty."[3] On the other side are international war crimes tribunals, which are charged to investigate large-scale killings but which may lack the resources or political will to undertake forensic investigations aimed at identifying all of the dead. When a tribunal does levy charges of genocide or crimes against humanity – the two most heinous of all state-sponsored crimes – against suspected high-level perpetrators of mass killings, personal identification of the victims may not be a necessary part of a legal investigation. The charge of genocide, for example, requires that the prosecution prove that the alleged perpetrators committed acts with the intent "to destroy, in whole or part, a national, ethnic, racial or religious group."[4] As such, particular persons became victims because of how they were perceived by the perpetrators.[5] A forensic investigation will then focus on ascertaining the "categorical identification" of the dead, such as the victims' ethnicity, religion, or race, and the cause and manner of death. Once these attributes have been established, the tribunal usually releases the remains to local forensic scientists to conduct the more difficult process of making personal identifications of the victims. Meanwhile, many families may continue to live with the uncertainty as to whether their missing loved ones are dead or alive.

Ideally, the relationship between the families of the missing and international war crimes tribunals should be symbiotic, benefiting both the relatives *and* the courts but, in reality, it rarely is. Since the establishment of the two *ad hoc* international criminal tribunals for the former Yugoslavia and Rwanda in the early 1990s, only a small fraction of the remains of the missing have been identified and returned to their families for proper burial. This can be attributed largely to the clandestine manner in which the bodies of the victims were disposed of, making their recovery difficult, if not impossible, without the cooperation of the actual perpetrators, who for obvious reasons would rather remain anonymous. In Rwanda, the sheer number of dead has made it virtually impossible for the country's government or the International Criminal Tribunal for Rwanda (ICTR) to undertake large-scale forensic investigations.[6] Finally, while the International Criminal Tribunal for the former Yugoslavia (ICTY) has been successful in identifying many of the dead at sites of small-scale massacres, it has chosen, largely for lack of resources, to forgo long-term identification projects at sites where the victims number in the thousands.

In this era of attention to international criminal justice and accountability, we need to develop a new, more comprehensive plan for identifying and treating the remains of the dead and working with their families and communities in the aftermath of war. We should develop a coordinated strategy that satisfies both the humanitarian needs of the families of the missing and the legal needs of international war crimes tribunals. This chapter looks at the rationale for developing such a strategy.

The search for the missing

Recent history is replete with examples of situations where the International Committee of the Red Cross (ICRC) and other humanitarian and human rights monitoring organizations have been rendered powerless by military commanders and civilian leaders who disregard their obligations under international humanitarian law and block access to detainees and other vulnerable groups. One such incident took place in the summer of 1992, when Bosnian Serb authorities repeatedly denied an ICRC delegate access to three concentration camps near the central Bosnian town of Prijedor where thousands of Bosnian Muslims and Bosnian Croats were imprisoned in appalling conditions.[7] Many of the detainees were summarily executed, while others died under torture or were starved to death.[8] It wasn't until a British television crew filmed the emaciated prisoners in one of the camps, sparking international outrage, that the camps were finally closed down.[9]

Another incident took place seven months earlier, on November 20, 1991, when a commander of the Yugoslav National Army (JNA), Army Major Veselin Sljivancanin, stopped an ICRC convoy from entering the grounds of the Vukovar hospital in eastern Croatia where hundreds of civilians were waiting to be evacuated.[10] While the ICRC delegate argued with the JNA officer in an effort to gain access, Yugoslav troops removed 200 lightly wounded soldiers and hospital workers from the hospital and bused them to a farm called Ovcara nine kilometers south of the city. As night descended, the soldiers forced the men to stand in a freshly dug pit and then opened fire.

In October 1992, largely as a result of the suspected massacre on the Ovcara farm and the existence of so-called "death camps" in central Bosnia, the UN Security Council appointed a Commission of Experts to investigate reports of massive violations of international humanitarian law in the former Yugoslavia.[11] Their findings, and some other factors (see Fletcher and Weinstein, Chaper 1 in this volume), in turn prompted the UN Security Council to establish the ICTY[12] in May 1993, and in November 1994 the UN Security Council established a second *ad hoc* tribunal, the ICTR. To gather physical evidence of war crimes the tribunals set up forensic units which themselves drew upon the expertise of forensic workers developed while investigating forced disappearances in Central and South America.

The first forensic investigation of the disappeared in Latin America took place shortly after civilian rule returned to Argentina in 1983. Trained by American forensic anthropologist Clyde Snow, a team of medical and archaeology students set out to document the whereabouts of over 10,000 persons who had disappeared during the previous seven years of military rule. Known as the Argentine Forensic Anthropology Team (EAAF), the young scientists began collecting evidence for the trial of the nine members of the military junta. This aspect of their work was short-lived, however, as the new civilian government, faced with a string of military rebellions, enacted a series of laws in the late 1980s that effectively amnestied all but a handful of military and police personnel. Still, the team persisted in their work, fueled by the conviction that the families of the missing had a right to know the fate of their loved ones and to give them a proper burial.[13]

Snow and his Argentine colleagues went on to train forensic teams in Chile and Guatemala in the early 1990s. The formation of the Guatemalan team was prompted by a declaration signed in 1992 by a coalition of family groups demanding a full accounting of the hundreds of thousands of people who were killed during Guatemala's thirty-six-year civil war. "Peace will not come to Guatemala," the family groups declared, "as long as the remains of our massacred relatives continue to be buried in clandestine cemeteries and we cannot give them Christian burials."[14]

Like their Argentine counterparts, the Guatemalan team soon discovered that their findings would be admitted as evidence in only a handful of criminal trials. As such, they placed a priority on performing exhumations for the families of the missing and their communities. During the first days of an exhumation, family members would cluster near the graves. At first, they were often reluctant to speak to the scientists – likewise, members of the forensic team recognized how important it was to let the relatives approach them at their own pace and in their own way. Invariably, after a day or so, a group of women would draw near. A widow might produce a photograph of her missing husband and recount how he had disappeared.

Often, not just families but entire villages would come to the exhumation sites in Guatemala. In the morning, women from surrounding villages would kneel next to the grave and pray for the deceased. They would cook hot meals for the scientists during the day and volunteer to heft buckets of earth out of the grave. In the evenings, men from the village would leave their fields and help the scientists cover the open pits with tarpaulins, and carry their shovels and picks back to the villages. Such encounters were extremely important for the families of the missing. For years – even decades – the military, police, and courts had denied them information about their loved ones. Now, in the presence of scientists whose sole aim was to establish the truth, the relatives could begin to regain a sense of control and help in the process of locating their missing relatives.

Led largely by the Argentine and Guatemalan teams, and by two American organizations – the American Association for the Advancement of Science (AAAS) and Physicians for Human Rights (PHR) – the search for the disappeared spread in the mid-1990s from Latin America to other parts of the world. By 1999, ninety-seven forensic scientists from twenty countries had traveled to the former Yugoslavia, Rwanda, and thirty other countries to investigate the whereabouts of the missing and to train local forensic scientists in the procedures of unearthing mass graves. They brought with them new technologies and scientific advances designed to bring greater accuracy to their investigations. Satellite imagery made it possible to generate maps to be used in pinpointing graves hidden in remote locations. Electronic mapping systems had replaced the standard archaeological technique of a baseline and string grid, which meant the teams now could save time and produce more accurate data. Most important, advancements in DNA analysis meant that the scientists could identify some remains that had confounded more traditional anthropological methods.[15]

The legal and evidentiary needs of war crimes tribunals

The first excavation of a mass grave under the auspices of the *ad hoc* international criminal tribunals for the former Yugoslavia and Rwanda took place in the grounds of a Roman Catholic Church in the western Rwandan town of Kibuye in December 1995. Out of the nearly 500 individuals exhumed at the church, leads could be established for only seventeen persons.[16] Six carried identifying documents and eleven more had clothing or personal effects recognizable to acquaintances. None had hospital X-rays or dental records. For only two of the victims could surviving blood relatives be located. Soon after the Kibuye exhumation, the Rwandan tribunal ended its forensic program. In the absence of other efforts to identify the dead, the remains of the vast majority of the victims – numbering in the hundreds of thousands – of the 1994 genocide have been left unidentified.

Meanwhile, in the former Yugoslavia, the Office of the Prosecutor (OTP) of the ICTY launched its first investigation of mass graves in the spring of 1996. One of the five sites was the pit on the Ovcara farm containing what were believed to be the remains of the 200 patients and staff from the Vukovar hospital.

The grave at Ovcara

The Ovcara investigation represents one of the best examples of how forensic efforts can satisfy both the legal and evidentiary needs of an international criminal tribunal and the humanitarian needs of families. As of October 2002, 184 of the Ovcara victims have been identified, largely on the basis of DNA analysis, and returned to relatives for burial.[17] This relatively high success rate of identification can be attributed to a concerted effort on the part of the Croatian government to identify the victims, combined with the fact that the war had left Croatia's infrastructure relatively unscathed. Prior to the OTP exhumation, four years were devoted to collecting ante-mortem information, and the Croatian government had built a modern, state-of-the-art morgue at the medical school of the University of Zagreb for the exclusive use of OTP investigators. The government also trained Croatian geneticists in DNA analysis so that they could begin analyzing the remains of those individuals whom the OTP investigators could not identify using traditional anthropological methods.

From a legal and forensic perspective, the prosecution's case against the four accused in the Ovcara indictment was fairly straightforward.[18] The Ovcara case, unlike subsequent investigations in Bosnia and Kosovo, involved a single crime – the murder of 200 people – at one location. Physical evidence of the crime was contained in a single mass grave that had been left undisturbed since the massacre. The OTP had numerous eye-witnesses who could confirm that one of the accused, then Army Major Veselin Sljivancanin, had ordered the hospital patients onto the buses that took them to their deaths on the Ovcara farm. Other witnesses, mostly survivors of the massacre, could testify that Sljivancanin and the other codefendants – three military or paramilitary officers – were on the Ovcara farm on the day of the killings.

Finally, a high level of cooperation and information exchange among the organizations of the relatives of the missing, the OTP, and the Croatian government further contributed to the successful outcome. During the investigation, the OTP investigators and Croatian forensic scientists took the time to keep the relatives of the missing informed about developments in the case. Davor Strinovic, the Croatian forensic pathologist who took over the case from the OTP investigators, was especially responsive to the needs of the families. "Dealing with the mothers has been the most painful part of my work," he said later. "For nearly five years, they have waited for some kind of news. Is he alive? Is he dead? Some mothers expected a miracle to happen, something God-sent, which would magically return their child. Then the day comes when the body's been identified and I have to inform the mother. I try to break the news kindly, but it is never easy. All those years of hope are shattered in a matter of seconds."[19]

Genocide at Srebrenica

In contrast to the Ovcara exhumation, the OTP's forensic investigation of the Srebrenica massacre rendered less salutary results for the families of the missing. Uprooted from their homes and villages, the survivors lived in squalid refugee camps and collective centers where they waited for news of their missing relatives. Because the massacre sites were behind enemy lines, they were unable to observe the exhumations and thus come to acknowledge, difficult though it was, that their loved ones might be dead. Denial nurtured hope, and when it was unfulfilled, frustration and anger took its place. At the same time, decisions were being made about the handling and investigation of the remains of the Srebrenica victims in which the families had no say.

The Srebrenica massacre began shortly after the Bosnian Serb army, under the command of General Ratko Mladic, seized the north-eastern Bosnian town on July 11, 1995. Declared a UN "safe area" two years earlier, the predominately Muslim community had swollen from a pre-war population of 9,000 to 40,000 people, many of whom had been "cleansed" from elsewhere in Bosnia. As Mladic's troops swarmed over the town, the women, children, and elderly took refuge two kilometers away in a UN base, staffed by a Dutch battalion, in the village of Potocari. Meanwhile, the remaining men and boys – some 10,000 to 15,000 – fled through the woods on foot, trying to reach Muslim-controlled territory nearly 40 miles away. Over the next three days, General Mladic's army attacked or captured and executed over 7,500 men and boys, leaving bodies where they fell or burying them in clandestine graves scattered throughout the hills. The women and children who had taken refuge at the UN base were later transferred to Bosnian Muslim-controlled territory outside of Tuzla. From collective centers and hastily erected tents, they began the wait for news of their missing relatives.[20]

On November 16, 1995, four months after the fall of the enclave, the ICTY chief prosecutor, Richard Goldstone, leveled additional charges of genocide against General Mladic and his civilian superior, Radovan Karadzic, for their role in planning and carrying out the Srebrenica massacre.[21] Four months earlier, the ICTY had also charged the two men with genocide for their role in the bombardment of civilians in Sarajevo.[22] In May 1996, after the spring thaw, Goldstone dispatched a forensic team, assembled by PHR, to begin the excavation of four of the suspected mass graves in the hills around Srebrenica. By the end of 1996, the scientists had unearthed approximately 517 bodies and assorted "disarticulated" body parts, autopsied them in a makeshift morgue to determine the cause and manner of death, and carefully preserved incriminatory evidence, such as ligatures and blindfolds.[23] The bodies – all unidentified – were then released to the custody of the local Bosnian authorities who, lacking the means to grapple with the Srebrenica identifications, placed them in an abandoned tunnel cut into a hillside in Tuzla. In effect, the OTP had decided that the establishment of the victims' ethnicity and cause and manner of death would be enough to build their case of genocide against the principal perpetrators of the massacre, and that individual identifications were unnecessary.

In the meantime, the Srebrenica survivors continued to insist that their relatives were alive. Rumors spread through the collective centers that their menfolk were languishing in Bosnian Serb prisons or working as forced laborers in mines across the border in Serbia. Many of the Srebrenica survivors blamed the Muslim authorities and the UN for failing to protect the enclave and for the loss of their men. Rallies held by the Srebrenica families on behalf of the missing often turned violent. The most serious incident took place on February 2, 1996, when hundreds of women stormed the ICRC headquarters in Tuzla, demanding that greater efforts be made to find their missing men.

Throughout 1998 and 1999, both OTP and local Bosnian investigators continued to recover thousands of bodies and body parts from the hills of Srebrenica. Meanwhile, PHR continued to collect ante-mortem information from the relatives of the missing. With no more space left in the tunnel, the remains were placed in containers in a parking lot, which further angered the family associations. Finally, in 2000, the International Commission on Missing Persons (ICMP), established by President Clinton in 1996 to assist the families of the missing throughout the former Yugoslavia, built a new storage and morgue facility for the Srebrenica remains. The Commission also began an ambitious program of DNA testing to identify the remains recovered from Srebrenica and throughout the former Yugoslavia.[24]

As of July 2003, seven years after the fall of Srebrenica, over 700 victims have been positively identified, largely through DNA analysis.[25] Although recent DNA testing is showing promising results, identifying the dead from Srebrenica has proved more difficult than naming the remains exhumed from other mass graves in Bosnia and Croatia. Indeed, the statistical odds have been stacked against the Srebrenica investigators. Unlike the deceased in the Ovcara grave, the remains of the Srebrenica victims were spread over a large area, and the vast majority had been stripped of personal documents, jewelry, and other potential leads to their identity. Bodies left in the open fell prey to scavengers which scattered the remains. In an effort to cover their tracks, Bosnian Serb soldiers used earth-moving equipment to exhume some of the graves and redeposit the remains in secondary graves. In the process, the remains were disarticulated, commingled, and crushed.[26] Rather than initiating or encouraging another international entity to make a long-term effort to identify the Srebrenica victims, the OTP turned over the remains to local forensic scientists who lacked the resources and skills to undertake such an enormous task.

Widespread killings and command responsibility in Kosovo

The OTP's next large-scale forensic investigation of war crimes in the former Yugoslavia began in mid-June 1999, days after NATO tanks rumbled into war-torn Kosovo. Over the next three months, the OTP shuttled over 300 forensic scientists from 14 countries in and out of the region in what soon became the largest international forensic investigation of war crimes – or possibly of any crime – in history. Scotland Yard, the Royal Canadian Mounted Police, and the FBI all sent teams, as did police agencies from Germany, Denmark, France, Belgium, the Netherlands, and Switzerland. The FBI team, consisting of 64 people and 107,000 pounds of equipment, even brought heavily armed agents from its Hostage Response Team to provide on-site security.

The forensic teams were charged with collecting physical evidence in support of an ICTY indictment issued against the Yugoslav president, Slobodan Milosevic, and four high-ranking military and civilian leaders on May 24, 1999. The indictment charged the five codefendants with crimes against humanity and violations of the laws of war for having "planned, instigated, ordered, committed or otherwise aided and abetted in a campaign of terror and violence directed against the Kosovo Albanian civilians living in Kosovo of the Federal Republic of Yugoslavia."[27] The core of the tribunal's indictment was based on detailed accounts of massacres that Yugoslav forces carried out against civilians in seven villages and towns throughout the province.

The most serious charge against Milosevic and his co-defendants was "crimes against humanity."[28] The term originated in the Preamble to the 1907 Hague Convention, which codified the customary law of armed conflict. In 1915, the Allies accused the Ottoman Empire of crimes against humanity. Thirty years later, in 1945, the United States and its Allies incorporated it into the Nuremberg Charter,[29] which served as the legal basis for levying charges against Nazi leaders following the Second World War. Crimes against humanity encompass a wide range of abominable acts – mass murder, extermination, enslavement, deportation, rape, torture – committed against civilians on a large scale.

While Milosevic and his codefendants faced serious charges for their actions in Kosovo, punishable with life imprisonment, the OTP's forensic investigators also had some serious investigative work ahead of them. In effect, they had to prove, beyond a reasonable doubt, that the crimes Yugoslav forces committed in villages and towns across Kosovo were not just an accident but had been planned and were *widespread and systematic*. As with Srebrenica, the investigators did not need to identify every victim. Instead, they had to establish whether the victims were civilians and whether the manner in which they were killed was similar in each of the seven villages and towns named in the indictment.

"In the absence of direct evidence of a plan to massacre these people," the OTP's deputy prosecutor, Graham Blewitt, said in July 1999, "we have to rely on circumstantial evidence. So proving patterns is important. We have to demonstrate that the tactics used by Yugoslav military, police, and paramilitary units in, say, village A were the same as those in village B on or about the same day and thereafter in village C and village D. We don't have to prove every single murder, or every single massacre, we just need to select a sample of these so that we can prove a pattern of killing and destruction aimed against civilians."[30]

Blewitt's most difficult task in Kosovo, as it had been in the Ovcara and Srebrenica cases, was establishing "command responsibility" – namely, that Milosevic and his co-accused had either ordered the acts in question or, having known that crimes were taking place, had failed to take all necessary and reasonable measures to prevent subordinates from committing such acts.[31] Establishing the chain of command in Kosovo would require gathering testimonies from Kosovar Albanians who had witnessed war crimes in the seven villages and towns named in the indictment. It also meant obtaining documentary evidence, such as orders of troop deployments, notes from high-level meetings, and intelligence intercepts of telephone conversations that would demonstrate a systematic plan, conceived and implemented at a high level, to kill and terrorize civilians in these seven locations. Finally, establishing the chain of command would require an enormous forensic effort to exhume the mass graves in these areas to determine how the victims had been killed and disposed of. In essence, the forensic experts were in Kosovo to corroborate witness testimonies and documentary evidence by identifying some of the victims of mass killings, determining how they had died, and demonstrating that the systematic and widespread nature of the killings suggested they had been planned in high places.

Given these evidentiary priorities, the OTP's forensic teams, with a few exceptions, did not set up formal procedures for gathering ante-mortem information from the relatives of the missing. Nor did they routinely take bone or teeth samples from the remains they exhumed for future DNA analysis. In addition, the teams were under a great deal of pressure to investigate as many massacre sites as possible and to report their findings back to The Hague. This put the investigators in a difficult position *vis-à-vis* the local villagers, who were waiting anxiously for the remains of their relatives to be exhumed and identified.

Forensic investigators recovered approximately 4,500 bodies from mass graves throughout Kosovo. Of these, half have been identified.[32] Some of the identifications are a legacy of the ICTY's efforts immediately following the war. But many of the dead have been identified by local and international teams working solely for humanitarian purposes. Many of the bodies originally autopsied by ICTY forensic teams were left unidentified and then reburied haphazardly, without proper identifying markers. This has caused problems for forensic teams working with the United Nations Interim Administration Mission in Kosovo (UNMIK) and the ICMP, which later re-exhumed the bodies for identification purposes. In September 2002, the ICMP launched a large-scale, DNA-led identification process, similar to the program underway in Bosnia.[33] In the meantime, the relatives of the missing have staged protests and hunger strikes throughout Kosovo demanding that the process of identifying the dead be accelerated.

The humanitarian needs of families

No large-scale, cross-cultural study has ever been conducted to understand the long-term psychological impact of disappearances on the relatives of the missing. However, anecdotal evidence and country- and population-specific studies suggest that relatives of the missing can suffer trauma-associated stress as a result of "the anguish and pain caused by the absence of a loved one."[34] Without the remains, some families may fall into a limbo of "ambiguous loss," torn between hope and grief, unable to return to the past or plan for the future.[35]

Lacking bodies and funerals, the relatives of the missing are often unable to visualize the death of their loved ones and accept it as real. Nor can they fulfill their religious and communal obligations to the dead. Funerals express the emotional links of the living to the dead, be they of respect or grief. In some cultures and religious groups, funerary rituals are explicitly carried out for the dead, but they are also rites of passages for the principal survivors, a mechanism for restoring the rent in the social fabric caused by death. Bosnian Muslims, for instance, view bereavement as an experience to be shared, strengthening the solidarity of family and community. For days and weeks after the burial, women and men may hold separate and, at times, collective prayers, or *tevhids*, for the departed. The most important aspect of the tevhid for the traditional Bosnian Muslim woman, in the words of anthropologist Tone Bringa, "is fulfilling her obligation to care for the spiritual well-being of deceased persons with whom her household has had close social relations, whether they were relatives, neighbors, or friends."[36] For the Srebrenica survivors, and especially the women, the absence of bodies robbed them not only of funerary ritual but of the visual cues that would enable them to acknowledge the death of their loved ones and to mourn.

When neighbors, friends, and relatives join together to recite, eat, and talk at a tevhid, they bring the loss of the individual into the larger community. In her study of the reburial of bones from the Second World War in Yugoslavia, Katherine Verdery found that "burials and reburials serve both to create and to reorder the community."[37] They do so by bringing people together, through exchanges of food and objects, and through limiting the "community of mourners, all of whom think they have some relation to the dead person." In defining a group of mourners, funerals strengthen the sense that the individual does not suffer the grief alone.

As the chapters in this volume suggest, mass violence and its sequel must be understood as both an individual and collective experience. Individuals lose family members, and communities are decimated.[38] In a post-war landscape, an individual dealing with the ambiguous loss of a relative must often confront the real loss of home and community and a sense of security and place in the world. Mental health problems, including post-traumatic stress symptoms, can increase when people are disconnected from their biological, personal, and historical past.[39] In this context, an important source of coping for families of the missing is the presence of a community to provide mutual support and to nurture problem-solving strategies.

Experience in several countries suggests that involving family members as observers at forensic exhumations can have positive results, especially if they are able to observe both the technical skills required and the care that is taken to honor the dead.[40] Involving family members in the collection of ante-mortem data, such as medical records and X-rays, to help identify the deceased may also help ease feelings of helplessness and survivor's guilt. At the community level, exhumations can become a commemorative event that can facilitate the process of mourning. If conducted under the aegis of local or international institutions, exhumations can help individual mourners and whole communities receive acknowledgment of their loss and move forward in the grieving process. The presence of family members at exhumations can also remind the forensic investigators of the human difference their work is making.[41]

These concerns cross cultures and traditions. According to the Amani Trust, a Zimbabwean human rights organization, many family members of the missing in the western province of Matabeland have experienced tremendous psychological suffering because they have been unable to bury and mourn their dead according to local custom. In the Ndebele culture the dead play a significant role in the well-being of the living, and those who have not been given a proper burial can return as "a restless and vengeful presence, innocent yet wronged, aggrieved and dangerous to the living."[42] In order for an ancestral spirit to fulfill its true task of protecting the family, it needs an honorable funeral followed by another traditional ritual whereby the spirit of the deceased is welcomed back into the family home.

In contrast to the legally motivated exhumations carried out by the *ad hoc* international criminal tribunals, the Amani Trust conducts exhumations and reburials solely at the request of the families of the missing. "Our work is not about the exhumation of hundreds or thousands of skeletons in a short space of time," writes Shari Eppel. "We are more concerned in exhuming a few graves and working closely with the families and communities over several years, in order to gain a more thorough understanding of how the process of exhumations and reburials can transform the lives of families and restore the social fabric" in the wake of widespread political violence.[43] For instance, in the five adjacent villages where the Amani Trust has worked for the past four years, the collection of ante-mortem records from family members is used to conduct informal "testimony therapy." Over consecutive visits, family members are encouraged to recall the complete history and habits of the deceased, something they may never have had the opportunity to do since the death. Amani workers also prepare family members for the pitfalls of exhumations, including the real possibility that the remains of the deceased may not be located or that the remains, upon post-mortem examination, may reveal that the deceased suffered great physical trauma prior to death.

Some individuals, families, and entire communities in post-war societies may find it too painful to go through the process of identifying the dead, especially if the effort will take years. Or they may have other cultural needs that preclude individual identifications. Many of the Srebrenica survivors, for instance, believe that the construction of a memorial and a collective burial site for the anonymous dead should take precedence over individual identifications. In 2000, these survivors lobbied successfully for a commemorative site to be built at a location near to where the massacres took place. Their active participation in choosing the site and in its planning and design gave the survivors a sense of control over their own needs and ultimately of the mourning process that had been denied them for so many years.[44]

In the 1990s, Guatemalan archeologists discovered a creative way of allowing families of the missing to participate in funeral ceremonies of the deceased even if the remains of their loved ones had not been identified. The incident took place in the village of Panzos, where the scientists had exhumed twenty-seven skeletons from a mass grave near the village. After weeks of analysis, the scientists could identify only two of the skeletons. In preparation for the funeral, the scientists placed the skeletons in small coffins and took them to the community center. Artifacts, such as pieces of burnt clothing or coins found in pockets, were placed on top of each coffin. Because the greatest desire of family members was to carry the remains of their loved ones in the burial procession, the scientists gave them an opportunity to look at the artifacts. Although these were not considered positive scientific identifications, when survivors recognized an artifact, they lined up beside the coffin. As other family members reached the end of the row of coffins without immediately recognizing anything, they would return and start over. Within a few minutes, a cluster of survivors was standing beside each coffin. When one of the scientists approached a family to find out what they had identified, they shook their heads and said "nothing." Then an elderly man added: "If this coffin doesn't have an owner, it is ours." That evening the families carried the anonymous coffins to the village cemetery and laid their dead to rest.[45]

Psychologists dealing with survivors of trauma have long postulated that personal efficacy is a major determinant in recovery. In recovering from trauma, Judith Herman argues that "no intervention that takes power away from the survivor can possibly foster her recovery, no matter how much it appears to be in her immediate best interest."[46] Another way of examining this phenomenon is through the "control over one's destiny" hypothesis, which postulates that gaining a sense of control in one's life often leads to better health outcomes.[47] Both the examples from Srebrenica and Panzos suggest that families should have more than just "a right to know the fate" of their missing loved ones: they should also be actively involved in the consultative and decision-making processes of locating, exhuming, reburying, and memorializing the dead.

Conclusion

In its 2002 report, the UN Office of the High Commissioner for Human Rights stressed that "the growing number of national conflicts generating gross and massive human rights violations has provided more impetus to the need to resort to forensic and related experts to identify the victims."[48] This demand has spawned the formation of nine forensic teams and programs within non-governmental organizations dedicated to the medico-legal investigation of violations of international human rights and humanitarian law. The UN, through its Commission on Human Rights, has also created a list of 487 forensic experts who are available for human rights fact-finding missions.[49]

As more forensic scientists enter this growing field, the international community needs to develop scientific and ethical standards and protocols relating to the exhumation and post-mortem examination of the remains of the missing. Such guidelines should ensure that forensic investigations into the fate of the missing are conducted in a manner that serves the best interests of the families and their communities as well as bringing those responsible for these crimes to justice. The ICRC, after a year of consultations with forensic scientists, military personnel, jurists, and representatives of family and human rights organizations, has called on forensic scientists working in the context of the missing to demonstrate a level of professionalism that goes beyond simply adhering to scientific standards. Forensic specialists, the ICRC argues, must also advocate the development of an identification process of the dead and observe and record all crime-scene and post-mortem information potentially relevant to identification; refrain from destroying material that may be used for future identification purposes; consider the families' rights and needs before, during, and after exhumation; and know the ethical boundaries of their work. The underlying message is that forensic scientists must recognize that they have an obligation to the legal institutions that retain their services *and* to the families of the missing.

There is also a need to establish an international network of forensic scientists to work on behalf of missing persons.[50] This network should be under the auspices of the ICRC in Geneva or be established as a wholly independent institution without affiliation to any government. Such an organization should be guided by the principle that "identification for purposes of informing the family and returning remains *is just as important as* providing evidence for criminal investigations and constitutes due recognition of the rights of the families [emphasis added]." It should, among other things, develop and disseminate guidelines and standards of practice and codes of ethical conduct; accredit laboratories to undertake DNA analysis; help train local and regional forensic teams which will be best suited to deal with local cultural customs and traditions; lobby governments to make forensic expertise and material resources available for national and international work; speak out on behalf of forensic scientists who face persecution for their professional activities; and develop mechanisms for debriefing and providing psychological assistance to forensic scientists.

In our view, such a network should be inclusive rather than exclusive. The network should facilitate rather than dictate. And it must not internationalize the search for the missing to such an extent that it undermines the capacity of local governmental and non-governmental institutions to develop culturally appropriate responses to what are ultimately local problems. The network must ensure that the families of the missing and the organizations that represent them have a voice at all times in the decision-making processes that guide forensic investigations into the fate of the missing.

The challenge that forensic scientists face in today's increasingly violent world is to keep the primacy of international criminal law from supplanting our obligations to the living. Forensic scientists must continue to be advocates for the dead. But, in doing so, they must not lose sight of the needs and rights of the survivors and their communities, for whom justice is also sought.

NOTES

1. Wislawa Szymborska, "Hunger Camp at Jasko." In Carolyn Forche, ed. *Against Forgetting: Twentieth Century Poetry of Witness* (New York: W. W. Norton, 1993), 459.
2. A version of this chapter appeared under the title "The Missing in the Aftermath of War: When Do the Needs of Victims' Families and International War Crimes Tribunals Clash?," *International Review of the Red Cross* 84:848 (2002): 845–866.
3. Mimi Doretti and Luis Fondebrider, "Science and Human Rights – Truth, Justice, Reparation and Reconciliation: A Long Way in Third World Countries." In V. Buchli and L. Gavin, eds. *Archaeologies of the Contemporary Past* (London: Routledge, 2001), 138–144.
4. *Convention on the Prevention and Punishment of the Crime of Genocide*, 78 UNTS. 277, adopted by Resolution 260 (III) A of the General Assembly of the United Nations on December 9, 1948.
5. See William D. Haglund, "Recent Mass Graves: An Introduction." In William D. Haglund and Marcell Sorg, eds. *Advances in Forensic Taphonomy* (New York: CPR Press, 2001), 243–262.
6. See *The Prosecutor v. Jean Kambanda*, International Criminal Tribunal for Rwanda, ICTR 97-23-S (1998).
7. One of the camps, Omarska, alone held a total of 3,000 or more prisoners. See *The Prosecutor v. Kvocka et al.*, International Criminal Tribunal for the former Yugoslavia, ICTY IT-98-30/1 (2001), 8.
8. In its judgment, the tribunal noted that: "The evidence is overwhelming that abusive treatment and inhuman conditions in the camps were standard operating procedure . . . Many detainees perished as a result of the inhumane conditions, in addition to those who died as a result of the physical violence inflicted upon them." See *The Prosecutor v. Kvocka et al.*
9. Roy Gutman, *Witness to Genocide* (New York: Macmillan Publishing, 1993), 63. Two of the camps, Omarska and Keraterm, were closed in August 1992 and a third, Trnopolje, was closed in October 1992.
10. See Eric Stover and Gilles Peress, *The Graves: Srebrenica and Vukovar* (Zurich: Scalo, 1998), 104–107.
11. See United Nations Security Council *Final Report of the Commission of Experts Established Pursuant to Security Council Resolution 780 (1992)*, S/1994/674,1994 and Annexes, S/1994/674/Add. 2 (Vol. I–V). 1994.
12. SC Res. 827, UN SCOR, 48th Session, 3217th Meeting, UN Document S/RES/827 (1993).
13. See Christopher Joyce and Eric Stover, *Witnesses from the Grave: The Stories Bones Tell* (Boston: Little, Brown, Inc., 1991), 215–305.
14. See Dawnie W. Steadman and William D. Haglund, "The Anthropologist/ Archaeologist in International Human Rights Investigations." Paper

presented at the *Annual Meeting of the American Academy of Forensic Sciences*, Seattle, Wash., February 2001.

15. See Stover and Peress, *The Graves*.
16. See Haglund, "Recent Mass Graves," 243–262.
17. Davor Strinovic, conversation with author, Institute for Forensic Medicine and Criminology, Zagreb, Croatia, 11 October 2002.
18. See *The Prosecutor v. Mile Mrksic, Miroslav Radic, Veselin Sljivancanin, and Slavko Dokmanovic*, International Criminal Tribunal for the former Yugoslavia, Case No. ICTY IT-95-13a-I (1997).
19. Davor Strenovic, quoted in Stover and Peress, *The Graves*, 210–211.
20. Jan Willem Honig and Norbert Both, *Srebrenica: Record of a War* (London: Penguin Books, 1996), 28–47.
21. See *The Prosecutor v. Karadzic & Mladic*, International Criminal Tribunal for the former Yugoslavia, ICTY IT-95-18 (1995).
22. Ibid.
23. See Stover and Peress, *The Graves*.
24. See the International Commission of Missing Persons at www.ic-mp.org/icfact.asp.
25. Ibid.
26. Testimony of William Haglund, *The Prosecutor v. Krstic*, International Criminal Tribunal for the former Yugoslavia, Case No. ICTY IT-98-33 (1999), T. 3722.
27. See *The Prosecutor v. Milosevic et al.*, International Criminal Tribunal for the former Yugoslavia, ICTY IT-02-54 (1999), para. 90.
28. United Nations Security Council *Statute of the International Criminal Tribunal for the former Yugoslavia*, adopted by UN Security Council Resolution 827 on May 25, 1993.
29. *The Charter of the International Military Tribunal*, annexed to the *London Agreement for the Prosecution and Punishment of the Major War Criminals of the European Axis*, of August 8, 1945, Art. 6(c).
30. Graham Blewitt, quoted in Fred Abrahams, Gilles Peress, and Eric Stover, *A Village Destroyed: May 14, 1999, War Crimes in Kosovo* (Berkeley, Calif.: University of California Press, 2002), 75.
31. The principle enunciating the responsibility of command derives from the principle of individual criminal responsibility applied by the Nuremberg and Tokyo Tribunals. It was subsequently codified in Article 86 of the Additional Protocol I of June 8, 1977 to the Geneva Conventions of 1949.
32. Jose-Pablo Baraybar, Director, Office on Missing Persons and Forensics, United Nations Interim Administration Mission in Kosovo (UNMIK), "29 September 2002 – UNMIK/PR/835 – Steiner Concludes Successful Visit to Slovenia." *UNMIK Press Releases 2002*, available at http://www.unmikonline.org/press/pressr02.htm.
33. United Nations Interim Administration Mission in Kosovo (UNMIK), "24 September 2002 – UNMIK/PR/828 – Plans Completed for Setting up Medical Examiners' Office of Kosovo." *UNMIK Press Releases 2002*, available at http://www.unmikonline.org/press/pressr02.htm.

34. Amnesty International, *'Disappearances': A Workbook* (New York: Amnesty International USA Publications, 1981), 109. Also, see Gregory J. Quirk and Leonel Casco, "Stress Disorders of Families of the Disappeared: A Controlled Study in Honduras," *Social Science and Medicine* 39:12 (1994): 1675–1679. Also, see Harvey M. Weinstein, "Where There Is No Body: Trauma and Bereavement in Communities Coping with the Aftermath of Mass Violence," *International Committee for the Red Cross Proceedings of Conference on the Missing: Action to Resolve the Problem of People Unaccounted for as a Result of Armed Conflict or Internal Violence and to Assist their Families* (ICRC, Geneva, June, 2002).

35. See Pauline Boss, *Ambiguous Loss: Learning to Live with Unresolved Grief* (Cambridge, Mass.: Harvard University Press, 1999).

36. See Tone Bringa, *Being Muslim the Bosnian Way: Identity and Community in a Central Bosnian Village* (Princeton, N.J.: Princeton University Press, 1995), 194.

37. Katherine Verdery, *The Political Lives of Dead Bodies: Reburial and Postsocialist Change* (New York: Columbia University Press, 1999), 107–108.

38. See Derek Summerfield, "Addressing Human Response to War and Atrocity: Major Challenges in Research and Practices and the Limitations of Western Psychiatric Models." In Rolf J. Kleber, Charles R. Figley, and Berthold P. R. Gersons, eds. *Beyond Trauma: Cultural and Societal Dynamics* (New York: Plenum Press, 1995), 19–22.

39. R. Lindheim and L. Symes, "Environments, People, and Health," *Annual Review of Public Health* 4 (1983): 335–359.

40. See Doretti and Fondebrider, "Science and Human Rights."

41. Luis Fondebrider, "Reflections of the Scientific Documentation of Human Rights Violations." Paper presented at the *ICRC Workshop on Human Remains: Law, Politics, and Ethics*, Geneva, Switzerland, May 2002.

42. See Shari Eppel, "Healing the Dead to Transform the Living: The Preventive Implications." Paper presented at the *International Seminar on Torture and Organized Violence in the 21st Century*, Copenhagen, Denmark, January 2001.

43. Ibid.

44. Craig Evan Pollack, "Burial at Srebrenica: Linking Place and Trauma," *Social Science & Medicine* 56 (2003): 793–801.

45. See Victoria Sanford, *Buried Secrets: Truth and Human Rights in Guatemala* (New York: Palgrave Macmillan, 2003), 234–235.

46. Judith Herman, *Trauma and Recovery: The Aftermath of Violence – From Domestic Abuse to Political Terror* (New York: Basic Books, 1992), 134.

47. See S. Leonard Syme, "Social and Economic Disparities in Health: Thoughts about Intervention," *The Millbank Quarterly* 76 (1998): 493–505.

48. United Nations High Commissioner for Refugees. *Report of the United Nations Office of the High Commissioner for Human Rights*, E/CN.4/2002/67, January 2002.

49. Ibid. The UN has also produced two documents – the *Manual for the Prevention of Extra-Legal, Arbitrary and Summary Executions* and the *Guidelines for the Conduct of United Nations Inquiries into Allegations of Massacres* – that set

out the standards and procedures for investigating war crimes and violations of human rights.

50. See ICRC, "The Missing: International Committee of the Red Cross Report (Summary of the Conclusions Arising from Events Held prior to the International Conference of Governmental and Non-Governmental Experts), 19–21 February 2003," working paper, International Committee of the Red Cross, Geneva, 2003.

5   Witnesses and the promise of justice in The Hague

Eric Stover

One day in February 1998, as a Croatia Airlines flight made its final descent into Zagreb, a man we will call Dean Levic leaned his forehead against the plane's window and gazed down on the red-tiled roofs of his homeland. The day before, in The Hague, he had held a courtroom spellbound as he described how, seven years earlier, Serb troops had removed over 200 men from a hospital in his hometown and gunned them down on a remote farm in eastern Croatia. Sitting only a few yards away from one of the men accused of ordering the massacre, Dean had been surprised, astonished even, at his own poise and confidence on the stand. Not even the defendant's attorney, a top Belgrade lawyer, was able to rattle him. But now, as the plane pressed down onto the tarmac, Dean began to wonder if he had done the right thing.

On his way home, Dean felt that fear was beginning to commandeer his thoughts. Although his name had not been disclosed at the trial, he was sure that word had already leaked out about his testimony. It had happened to other protected witnesses, including a neighbor who had returned home to find a death threat spray-painted across the windshield of his car. If his boss, a Serb, caught wind of his testimony, Dean was sure he would be fired on the spot. Then there was the problem of his wife. On the day he left for The Hague, she had stormed out of the house with their daughter, furious that he would put his family in danger. "In The Hague I had felt like I was serving justice. You know, actually doing some good for my community," Dean said later. "Then suddenly it all changed. I was back in my country playing life's fool."

By the end of 2003 hundreds of prosecution witnesses like Dean Levic had traveled to The Hague to testify before the International Criminal Tribunal for the former Yugoslavia (ICTY). Like Levic, most of them had witnessed wartime atrocities, including mass killings, torture, rape, inhumane imprisonment, forced expulsion, and the destruction of their homes and villages. For many witnesses the act of testifying in an international court required an act of great courage, especially as they were well aware that war criminals still walked the streets of their villages and towns. Yet despite these risks, little attention has been paid to the fate of witnesses like Levic. Nor do we know much about their experiences testifying before an international tribunal or the effect of such testimony on their return to their post-war communities.

In 2001, I interviewed eighty-seven ICTY witnesses, including Dean Levic, to understand their experiences, thoughts, and feelings about the tribunal and its effects on their communities in the aftermath of the recent Balkan wars.[1] I also interviewed seven potential witnesses who had given statements to tribunal investigators in their countries of residence but who were not called to testify. All of the witnesses had testified on behalf of the prosecution. Sixty-two (72 percent) of the witnesses interviewed were Bosnian Muslims who had testified in one of five trials involving alleged war crimes committed during the siege of the Lasva Valley by Bosnian Croat troops in April 1993. Twenty respondents (23 percent) were Croats who had testified in the trial of the former mayor of Vukovar, Slavko Dokmanovic. Five respondents (5 percent) were Bosnian Serbs who had testified in the trial of four codefendants who, for a period of several months in 1992, were commanders or guards at the Celibici prison camp in southern Bosnia. The majority of the study participants had been non-combatants at the time they experienced or witnessed an alleged war crime.

Victims and witnesses are the "lifeblood of ICTY trials," writes a former tribunal judge.[2] Indeed, because the Balkan offenders did not keep meticulous records of their bloody deeds, prosecutors have needed a substantial number of eyewitnesses to make their charges stick. At the same time, the tribunal has said that one of its objectives is to provide justice to victims of war crimes. Yet is that goal being achieved?

The moral duty to testify

The study's principal finding suggests that *under the right conditions* international criminal courts, while striving to guarantee defendants a fair and public trial, can acknowledge the suffering of those most directly affected by war crimes and help them discharge their moral duty to testify on behalf of the dead. Seventy-nine study participants (90 percent), whatever their national identity, said it was their moral obligation to testify before the Hague Tribunal. "It was my wish, my desire, and my duty to my family to testify," a witness said. Indeed, the need to speak for those who were missing or dead was so pervasive that even if they had complaints or misgivings about the ICTY, most respondents said they would testify again if only to ensure that the fate of their families and neighbors would never be forgotten.

The witnesses went to The Hague not on a quest for vengeance – time had dimmed such fantasies, if they had existed at all – but to set the record straight about the suffering of their families and communities in the presence of the accused. "It was not a question of revenge," a witness said. "I just wanted to meet the accused on the same level and to remind him of what he did to me and my family." Some witnesses, at least in their own minds, had struck a deal with the ICTY: they would provide the court with the "factual truth" – who killed whom, at what range, and on what day and hour – but in return they wanted the tribunal to help them find meaning in their loss and suffering. Many witnesses yearned to understand *why* the defendants – who were their fellow citizens and in some cases neighbors – had committed, or let their subordinates commit, such abominable acts. A 55-year-old housewife waited anxiously for the day she could confront the three neighbors she held responsible for the death of her husband and neighbors. "I wanted to see the [three defendants] in the courtroom and to ask them why they did it. Why did they kill all these people? Why did they destroy our village? We had such good relations. We were good neighbors. I just wanted one of them . . . to tell me why they did that."

Such expectations place a heavy – and, perhaps, an unrealistic – burden on international criminal courts. War crimes trials, at their best, can create an aura of fairness, establish a public record, and produce some sense of accountability by acknowledging the losses that victims have suffered and punishing the perpetrators for the harms inflicted. Trials also can create credible documents and events that acknowledge and condemn horrors.[3] For some victims, testifying can help bring about a sense of acceptance of loss and facilitate a positive change in their perception of the future. But, by and large, war crimes trials are generally ill-suited for the sort of expansive and nuanced storytelling so many witnesses seek.

Courtrooms are hardly safe and secure environments for the recounting of traumatic events. Judges can – and often do – admonish witnesses who stray from the facts, which in turn can frustrate victims who have waited years to tell their story publicly. The adversarial nature of trials also can result in unanticipated and unexpected events in the courtroom. A long-suppressed memory or the sight of a photograph of a loved one can devastate even the most confident witness. So can the hardscrabble cross-examination by defense attorneys as they set out to poke holes in a witness's testimony or impugn his or her credibility. On leaving the courtroom, witnesses are generally anxious to receive appreciation from their prosecutors, but sometimes the lawyers are not available to debrief or even thank them. Witnesses also may feel that the court did not "respect" them, especially if they had to endure an intense cross-examination or were not given extra time to say what they wanted at the end of their final testimony. And, in a few cases, witnesses may even travel to The Hague but end up not testifying, for trial-related reasons.

Human rights activists often valorize the "therapeutic value" of war crimes trials for victims and witnesses.[4] They argue that victims who are able to recount horrific events in a context of acknowledgment and support will often find closure and be able to move on with their lives. The findings of this study (and corroborating data from our parallel studies – see Chapters 9 and 10 in this volume), however, suggest that such claims so far as war crimes trials are concerned reflect more wishful thinking than fact. The few participants who experienced cathartic feelings immediately or soon after testifying before the ICTY found that the glow quickly faded once they returned home to their shattered villages and towns. This was especially true for witnesses who faced uncertainties in their lives, including the loss of a job, death of a loved one, or eviction from their homes. Respondents also reported feelings of helplessness, abandonment, and anger when they learned of the light sentences meted out by the tribunal, or of the reversal of an earlier conviction on appeal. Still others who had testified against high-level defendants said that their "work as a witness" would be complete only once they had testified against *local* war criminals whom they held directly responsible for the deaths of family members and neighbors.

The idea that war crimes trials can be healing for victims and witnesses is further undermined by the sense of abandonment that many of the witnesses felt on their return home. Some had developed unreasonable expectations of what a war crimes tribunal can do, expecting it to make all things right. Others attributed this sense of desertion to the lenient sentences meted out to the accused, the lack of information about their cases, or their inability to gain immediate access to ICTY personnel when they and their families were threatened. The most disgruntled study participants were those witnesses who had testified in a case that was later overturned on appeal. "When I heard about the appellate ruling," one female witness said, "I immediately took five valiums. No one from The Hague called, no one came or even bothered to explain what had happened . . . [The ICTY investigators] lured us to testify, but that was all about them, making money for themselves. I would go to The Hague just to tell them what I think of it."

These findings underscore what mental health professionals have long recognized as the basic components of recovery from personal trauma or loss: namely, that recovery takes place over time and in stages, and that it must be accompanied by a sense of safety, restoration of control over one's life, and the ability to reconnect with others.[5] Recovery from trauma rarely results from a single cathartic experience. The impact of a traumatic event can continue to reverberate throughout a victim's life. Changes in the life cycle, such as marriage or divorce, a birth or death in the family, the loss of a job, illness, or retirement can trigger a resurgence of traumatic memories. For survivors of ethnic cleansing, recovery is further complicated by the fact that many – if not most – of its victims suffered multiple traumatic events, including imprisonment, personal violence, loss of family members and friends, destruction of property, and forced displacement (see Longman et al., Chapter 10). Post-war destruction throughout the countryside can further compound trauma by constantly reminding survivors of the past conflict and their losses.

Most survivors of violent crime seek to resolve their traumatic experience within the confines of their personal lives. "But a significant minority," writes Judith Herman, "feel called upon to engage in a wider world." These survivors find that they can transform the meaning of their personal tragedy through social action, including the pursuit of justice. Survivors who elect to engage in legal battle, she argues, will discover an inner "source of power that draws upon [their] own initiative, energy, and resourcefulness." Joining with other survivors, they can forge an alliance based on shared cooperation and purpose. Thus, survivors who choose legal action recognize that holding perpetrators accountable for their crimes "is important not only for . . . personal well-being but also for the health of the larger society."[6]

Herman's notion of a "survivor mission" resonated in the interviews conducted for this study, but in a slightly altered form. Indeed, only two of the eighty-seven witnesses said they went to The Hague to perform a universal good for, say, the Bosnian or Croatian or Serbian nation, or for all victims of war crimes. One of them, a medical doctor, said that he "wanted to describe what can happen when you follow people who use propaganda, religion, and nationality as a vehicle for accomplishing so-called national interests. I wanted to prevent the same thing from happening anywhere else in the world."

Most study participants described their obligation to testify in more intrinsic terms, grounded in moral obligations to family and community. This finding should be encouraging news for the ICTY and future tribunals, because it suggests that international criminal tribunals, despite their shortcomings, can provide victims and witnesses with a forum for discharging their perceived moral duty. But it also places a grave responsibility on tribunals to do their utmost to protect the physical safety and psychological well-being of witnesses, and to ensure that their interaction with the court is a dignified one.

War crimes tribunals, like all courts, have much to gain by going out of their way to treat witnesses in a respectful manner; witnesses who felt respected fared better in the courtroom and were more inclined to encourage others to testify. Witnesses in other court settings have also expressed this sentiment. For instance, a survivor of the 1995 bombing of the Alfred P. Murrah federal building in Oklahoma City who later testified in the trial of Timothy McVeigh and Terry Nichols told a meeting of federal and state attorneys involved in the case: "There are three things that I encourage you to keep in mind when working with victims: Care about us, keep us informed, and create a feeling of 'us' – the prosecutors and the victims – as part of the same team. If you do these things, the results will benefit you because just as you are my advocate in the courtroom I am your advocate to the public."[7]

The witness's moral duty to testify places an onus on governments and the United Nations (UN) to provide courts with adequate financial support to make such testimony possible. While the UN's financial and moral commitment to the ICTY and the Rwandan Tribunal has grown in recent years, its understanding of what a tribunal needs in order to function effectively in local settings has yet to catch up.[8] Nowhere is this more apparent than at the ICTY's victims and witness unit, where an understaffed office still struggles to provide services to an increasing number of witnesses.

As the world community turns increasingly to international criminal courts to respond to mass violence, it is paramount that we re-examine how we think about and interact with victims and witnesses who enter these new judicial processes. We must shed the assumption that "revealing is healing"; testifying in a criminal trial can have both good and ill effects. Exposure to massive trauma in war and its aftermath is often considerably different from exposure to individual acts of violent crime in domestic settings. War trauma and atrocity is not only a personal experience, it also involves whole families and communities.[9] Many study participants insisted that their suffering was nothing in comparison with the disappearance of a younger brother, the witnessing of the gruesome death of a close friend, or the destruction of their neighborhood. As such, we need to develop support systems for court witnesses that take into account both the needs of individual witnesses and groups of witnesses, such as rape victims, and how these individuals fit within the communal dynamics of their post-war societies.

Rights and obligations

Should international criminal tribunals provide victims of and witnesses to war crimes with certain rights and entitlements? If so, what should they cover? Similarly, do tribunals have obligations to witnesses? And, if so, when do they begin and end?

Neither the statute of the ICTY nor its rules of evidence and procedure provide victims and witnesses with specific "rights." Instead, the ICTY staff refer to witness services as "entitlements." In 1998, four years after the establishment of the tribunal and at a point when the number of trials and witnesses had become significant, the ICTY's victims and witnesses unit began distributing a brochure in Serbo-Croatian to prospective witnesses. The brochure describes the mandate of the ICTY, the role of witnesses, and their entitlements, including travel arrangements, protective measures, and other pertinent information, yet it makes no mention of any *rights* afforded victims and witnesses. The brochure also does not provide witnesses with a right to be informed about the conviction and subsequent appeals hearings, imprisonment, and release of the accused. ICTY prosecutors and investigators, as well as defense attorneys, are supposed to give the brochure to potential witnesses, but most witnesses never receive it.

Of all the entitlements, protective measures are the most vital. The ICTY provides that judges can order a witness's name and identifying information expunged from tribunal records. They also can have a witness's identity obscured in the courtroom through image- or voice-altering devices or closed-circuit television and the assignment of a pseudonym. Many study participants only learned about the availability of protective measures once they came to The Hague. They usually acquired the information from other witnesses encountered at their hotel or at the ICTY.

The somewhat arbitrary manner in which potential witnesses are informed of their entitlements may actually be undermining the ICTY's work. Participants said they placed a high premium on maintaining *clear and open communications* with prosecutors and investigators. From their point of first contact with tribunal staff, the witnesses wanted to know what the ICTY expected from them and what they could expect from the tribunal. Indeed, witnesses who had been thoroughly briefed on their entitlements by prosecutors and investigators and who remained in fairly regular contact with them had a more positive view of the tribunal.

Listing witness entitlements in a brochure is helpful, but it is not enough. During their first encounter with witnesses, prosecutors and investigators must take special care to tell potential witnesses what they are entitled to, the risks and benefits of testifying, and the full range of protective measures available to them. It is also of paramount importance that witnesses know that protection measures are not infallible. This is especially true if they are testifying against defendants from their own towns and villages. The majority of protected witnesses interviewed for this study said the protection measures in The Hague failed to guard their anonymity, thus leaving them open to recriminations on their return home. The protected witnesses speculated that those most likely to have revealed their identities were the defendants and their lawyers.

The handling of witnesses by lawyers and investigators from the Office of the Prosecutor (OTP) is uneven, at best. This imbalance may be largely a result of the amount of exposure that individual OTP staff have had to witnesses before coming to the ICTY. In the common law tradition, prosecutors are used to working closely with witnesses. Live witness testimony is the preferred and often the only way to present evidence on what, when, where, and even why critical events occurred. In civil law systems, however, there is a far wider use of written witness statements and of hearsay, especially during the initial period presided over by an investigative judge who produces the "dossier" on which the actual trial is based. As such, the investigating judge often has greater interaction with witnesses then do prosecutors. A former ICTY judge has suggested that prosecutors should "prepare their witnesses more carefully for what they will encounter by way of cross-examination . . . Counsel should certainly acquaint the witness with prior statements on which he may be quizzed and even try to build the witness's emotional stamina so that he will not blow up or break down on the stand. For whatever reasons – time constraints or unawareness – that kind of minimal witness care does not seem to be a universal prerequisite in trial preparation at [the ICTY]."[10]

Providing certain rights and entitlements to witnesses raises the question of when a tribunal's obligations to them should end. Technically speaking, neither the ICTY statute nor its rules of evidence and procedure require that the OTP or the Victims and Witnesses Section (VWS) maintain contact with witnesses in the post-trial phase. Indeed, the prevailing view at the tribunal is that once witnesses have returned to their country of residence, local authorities should handle their protection. Given the ICTY's limited resources, such a position is understandable, although it leaves in a vulnerable position witnesses who live in areas where they are in the minority. A significant number of Bosnian Muslim witnesses from the Lasva Valley, and especially those who lived in the predominately Croat town of Vitez, feared reporting threats and other forms of harassment to the local authorities, who were Croats. Croat witnesses in Vukovar were less fearful of approaching their authorities, since their national group predominates in local government. Still, they remained suspicious of the local police force, which is composed of both Serbs and Croats.

Finally, the ICTY needs to put stronger teeth into its rules that provide for sanctions against any person guilty of attempting to interfere with or intimidate a witness. This study found that the ICTY had failed to adequately investigate, let alone punish, anyone for "witness tampering." A protected witness frequently called the ICTY to say that the wife of the accused and her two brothers had repeatedly threatened her if she went to testify in The Hague. Yet neither the ICTY nor the local authorities investigated these charges in any meaningful way. In another case, a woman who had testified as a protected witness in three trials told me a group of masked men had attacked her on the street. She believes some of her assailants were members of the paramilitary group that had held her captive and raped her in 1993. A few weeks later, she received an anonymous letter warning her that she would be killed if she ever testified in The Hague again. The woman and her husband, who also testified before the ICTY, repeatedly asked the tribunal to investigate these threats and to provide them with some form of protection, but to no avail. Then, the woman said, the ultimate irony occurred: "Some defense attorneys came to visit me. They tried to convince me to change my statement against their clients because the ICTY would not provide me with protection!" Similarly, in the Celibici case, the leaking of the names of witnesses (many of whom were protected) to the Bosnian press was never fully investigated, nor was anyone ever punished for the offense.

Given these findings, I suggest that the ICTY and other international criminal tribunals should take the proactive, rights-centered approach to witnesses that is the preferred model in many countries. In the United States, for instance, victims testifying in federal trials are given a bill of victims' rights that mandates employees of the Department of Justice and other federal agencies to respect these rights.[11] The 1990 bill states that victims have a right to be kept informed of developments in their cases, including details about the progress of the case and the offender's status, be treated in a dignified manner, and be reasonably protected from the accused offender.[12] The bill apprises federal prosecutors and law enforcement officers that victims of crime should be regarded as *active and engaged participants in* – not merely *auxiliaries to* – the criminal justice system. The bill is intended to give crime victims a sense of personal efficacy and control. As rights-bearing agents, they are in a better position to regain control over their lives and influence the events that impinge on them as they pass through the criminal justice system.

During the past two decades the UN also has undertaken a number of initiatives to address the rights and needs of crime victims at the international level. One of the most significant is the *Declaration of Basic Principles of Justice for Victims of Crimes and Abuse of Power*, adopted by the UN General Assembly on November 29, 1985.[13] Hailed as the "Magna Carta" for crime victims around the world, the declaration sets out basic principles of justice for crime victims, including the right of victims to have access to the judicial process and to receive prompt redress for the harm they have suffered. The UN provides that, among other services, the responsiveness of judicial and administrative processes to the rights and needs of victims should include:

(1) informing victims of their role and the scope, timing, and progress of the proceedings and of the disposition of their cases, especially where serious crimes are involved and where victims have requested such information

(2) allowing the views and concerns of victims to be presented and considered at appropriate stages of the proceedings where their personal interests are affected, without prejudice to the accused and consistent with the relevant national criminal justice system

(3) providing proper assistance to victims throughout the legal process

(4) taking measures to minimize inconvenience to victims, protect their privacy, when necessary, and ensure their safety, as well as that of their families and witnesses on their behalf, from intimidation and retaliation

(5) avoiding unnecessary delay in the disposition of cases and the execution of orders or decrees granting awards to victims.

Rights also have their limits. A victim's rights to privacy and protection, for example, must, in the words of the UN declaration, "be exercised in a manner which is not prejudicial to or inconsistent with the rights of the accused and a fair and impartial trial." This right is one of the minimum guarantees for a fair trial enshrined in international instruments[14] and is particularly important with respect to charges of genocide and crimes against humanity where the accused may be sentenced to life imprisonment. Article 14 of the International Convention of Civil and Political Rights (ICCPR), for example, provides that the right to a fair trial means that the accused must be able "to examine, or have examined, the witnesses against him" to test the veracity of the testimony and identify potential bias, and "to obtain the attendance and examination of witnesses on his behalf under the same conditions as witnesses against him."

Similarly, the accused must know the identity of all prosecution witnesses and be able to cross-examine them in depth; otherwise a court runs the risk of convicting innocent persons based on evidence that has not been fully scrutinized. Admission of anonymous or secret witnesses also leaves open the possibility that revisionists will attack the validity of a court's judgments. Amnesty International drives home this point by insisting that trials before international criminal tribunals "be perceived by the entire international community, including the ethnic, racial, national, religious and political groups of which the convicted person is a member, as scrupulously fair."[15] Ultimately, justice must not only be fair, it must be seen to be fair.

Patricia Wald, a former ICTY judge, is concerned that the ICTY has come dangerously close in some trials to not honoring that right of the accused to a public trial because of the trial chamber's overuse of protective measures.[16] Wald points to the Kristic trial, where 58 of the 118 witnesses testified under a pseudonym or with face or voice distortion, and 9 gave their evidence in closed session. Thus, just under 50 percent of the witnesses did not testify publicly in the usual sense of the word. Data collected by the ICTY shows that some form of protective measures has been employed for 41 percent of all witnesses appearing at the ICTY since January 1998.

Wald found in her experience at the tribunal that the need for protective measures often depended on the personality and attitude of the witness; some from the same locale and background asked for protection while others were willing to speak openly. "In my view," writes Wald, "prosecutors, who generally have more witnesses than the defense, should consider whether a witness will testify in person when soliciting testimony for a case . . . Given a choice between a witness who will testify openly and one who requires protection, the former should have the edge."[17] The present study suggests that Wald's concern about the ICTY's overuse of protective measures has merit. The fact that 39 percent of the protected witnesses interviewed for this study allowed their names to be mentioned in this report because, in the words of one respondent, "being a protected witness didn't mean much" suggests that the protection measures are inadequate or that the tribunal may be using these measures too liberally, or both. It also suggests that prosecutors and investigators need to do a better job of informing witnesses of the limitations of protection measures. In other words, witness protection measures must be strong enough to encourage victims of war crimes to testify, but they must not be so strong as to make war crimes trials secretive affairs hidden from the public eye. In general, more thought needs to be given to the intrinsic conflict between witness protection and the rights of the accused.

The meaning of justice

"Justice," wrote the American legal scholar Edmond N. Cahn in 1949, "is unwilling to be captured in a formula. Nevertheless, it somehow remains a word of magic evocations."[18] Cahn's admonition resonated in the interviews for this study. By and large, the study respondents scorned the notion that justice somehow possessed "miracle-working" powers. Instead, they spoke of justice as being highly intimate and idiosyncratic and, at times, ephemeral. "How can you measure justice against all that I have suffered?" asked a witness whose husband and two sons had perished during an assault on her village. "It's just a word. It means nothing."

Although the vast majority of witnesses supported war crimes trials, they were far less certain about whether justice had been rendered in the cases in which they had testified. Tribunal justice, they said, was capricious, unpredictable, and inevitably incomplete: defendants could be acquitted; sentences could be trifling, even laughable, given the enormity of the crimes; and verdicts could be overturned.

For the witnesses, "full justice" was far larger than criminal trials and the *ex cathedra* pronouncements of foreign judges in The Hague. It meant the return of stolen property; locating and identifying the bodies of the missing; capturing and trying *all* war criminals, from the garden-variety killers (the so-called "small fry") in their communities all the way up to the nationalist ideologues who had poisoned their neighbors with ethnic hatred; securing reparations and apologies; leading lives devoid of fear; securing meaningful jobs; providing their children with good schools; and helping those traumatized by atrocities to recover.

Justice, the witnesses said, meant piercing the veil of denial about past war crimes that had lain over their divided communities since the war. The witnesses felt betrayed by neighbors of other ethnic groups who had supported radical nationalist leaders or had aided and abetted paramilitary groups. For many witnesses, reconciliation would only take hold once their neighbors from the opposing group had acknowledged their complicity in war crimes. These are, of course, matters over which the ICTY has little, if any, influence. But they remind us that tribunal justice should never be regarded as a panacea for communities divided by genocide and ethnic cleansing.

Still, there are a small but growing number of legal theorists who argue that war crimes proceedings should function as a kind of "moral theater," a theatrical performance that is carefully orchestrated to teach history to a world audience. Proponents of this argument believe that post-genocide trials should not be about applying legal rules to the narrow facts of one individual's case: the trials should aim more broadly, offering a stage for survival testimony and the creation of an official historical record that can be relied upon for years to come.[19] Mark Osiel, a professor at Iowa law school who has studied the Argentine military trials of the late 1980s, envisions trials in the aftermath of large-scale brutality as a "transformative opportunity in the lives of individuals and societies." Such proceedings, he writes, should "shape collective memory of horrible events." As in a theater, lawyers and judges should heed the "poetics" of "legal storytelling." Judges should use the law "to recast the courtroom drama in terms of the 'theater of ideas,' where large questions of collective memory and even national identity are engaged . . . To maximize their pedagogic impact, such trials should be unabashedly designed as monumental spectacles."[20]

But not everyone accepts the role of judge as dramaturge. One critic is Ian Buruma, who writes in *The Wages of Guilt: Memories of War in Germany and Japan*: "Just as belief belongs in the church, surely history education belongs in school. When the court of law is used for history lessons, then the risk of show trials cannot be far off. It may be that show trials are good politics . . . but good politics don't necessarily serve the truth."[21] This is why legal proceedings should not be designed to tell a historical narrative or construct didactic narratives. It is an illusion to suppose that the ICTY, located over a thousand miles away from the former Yugoslavia, can forge a common version of the history of the Yugoslav conflict that would be accepted by all sides (see Freedman et al., Chapter 12 in this volume, for a discussion of the complications of teaching history). Even if the tribunal establishes a factual record of what happened, it cannot contribute to national reconciliation if the peoples of the former Yugoslavia are unable or unwilling to recognize and internalize this record. As history constantly reminds us, memories of wartime atrocities, like all memories, are local; they are embedded in the psyche of those who have experienced the events and, through the process of retelling and memorialization, they are deposited in the collective memory of the community. This is why so-called "impartial" or "objective" outsiders who try to recast localized memories to fit a larger truth will always be viewed with suspicion.[22]

What a community chooses *to deny* about its past is largely defined by its group identity. Communities that believe they are victims of aggression are often unable to acknowledge that their side also committed atrocities (see Biro et al., Chapter 9 in this volume). Witness the ethnically mixed village of Ahmici in the Lasva valley of central Bosnia, which is inhabited by Croats and Muslims. To date, the ICTY has convened four trials focusing on the Bosnian Croat troops' assault on the village on April 16, 1993. The ICTY proceedings have involved over a dozen Bosnian Croat defendants, ranging from foot soldiers to high-ranking military and civilian leaders. Yet according to study participants, there is absolutely no indication that these trials have in any way transformed the way in which Croats in the village interpret what happened. "The trials have changed nothing," commented a Bosnian Muslim resident. "If anything, things are worse than before." Adding insult to injury, in 1998, when Bosnian Muslim residents began returning to Ahmici, the Croats erected a large neon cross near the access road to the village. At the base of the cross, a plaque memorializes Croats who died during the war, but nowhere does it mention the fate of Muslim residents who perished during the 1993 massacre. Today, Ahmici remains a divided village, where Croat and Muslim neighbors remember and mourn separately.

Betrayal and denial

Since the end of the war, a deep sense of betrayal and denial has settled over many communities in the former Yugoslavia like an impenetrable fog, its fingers working its way into nearly every institution – the media, the places of worship, the schools. Nationalists hold considerable sway over these communities through their positions in local government, political rallies, and their control of media outlets, including newspapers, radio, and television. Unemployment is rampant, and employers often favor hiring members of their own national group. Religious leaders generally avoid the topic of reconciliation and, in some cases, use their authority to cast suspicion on other national groups. In some towns children from different national groups attend school in separate classrooms and study a different school curriculum.

Study participants said that the *inability* and *unwillingness* of their neighbors from other national groups to acknowledge that they stood by as other members of their group committed war crimes in their name was one of the biggest hindrances to reconciliation (see Ajdukovic and Corkalo, Chapter 14 in this volume). Consider the sentiments of a Muslim witness who ran to her best friend's house after Bosnian Croat soldiers had shot her husband and set her house on fire. Her friend, a Croat, turned her away, and she was eventually captured and taken to a prison camp. "Believe me, what my so-called friend did went straight to my heart," she said. "I've tried so hard, but I can't find a reasonable explanation for what she did . . . She betrayed me, and I can never forgive her for that." Many witnesses rejected the notion that feelings of betrayal and denial could be overcome with the passage of time. "Sure time will help," a witness said. "And, of course, we have to move ahead – that's for certain. People who didn't suffer certain things, maybe they can forget. But for people who've really suffered, it will be hard. Maybe we can forgive, but forget, that won't be possible."

While most study participants felt their participation as ICTY witnesses had been beneficial, they also said it had not changed, either positively or negatively, their attitudes about other national groups. Indeed, younger respondents in this study were more pessimistic about living together with other national groups than their elders, a consistent finding that does not augur well for the future. The respondents also said that more had to be done – arresting local war criminals, finding the missing, providing jobs and adequate housing, repairing factories and public buildings, reintegrating primary and secondary schools – before true reconciliation could take hold in their communities. They said the ICTY could contribute to this process by arresting and prosecuting the middling and high-level war criminals. Lifting the fog of betrayal and denial, they said, would require the creation of local processes whereby neighbors from opposing groups recognized and acknowledged that their silence had allowed others to commit war crimes in their name.

Conclusion

The ICTY has achieved much since its creation in 1993. Over two thousand prosecution and defense witnesses have testified before the court, with few serious mishaps. It is delivering fair trials to some of the principal alleged perpetrators of the atrocities in the former Yugoslavia. It is also capable of overturning poorly reasoned judgments and thus upholding the right of the accused to a fair trial. In late 2002, the tribunal facilitated the extraordinary confession of Biljana Plavsic, the former president and wartime leader of the Bosnian Serb republic, who admitted responsibility for horrific crimes against non-Serbs and expressed her remorse to the victims. Unlike the Nuremberg and Tokyo tribunals, the Yugoslav Tribunal has not fallen prey to charges of "victor's justice." Indeed, Slobodan Milosevic's claim that the ICTY is a "political tribunal" that issues "false indictments" carries little weight. He too will receive a fair trial, and justice will be rendered. The tribunal has also forged a set of procedures and rules of evidence, drawing from both civil and common law traditions, and served as the *sine qua non* for the newly established International Criminal Court.[23]

From the perspective of the witnesses interviewed for this study, the trials in The Hague had three prevailing purposes. The first, in the words of one witness, was "to capture suspected war criminals, give them a fair trial, convict them, and let them serve their sentences. And let this be a message to others." The second was to provide victims, however briefly, with a public forum where they could discharge their "moral duty" to "bear witness" on behalf of their deceased family members and neighbors. Finally, the witnesses said the trials provided them and other victims with the opportunity to confront their tormentors with what one witness called "unfinished business." For many study respondents, merely being in the courtroom with the accused while he was under guard helped to restore their confidence in the order of things. Power, one witness said, "flowed back from the accused to me." If only for a brief while, this witness finally held sway over his personal tormentor, and his community's wrong-doer. It was at moments like these that tribunal justice was at its most intimate.

As the world community turns increasingly to international criminal justice to respond to mass violence, we must re-examine how we think about and interact with victims and witnesses who enter these new judicial processes. If potential witnesses come to regard their treatment as demeaning, unfair, too remote, or little concerned with their rights and interests, this neglect may hinder the future cooperation of the very people we are trying to serve. We must take a more realistic view of what criminal trials can accomplish in societies struggling with the immediate aftermath of war, and more attention needs to be paid to the impact that testifying has on witnesses as they try to reintegrate into their communities. Most of all, we have a duty to victims and witnesses to make the process of testifying in war crimes trials as respectful and dignified an experience as possible.

NOTES

1. In addition to the ICTY witnesses, I interviewed two other groups of people for the study. One group consisted of six people who had given pre-trial statements to ICTY investigators but who, for one reason or another, did not testify. The other group consisted of thirty-six members of the ICTY staff, including judges, investigators, prosecutors, interpreters, and social workers, as well as journalists, human rights workers, and psychologists working in Croatia and in Bosnia and Herzegovina.
2. See Patrica M. Wald, "Dealing with Witnesses in War Crimes Trials," *Yale Human Rights and Development Law Journal* 5 (2002): 222–233.
3. See Martha Minow, *Between Vengeance and Forgiveness: Facing History after Genocide and Mass Violence* (Boston: Beacon Press, 1998), 25–51.
4. See, for example, Laurel E. Fletcher and Harvey M. Weinstein, "Violence and Social Repair: Rethinking the Contribution of Justice to Reconciliation," *Human Rights Quarterly* 24 (2002): 593–595; Neil J. Kritz, "Coming to Terms with Atrocities: A Review of Accountability Mechanisms for Mass Violations of Human Rights," *Legal and Contemporary Problems* 127 (1996): 128; Martha Minow, *Between Vengeance and Forgiveness*, 22; and Julie Mertus, "Only a War Crimes Tribunal: Triumph of the International Community, Pain of the Survivors," in Belinda Cooper, ed. *War Crimes: The Legacy of Nuremberg* (New York: TV Books, 1999), 232–237.
5. See Judith Herman, *Trauma and Recovery: The Aftermath of Violence – from Domestic Abuse to Political Terror* (New York: Basic Books, 1992), 213.
6. Ibid., 207–211.
7. Quoted in Susan Urbach, "A Victim's Voice," *United States Attorneys' USA Bulletin* 47:1 (January 1999): 54–57.

8. See David Tolbert, "The International Criminal Tribunal for the former Yugoslavia: Unforeseen Successes and Foreseeable Shortcomings," *The Fletcher Forum of World Affairs* 26:2 (summer/fall 2002): 15–16.

9. See Derek Summerfield, "Addressing Human Response to War and Atrocity: Major Challenges in Research and Practices and the Limitations of Western Psychiatric Models." In Rolf J. Kleber, Charles R. Figley, and Berthold P. R. Gersons, eds. *Beyond Trauma: Cultural and Societal Dynamics* (New York: Plenum Press, 1995), 17–29.

10. Wald, "Dealing with Witnesses," 222–233.

11. See the *Crime Control Act, U.S. Code*, vol. 24, secs. 10606–10607 (1990) and the *Victims' Rights Clarification Act, U.S. Code*, vol. 9, sec. 3510 (1997).

12. See US Department of Justice, Office of the Attorney General, *Attorney General Guidelines for Victims and Witness Assistance* (Washington, D.C.: Government Printing Office, 2000), 26. Also, see Council of Europe, *Council Framework Decision of 15 March 2001 on the Standing of Victims of Crime in Criminal Proceedings* (2001/220/JHA), OJ,L82, March 22, 2001, and the Commission of the European Communities, *Council Directive on Compensation to Crime Victims* (Brussels: European Commission, 2002), 562, final.

13. See United Nations, A/Res/40/34 (1985).

14. See, for example, Article 6 of the European Convention for the Protection of Human Rights and Fundamental Freedoms and Article 8 of the American Convention of Human Rights.

15. Amnesty International, *The International Criminal Court: Ensuring an Effective Role for Victims – Memorandum for the Paris Seminar, April 1999*, AI Index: IOR 40/06/99, available at http://web.amnesty.org/library/Index/ENGIOR400061999?open&of=ENG-385. Both the ICCPR and the American Convention of Human Rights prohibit the use of secret witnesses.

16. Wald, "Dealing with Witnesses," 224.

17. Ibid.

18. Edmond N. Cahn, *The Sense of Injustice* (New York: New York Press, 1949), 13.

19. See Lawrence Douglas, *The Memory of Judgment: Making Law and History in the Trials of the Holocaust* (New Haven, Conn.: Yale University Press, 2001).

20. See Mark Osiel, *Mass Atrocity, Collective Memory, and the Law* (New Brunswick, N.J.: Transaction Publishers, 1997).

21. See Ian Buruma, *The Wages of Guilt: Memories of War in Germany and Japan* (New York: Farrar, Straus, and Giroux, 1994).

22. See Michael Ignatieff, "Articles of Faith," *Index on Censorship* 5 (1996): 114.

23. Tolbert, "The International Criminal Tribunal for the former Yugoslavia," 17–18.

6 Reparations in the aftermath of repression and mass violence

Naomi Roht-Arriaza

It is a basic maxim of law that harms should be remedied. Every legal system insists on it, in some form. Under international law, states are obliged to provide remedies for violations of human rights, both as a matter of treaty law and as part of the general rules of state responsibility. Recent United Nations (UN) formulations view restitution, rehabilitation, and compensation as interlinked but distinct state obligations.[1] Not only states must remedy past harms: the statute of the newly created International Criminal Court allows for individual offenders to pay reparations to victims, as well as for the creation of a trust fund to be used where individual awards are impracticable.

Despite these remedies, few reparations have actually been paid to victims of war crimes and human rights abuses in the wake of mass violence. So far, Germany has paid the largest reparations (for Nazi-era crimes). The United States paid reparations to surviving Japanese-American internees, but other claims from the Second World War, like those against Japan for "comfort women" and slave laborers, have fared less well. Outside the context of the Second World War, examples of large-scale reparations programs become scarcer. Chile and Argentina provided compensation, rehabilitation, and services to some (but not all) of the victims of their respective military dictatorships. The UN set up a compensation mechanism for victims of Iraq's invasion of Kuwait, some of whom suffered what could be characterized as violations of human rights. The International Criminal Tribunal for the former Yugoslavia (ICTY) allows victims to pursue compensation claims in their national courts. Truth commissions in South Africa, Guatemala, El Salvador, and Panama have recommended reparations programs, but to date the governments of those countries have been slow to act on their proposals. The Rwandan government has an elaborate plan for reparations for victims of the 1994 genocide, but it is too soon to tell if the process will work effectively.

Why the discrepancy between word and deed? If reparations are so universally accepted as part of a state's human rights obligations, why have so few states emerging from periods of armed conflict or mass violence put viable programs into place? In this chapter I consider some of the difficulties in thinking about reparations in the wake of genocide and other forms of mass violence, both in general and in the context of poor countries where there may be many victims and multiple claims on scarce resources. I also examine past practices for ideas and insights that might be applicable in the context of mass violence. In a final section, I propose three distinct yet interrelated ways of thinking about reparations, all of which eschew the classic view of individual, court-ordered reparations in favor of more community-oriented, flexible approaches.

Defining reparations

There is a basic paradox at the heart of the idea of reparations: they are intended to return victims to the state they would have been in had the violations not occurred – something that it is impossible to do. They are also supposed to be the physical embodiment of a society's recognition of, and remorse and atonement for, harms inflicted. This view of reparations emerges both from the law of civil wrongs and from the law and jurisprudence around state responsibility for wrongs done, at least initially, to other states. But what could replace lost health and serenity, the loss of a loved one or of a whole extended family, a generation of friends, the destruction of culture or an entire community?

Reparations serve multiple functions. They are both backward- and forward-looking. They aim to recompense for loss and to restore the good name of those defamed, but also to reintegrate the marginalized and isolated into society so that they can contribute to the future rebuilding of the country. Reparations can be both moral and material. Material reparations for an individual victim can include restitution of lost or stolen property, a job, a pension, or a person's good name. If needed, they can provide rehabilitative services to victims, including medical, psychiatric or occupational therapies. They can encompass monetary compensation in the form of a one-time payment, a pension, or a package of services for victims and survivors. For collectivities such as a village or religious community, restitution can include restitution of cultural or religious property, communal lands, and education and health facilities, and compensation in the form of money or services to the community.

History has shown that moral reparations are essential for victims and, in some cases, more important than material ones. They can encompass the disclosure of the facts of a victim's mistreatment or a loved one's death, and the public naming of those responsible for these crimes. They can include official apologies and acknowledgment of wrongdoing and, most importantly for many victims, judicial proceedings or administrative procedures, including the removal of perpetrators from positions of power.

Moral reparations can be as fundamental as the exhumation and identification of the remains of victims, and assistance in reburials and mourning ceremonies. They can have a collective aspect, including public memorials, days of remembrance, parks or other public monuments, renaming of streets or schools, preservation of repressive sites as museums, or other ways of creating public memory. Reform of education, re-writing of history texts, and education in human rights and tolerance embrace the notion of reparations. However, there is a danger that such moral reparations can be used politically to stigmatize and marginalize those groups whose members perpetrated the abuse. Reparations must be offered in ways that acknowledge the suffering of victims but do not victimize others who did not actively engage in the violence.

Modalities of reparations

Reparations to victims can come about through complaints filed in the courts, or through specially designed administrative schemes. Most reparations programs have elements of both approaches. In a number of cases, settlements of court cases have included or have triggered administrative compensation schemes. In addition to national courts, which hear claims based on acts committed in the victim's home country and, occasionally, abroad, regional courts in Europe and the Americas have assessed damages against states, and friendly settlements of cases before regional bodies have sometimes provided for individual reparations.

Court-based mechanisms function best when the plaintiffs are single individuals or, at most, small numbers of victims. In situations where large numbers of people were affected but only a few sue, a few victims can receive large amounts of compensation while others, similarly situated, receive nothing because they never filed claims. Better-educated, middle-class victims often have greater access to courts than those in the lower echelons of society. Court procedure often can be protracted or obscure, or seem to favor defendants. Judgments may be hard to collect. Moreover, individual reparations may fail to capture the collective element of the harm in situations of mass conflict or repression. In counter-insurgencies and civil conflicts, those who plan and carry out atrocities often target specific communities in an effort to end the community's support for rebels, to disperse any organized opposition, or to force the population to flee. Military forces may seek to make local civilians complicit in atrocities, forcing them to watch or even to participate in the violations of their families' or neighbors' basic human rights. These harms to community life and trust cannot easily be redressed through individual awards. For all these reasons, access to courts, national or regional, will be insufficient in most cases of mass violence.

Few governments have instituted administrative schemes to pay reparations to victims and survivors of massive violations of human rights. In general, existing reparations programs have involved relatively well-off countries, or those where there is a limited and easily identifiable set of victims. They also have involved abuses committed by state security forces against a largely unarmed opposition, such as those in the Southern Cone of South America or Eastern Europe.

German reparations to the victims of the Holocaust have served as the model for subsequent reparations programs. Claimants who could prove they had survived a concentration camp received a lump sum for deprivation of liberty, while another lump sum went to a coordinating body of Jewish organizations for the settlement of Jewish victims living outside Israel.[2] Compensatable categories of harm included loss of life, damage to health, and loss of liberty. Despite the billion-dollar sums involved, many victims remained unsatisfied with the German effort. The administrative procedure was intimidating and degrading, officials tried to weed out claims rather than support victims, and professionals were treated far better than ordinary workers. Retraumatization and a sense of injustice followed, and the lesson that design and attitude matter carried forward to more recent reparations efforts.

In the wake of military dictatorships during the 1970s and 1980s in Chile, Argentina, and Brazil, the newly elected civilian governments of those countries agreed to institute reparations programs for victims of the human rights abuses of the dictatorship. The scale of the programs, like the scale of the repression, differed greatly from one country to the next. For example, following the 1973 military coup in Chile, security forces killed some 3,000 people, and over 1,000 disappeared. The Chilean Congress agreed to provide a lump-sum payment equal to a year's pension, and a monthly pension, based on the average wage, for the spouses, parents, and children of those killed or disappeared. Scholarships for the children of those killed or disappeared, and free medical and psychological care were also available. Argentina compensated political prisoners and the families of the over 10,000 disappeared, and created a legal figure of "absent due to forced disappearance" which allowed the families of the disappeared to remarry or claim inheritance rights without having to concede that the disappeared person was dead.[3] In addition, both Chile and Argentina have provided some degree of moral reparations, including official acknowledgment and public memorials.

In the 1980s, several Eastern European countries established compensation for those killed or imprisoned under Communist regimes. Meanwhile, South Africa's Truth and Reconciliation Commission (TRC), formed to investigate gross human rights violations during the years of *apartheid* rule, recommended payment of some R50 million (approximately US $8 million at the current exchange rate) to 18,000 people as immediate interim reparations, and individual reparation grants of about US $3,500 a year for six years to victims, an amount the commission considered "sufficient to make a meaningful and substantial impact on the quality of [victims'] lives."[4] It also recommended provision of medical and psychological care, fulfillment of significant personal and community needs (like health care, mental health facilities, education and housing, and headstones for graves), and symbolic reparations.

Truth commissions in El Salvador and Guatemala recommended a range of reparatory measures, few of which have been carried out. The Salvadoran Truth Commission, made up entirely of non-Salvadorans, called for the creation of a Special Fund, financed by government and international aid funds, to pay compensation to victims. It also recommended moral reparations and a follow-up body to monitor compliance with the recommendations. In Guatemala, the UN-backed Commission on Historical Clarification (CHC) called for official acknowledgment, construction of parks and monuments, naming public buildings after victims, a day of remembrance, and restoration of Mayan sacred sites. It also recommended a National Reparation Program, to include restitution of material possessions, especially land; compensation for the "most serious injuries and losses"; psychosocial rehabilitation; and moral and symbolic reparations. However, neither of the parties to the conflict has expressed much interest in carrying out these recommendations.[5]

Administrative reparations also can include restitution of land and property. In Bosnia and Herzegovina, the Dayton Peace Agreement included provisions delegalizing transfers of property made under threat or duress or otherwise connected to ethnic cleansing, and created a special Commission on Real Property Claims to provide restitution or compensate citizens who lost land and property during the 1992–1995 war. In South Africa, the government established Land Claims Courts. Under the South African Restitution Act, plaintiffs must show that they are communities or individuals who themselves or through their forebears had land rights of which they were dispossessed after June 19, 1913 by racially discriminatory laws or practices. The difficulties of proving land rights that go back generations and where land was often held communally and without written title are formidable, and the Land Claims Courts have used testimony from historians and anthropologists, as well

as local elders, to substantiate claims. Remedies can include full ownership, partial rights to the land, rights to equivalent land, or compensation.
The present landowners are compensated by the state at market value.[6]

Another compensatory mechanism is the creation of trust funds at a
national or international level. In the wake of Iraq's invasion of Kuwait in
1990, the UN established a Compensation Commission to provide reparations to foreign governments, corporations, and individuals injured by
Iraq's actions. The compensation comes from sales of a fixed percentage
of Iraqi oil, held in a fund. The UN has a number of trust funds, including one for victims of torture. Sierra Leone set up a Special Fund for
Victims, which it hopes to finance through international donations.

These compensation schemes share a number of vexing problems.
First, and perhaps most difficult, is defining who is a "victim." At least
in three countries, the results have not been very satisfying. In Chile, the
government decided to focus solely on those killed and disappeared by
the security forces, leaving aside the vastly larger number of those who
were tortured while in detention and survived, and those who were forced
into exile. While justified as a way to spend limited funds on the "worst"
violations, the effect was to infuriate survivors, who read this as a lack
of recognition of the severity of their own suffering and an attempt to
paper over the extent of the crimes.[7] In South Africa, the TRC defined
"victims" as those who suffered from the gross violations – killing, torture, abduction – prohibited under South African and international law.
Critics pointed out that this limited mandate excluded the legal pillars of
apartheid: forced removals, pass laws, residential segregation, and other
forms of racial discrimination and detention without trial.[8] By doing so,
it shifted the focus from complicity in and the benefits of *apartheid* as
regards whites as a group to the misdeeds of a smaller group of security
force operatives, easily characterized as "bad apples." In this case, individual guilt promoted a myth of collective innocence for the beneficiaries of
the *apartheid* system. Finally, in Guatemala, members of the paramilitary
Civil Self-Defense Patrols ((PACs), who were used as human shields and
to do the military's dirty work, claimed compensation for their unpaid
government service. The government agreed to pay each PAC member
some Q5,000 (US $675), while reparations for civilian victims of war
crimes languished. In all three cases, the identification of "victimhood"
has been highly contested.

The range of reparatory measures may also be open to debate. The
largest study to actually interview victims was carried out by the Chilean
human rights organization CODEPU under the auspices of the Association for the Prevention of Torture. The study interviewed about 100
individuals and groups of family members of disappeared and summarily

executed victims in Chile, Argentina, El Salvador, and Guatemala (it relied on secondary research for a section on South Africa). The study emphasized that, for the victims, moral and legal measures of reparation are fundamental, while monetary compensation is controversial and problematic. One striking finding of the CODEPU study is the emphasis that survivors placed on education for the children of those killed.[9]

Why collective reparations?

In recent years, episodes of genocide and mass violence involving the deaths of tens or even hundreds of thousands of people usually have taken place in poor countries with scarce resources. Often they follow or coincide with a civil conflict that has devastated the country's infrastructure and displaced large segments of the population. In these situations, individualized monetary reparations are difficult to imagine without a substantial financial commitment from the international community.

Because the number of victims is so large, episodes of mass violence can exacerbate the limitations of individual reparations schemes. Reparations through courts or administrative compensation schemes require a generally functioning system, not one suffering massive breakdowns in every facet of life and governance. Moreover, in mass conflicts, the collective nature of the harm becomes more salient. Where there is attempted genocide, the harm is defined in terms of an attempt to destroy a group, and so reparation should be similarly defined. Genocidal (or large-scale political conflicts) often have been characterized by the displacement and destruction of whole communities, the setting of neighbor against neighbor, the breeding of forced complicity, and of atomization and distrust. In such situations the lines between victim, bystander, accomplice, and perpetrator are often blurred.

By and large, courts have been reluctant to award collective reparations in the wake of mass violence, and in any case have found themselves ill-equipped to do so. For example, the International Criminal Tribunal for Rwanda (ICTR), through the Office of the Registrar, attempted at one point to provide minimal support for witnesses coming before the tribunal. In September 2000, the Registrar's office launched an initiative to provide legal advice, psychological counseling, physical therapy, and monetary assistance to the Taba Township. In this locality, where the mayor had been convicted of genocide, there were hundreds of survivors, most of them destitute women. However, the tribunal soon found that the needs far exceeded its capacity, that it was ill-equipped to design and administer reparations schemes, and that to do so adequately would require amendment of the tribunal's statute and rules. The effort was scaled back, although the judges and prosecutor agreed that the UN Security Council should amend the tribunal's statute to allow it a greater role in compensation.[10] This dilemma raises the important question of whether an international court should differ in its responsibilities to victims and their communities from domestic courts, where collective harm is usually minimal (see also Stover, Chapter 5, and Fletcher and Weinstein, Chapter 1, in this volume).

Court-based mechanisms tend to function most effectively for individual litigants or small groups. Nevertheless, the Inter-American Court of Human Rights (IACHR or the Court) has taken some steps in a number of cases to use the court system to award collective reparations. In one case involving summary executions in Suriname, the IACHR awarded collective reparations by ordering the construction of a school and medical dispensary as part of a formal judgment, while denying monetary compensation to the affected community as a collective.[11] In a massacre case in Guatemala, the parties agreed on collective as well as individual reparations, to be decided by a community consultation process.[12] In each of these cases the limitations of court-based procedures for granting collective awards is apparent: only a relatively small number of actual victims were involved in either case, and significant amounts of time passed between the violation and the reparations settlement or judgment.

The most comprehensive collective reparations program has been the German payments to Jewish organizations and to the State of Israel following the Holocaust. Jewish organizations asked for collective reparations to compensate for the damage caused to the "very fabric of the Jewish people's existence," including the loss of life, destruction of property, and suffering of those with no living heirs or dependants.[13] Germany eventually paid a total of approximately US $824 million to Israel for acts against the Jewish people, in addition to substantial amounts of compensation to other European states, and to individual victims and survivors.

Other group claims relating to the Second World War have fared less well. For example, after decades of silence, Asian "comfort women" began in the late 1980s to organize to seek redress for their sexual enslavement by the Japanese army during the war. The women unsuccessfully sought official acknowledgment and apologies, a memorial, compensation for survivors and their families, and changes in the teaching of history in Japanese schools. In 1991, one woman, Kim Hak Sun, filed suit against the Japanese government. While the government refused to provide individual compensation, it did attempt a form of collective reparations. Eventually, an Asian Women's Fund (AWF) was established through private donations to improve the livelihoods of the women. Some survivors have criticized this approach as being based on socio-economic need rather than on moral restitution. They have held out for individual reparations fully funded by the government and accompanied by a formal apology from the Diet (Japanese Parliament).[14] The Japanese government's resistance to collective reparations may reflect on-going denial of responsibility for the actions of Japan during the Second World War, covert racism, or a reflection of the role of women in Japanese society. Whatever the explanation, this kind of governmental resistance sends a message that the wrong has not been acknowledged; the victims are not likely to feel relief and are revictimized.

Modalities of collective reparations

Collective reparations in the wake of mass violence can fit into three broadly defined and overlapping models: reparations as community development, reparations as community-level acknowledgment and atonement, and reparations as preferential access. I will explore the advantages and complications of each in turn.

Community development

Communities affected by mass violence are usually poor. In some cases, the key underlying causes of the violence have been poverty and inequality. In these situations, widespread destruction of property, crops, infrastructure, and services only exacerbates poverty. Women and children are particularly vulnerable and often are the majority of victims. In some countries, property and inheritance laws that disfavor women may leave widows landless. Economic development at the community level is thus a sorely needed commodity.

Community development as a form of reparation can have several benefits. Projects, such as the construction of schools and community centers, can provide recognition of the wrong done to a community as a whole and give members of divided communities a focus around which to begin rebuilding the fragile ties among neighbors stretched or broken during the conflict. It is essential, however, that the beneficiaries themselves participate in defining the priorities and design of such projects.[15]

The most attractive feature of linking collective reparations with local development is that it avoids the dilemma of choosing between reparations and other, equally pressing, spending priorities like water or housing. The South African government, for example, justified the small size of its proposed individual reparations grants for victims of *apartheid*-era abuses by arguing that the overall goal of fundamental social transformation is paramount, and that the TRC's reparations proposals could only be accommodated within that larger goal.[16]

Reparation as a form of development has a number of drawbacks. First, it conflates two separate obligations of government: to make reparation for wrongs and to provide essential services to the population. Why should governments, which are obligated to improve the well-being of their citizenry, be allowed to slap a "reparations" label on a development project and get off cheaply? Human rights groups have objected to this conflation of obligations as an abdication of a state's legal obligation to respond to past injustices.

Second, it is often impossible to appropriately target development projects as reparations to the victims and survivors. Where the country is ethnically or politically divided along geographic lines, it may be possible to funnel development aid and projects to the hardest-hit areas, where most victims and survivors reside. Doing so may foster new resentments over perceived favoritism, however. The development of new infrastructure and services may even tend to disproportionately favor those with the economic and social power to take most advantage. In countries like Rwanda, where Hutu and Tutsi live intertwined, services and infrastructure cannot feasibly be reserved to the "victim" group, and so development projects framed as reparations are of equal benefit to victims, bystanders, and even, at times, perpetrators. The Guatemalan Truth Commission recognized this conundrum and advised in its report that:

Collective reparatory measures for survivors of collective human rights violations and acts of violence, and their relatives, should be carried out within a framework of territorially based projects to promote reconciliation, so that in addition to addressing reparation, their other actions and benefits also favor the entire population, without distinction between victims and perpetrators.[17]

Depending upon the country's unique characteristics, the nature of the conflict, and the structure of the post-conflict government and of other development efforts, collective reparations must carefully consider the balance between acknowledging the special claims of some and avoiding the creation of new inequalities and resentments.

Finally, the "reparations as community development" paradigm can potentially negate or underrate the moral or symbolic elements of reparations, which studies have shown are the most important for victims.[18] Governments could add a commemorative element to their provision of basic services, such as naming a new school or health center after victims, combining the road opening with a monument. But this has to be done conscientiously, and the project has to be framed not just as development but also as redress. This is particularly important in rural areas where such projects, although no substitute for individualized reparations, may be the best that can be expected.

One of the obstacles to pursuing a "reparations as community development" framework is the differing mandates, cultures, and conceptualization of goals that exist among the various institutions usually involved in post-conflict reconstruction and development. On one side are human rights and survivors' organizations that often view reparations and accountability for past crimes as a priority. Even here, our studies (see Biro et al. Chapter 9 and Longman et al. Chapter 10 in this volume), suggest that the relationship between trauma and justice is not straightforward. On the other side are governments, which may wish to avoid dredging up old animosities, and international development agencies, which wish not to become bogged down in political issues.

These two visions have moved closer together in recent years, as the UN Development Programme (UNDP) and the World Bank, as well as major European, Canadian, and US development agencies, have realized the need for a more comprehensive approach to their post-conflict interventions. The UNDP, the World Bank, and national development agencies such as the United States Agency for International Development (USAID) now have specific units or bureaus devoted to post-conflict recovery and reconstruction. The UNDP's list of recovery priorities includes "reduction of conflict and promotion of reconciliation," while the World Bank's human rights manifesto lists "victims of war and violence" as among the vulnerable groups most needing protection.[19] The integration of post-conflict reconstruction and collective reparations seems, therefore, promising. However, difficulties persist based on differences in vocabulary, professional biases, restrictive mandates, and ease of goals. Neither the UNDP nor the World Bank frames issues in terms of justice or dealing with legacies of the past, but rather in terms of repair and economic growth. In part, this may be due to the predominance of lawyers in framing reparations issues, and the predominance of economists and engineers in the development assistance world. Post-conflict work also involves merging the different perspectives of conflict management, humanitarian assistance, human rights monitoring, and traditional development cultures, each with its own "turf," time frame and policy prescriptions. Development aid involves different, often shorter-term, and more measurable goals. As a World Bank report stated in 1998: "It is easier to rebuild roads and bridges than it is to reconstruct institutions and strengthen the social fabric of a society."[20] It is also easier to quantify payback periods and break-even points in the former enterprise than the latter.

A reparations perspective, especially if politically sensitive, might also be considered interference in the political affairs of a state, which is prohibited by the World Bank's Articles of Agreement.[21] To the extent that identified victims and all local residents benefit from projects, this problem would be mitigated. The World Bank has come a long way toward recognizing human rights, considering "rights-based" approaches to its work, and incorporating demobilization of former combatants and reintegration of displaced groups into its mandate.[22] However, the kind of market-opening, social-service-restricting, large project development often espoused by agencies like the World Bank and the International Monetary Fund (IMF) may actually run counter to the local-level, service-providing, participatory focus of a reparations policy. Development strategies such as micro lending and small grants seem better suited to integrating development into a reparations perspective – and reparations into a development plan.

Community-level acknowledgment and service

Collective reparations in the aftermath of genocide and other forms of mass violence form only a small part of a larger agenda for social reconstruction. That agenda, explored in the rest of this volume, includes such mechanisms as prosecutions; disclosure of the nature, pattern, extent, and consequences of abuses through various approaches; removal of those responsible for past crimes from positions of public trust; psychosocial interventions; education reform; refugee returns; community-building; and commemoration.

In a number of post-conflict countries – Rwanda, East Timor, Sierra Leone – the new governments have turned to quasi-traditional mechanisms to provide some measure of justice while fostering the reintegration of low-level offenders into local communities. Although discussed mainly in terms of punishment, such quasi-traditional mechanisms have a clear reparatory element, one which should be further emphasized and developed. For example, in Rwanda (as described by Karekezi et al. in Chapter 3 in this volume), the post-genocide government opted to revive the gacaca system of traditional justice. The courts consist of some tens of thousands of elected lay judges who hear testimony from assembled villagers on the participation of suspects in genocide, and may sentence them to jail time or, in the case of property crimes, to compensatory payments. The primary emphasis is on restoring some of the damage done to the community, but the public hearings also allow for truth-telling; confrontation of victims and accused; and opportunities for acts of contrition and apology on the part of perpetrators and bystanders; and, when possible, acceptance by victims. During the public village hearing, civil claimants can make their case for compensation, and the accused, or others, can present arguments against the civil claim.[23] The gacaca judges compile a list of victims who suffered material losses or bodily harm, and create an inventory (including an amount) of losses according to a schedule set out by law. This list is to be forwarded to a compensation fund, which will be in charge of implementation. The compensation fund is to be financed by a combination of state funds, voluntary foreign contributions, reparations taken from individual offenders tried in the domestic courts, and profit from community service works. Because the amounts awarded by thousands of gacaca courts may well exceed the amount collected for the fund, the fund's board can draw up a scale of payments, and payments may be made in decreasing installments.[24]

If the suspect (except for leaders and organizers) confesses, half the sentence may be converted to a community service order; for lesser (Category 3) offenders the whole sentence may be replaced by community service. A draft decree on community service would create "Committees for Community Service" which will place prisoners in host institutions. Community service may involve rebuilding destroyed schools, houses, or clinics, maintenance work on buildings, roads, or gardens, crop cultivation to feed the prison population, educational and motivational activities, first aid, or personal care. Thus, a form of collective reparation would replace punishment. Ideally, this will be of benefit both to victims and perpetrators, and thus encourage the social reconstruction of community life.

However, there are a few potential drawbacks: while the labor may be free, many building and maintenance materials still have to come from somewhere, and it is unclear whether adequate state resources will be available. In addition, community service by mostly Hutu offenders may reawaken memories of old injustices, when Belgian colonialists imposed forced labor "uburetwa" on the mostly Hutu peasantry.[25] It is unclear whether enough judges with clean hands or witnesses can be found or, as Karekezi and colleagues describe, that the population will be willing to participate in a process that can be time-consuming and take years to complete. Finally, the gacaca courts do not have a mandate to examine crimes committed by the Rwandan Patriotic Front (RPF); this leaves victims of RPF abuses unrecognized and unacknowledged (see Des Forges and Longman, Chapter 2 in this volume).

A traditional approach to reparations has also been undertaken in East Timor, where widespread looting and burning, along with murder and rape, accompanied the 1999 rampage of pro-Indonesia militias, a culmination of years of repressive acts and human rights violations by the

Indonesian military following its 1974 annexation of the island nation. After the violence ended, a national Commission for Reception, Truth, and Reconciliation was formed to assist in reconciliation. The Commission has the normal truth-seeking, statement-taking, and report-writing functions, but it contains a significant innovation. Those who committed less serious crimes (theft, minor assault, house-burning, stealing or destroying crops or animals) may approach the Commission and ask it to convene a meeting with victims and local community members. These parties are to discuss the crimes and propose an agreement whereby the perpetrator agrees to undertake some form of community service, including community work, a repayment or public apology, or to undertake some other "act of reconciliation." Once this process is completed, the District Court is to enter an order that those acts cannot be prosecuted or be subject to civil liability in the future, and the community is to agree that the perpetrator may return home without fear. Failure to fulfill the agreement is itself a criminal offense punishable by up to one year's imprisonment and/or a fine, while failure to apply to the Commission process leaves the offender at risk of future prosecution. Serious crimes, including rape, murder, organizing or planning crimes, and crimes against humanity are dealt with separately by a Serious Criminal Offenses Panel.[26]

The hearings have been ceremonial affairs making extensive use of traditional symbols and rituals, including traditional law-givers. Before a panel of community elders and the assembled village, including the victims, those seeking reintegration tell their story and respond to questions. Victims then are able to respond, the public can contribute additional information about the deponents, and negotiations ensue over appropriate reparatory acts. In the hearings to date, these have ranged from a formal apology, to payment in livestock, traditional fabric, coins, and liquor. In a few cases, the accused have agreed to work repairing a school (together with the victim after he volunteered to help) or building a church. According to one observer, "[d]eeply embedded in the strong local culture and custom, community members affirmed that this process had real meaning for their lives – that it was important for them to publicly acknowledge what had happened in the community and to deal with the rift that had divided them."[27]

These types of local-level community reconciliation program might prove an effective form of reparation where there are many low-level perpetrators, where victims and perpetrators (and everyone in between) must coexist, and where neither the state nor the perpetrators have the resources to pay monetary compensation. These approaches emphasize moral reparations to the community as a whole, a recognition that wrong was done both to individual victims and to the fabric of community life.

Other attractive features include the perpetrators' public recognition and atonement for their wrongs, and the involvement of the whole community in the process of hearing and challenging the defendant/deponents' story, and in the ultimate resolution and reintegration of all concerned. These efforts allow victims to confront those who harmed them, and encourage apologies and atonement. They also are able to reflect and affirm local cultural traditions and values, and can be tailored to the specific dynamics of each culture.

And yet, to date, the primary focus has been not on reparations but on punishment (Rwanda) and reconciliation (East Timor). There is the danger that issues of reparation could be short-changed, and that victims could feel pressured not to demand too much from perpetrators in order not to interfere with community reconciliation. Community reparations programs like these will also work well only where there is a sense that the higher-ups who perpetrated the violence are being adequately dealt with elsewhere. Finally, there may be certain cultural preconditions for such programs. In rural societies like East Timor, for example, community unity and harmony may be more salient values than, say, in cities in Bosnia or in Latin America. Cultural determinants may condition these kinds of community service/reconciliation program.

Preferential access

A third way of thinking about reparations after genocide or mass violence is the provision of preferential access to services and public goods to victims: a "go-to-the-head-of-the-line" approach. From a position of ostracism and marginalization, the victims' status as worthy members of society is restored and acknowledged, through priority access to government services such as state-subsidized or state-built housing, education, public transportation passes, and the like.

Most countries provide their war veterans with preferential access to certain state benefits. It takes only a small leap of the imagination to analogize the risks and burdens borne by veterans with those borne by victims of state repression or targeted by *génocidaires*. Like veterans, victims of mass atrocity have made extraordinary sacrifices; they arguably deserve a privileged place in rebuilding society. Indeed, in the Gorbachev-era Soviet Union, many cities awarded survivors of the Gulag the privileges enjoyed by veterans, including the right to shop in special stores, free passage on local transport, and priority access to better housing and medical care.[28]

The approach in practice may not differ much from a "reparations as development" paradigm, but the underlying rationale is focused on repairing individual harms and on foregrounding recognition that society owes a debt to victims. It also allows an emphasis on the educational and health benefits that victims and survivors seem to value most highly, with less focus on more controversial monetary compensation. It does not confuse the state's obligation to all inhabitants to provide infrastructure and public services with its separate obligation to remedy past harms to some.

A preferential access approach does, however, entail certain risks and drawbacks. To begin with, if a large enough percentage of the population qualifies as "victims," there may be little point to being moved to the front of a very long line for services. It is also unclear how long such programs should last before the debt is paid, and what kind of administrative apparatus is needed to register the individual's special status. More fundamentally, a preference-based approach can create new resentments and a sense of victimization among those who are not the beneficiaries of preferences. Moreover, in some circumstances, victims may not want to have to publicly identify themselves as such in order to gain access to services. It is hard to imagine, for example, Tutsi victims of the Rwandan genocide wanting to carry any identification giving them preferential access to government services, after identification cards marked with ethnic identity served as death warrants during the 1994 genocide.

Conclusion

States may combine elements of these three approaches to reparations in cases of mass violence. Rwanda's compensation fund, for example, contemplates payment in services as well as cash. One could imagine preferential access to microcredit as a combination approach. Much will depend on the specific culture and the relationships among organized state power, perpetrators, and victims. The use of one or more of these three approaches should keep the focus on inclusion, moral reparation, community-level solutions, and access to necessary resources. A constant under all these approaches is the need to involve the victims and their organizations in discussions about what reparations, like other post-conflict strategies, should look like.

Reparations are also part of a larger, multi-faceted approach to post-conflict justice and social reconstruction, and should be seen within that context. Reparations may be the most tangible and visible expression of both acknowledgment and change, and in that sense an important contributor to reconciliation and social reconstruction. Reparations also serve as a bridge between the notions of reparatory and distributive justice, between the spheres of political/moral life and economic well-being. Much empirical research on the effects of different kinds of reparations policy on victims, perpetrators, and the larger society remains to be done before we can pinpoint the contribution of reparations to the larger goals of peace, justice, and equity. It will take a good deal of experimentation and flexibility, as well as adherence to the principle that reparations must eventually be provided to victims of mass violence, to find the right approach for each society.

NOTES

1. Sub-Commission on the Protection and Promotion of Human Rights, *Basic Principles and Guidelines on the Right to a Remedy and Reparation for Victims of Violations of International Human Rights and Humanitarian Law*, UN Doc. E/CN.4/2000/62 (18 Jan. 2000) (annex).
2. Kurt Schwerin, "German Compensation for Victims of Nazi Persecution," *Northwestern University Law Review* 67 (1972): 479–527; Dinah Shelton, *Remedies in International Human Rights Law* (Oxford: Oxford University Press, 2000), 334–336.
3. Marcelo Sancinetti and Marcelo Ferrante, *El Derecho Penal en la Protección de los Derechos Humanos* (Buenos Aires, Ediciones Hammurabi, 1999), 360–377.
4. South African Truth and Reconciliation Commission, "A Summary of Reparation and Rehabilitation Policy, Including Proposals to be Considered by the President," available at http://www.doj.gov.za/trc/reparations/summary.htm.
5. Victor Espinoza Cuevas, Maria Luisa Ortiz Rojas, Paz Rojas Baeza, "Comisiones de Verdad: Un Camino Incierto? Estudio Comparativo de Comisiones de la Verdad en Argentina, Chile, El Salvador, Guatemala y Sudáfrica desde las víctimas y las organizaciones de derechos humanos" (Santiago, Chile: CODEPU/APT, 2002), 139. Available at http://www.apt.ch/pub/library/Estudio2.pdf.
6. South Africa Restitution Act, as amended by Land Restitution and Reform Laws Amendment Act 63 of 1997, available on World Wide Web at http://www.polity.org.za/html/govdocs/legislation/1997/act63.pdf.
7. Cuevas, Rojas, and Baeza, "Comisiones de Verdad."
8. Richard A. Wilson, "Justice and Legitimacy in the South African Transition." In Alexandra Barahona de Brito et al., eds. *The Politics of Memory* (Oxford: Oxford University Press, 2001), 207; Mahmood Mamdani, "Reconciliation Without Justice," *Southern African Review of Books* (1996), 45.
9. Cuevas, Rojas, and Baeza, "Comisiones de Verdad."
10. United Nations Security Council, "Letter Dated 14 December 2000 from the Secretary General Addressed to the President of the Security Council," S/2000/1198, December 15, 2000. The ICTY came to similar conclusions – see United Nations Security Council, "Letter Dated 2 November 2000 from the Secretary General Addressed to the President of the Security Council," S/2000/1063, November 2, 2000.
11. Aloeboetoe et al., Judgment of 10 Sept. 1993, 15 Inter-Amer. Ct. H. R. (ser. C) (1994).

12. Report 19/97, Case 11.212, *Juan Chamay Pablo v. Guatemala* (Colotenango case), 13 March 1997.
13. Elazar Barkan, *The Guilt of Nations: Restitution and Negotiating Historical Injustices* (Baltimore: Johns Hopkins University Press, 2000), 6.
14. K. Parker and J. F. Chew, "The *Jugun Ianfu* ('Comfort Women') System." In R. L. Brooks, ed. *When Sorry Isn't Enough: The Controversy over Apologies and Reparations for Human Injustice* (New York and London: NYU Press, 1999), 89.
15. The Guatemalan and South African Truth Commissions recognized the need for community involvement and empowerment. Commission for Historical Clarification, "Memory of Silence: Report of the Commission for Historical Clarification, Conclusions and Recommendations" (Guatemala: Commission for Historical Clarification, 1999), recommendations, para. 11. Available on World Wide Web at http://shr.aaas.org/guatemala/ceh/report/english/recs3.html; Hlengiwe Mkize, "Introductory Notes to the Presentation of the Truth and Reconciliation Commission's Proposed Reparation and Rehabilitation Policies, 23 Oct. 1997." In Brooks, ed. *When Sorry Isn't Enough*, 501.
16. See, eg, Matome Sebelebele, "Mbeki Says No to 'Wealth Tax'," *BuaNews*, April 15, 2003. Available on World Wide Web at http://www.safrica.info/ess_info/sa_glance/constitution/wealthtax.htm.
17. Commission for Historical Clarification, "Memory of Silence."
18. Cuevas, Rojas, and Baeza, "Comisiones de Verdad."
19. The UNDP has a Bureau for Crisis Prevention and Recovery, while the World Bank has a Conflict Prevention and Reconstruction Unit. The US Agency for International Development's Office for Transition Initiatives plays a similar role. See the website on World Wide Web at http://www.undp.org/erd/recovery/recoverypriorities.htm; World Bank, Conflict Prevention and Reconstruction Unit, "Post-Conflict Reconstruction: The Role of the World Bank," available on World Wide Web at http://lnweb18.worldbank.org/ESSD/sdvext.nsf/67ByDocName/FrameworkforWorldBankInvevolvement-inPost-ConflictReconstruction/$FILE/pcr-role-of-bank.pdf; World Bank, *Development and Human Rights: The Role of the World Bank* (Washington, D.C.: World Bank, 1998).
20. World Bank, *Development and Human Rights*, 8.
21. See Maurizio Ragazzi, "Role of the World Bank in Conflict-Afflicted Areas," *The American Society of International Law Proceedings* 95 (2001): 240–244.
22. World Bank, *Development Cooperation and Conflict Operational Policy 2.30* (Washington, D.C.: World Bank, 2001), para. 2.
23. Stef Vandeginste, "Victims of Genocide, Crimes Against Humanity, and War Crimes in Rwanda: The Legal and Institutional Framework of Their Right to Reparation." In John Torpey, ed. *Politics and the Past: On Repairing Historical Injustices* (Lanham, Md.: Rowman and Littlefield, 2003), 249–276.
24. Ibid.
25. Ibid.
26. Information about the Commission and its work can be found on World Wide Web at http://www.easttimor-reconciliation.org.

27. Kieran Dwyer (observer at a November 2002 hearing), "Report on a Community Reconciliation Process in Suco Lela-Ufe, Nitibe, Oecussi on 22 November 2002," reported in Commission for Reception, Truth, and Reconciliation in East Timor, "Update: October–November 2002," available on the World Wide Web at http://www.easttimor-reconciliation.org/Update-OctNov.htm#English.

28. Kathleen Smith, "Destalinization in the Former Soviet Union." In Naomi Roht-Arriaza, ed. *Impunity and Human Rights in International Law and Practice* (Oxford: Oxford University Press, 1995), 117.

Part II

Social reconstruction and justice

How do multi-ethnic communities torn asunder by war and communal violence remember the past? Do they become mired in feelings of betrayal and revenge? What should children be taught about human rights, tolerance, the recent wars, and the history of their country? Do trials of suspected war criminals make a difference? What will it take for divided communities to live together again in peace? These are the questions that the authors in Part 2 address.

Rebuilding a post-war society involves repairing both its physical infrastructure and social fabric. While physical reconstruction suggests a coherent process similar to the rebuilding of a city after a natural disaster, the process of social reconstruction presents a far more challenging and complex task. This process takes place at all levels of society and entails constructing social networks, renewing old relationships, working with former enemies, and setting common goals that will benefit all citizens. In the opening two chapters of Part 2, Dinka Corkalo et al. and then Timothy Longman and Théonèste Rutagengwa examine the process of social reconstruction through the lens of collective memory. Using data collected from qualitative studies in Rwanda and the countries of the former Yugoslavia, they describe how ethnicity molds collective memory, and how governments and nationalist discourses influence that process. The authors provide accounts by ordinary people of what it is like to rebuild a community in an environment of on-going ethnic and nationalist manipulation.

In Chapters 9 and 10, Miklos Biro and Timothy Longman and their colleagues report on quantitative surveys they conducted in the same locales described in the preceding chapters. These quantitative studies allow us to develop models that show the complex relationships between trauma, justice, reconciliation, ethnicity, and social interaction with former enemies. Both studies suggest that ethnicity in Rwanda and the former Yugoslavia continues to shape people's perceptions about their social identity, their attitudes toward accountability, and their willingness to be reconciled with former enemies.

In the final chapters of Part 2, Sarah Freedman and her colleagues examine the role education can play in shaping attitudes toward ethnicity, justice, and social reconstruction in post-war countries. They highlight the lack of attention to schools as a critical component of the process of social reconstruction and note that many children in Rwanda and the former Yugoslavia have been caught in the crossfire of competing ideologies, with little guidance from their teachers on how to make sense of these "contested truths." The authors conclude that education reform must proceed along a parallel process to that of trials, judicial reform, economic reform, and democratic change. The opinions of students, teachers, and parents lead to the recommendation that schools in these divided communities adopt unified history curricula that encourage critical thinking about the past and explore multiple perspectives in an open and democratic manner.

Neighbors again? Intercommunity relations
after ethnic cleansing

*Dinka Corkalo, Dean Ajdukovic, Harvey M.
Weinstein, Eric Stover, Dino Djipa, and
Miklos Biro*

How can survivors of wars inflamed by ethnic hatred rebuild their lives? How do they describe their former enemies, now their neighbors? What role does justice play in the process of rebuilding communities? And what will it take to re-establish trust among former neighbors torn apart by communal violence?

In the summer of 2000, we set out to answer those questions through a series of long-term studies in three war-ravaged cities in Bosnia and Herzegovina (Mostar and Prijedor) and Croatia (Vukovar). As Weinstein and Stover have noted in the Introduction to this volume, these cities, once vibrant and thriving urban centers, are now deeply divided along ethnic lines. While the "ethnic divide" in Mostar is facilitated by the River Neretva, with Bosniaks living on the east bank and Croats living on the west bank, neither Vukovar nor Prijedor has such a physical demarcation. Instead, a "psychological wall" exists in both these cities, separating Croats from Serbs in Vukovar, and Bosniaks from Serbs in Prijedor. In all three cities, people from opposing ethnic groups who once lived together peacefully now harbor deep-seated resentments and suspicions of one another, making it difficult to renew social relationships or to form new ones.

Our studies examined the views of residents in these three cities regarding war, justice, and the prospects for reconciliation. In Mostar and Vukovar, we studied the daily lives of residents over a two-year period. This intensive field study was complemented by focus group research in both cities, and by data collected during key informant interviews with social and political figures. Interview data also were collected from refugees in Serbia who had left Croatia during Operation Storm in 1995. In the third city, Prijedor, where some 15,000 Bosniak returnees now live among the Serbs that expelled them, we did not conduct a field study but collected data from key informants and focus groups.

Methodology

These studies are based on the principle of triangulation. By combining research methods, we are able to maximize the reliability and validity of our findings. First, we employed field studies in the cities of Vukovar and Mostar that began in September 2000 and lasted two years. Every four months a researcher visited each city and remained there for four weeks. They introduced themselves in the communities as researchers collecting data for a study of social reconstruction. As participant-observers, their task was to make contacts and communicate with city residents, to observe interactions among inhabitants, and to chronicle their way of life. Field data included analyses of perceptions of objective changes over time in the areas of reconstruction, economic growth, employment, schooling, health care, culture and sporting events, religion, media, civil society, safety, politics, and everyday life.

Second, in all three cities we conducted focus groups with representatives of war victims, non-governmental organizations (NGOs), young people (age range from 18 to 30 years), and entrepreneurs. Focus groups, consisting of six to eight people, were homogeneous, based on our recruitment criteria and according to national origin. In total, eight focus groups were conducted in each city. The focus group protocol addressed such issues as outcomes and consequences of the war; the role of the international community; the effects of war on physical and mental health; relations among ethnic groups before, during, and after the war; problems of living in each city; war crimes; perceptions of the International Criminal Tribunal for the former Yugoslavia (ICTY); and reconciliation. The focus groups took place in Mostar and Vukovar during December 2000, and in Prijedor during September 2001. During the same month, focus groups also were held in Novi Sad (Serbia) with Croatian Serb refugees from Vukovar and other parts of Croatia that were not under the control of Croatian authorities during the war (the so-called "Serbian Republic of Krajina").

Finally, we carried out key informant interviews in these cities during the summers of 2000 and 2001 to ascertain the opinions and attitudes of key community figures (N = 90) regarding the impact of the war; experiences with other national groups; and attitudes toward domestic and international war crimes trials, the international community, and the relationship of justice to reconciliation.

Communities in war

Disintegration of pre-war life

All of our informants reported positive, almost nostalgic, memories of a good quality of life before the war. Most participants said that relations among the different ethnic groups were harmonious during the pre-war years. It was irrelevant whether their neighbors, co-workers, and friends belonged to a different ethnic group. "We lived normally," an informant said. "We did not even know who was who [meaning who was from which ethnic group]. We visited each other at our homes and celebrated each other's religious holidays together." Both Vukovar and Mostar residents proudly noted their cities' long and celebrated history of multi-culturalism and tolerance. Many Croats from Vukovar, however, spoke bitterly about their former Serbian friends and neighbors who, they claimed, failed to warn them about the ensuing assault on the city by Yugoslav troops and Serb paramilitaries. Our data show that this feeling of betrayal is a profound obstacle to the process of social repair in the aftermath of communal violence (see Stover, Chapter 5; Ajdukovic and Corkalo, Chapter 14; and Halpern and Weinstein, Chapter 15 in this volume).

Although the political and social collapse of the former Yugoslavia occurred gradually,[1] our participants viewed it somewhat differently. They spoke of changes taking place "as if overnight," including the abrupt termination of relationships with old friends and neighbors, and the rapid formation of ethnically homogeneous political and social groups. A Serb man who is an entrepreneur in Prijedor said: "War exploded in this area within forty-eight hours. We were caught by it suddenly." A Croat man who belonged to an NGO in Vukovar put it this way:

We all used to be friends and this is the reason for the pain we now feel. We used to share happiness and sorrow with them. And suddenly in 1991 you come to seek protection from a person [from another ethnic group] who until yesterday was your very good friend, and he almost does not recognize you any more. He would not dare to be your friend any more.

Whether because of horrific war experiences and trauma, the sense of disillusionment and betrayal, or simply because of the process of selective remembering, most participants failed to acknowledge that ethnic divisions had begun to occur in the years and months before the war. For all that things were harmonious on the surface, there was at least some consciousness about national identity and ethnic difference in the pre-war years, although it was not publicly emphasized. Consider this comment from a young Serb man from Prijedor: "When I was 10 I moved to the part of city inhabited mainly by Muslims, and the first thing they asked was my name, whether I was 'Vlah,'[2] and what was my nationality. I did not know how to answer them." Or that of a Serb man from Croatia who now lives as a refugee in Serbia: "We all thought that there had been 'Brotherhood and Unity,' but it became apparent that Croatian nationalism smoldered underneath and that they were always plotting against us."

Whether we accept the hypothesis that ethnic divisions appeared suddenly or that they had always been present, the experiences of participants indicate that the delineation of intergroup boundaries took place quite swiftly. The Vukovar group described a period of two years to several months before the war when ethnic divisions began to intensify and when nationalist identities started to take shape and impose themselves on the life of the city.[3] Before the war "we didn't know who was a Serb and who was a Croat," said a Croat woman from Vukovar. "At that time none of them ever used Cyrillic letters even to sign their names. Then, all of sudden in 1991 they started to emphasize that they were Serbs, which means that they were brought up in such a way."

Despite Tito's call for "Brotherhood and Unity," a Yugoslav identity (as opposed to, say, a Serb, Croat, or Muslim identity) never fully took hold in the former federation. Sekulic et al. report that in 1989 less than 15 percent of the people in Bosnia declared themselves to be Yugoslavs, while in more ethnically homogeneous republics – Croatia, Slovenia, Serbia, and Macedonia – that number was significantly smaller.[4] Just prior to the war, nationalist politicians revived and reconstructed national identities by introducing cultural elements of ethnicity that until then were not regarded as important or necessary. Examples of these included the use of Cyrillic letters, language purification, and the introduction of religious symbols and national signs (coats of arms) and songs. Historical debts were emphasized, as well as complaints of discrimination and abuse of national rights. Many nationalist politicians encouraged the use of national signs and symbols as a way of threatening other national groups. With their security under attack, many people, either willingly or unwillingly, sought refuge in the confines of their own ethnic group. Issues of individual and group identity became paramount, and the boundaries between "us" and "them" were solidified. As we will see when we explore how social life evolved after the war, it is extraordinarily difficult to reverse this process. However, the fluidity of social identity can be seen in how many residents in all three cities still try to overcome ethnic boundaries by emphasizing their urban identity as "true Mostarians" or the "old Vukovar inhabitants." The civic identity simultaneously reflects nostalgia for the old life and a rejection of the boxes in which people find themselves.

War crimes

Most focus group participants from all national groups, as well as other informants, said that the international community failed to play an honorable role during the war, and that more could have been done to stop genocide and ethnic cleansing. While participants (especially those from Bosnia and Herzegovina) recognized that the international community finally took action to stop the war, they said that the international community's principal motivation was based not on concern for the conflicted national groups but solely on its own interests. Although often expressed as a vague suspicion, one common element was the belief that a strong Yugoslavia was perceived as unacceptable to the countries of the West. A comment by a Croat woman from Vukovar reflected the sentiments of many participants: "The international community did not even do the minimum that it should have done. If they could not prevent the destruction [of a city], then they should have at least stopped it, and not allowed [atrocities] to happen . . . They should have served as a barrier to stop what was happening."

Focus group participants often became emotional when discussion turned to the topic of war crimes and the trials of suspected war criminals by the ICTY. Most participants agreed that war crimes had been committed and that perpetrators should be punished, but many said the local courts could not properly conduct war crimes trials because the judges would not be objective (Stover describes a similar attitude among ICTY witnesses in Chapter 5 in this volume). Further, study participants raised doubts about the judicial impartiality of the ICTY.[5] Many said the tribunal was a political court whose goal was not to execute justice but to exert political control. "The Hague Tribunal is a big mockery," a young Croat woman from Vukovar said. "I do not consider it competent. It seems that it was made only for us. What about America? What about Iraq and Iran? Nobody is asking them anything, but they are asking us because we allow it." A Serb man, also from Vukovar, said: "The Hague is dictated by the Americans. Those that they want to send to The Hague are sent there. And the wrong people are being tried. Take Blaskic – he didn't even know what was going on."[6]

Representatives of all national groups felt victimized by the war. Although study participants recognized the existence of war criminals within their own ranks, they considered their national group to be the greatest victim.[7] They also felt the ICTY was prejudicial to their own group, as this comment by a Croat man from Vukovar illustrates: "Many more people have been killed in Ovcara than compared to Gospic and Ahmici, and the tribunal is trying only Croats. Among Bosnian Serbs who have been sentenced, nobody got forty-five years as Blaskic did. This is a political court and [Blaskic] was tried for political reasons . . . It was only important that he was a Croat and to give him a long sentence." A Serb woman from Vukovar, now living as a refugee in Serbia, said: "The tribunal condemns only Serbs. Everyone points out Srebrenica, but what about [the other crimes] that preceded it?"

Some Croat and Bosniak participants believed that their side could not have committed war crimes, because their national groups were being attacked. "It is important [to punish war crimes]," a young Croat man from Vukovar said, "but in Vukovar our side could not have committed war crimes, because people were defending themselves." Or as a Bosniak man put it: "A nation that is subjected to war crimes cannot commit war crimes itself."

Since members of all national groups consider themselves victims, Croats and Bosniaks particularly, bringing their compatriots before a court implies repeated victimization of the actual victims. This attitude has important psychological implications for analysis of the relationship between individual and collective responsibility. On the one hand, the intention of the court is to individualize guilt and to take the burden off a whole nation. (Most participants agreed with this notion.) On the other hand, members of the national group from which the convicted persons originated often personalized those trials and experienced them as trials directed against "their" collective. Hence the oft-repeated admonition: "We are the only ones that are tried in The Hague."

Many study participants said they felt torn in two directions. As bystanders, they do not want to be held collectively responsible for war crimes committed by other members of their ethnic group. At the same time, they cannot separate themselves from the national group, for to do so would mean jeopardizing their sense of self, their identity. Caught in this untenable position, they cannot free themselves of the guilt, so they criticize the ICTY as biased against their group, as this is the most socially acceptable option.

Baumeister and Hasting[8] argue that social groups, like individuals,[9] need to maintain and preserve a positive self-image. Taking into account the reconstructive nature of human memory, we would add to this argument that groups are especially motivated to remember events and memories that enhance their self-image. Baumeister and Hasting infer that these biases are motivated forms of group self-deception. We found the three most apparent forms of group self-deception among our participants were denial of what happened during the war, biased memories of the events or embellishment of particular historical episodes, and the downplaying of war crimes committed by members of their own national group. These manifestations of group self-deception offer fertile ground for building national myths instead of national history.

Although the participants largely agreed that all national groups committed war crimes, they tended to regard crimes in their own ranks as "individual excesses," while crimes committed by the other side were premeditated and sanctioned. A young Croat man who works for an NGO in Vukovar put it this way: "War crimes should be punished, regardless of which side committed them . . . Perhaps my countrymen also committed crimes, but this was so seldom that it is not worth mentioning." A Serb woman from Prijedor expressed a similar sentiment: "It is very hard for me to hear that something happened in Trnopolje which is not true.[10] I was a member of Red Cross and used to go there every day. And this faked video with people behind a barbed wire. They were in front of the wire, but nobody talks about it. I would never have allowed myself to work in a concentration camp." These statements illustrate why the full disclosure of past crimes is necessary for the construction of an unbiased history. Such public disclosures also offer opportunities for the offending group to express basic compassion to the victims. "We must be open, we must talk about some things, and we must clarify and admit what happened," a Croat woman from Mostar said. "Only then will reconciliation be possible. We all know what happened, but it is easier when you hear a criminal confessing his crimes. What happened has happened and it cannot be changed, but it means a lot to you when you hear a confession. That is something very important."

Reconstructing community

Our data suggest that post-war communities inherit features from both their pre-war existence and their experiences of war and its aftermath. Above all, a community will never be the same in the wake of war and communal violence. Many people will have died or fled the violence. Some refugees will never return, and those who do are encumbered with experiences of violence, exodus, exile, and return. Those who remained often resent those who fled, and they too have been changed by their experience of the war. During the course of the protracted war, a new generation grew up, adopting normative patterns that differ from those of previous generations.

The physical environment

We found that rebuilding in post-war communities usually begins with physical repair of houses and the city infrastructure. The more quickly destroyed houses are repaired and new ones built, the more rapid the return of refugees and the internally displaced. We observed this phenomenon in Mostar between 2000 and 2001. During our first field visit, in October 2000, only 5 to 8 percent of the pre-war population had returned to Mostar, which was one of the lowest percentages in all the Federation (the average return to the Federation of Bosnia and Herzegovina stood at around 15 percent). The situation was almost the same as in Republika Srpska, where the rate of return of refugees and displaced persons is lowest. A year later, the percentage of return to Mostar had more than doubled (on average, to approximately 18 percent).[11] In Mostar, the progress of return has reverberated more powerfully on the east than on the west bank. In addition, there have been no dramatic changes in economic investments and employment during these two years. The words of the Mostar field researcher illustrate the slow process of reconstruction on the west bank in late 2001:

Generally, the comments of the local people on the changes in the town are different: while the newcomers generally have no opinions on this, the old inhabitants are generally unhappy with the speed of changes, they believe the changes are too slow. I already said that I saw more cranes and bulldozers in the west part than in the east but I must say that I saw some of this machinery in the same places and in the same phase of construction during my first visit to Mostar, which would imply that not much has been done.

Another field researcher provided a mirror image of the same situation in Vukovar in early 2002:

I would like to point out that it's getting harder and harder for me to notice the changes that are happening. I have a feeling that I'm becoming like a resident of the city who, when asked in a general way, "Are there any changes?" will, at first, respond: "Nothing has changed." Only after saying that will they begin listing the little things that might be interesting. The other thing I noticed is the mind-boggling construction rate of new family houses. The restorative work is not, I believe, any faster than before, but I am left completely stunned when I see with my own eyes the spectacle of a street full of new homes where there was nothing but ruins only a few months before. So, with an eye towards previous periods, I would say that Vukovar is acquiring the contours of a city after all. Of course, this relates only to its physical appearance and only when compared to earlier times, because destroyed and unusable buildings are apparent every step of the way.

While Vukovar and Mostar have experienced a certain degree of physical renewal, the effects of the war are still apparent. This is especially the case with respect to certain characteristic sights and structures that had great symbolic meaning for city residents and visitors alike. The destruction of these symbols of civic identity facilitated the creation of ethnic divisions when a unifying whole was lost. One such symbol is the centuries-old bridge of Mostar, the Stari Most, destroyed by the Bosnian Croat Army in 1993. The bridge, built in 1566, was considered a masterpiece of Islamic architecture and a unique symbol of an undivided city. It was the place where high-divers from all around the region competed every year, dropping from a height of 21 meters to the churning surface of the Neretva River. Destruction of the bridge represented an attack on the city's rich cultural, historical, and multi-cultural heritage. The implicit message of this act was that the city should be divided into two sides, Bosniak and Croat, which would then have nothing in common.

One of the men who used to dive from the bridge is planning to organize a diving competition as soon as reconstruction of the bridge is completed. He intends to invite divers from around the world who have previously made the plunge. When asked whether he would invite Croatian divers, he became offended: "Of course we will. The criterion on this bridge is not your nationality but whether you are brave enough to dive. Nothing else is important."

The slow pace of the bridge's reconstruction is emblematic of the reluctance of many Bosniak and Croat residents of Mostar to reconcile their differences as a result of the war. In November 2001, our field researcher in Mostar reported that the anniversary of the destruction of the bridge:

was commemorated by pupils of elementary schools from the eastern part of Mostar tossing flowers into the Neretva river at the spot where the bridge once stood. The town authorities were represented only by the Bosniak deputy mayor, Hamdija Jahic. The pupils from the western part of Mostar did not participate in the ceremony, nor did the West Mostar media inform about this event . . . and other inhabitants of the Old Town took this as a proof that the Croat side does not wish to unite the town . . . On the other hand, I heard from the Croats that it suits the Bosniaks better to have the bridge unfinished, or rather a bridge that is permanently under construction, because they can get more money out of international organizations.

Here, too, there is considerable ambivalence toward the international community for not doing more to complete the construction of the bridge. As one Bosniak tradesman noted: "Every spring the foreign politicians come and say, 'We will build the Stari Most. We broke down the Berlin Wall and will break down the Mostar one.' The people don't believe them any more." Whether the problems were primarily internal to Mostar or external, emanating from the international community, the ten-year lag in rebuilding the bridge is symbolic of the fragmented nature of the reconciliation process.

The social environment

The rebuilding of post-war communities is a process that embodies a series of social elements.[12] "Social reconstruction or renewal," writes Ajdukovic, "is a process within a community, which returns the community's damaged social functioning to a normal level of its inhabitants' interpersonal and group relationships in a way that renews the social tissue of the community."[13] The term "normal" in this definition does not imply "the way it was before," but refers to the needs of community members; thus, the pace of social reconstruction is set by them, and it cannot, and should not, be rushed. Ajdukovic suggests: "The social reconstruction of a community in a certain period can reach only the level of social functioning that is acceptable to the majority of its members. It is a level on which they recognize that some common interests cannot be accomplished through individual efforts, or through separate interest groups, or by the state, but that the members of that community need to reach an agreement."[14] We would add that when a certain level of social reconstruction is reached, it will be sustained until it becomes dysfunctional in some other area of community life.

Social reconstruction is not a linear process. While being significantly improved in some aspects of the social world, in others the "social tissue" or social network can be remarkably weaker or even non-existent. For example, an improvement in business or work relations between members of different ethnic groups may not necessarily be present in private, social encounters. Consider, for example, the remark by a young Croat woman from Vukovar: "I work with a Serb whom I very much respect and this is the only Serb who has entered into my home. The rules are clear: we work together, but Croats visit Croats in their homes, and Serbs visit Serbs . . . The Serbs who have done nothing are suffering because of those who behaved like savages."

At some point it might be possible to socialize publicly with members of other national groups, but not privately, or vice versa – people may be ready to let a member of another group into their home and to socialize privately, particularly when "the other" is an old friend, but they feel uneasy or see it as socially undesirable to socialize outside the house. "Home visits are less frequent than before the war," said a Serb man from Vukovar, "but we meet each other on the street and in cafés. I met a friend in 1997, but he told me not to call him at home and he will not call me at home either."

A city we have (not) known

Mostar and Vukovar have developed an almost rural character as a result of the war, changes in the population, and the manner in which residents must survive to make ends meet. Communal violence has not only brought about ethnic division of the urban space but has redefined the space itself. As the cities become more rural in appearance, customs, and manners, they are less recognizable to their pre-war inhabitants. Many older inhabitants find themselves in an uncomfortable state of "liminality," living neither in the city nor in the country. As our field researcher in Vukovar reported in December 2001:

There are an insignificant number of people out in the streets after five o'clock in the afternoon. In some places, the streets are completely empty. Even during the day there are no children playing in front of their houses in the suburbs. There are no groups of people engaged in any kind of social activity, including bowling, which used to be common in the buildings in the Borovo Naselje or basketball on the playgrounds in certain neighborhoods.

A young woman lamented to our field researcher in Vukovar the loss of "spirit" which once prevailed in the town:

A lot has changed since reintegration. When I go to work now, I think about how it's already been five years. Now, I have almost no friends. My best friends before the war were Croats and they didn't come back because that was the very generation that got married or found jobs somewhere else . . . This city no longer has a spirit. It isn't like it was before and it will definitely never be like that again . . . It can barely be called a city now. It is pretty and idealistic only in the way we remember it. But people don't understand that how it was in the past has nothing to do with the way it is today.

Unlike before the war, many residents in Vukovar and Mostar have taken to raising livestock, such as pigs or chickens, to supplement their meager incomes. A young woman from Vukovar noted: "The city has turned into a village because people are forced to live off something." Cultural activities also have dropped perceptively. "Our past cultural life has split apart, and nothing new has replaced it," said an official at the Vukovar museum. "In the past, people didn't need to create a cultural life, it was always there. Now we have to build it on new foundations. The young people have to recognize a cultural life is necessary. Not everyone will return because of the reconstruction of a factory. There has to be a spirit of culture here as well." (Blotner describes a similar need to rebuild the arts in post-war Croatia and Bosnia and Herzegovina in Chapter 13 in this volume.)

Many older residents find it difficult to accept the social norms that now exist in their hometowns. A resident of Mostar said:

My generation, 1965–1975, was worse off than any other generation. The largest proportion of those killed and forced to flee were from that generation. The younger ones, who were 10 or 12 years old when the war broke out, they tend to go to the other side in larger numbers. They don't know how it used to be and they are satisfied with how things are now. We, the older ones, when we remember what it used to be like and compare it with what it's like now, the only thing we can do is cry. Never again will Mostar be as it used to be and have the spirit it used to have, because less than 20 percent of the old crowd have remained in Mostar on both sides.

An example of how a common urban vocabulary has succumbed to the worsening of interethnic relations since the war in Vukovar can be found in the greeting that inhabitants exchange when they meet on the street. In the years leading up to the war, the traditional greeting *Zdravo* gradually became associated with the Serbian ethnic community exclusively, while the Croats replaced it with *Bog* or *Bok*, which was a very common greeting before the war in other parts of Croatia. Thus, a greeting assumed a form of ethnic legitimation, an ethnic marker of urban space. The usual polite greetings, *Dobar dan* or *Do vidjenja*, are used only in very formal situations and when people expect the interaction to be brief enough that one's identity will not be revealed.[15]

In Mostar, a change of greeting patterns has developed whereby the indigenous urban youth from both sides of the river use the pre-war greeting *Ciao*. Meanwhile, in the Bosniak (Eastern) part of Mostar, the salutation *Bok* used by new Croatian residents of West Mostar is perceived by old inhabitants as an Ustasha greeting,[16] while in the Croatian part of the city it is considered a greeting introduced by peasants from the countryside. As our field researcher in Mostar reported in October 2000, these linguistic differences belie a split between the old inhabitants and the mostly rural "newcomers":

The old residents of Mostar use pre-war slang, including about fifty expressions not used by newcomers. The old residents consider themselves (and their friends on the other side of the river) as the "protectors of the town," claiming that the "spirit of Mostar" is most jeopardized by the newcomers, no matter their nationality, from the countryside who have not accepted urban standards of behavior.

A very important element of pre-war social life throughout the former Yugoslavia had been the custom of taking time to drink coffee with a friend or colleague. The invitation "Let's have a coffee" does not mean that coffee will necessarily be consumed, but serves as an invitation to spend time together in friendly conversation. The disappearance of this custom between national groups in post-war Vukovar and Mostar is another indicator of disturbed social connections.[17] These changes demonstrate the extent to which people from different national groups have withdrawn from one another and feel insecure in social situations that go beyond family and close friends. A Bosniak who fled Mostar during the war describes his visits to his former home:

My old neighbors are Croats and when we first returned to visit, they approached us and we shook hands and greeted each other. They asked how we were and so on. When we come these days, they only say "Good afternoon." It isn't like it used to be before the war. There is no "Come on, let's have a coffee." There is nothing like that any more. And when there is nothing like that, I do not feel like going there.

In Vukovar as well, social relations have changed considerably, even within the same ethnic group, as our field researcher reported in 2001:

[O]ld social relationships have been broken. Croats say hello to each other but they don't visit each other for coffee as much as they did before. The old friendships have fallen apart or grown weak . . . There are no contacts with the Serbs.

While the most significant change has been across national groups, field data suggest that social life as a whole has been curtailed in Vukovar. A young returnee to Vukovar describes how her parents have retreated from any form of social life:

[Serbs and Croats] only greet one another or chat about something unimportant and that's that. Nobody goes for coffee or a visit. Those things don't happen any more. It's only with family. Everyone's in their own apartment and there is no social life. Before, my parents used to go somewhere non-stop, but now they just sit at home. I feel sorry for them. They have money because they both work, but they no longer have anyone to go out with.

While the fundamental social divisions fall on ethnic lines, it would be an oversimplification of the social reality to base these social changes merely on ethnic identity. In fact, ethnic categories are mentioned rarely in the inhabitants' discourse. Terms used most often are "we" and "they." Vukovar Serbs, for example, rarely use the term "Croats"; they mostly use the term "returnees."[18] Further, the burden of people who decided not to choose sides is well illustrated by a Croat who remained in the city after the fall of Vukovar: "Imagine how it is when all your colleagues leave and you decide to stay, working the worst jobs not because you want to or because you're paid, but because you must. It's degrading professionally and in all other ways and, in the end, they consider you a traitor and they don't renovate your apartment and you can't get a job." Such stratification at many levels within communities actually hinders the possibility of forming a critical mass of individuals who could instigate the process of growing closer. Local political elites are not of much help, since they continue to support separation covertly.

Nowhere is the policy of ethnic division in Mostar and Vukovar more starkly apparent than in the school system, where both schools and classrooms are divided along ethnic lines. In some Vukovar schools, Croat and Serb children attend the same classes but in different classrooms. In others, children of different national groups attend the same school in different shifts. Croat children are taught in Croatian, while Serb children learn in the Serbian language. A similar situation exists in Mostar between Croat and Bosniak children, although change is being mandated in the old Gymnasium. (Freedman et al. discuss the repercussions of separated education in Chapter 11 in this volume.) Since the ethnic division of the urban space is so complete, leaving no possibility for children to socialize after school hours, school segregation may have especially detrimental social consequences. In the words of a teacher from Vukovar who teaches in a school in Serbian language and letters: "Schools should be places where segregation doesn't exist. These children have not lived together before the war like our generation has, and so they should be taught together from the beginning. If there is segregation in schools one cannot expect the children to be together on the street." Many parents both from Mostar and Vukovar report similar misgivings. One of our Mostar informants said: "Children who finish these schools can only add, subtract, and divide in the same way. Everything else is different."

A divided school system points to a dysfunctional state and community, where distrust between its members prevents cooperation around any common objective, even though in Bosnia and Herzegovina, where there are three constituent peoples, integrated schools would serve everyone's – and especially the state's – interest. Given European tradition and the current re-emphasis on minority rights, balanced solutions to ethnic segregation in schools and rights to an education that safeguards minority ethnic identity require creative solutions. This is a critical issue in Croatia, where Serbs are a minority population. Education policy in that country is caught between the dangers of exclusivity or special programs that may promote ethnic identity, and options such as integration that may facilitate societal reconciliation but that may challenge minority rights. If schools are to play a positive role in rebuilding post-war Vukovar, we suggest that at present the extreme positions of "either integration or separation" should not be the only possible solutions for educating minority and majority children.

Economic uncertainty, few jobs, and the lack of domestic and foreign investment are related to another ominous trend – the departure of youth. Once refugees or internally displaced, many young people have now returned to their cities of origin, not by choice but because of their parents' nostalgia and the pressures placed on them by the host countries to leave. Many feel that they have sacrificed their childhood and adolescent years. "After finishing school, a lot of young people in Mostar want to leave the country and go abroad," our field researcher reported in July 2001. "They don't see a future in Bosnia and Herzegovina. One of those is Sead, a Bosniak who was expelled from Stolac in 1993 and, together with his family, fled to East Mostar . . . He says that his parents want to go back to Stolac and that he wants to finish school and go abroad, as do most educated young people." Another young man notes: "I have nothing to wait for any longer. I have been waiting long enough. That is actually all I do. Just wait." Many young people who were educated abroad during the exile see this experience as an advantage that will facilitate their new departure, but not as capital that they might utilize in their own country. Apathy is also prevalent among the younger generation, and few profess a desire to promote change in their community. Although no reliable statistics exist on the number of young people who have moved away, our data suggest that it is a troubling trend that will continue for many years to come. A demographic shift to a more elderly population has implications as well for economic recovery.

Most participants view their economic difficulties as a serious obstacle to overcoming the current social divisions. Both unemployment and low incomes contribute to the feeling of being disadvantaged because of national origin. All national groups believe that their group is discriminated against in employment and realization of their rights; all feel that the other group is privileged. "The Serbs have more opportunity to get jobs," a Croat woman from Vukovar said. "They can find jobs in Serbia, and they also can get jobs here more easily because they can claim discrimination. There are many Serbs who do not live here, they live in Yugoslavia and cross the border to work here." At the same time, a young Serb woman from Vukovar took this perspective: "The Croats are those who mostly have jobs. The Serbs are at home, unemployed . . . None of my friends work . . . Those who work and get salaries will always dominate those who do not . . . Unemployment is what is forcing us to leave."

Memory and ethnicity

The diversity of experiences during the war brought about a phenomenon that might be described as an "ethnization" of memories. By this term we mean that a memory itself and interpretation of the past become ethnically exclusive, creating subjective, psychological realities and different symbolic meanings of common events in people who belong to different ethnic groups. The many individual experiences have merged into the collective memory of the opposing ethnic groups. They interpret the same events in utterly different ways and show great differences in their willingness to talk about them, particularly their relevance to daily life. For instance, when discussing the onset of the war, Vukovar Serbs, in focus groups, will date its beginning to the period a few months prior to the bombardment of Vukovar. "A few months before the war began, there was not a day in Vukovar that a Serb store, a café, or a car was not blown up," a Serb informant said. "It was very chaotic, the people would not dare to go out of their homes." Meanwhile, most Vukovar Croats never mention this period. They point out that the Serbs knew that there would be a war, formed closed groups, and failed to warn their closest friends to take precautions (Ajdukovic and Corkalo discuss this further in Chapter 14 in this volume). Nor is there a consensus about the end of the war: Serbs claim that it began and ended in 1991; for the Croats, it ended in 1997 through the process of peaceful reintegration, when they were allowed to return to Vukovar.

The ethnic difference in interpreting what happened in Vukovar is well illustrated by the term used by Vukovar Serbs and Croats when referring to November 18, 1991, when Yugoslav Army and Serbian paramilitary units captured the town. While, for the Croats, this date is named the "Day of the Fall of Vukovar," the Serbs refer to this date as "Liberation Day." A sign of concession in speech is to make reference to the date without mentioning a name. The commemoration of this anniversary always brings about a disquieting atmosphere in the town, a sign of the failure to reconcile different attitudes. Distinctions between defendants and aggressors become blurred depending upon national interpretation. As our field researcher observed in November 2001:

On the 18th the whole town was almost desolate (unusually so, although it was Sunday). The shops were closed, and so were some Serb coffee bars, and the market. The Serb coffee bars that were open were empty all day. The town was full of police, who gathered especially in the center and at the market. A few institutions asked to have police near their building (Yugoslav consulate, and a few political parties). The majority of Serbs that I talked to said they spent the day at home, since they did not want to be seen as provocateurs.

Conclusion

The post-war period in Vukovar and Mostar reflects uncertainty and an uneasy sense of transition. While we lack field data for Prijedor, interview and focus group data are consistent with the findings in the other cities. On the whole, we find that physical reconstruction has developed much faster than social renewal. Our data also suggests that social reconstruction must address at least four levels. At the individual level, there is the need for psychological interventions to help those most affected by the war and its aftermath cope with the trauma. At the level of community, the pre-war network of social relationships, although now changed in quality, must be re-established. Further, new relationships must be developed as a precondition for the renewal of the community as the basic unit. A vital element of these relationships is the renewal of trust. At the societal level, there is a need to establish relationships that pursue common interests, create civic initiatives, and develop cooperative relationships between different social groups. Finally, at the state level, the rule of law must be established to protect the rights of *all* individuals. Post-war policy and practice must simultaneously address all of these to build peaceful and stable communities.[19]

NOTES

We wish to thank our collaborators, Damir Pilic, a psychologist, and Kruno Kardov, a sociologist, who collected the field data. We also express our thanks to Professor Marita Eastmond from the University of Gothenburg, Sweden, for her valuable help and advice during the course of our field research. Our deepest gratitude and respect go to the people of Vukovar, Mostar, Prijedor, and Novi Sad who have shared their stories with us.

1. Sabrina P. Ramet, *Balkan Babel: The Disintegration of Yugoslavia from the Death of Tito to Ethnic War* (Oxford: Westview Press, 1996).
2. That is, if he was a Serb. "Vlah" is in fact a label for a Christian. This is what the Turks called all Christians during the Ottoman era.
3. Roger Brubaker, *Nationalism Reframed: Nationhood and the National Question in the New Europe* (Cambridge: Cambridge University Press, 1996). Brubaker's concept of the suddenness and "eventfulness" of the experience of the overwhelming nationalization of social and private life offers one way to think about the speed with which the Communist regime fell and the states of the Eastern Block disassociated during this nationalist ascendancy. However, even eventfulness has a history, as illustrated by the narratives of our informants.
4. Dusko Sekulic, Garth Massey, and Randy Hodson, "Who Were the Yugoslavs? Failed Source of a Common Identity in the Former Yugoslavia," *American Sociological Review* 59 (1994): 83–97.
5. Bosniaks, and particularly Bosniaks in Prijedor, showed the greatest confidence in the ICTY.
6. General Tihomir Blaskic, a commander in the Croatian Defense Council, or HVO, in central Bosnia voluntarily gave himself up to the tribunal in April 1996. Four years later the trial chamber found him guilty and unrepentant of crimes against humanity, grave breaches of the Geneva Conventions, and war crimes committed against Bosnian Muslim and Serb civilians in the Lasva

Valley, and sentenced him to forty-five years' imprisonment – the longest sentence at that time.

7. The Human Rights Center and the International Human Rights Law Clinic, University of California, Berkeley, and the Center for Human Rights, University of Sarajevo, "Justice, Accountability and Social Reconstruction: An Interview Study of Bosnian Judges and Prosecutors," *Berkeley Journal of International Law* 18 (1999): 102, 133. In this study of Bosnian legal professionals, researchers found that no matter what facts emerged in the judicial record, the so-called truth would be distorted by national group narratives reflecting the group's sense of victimhood.

8. Roy F. Baumeister and Stephen Hasting, "Distortions of Collective Memory: How Groups Flatter and Deceive Themselves." In James W. Pennebaker, Dario Paez and Bernard Rime, eds. *Collective Memory and Political Events: Social Psychological Perspective* (Mahwah, N.J.: Lawrence Erlbaum Associates, 1997), 276–293.

9. Henri Tajfel and John C. Turner, "Theory of Intergroup Behavior." In Stephen Worchel and William G. Austin, eds. *Psychology of Intergroup Relations* (Chicago: Nelson-Hall Publishers, 1986), 7–24.

10. Trnopolje and Omarska refer to Serb-run concentration camps near Prijedor, discovered in August 1992 by journalist Ed Vulliamy and his colleagues from the British television network ITN. See R. Gutman and D. Rief, eds. *Crimes of War: What the Public Should Know* (New York: W.W. Norton and Company, 1999).

11. Damir Pilic, "Field report from Mostar," July 2001, Zagreb, Croatia. (Unpublished.)

12. Laurel E. Fletcher and Harvey M. Weinstein, "Violence and Social Repair: Rethinking the Contribution of Justice to Reconciliation," *Human Rights Quarterly* 24 (2002): 573–639.

13. Dean Ajdukovic, "Socijalna rekonstrukcija zajednice" (Community social reconstruction). In Dean Adjukovic, ed. *Socijalna rekonstrukcija zajednice: psiholoski procesi, rjesavanje sukoba i socijalna akcija* (Community social reconstruction: psychological processes, conflict management and social action) (Zagreb: Society for Psychological Assistance, 2003), 11–39.

14. Social reconstruction is a process whose description varies with discipline perspective. At a 2003 meeting of the authors and invitees from many disciplines titled "Justice in the Balance: Justice, Accountability and Social Reconstruction in Rwanda and former Yugoslavia," held at the Rockefeller Study Center in Bellagio, Italy, the following definition was adopted:

> Social reconstruction is a process of reaffirming and developing a society based on shared values and human rights in which formal and informal institutions reflect those values. It includes a broad range of programmatic interventions including justice, education and other programs to address the factors that led to the conflict. No single institution or program will be able to address all the requisite dimensions of the process that occurs at multiple levels – neighborhood, community, and society.

15. The greeting is only at the beginning of an interaction, which can be immediately posed on an ethnic basis, if a greeting is used which is related only to a certain ethnic group. But even in cases when the initial interaction is posed

quite neutrally, one's national belonging can be discovered very quickly. And although Croats and Serbs understand each other completely, it is impossible to fail in one's ethnic identification according to their speech. Thus, in the course of a meeting, a conversation can continue if the language is perceived primarily as a communication tool, or it can be stopped if the language is perceived as primarily an ethnic marker.

16. Ustashas were members of the Croatian quisling military forces during the Second World War.

17. Urban space is divided into private and public. As a public zone, coffee shops are examples illustrating not only the processes of ethnic division of the space but attempts to overcome that as well. In Vukovar, for example, in the center of the town there is a coffee shop at the entrance of which there is a huge Croatian checker-board (a Croatian heraldic sign). There is no need to guess which national group gathers there, and which is not welcomed. In the central zone of Mostar, on the eastern side, where there is a Bosniak population, the *American Pub* was opened, originally intended to be a gathering place for young people from both sides of the river. Unfortunately, this attempt to renew social connections in this way did not succeed, and the coffee shop was closed. While, at the beginning, the ethnic division of coffee shops was quite firm, the situation today is somewhat more relaxed. There are some secure zones where people of different nationalities want to have coffee together. It is interesting how those who made friends with those "from the other side" interpret their own disinclination to visit their ethnic group's coffee shop with their friend. They deny that they succumb to group pressure and at the same time they emphasize their care for the other person. The explanation most often heard in such cases is: "I really do not care. It is not for my sake, I don't want her/him to have any inconveniencies."

18. Categories of Croats and Serbs in the context of Vukovar correspond mostly to the other frequently used term – returnees and remainees. It derives not only from the fact that most displaced persons indeed were Croats but also from the fact that not all those who stayed were Serbs. This is an example of where the process of creating and ascribing identity can be observed. The ethnic Croats who stayed are not well perceived by those Croats who were displaced; they don't consider them "right" Croats. They are also not welcomed by the Serbian community because of their different ethnic origin, although, for example, their manner of speaking is similar. Likewise, those Serbs who shared the destiny of displaced persons with Croats are also classified in the category of returnees together with Croats, and are not well perceived by Serbs. The complex multi-ethnic reality of the pre-war Vukovar community is simplified by division into returnees and those who stayed.

19. Dinka Corkalo, "Croatia: For Peace Education in New Democracies." In Gavriel Salomon and Baruch Nevo, eds. *Peace Education: The Concept, Principles, and Practices Around the World* (Mahwah, N.J.: Lawrence Erlbaum, 2002), 177–187.

8 Memory, identity, and community in Rwanda

Timothy Longman and Théonèste Rutagengwa

Commemoration is necessary, and the work of memory is indispensable.
Hutu Man, Butare, Rwanda September 8, 2001

Ahabaye inkovu hadasubirana.
A wound does not heal completely.

Rwandan proverb

Since taking power in July 1994, the Rwandan government has under-taken an ambitious social engineering program intended to prevent future ethnic violence in the country. Believing that the 1994 genocide grew out of problems rooted deeply in Rwandan culture, the government has implemented a series of policies to foster a unified national identity, encourage respect for rule of law, create a socially responsible citizenry, and promote a democratic political culture. The government has used trials, public addresses, commemorations and memorialization, school programs, re-education camps, and new national symbols to shape the collective memory of Rwandan history. Through these policies, the regime hopes to transform how Rwandans understand their social identities and replace them with a unified national identity. At the same time that the government is seeking to force the population to come to terms with the 1994 genocide, it has dismissed accusations of its own engagement in war crimes and human rights abuses, leading to a perception of a double standard that has created political tensions and further divided the country. Leaders of the government, which is dominated by the Rwandan Patriotic Front (RPF), are driven by a strong sense of their own moral rectitude and right to rule, and a lingering distrust of the population. This creates a situation in which the regime theoretically allows freedom of speech and assembly but, in practice, uses its authority to persecute those who criticize its policies or even articulate a different vision for the country's future.

In this chapter, we present the findings of a two-year study in Rwanda that examined how the policies of the RPF-dominated regime have affected the ways in which the Rwandan population remembers the past.

162

Our particular focus is on the relationship between memory and identity. We begin by examining the Rwandan government's "official" interpretation of Rwandan history and review the programs it has used to shape collective memory. We then turn to data collected from ethnographic observation, survey research, individual interviews, and focus groups in three case study communities to explore how Rwandans are themselves discussing what happened in their country in 1994, what caused the violence, how to achieve reconciliation, and what all of this means for group identities.

The research project

The research for this chapter was conducted at two levels. First, at the national level, we monitored the local and international press, particularly the radio, for speeches, official statements, laws, and other official declarations. We examined government publications and documents for official interpretations of Rwandan history and conducted interviews with governmental officials, political party leaders, religious leaders, representatives of civil society, including human rights organizations, and organizations for genocide survivors.[1]

In addition to this national-level research, we conducted case studies of three of the local communities described in the introductory chapter to this volume. The communes[2] we studied – Ngoma, Mabanza, and Buyoga – reflected the diversity of Rwanda according to region, level of urbanization, ethnic distribution, and experience during and after the genocide. Ngoma is located in the south of the country and includes Rwanda's second-largest city, Butare, home to the national university. The other two case studies were in the rural communes of Mabanza in the central-western prefecture of Kibuye, and Buyoga in the northern prefecture of Byumba.

These three communes experienced the 1994 genocide in distinct ways, with Buyoga (mostly under RPF control) having a low incidence of the genocide but many RPF massacres, Mabanza having a high incidence of genocide but (under French control) few revenge massacres, and Ngoma (Butare) experiencing both genocide and massacres.

In each of these communes, we employed a range of data collection methods. Focusing on a selection of sectors within each commune,[3] we interviewed twenty-five to thirty-five individuals, and we conducted focus group interviews with genocide survivors, women, youth (aged 18 to 30), and older adults (aged 55 and older).[4] A total of 104 individuals participated in the focus groups. Our findings in these communities were augmented by the survey discussed in Chapter 10 and the education project described in Chapter 12 in this volume. Finally, we conducted ethnographic observation in each community, including visits to genocide memorials, massacre sites, gacaca trials, and polling stations.

The research was affected by several limitations. Because the study covered only three communes, it obviously has certain geographic limitations. Even so, we believe it is representative of the Rwandan population as a whole. Moreover, the political climate, violence, and restriction of civil liberties in Rwanda at the time of the research hindered open discussion of certain politically sensitive topics in the individual interviews and focus groups. We found this reluctance most pronounced in Buyoga, where RPF repression was most widely experienced. Nevertheless, the diversity of methodologies and the fact that the research was conducted by several distinct teams created a wealth of data and helped to correct these limitations.

Creating an official narrative of memory

The government program for reshaping Rwandan society grows out of a particular interpretation not only of the tragic events of the early 1990s but of the century of history that led up to the 1994 genocide. According to the historical interpretation promoted by the government, Rwandan society was essentially unified before the arrival of colonial rulers and the Catholic Church. Until then, the categories of Hutu, Tutsi, and Twa had limited social significance, representing mere occupational divisions but not status differences. The three groups were unified by religion, language, cross-cutting clan membership, loyalty to one king, and social and economic interdependence. According to this official narrative, when conflicts arose, they involved divisions such as regional or clan identities rather than ethnicity. According to the official narrative, colonial rule divided the Rwandan population and transformed Hutu, Tutsi, and Twa into ethnic identities.

This official narrative is widely accepted by former Tutsi refugees who have returned to Rwanda since the genocide and now dominate the country's social, political, and intellectual life.[5] Many formerly exiled intellectuals now occupy university, governmental, and religious posts in Rwanda and have reinterpreted and rewritten Rwanda's history in various domestic publications.[6] They review the rich historiography of Rwanda for evidence of the essential unity of Rwanda's pre-colonial population and the role of colonialism in creating divisions. For example, in an article on "The Family as the Principle of Coherence in Traditional Rwandan Society," Déogratias Byanafashe writes of the consolidation of the state of

Rwanda under the Nyiginya dynasty that dominated Rwanda for several centuries until the removal of the king in 1961:

The result of this centralism and this uniformization of the management of the country was a consciousness of the population's unity. "One king, one law, one people," that was Rwanda in this pre-colonial "Nyiginya" period. This step in the development of the country was the supreme realization of Rwanda as a family whose members were named the Rwandans or Rwandan people. In fact, it required the recent colonial intervention to break this people into three sections called "ethnicities."[7]

A similar expression of the official line is found in the report of a presidential commission that formed part of discussions on Rwanda's future held in 1998–1999. The authors, both politicians and intellectuals, write that:

The King was the crux for all Rwandans . . . [A]fter he was enthroned, people said that "he was no umututsi anymore," but the King for the people . . . In the programme of expanding Rwanda, there was no room for disputes between Hutu, Tutsi, and Twa. The King brought all of them together.[8]

According to this official narrative, the divisions imposed on Rwanda by colonial rule were the root cause of the 1994 genocide. The official government narrative argues that attacks against Tutsi in 1959 that began the exodus of Tutsi into exile were not a "revolution," as claimed by previous governments, but were the first instance of genocide in Rwanda's history, and they are directly attributable to the cynical manipulations of identity by Catholic missionaries and colonial administrators who wanted to guarantee continued influence even after formal independence.[9] According to the current Rwandan government, the post-colonial governments under Presidents Kayibanda (1962–1973) and Habyarimana (1973–1994) continued to use ethnicity as a wedge, falsely teaching that Tutsi were foreign invaders who had always subjugated and exploited the Hutu majority. These false teachings, it is claimed, created hatred of the Tutsi among the Hutu, who came to view Tutsi as less human and less deserving of basic rights. At the same time, the authoritarian post-colonial regimes encouraged obedience and docility from the population. In the view of the government, this combination of an ideology that fostered ethnic hatred and an obedient population were key to the 1994 genocide,[10] which is the defining event in the history of Rwanda and represents the culmination of the failed policies of international exploitation, ethnic division, and authoritarian government.

Given this interpretation of Rwandan history and the sources of genocide, the current Rwandan government argues that reconciliation can only take place once the country recovers the national unity that existed in pre-colonial Rwanda.[11] In short, the Rwandan people must reject the myth of ethnicity and, in the words of the presidential report, put "Rwandan citizenship first."[12] This official view also holds that reconciliation requires the development of a democratic political culture, so that people will think independently and be resistant to irresponsible leaders who want to manipulate them to undertake future ethnic violence. The Rwandan people need to develop "respect of human rights,"[13] which requires the population to take responsibility for their actions during the genocide and to judge those who participated in atrocities in order to fight impunity.

Since 1994, the government has introduced a variety of social programs to promote these ideas. Solidarity camps, called *ingando*, have been established for the "re-education" of politicians, entering university students, returned refugees, and released prisoners, among others, who have been required to attend for one to three months. In addition to providing paramilitary training, the camps use a teaching method that emphasizes leading discussions and asking questions in an effort to encourage participants to embrace the government interpretation of Rwandan history and the genocide. Memorials at massacre sites and annual commemorations are used to preserve the memory of the genocide and to show the dangerous results of ethnic divisions. In a number of sites, bodies of victims have been left exposed, displayed either in the rooms where the massacres took place or in semi-enclosed tombs. Each year, a national gathering is held on April 7 at one of these sites, where the president and other dignitaries present speeches about the genocide and how to avoid similar future tragedies. An annual national Day of Heroes highlights courageous individuals, primarily those who have fought ethnic division. Trials, both at the national and local level, are important tools for asserting the reprehensibility of the genocide and demonstrating that persecuting Tutsi has negative consequences.[14] The government in 2001 adopted a new flag, national anthem, and national seal, claiming that the old national symbols had associations with the genocide and that new symbols could mark a break with the past.[15]

Contrary tendencies

Although the desires to promote national unity and foster responsible citizenship have motivated many government policies, other interests have tempered the government's social agenda. The RPF leadership has a strong desire to hold on to power, which pushes it to maintain tight control on the political system even as the government creates limited democratic openings. They see themselves as enlightened leaders who liberated Rwanda from tyranny and ended the genocide, and they regard criticism and disagreement as indicators of a lack of political maturity and a continuing "divisionist" ethic. While supporting free political choice in principle, the regime is not yet confident in the population. In practice the population can only demonstrate its maturity for democracy by supporting the RPF. These concerns lead the government to continue to use considerable political repression and to retain tight control on the inner circles of power, even as they talk about democracy and civil rights and maintain a government that appears diverse on the surface.[16]

The government is particularly sensitive to implications that it is itself guilty of human rights abuses or that it is discriminatory. Although abundant evidence implicates the RPF in carrying out massacres as it advanced across Rwanda in 1994, in the months immediately after taking power, and in its two military incursions in Congo,[17] the government vociferously rejects any suggestion that it has engaged in systematic human rights abuses. Government officials claim that such abuses were carried out by renegade troops in violation of official RPF policy and, as such, have no moral equivalency to the genocide.[18] Although the government maintains numerous genocide memorial sites, there is not a single site commemorating the victims of RPF massacres. Government officials rarely, if ever, refer to RPF massacres in their speeches, and very few trials of those allegedly responsible have been held. Moreover, the gacaca courts are expressly forbidden from treating cases of human rights abuses allegedly perpetrated by the RPF or its supporters.

Those who criticize the RPF for its human rights abuses or for its perceived record of exclusion are accused of sowing division and are brutally silenced. For example, when Ibuka, the organization for survivors, began to articulate criticisms of the regime for failing to adequately address the needs of survivors, one of the organization's leaders was assassinated, and all of the other leaders fled the country. The former president Pasteur Bizimungu was harassed and then arrested after he criticized the RPF for being the cabal of a small minority; he formed a new political party that, he claimed, would be truly inclusive. His party was banned, and Bizimungu and those associated with him were thrown in prison. In the presidential elections on August 25, 2003, three candidates were allowed to compete, but in practice only the RPF candidate, President Paul Kagame, was free to campaign. Other candidates faced harassment and public denunciation, creating a climate of intimidation that allowed Kagame to win with 95 percent of the vote. Such actions inhibit discourse about the war and how to achieve reconciliation.[19]

Popular narratives of memory

Since the Rwandan government is plainly invoking Rwanda's history selectively and with obvious political intent, Rwanda presents an interesting case study of the limits of a government's ability to shape the collective memory of its citizenry. The construction of collective memory has become a major area of academic interest in recent years. Inspired by Pierre Nora's groundbreaking work in the 1980s on the use of symbols to create French national identity,[20] scholars have subsequently focused in particular on the construction of collective memory in the aftermath of violence.[21] Understanding collective memories and how they are formed and preserved can provide important insights into how programs to promote reconciliation can most effectively be constructed and what barriers they are likely to confront.

Rwandan history

Presenting a detailed account of Rwandan historiography is beyond the scope of this chapter. It is important to note, however, that the account of Rwanda's past offered by most specialists in Rwandan history differs substantially not only from the history taught by those in power prior to 1994 but also from the version of history promulgated by the current regime and its supporters. The pre-1994 governments taught a version of history developed during the colonial era that claimed that the Twa, Hutu, and Tutsi were distinct racial groups that had migrated into Rwanda at different times. The idea that the Tutsi were foreign invaders who had conquered Rwanda several centuries earlier and had since oppressed and exploited the larger Hutu population was a key element in the ideology used to promote the 1994 genocide.[22]

The account of history promulgated by the current regime and its supporters, however, also differs substantially from the view shared by most historians, suggesting the degree to which current interpretations of the Rwandan past are also being shaped by ideological considerations, albeit an ideology that may be intended to promote national unity rather than division. Few scholars would support the idea promoted by the current regime that Rwanda was a nation-state prior to colonial rule,[23] given the diversity of regional and other identities, and the complexity of political arrangements. On ethnicity, the scholarly community is more divided. Nearly all scholars agree that the meaning of Hutu and Tutsi as social categories changed during the colonial period, but many scholars reject the idea that colonial rulers "created" ethnic categories. Catharine Newbury, for example, has demonstrated how the last pre-colonial regime used ethnic differentiation as a means of dividing and dominating the population of regions being integrated into the Rwandan kingdom.[24] Meanwhile, Jan Vansina, the dean of Rwandan historians, goes so far as to assert that armed conflicts in the late pre-colonial period took on an ethnic character.[25] As one of the present authors has argued elsewhere, the key impact of colonial rule on identities in Rwanda was to racialize them and remove their mutability.[26]

Despite the contested nature of the historical narrative currently being promoted, we found that the population was remarkably familiar with the official narrative. When asked their impression of Rwandan history and of the development of ethnic conflict, most study participants said that Rwandans were historically unified and that it was colonial rule that had divided them. This discussion in a focus group of youths was typical:

QUESTIONER: Is it true that ethnicity played a role in the genocide?
SPEAKER 1: Yes, because in times past, there was no ethnicity. Everyone was called Rwandan. The policies of the Whites sowed the problem of ethnicity, the origin of the segregation of Rwandans. If there had been no ethnicity, there would have been no genocide.
SPEAKER 2: Wherever a Rwandan is, he should be considered as a Rwandan, not as a Tutsi or Hutu.
SPEAKER 3: In historic Rwanda, there was no ethnicity, but the herders were designated as Tutsi and the farmers as Hutu. And when a herder, that is to say a Tutsi, became poor, when his cattle disappeared, he was called a Hutu and vice versa for Hutu who became rich, they were called Tutsi.[27]

Despite widespread familiarity with the government's "politically correct" narrative of Rwandan history, participants rarely volunteered historical explanations for the genocide unless asked specifically about history and ethnicity. While the government regards the genocide as deeply rooted in Rwandan history, study participants were more likely to blame the genocide on immediate causes, such as bad politicians and greed. This divergence may be explained in part by the different attitudes toward the role of ideology. While the current regime sees ideology as a key factor that inspired popular participation in the genocide, the people we interviewed saw the genocide as an affair more of the elite, with people participating primarily out of fear and ignorance. People generally agreed that the previous regime had taught a biased version of history that encouraged ethnic hatred and division, but they did not volunteer this as a major cause of the genocide, at least not at the local level.

Furthermore, while most respondents were able to present an account of the government's narrative of Rwandan history, many also expressed skepticism about how history is interpreted and used by those in power. For example, a 50-year-old man in a Kibuye focus group said, after a long discussion of Rwanda's history: "The reason for our preoccupation [with history] is that whoever achieves power wants to refashion the history of Rwanda. There is no consensus and no general national vision."[28] In our survey, 49.2 percent of respondents agreed or strongly agreed with the statement "Whoever is in power rewrites Rwandan history to serve their own interests," while only 21.7 percent disagreed or strongly disagreed.

The war and genocide

Explaining the nature and the causes of the violent events that took place in Rwanda in the early 1990s was a major focus of both interviews and focus groups. We asked about the specific events that took place in each community as well as the participants' interpretation of the events at a national level. We found that Tutsi survivors of the genocide held a substantially different view of the genocide from that of others, especially Hutu. For example, when we asked "Can you explain in your own words what happened in Rwanda in 1994?" genocide survivors almost universally invoked the Kinyarwanda phrase that the government and survivors' organizations have adopted for genocide, *itsemba bwoko*, literally "to decimate an ethnic group," an expression that did not exist in Kinyarwanda prior to 1994. Hutu were more likely to refer to *intambara*, the war, *ubwicanyi*, the killings, or more vaguely *ibyabaye*, the happenings, or *amahano*, horror or tragedy. They tended to employ *itsemba bwoko*, if at all, only secondarily. Some Hutu mentioned as well *itsemba tsemba*, massacres, implying massacres of Hutu, which very few Tutsi, whether survivors or repatriated Tutsi refugees, mentioned. Nevertheless, the language of most interview subjects, regardless of ethnicity, indicated awareness of the official explanation of events. One man's response is typical: "They've said that it was a genocide and massacres, so I call it like that as well."[29]

While the official discourse on the genocide emphasizes the mass nature of the violence, participants in our three case study communities interpreted the violence as an affair of the elite, particularly national leaders, while de-emphasizing the role of popular participation. Political explanations for the violence were most common. Many participants mentioned the expansion of political party activity in the 1990–1994 period as something that divided the country and created instability. For example, one young man in Butare explained, "It all got worse with multi-party politics. Then the different members of the political parties confronted each other often, and in most cases this had an ethnic connotation. They said that there were parties of Hutu and those of Tutsi fanatics of the RPF who were at war against the Habyarimana regime."[30] Others talked about the greed for power and "bad governance" in general.

When discussing their own communities, study participants almost universally said that the violence initially came to their community from elsewhere.[31] In Butare, people claimed that the violence began with the arrival of presidential guard troops from Kigali and the intervention of interim president Théodore Sindikubwabo. In Mabanza, people insisted that there had not been militia training and claimed that local violence began with attacks of militia groups from other communes, particularly in President Habyarimana's home prefecture, Gisenyi. In Buyoga, people said that soldiers fleeing from the RPF's advance on the town of Byumba brought the violence into their commune.[32] Genocide survivors sometimes spoke about the violence beginning with anti-Tutsi massacres in 1959, 1963, and 1973, while most Hutu asserted that ethnic relations were peaceful in their community prior to 1994 – or at least prior to 1990 – and that only the intervention of outside forces led to violence.

While portraying the violence as organized by national elites and initiated by outside groups, people we interviewed generally did not deny that members of their community ultimately did participate in the genocide, but the degree to which they held the local population responsible varied. Genocide survivors were more likely to emphasize local participation and to hold the local population responsible. An exchange between a Hutu man and a Tutsi survivor in one of the focus groups demonstrates this point:

FIRST SPEAKER (HUTU): The fact that the situation went on for two months made it so that some people from Rubengera [Mabanza], those weak in spirit, of course, were ultimately implicated in the massacres. But the population at the beginning refused to give in to temptations.

SECOND SPEAKER (TUTSI): I find all the same that we should not minimize too much the role played by the local population in the massacres. There was also a certain complicity evident on the part of some people, because the killers from, for example, Gisenyi or Rutsiro couldn't have known the Tutsi in the Gacaca Sector if people hadn't served to indicate them. That is a sign of the previous existence of a certain mistrust, of interethnic hatred in Rubengera.[33]

Many respondents blamed popular participation on simple "evil" or "meanness." Others discussed the ignorance of the population, which allowed them to be misled by corrupt authorities. Our informants claimed that many people participated in the killings because they were intimidated by the authorities and feared being labeled *ibiyitso*, accomplices. According to the informants in our research, other factors that contributed to the genocide included radio broadcasts[34] encouraging Hutu to kill their Tutsi neighbors, and a general sense of insecurity caused by the displacement of Tutsi fleeing the genocide and Hutu fleeing the advance of the RPF who spread rumors about the RPF attacks. Study participants also identified greed and poverty as major factors driving active involvement in the genocide. For example, an older man in Mabanza claimed that some people exposed their Tutsi neighbors or joined in the killing in exchange for food or calabashes of beer.[35] Significantly, few people mentioned hatred of Tutsi as a cause for the genocide. Consistent with the claim that ethnic relations were good prior to the genocide, Hutu in particular tended to attribute the anti-Tutsi violence to non-ideological causes.

One significant variation from the official narrative of events concerned the role that the RPF invasion of Rwanda played in creating a climate where genocide was possible. Many people we interviewed identified the RPF invasion that began in 1990 and the desire for Tutsi refugees to return to Rwanda as important causal factors. A woman in Butare said that the genocidal spirit began "with the entry of the RPF into the history of Rwanda."[36] When asked to describe what happened in Rwanda in 1994, 10.8 percent of the survey respondents chose the response, "The RPF waged war against Rwanda." When asked to choose the principal cause of the violence in 1994, 9.2 percent chose the RPF invasion. It is surprising that people would select these responses, given their controversial nature and the politically charged environment, but it reflects a sentiment held by many Rwandans that the RPF itself bears some of the blame for the violence that has occurred in Rwanda.

Justice, commemoration, and reconciliation

Nearly all study participants said that Rwanda needed reconciliation, and they generally shared a common understanding that reconciliation was an effort to bring together victims and the victimizers in order to rebuild community. They disagreed sharply, however, on how reconciliation can be achieved. While nearly everyone agreed that those responsible for the genocide should be judged and that those who committed offenses should admit their errors publicly and receive forgiveness, they differed over how these activities should be put into practice. Participants in our study also disagreed about the effect of commemoration and memorialization, and the need to change the flag, national anthem, and national seal. As one older man told us, "Reconciliation is part of Rwandan culture. It is for forgetting the wrong committed or suffered. Without this, Rwandans will arrive at nothing."[37] The word for reconciliation in Kinyarwanda is *ubwiyunge*, which comes from the same root used to discuss setting a broken bone, and this Rwandan concept of bringing together people whose relations have been ruptured was widely shared among the people we interviewed. One survivor in Kibuye explained, "Reconciliation is the fact that those who did wrong ask forgiveness from those whom they offended and thus the two parties renew their social relations as before."[38]

While most participants said that trials of the accused were a necessary part of the reconciliation process,[39] there were subtle differences in how Tutsi genocide survivors and Hutu understood the function of trials.

Many survivors said that the role of justice is important primarily because it brings people to account for the wrongs they committed and facilitates the process of compensation. They also expressed concern that they were called upon simply to forgive, when emphasis should instead be placed on those who carried out the killing to ask for forgiveness:

The problem is that they ask us for reconciliation. It is true that it is necessary, because we can't continue with cyclical massacres. But you feel bad when you see those who killed your family strolling around with impunity. I say this because it is the case for me. I lost all my family in the genocide. My home was destroyed, and I live badly. But I feel bad when I know that the author of all this lives in Kigali. I know that [when he visits] he arrives at night and leaves early the next day [to avoid arrest]. How can I be reconciled with him when he doesn't come to ask my forgiveness or at least to reimburse my goods that he destroyed?[40]

Many survivors seemed less interested in the punishment of those who killed their families and destroyed their homes than in having them come forward and admit their wrong. Survivors also expressed considerable interest in compensation, both because this is consistent with historical practices of reconciliation in Rwanda and because of the dire economic circumstances in which many survivors live. (Naomi Roht-Arriaza examines the role of reparations in post-war societies in Chapter 6 in this volume.) Survivors expressed generally negative attitudes toward trials in classical courts because they neither require penitence on the part of the convicted nor facilitate face-to-face contact between the victims and their victimizers, and because they lack the means for providing compensation. In contrast, many survivors felt that gacaca could encourage positive confrontation with the accused and could help bring reparations, although many expressed concerns about gacaca as proposed. At the same time, a substantial number of survivors expressed support for seeing those who had wronged them punished, but this generally seemed a secondary concern.

Meanwhile, the Hutu in general expressed greater support for judicial action whether in classical or gacaca courts. When they spoke of judging the guilty, many Hutu emphasized the need to identify those who were actually responsible for the wrong done, thereby eliminating collective guilt. Their principal concern, however, was the release of the innocent. Like the Tutsi survivors, many Hutu spoke of the need for wrongdoers to ask forgiveness, but they tended to see forgiveness as an obligation on survivors. At the same time, most Hutu were suspicious of calls for reparations, perhaps fearful of the burden that reparations might place upon them. Few Hutu saw a relationship between reparations and reconciliation. In the survey, only 25.6 percent of Hutu respondents agreed or strongly agreed that trials should be concerned with providing reparations.

Study participants were deeply divided over the role that memorials and commemorations play in reconciliation. Many said they serve an important function in keeping alive the memory of the violence that Rwanda has experienced. The comments of genocide survivors in a focus group in Butare were typical:

SPEAKER 1: You can't forget the genocide and its consequences. These are living facts of what was committed in the light of day. Children who are born today ought to learn that Rwanda experienced a massacre and that it is bad. Forgetting is not possible, but I want commemoration to continue and to be done regularly.
SPEAKER 2: Another thing is that the fact of remembering our innocent victims is in itself a moral obligation. One should construct and manage memorial sites in a more impressive fashion, in a fashion where everyone would notice and understand their significance.[41]

Others, however, expressed objections on several grounds to such commemoration. Some felt that memorialization was divisive, filling survivors with anger and Hutu with fear and shame. A woman in Butare whose children died of disease in a refugee camp in Zaire said:

For me, to commemorate the genocide, I don't find it useful. Even those [implying the repatriated Tutsi] who did not see the genocide, when they talk about it all the time, it makes it seem like it will happen again . . . When others go to the site to commemorate, I stay home and think about what I have lost. What happened to me has no place in this [official] commemoration, because my children died differently and elsewhere.[42]

Others expressed concern that continually reminding people of what happened keeps injuries fresh and prevents victims – and society at large – from moving on. For example, one woman in Butare claimed, "The commemoration done each year could damage the process [of reconciliation]. Hearts remain injured with this repeated commemoration."[43] Interestingly, while Tutsi were generally more supportive of commemoration and memorialization, attitudes did not break down clearly along ethnic lines. For example, a genocide survivor in Kibuye offers similar concerns about commemoration: "To continue to talk about what happened risks infecting your children, who didn't even see it. It is better that they don't hear that there were others who killed with machetes."[44] We found a significant difference in the survey between Hutu and Tutsi in their attitudes toward memory, with 70.1 percent of Hutu agreeing or strongly agreeing with the statement, "It is better to try to forget what happened and move on," compared with 43.4 percent of Tutsi who agreed or strongly agreed.

Study participants also gave diverse meanings to commemorations and memorial sites. Survivors almost universally believed that these events and sites were intended to honor their suffering and loss, while Hutu were divided in their interpretations. Some expressed anger or frustration over the one-sided nature of commemoration that focuses on the suffering of Tutsi while ignoring the suffering of Hutu.[45] Others recognized that the sites focus on the Tutsi but felt that this was just, given what happened in the country.[46] Many other Hutu simply interpreted the commemorations and memorials in an inclusive fashion. For example, a Hutu woman in Rubengera Kibuye, whose husband was in prison under accusations of participation in the genocide, said:

Personally, I commemorate what happened. I think I have suffered like others have suffered. I suffer because I can't raise my children well . . . I find that what I had happen has a place in the commemorations, because we commemorate the suffering that everyone suffered. If it hadn't been for the war, we wouldn't have suffered.[47]

Participants also were divided over the changing of national symbols. Many survivors made claims similar to those of government officials[48] that the old national seal, which contained a machete, brought back negative memories of the machetes used to kill during the genocide, and that the mention of ethnicity in the national anthem was dangerous, and many Hutu were sympathetic. Others, however, regarded the changes as a cynical political manipulation with little serious impact on the society. As one participant said:

Personally, I find that Rwanda risks continuing to have problems if each politician who gets into power has to change all the symbols of the country. I am afraid that what we praise today will be repudiated by another regime! I don't even see why they changed the symbols. I find that Rwandans are used to accepting whatever the authorities decide. As for myself, I would hope that Rwandans would adopt the only and the same symbols once and for all! We need something lasting.[49]

Memory, identity, and culture

Our study provides a mixed picture of the Rwandan government's ability to reshape memory and culture after mass violence. On the one hand, the government has done a good job of disseminating its message about Rwandan history and culture. People we interviewed were widely aware of the government's interpretation of Rwanda's essential unity in the pre-colonial era and the artificiality of ethnic identities. They also knew the new term used for genocide, and nearly everyone condemned the violence. On the other hand, many people felt that those in the ruling elite were manipulating remembrance of the genocide to maintain their own positions of power rather than truly seeking to unify the country. People felt severely constrained in their ability to discuss openly the social and political situation in Rwanda. As someone in Kibuye told us: "We can't speak freely, only in whispers. It is this fear that stays in people's hearts. They are afraid that if they speak about ethnicity, they may be accused of supporting hostilities."[50] A few participants, particularly genocide survivors, openly criticized the current regime, but most others challenged the regime only indirectly. Participants in our interviews often prefaced their responses with statements such as "We have been told" or "I have heard on the radio," whereas later in the interview they revealed that their own ideas about history, ethnicity, reconciliation, and other issues were not in complete accord with the official positions.

While the current regime has been able to dominate public discourse about what went wrong in Rwanda and how to achieve reconciliation, alternative narratives are being formed privately. The government's attempt to fashion a collective memory of the 1994 war and genocide have been undermined by the perception that the presentation of the past is self-serving. Most people publicly espouse essential elements of the official discourse, yet they mix it with elements drawn from the discourse of the previous regime or from their own experience.

Significantly, ethnicity remains a central factor for Rwandan social identity. Some study participants sincerely and forcefully reject ethnic differentiation because of the suffering that it has brought upon the country. Yet for many, ethnicity remains key. As an older woman in Kibuye said: "It is true that in the official documents, like the identity card, the ethnic label has been eliminated. Yet the truth is that this ethnic label remains in people's hearts."[51] Many Hutu resent the fact that their experience of suffering is excluded from official discourse:

There will be no reconciliation between Hutu and Tutsi, because Tutsi have a tendency to see themselves as the only survivors, the only victims of the genocide. When a Hutu dares to say that he is also a victim, he is quickly blamed and made to feel uneasy. So how can there be reconciliation in such a situation?[52]

Even those who sought to reject ethnic labels had difficulty leaving them behind. Several times in our interviews, participants would refuse to give their ethnic identity, claiming that ethnicity no longer exists. Yet later in the interview, when asked if they had relatives from another ethnic group, they would freely volunteer that they had a Hutu sister-in-law or a Tutsi mother.

Continuing ethnic consciousness does not necessarily mean that ethnic hatred remains strong or that an ideology of ethnic division continues to hold sway. Instead, it may reflect the fact that people continue to relate to society differently depending upon their ethnic background. Certainly, Hutu and Tutsi experienced the violence in 1994 very differently. But the substantial divergence in responses in our research between Hutu and Tutsi, especially the survivors, suggests strongly that the two groups continue to experience the current situation differently.

In post-genocide Rwanda, Tutsi genocide survivors generally feel freer to speak, but many feel that they lack real influence in a regime that is dominated by former refugees who were not in Rwanda at the time of the genocide. They also feel that the government is not adequately address-ing social and economic problems that they face, including insecurity and poverty. Most Hutu feel limited in their ability to speak freely, particularly to express criticisms, because of fears that they will be accused of partic-ipating in the genocide or of promoting division. Those who have dared to claim publicly that the regime is exclusionary and favors a particular ethnic group have faced dire consequences, as with the case of former President Pasteur Bizimungu, a case to which many of the participants in our interviews referred.

The current government's repressive tactics undermine attempts to democratize Rwanda's political culture. Rather than creating responsible citizens, the regime is in some ways encouraging the type of obedience that was a factor in public participation in the genocide. One young man's ethnic self-identification is a troubling indication of the degree to which Rwandans may seek to follow the messages they are told: "When I was still in the refugee camps in Zaire, they told us that we were Hutu. Today on returning to my country, they say that there are no longer Hutu nor Tutsi. So, it is perhaps best to say that I was Hutu until January 1997, and I am Rwandan since I returned to Rwanda."[53] Whether he actually believes that his identity has changed is unclear; however, his effort to adapt to the message of the regime – at least publicly – is common to many of the people we interviewed.

If people still find ethnicity important, they also do not see it as the continuing source of their conflicts. We found that the vast majority of participants wanted to avoid future ethnic conflict, and many felt that the population, if left to its own devices, would be able to achieve reconcili-ation and maintain peace. As an older man in Kibuye said:

We folks in the countryside, we have already achieved our reconciliation. The survivors and others share everything together and have even started marrying one another again. But at the same time, we see problems at the top. The ruling class has not arrived at reconciliation, even though it is at the base of this war that has ravaged Rwanda. It [the ruling class] ought to shine as an example. It is enough to hear all the time of someone going into exile, that some other has been arrested, to see that they still need to be reconciled at the top. We here have no problems.[54]

Indeed, our survey found that 76.7 percent of respondents agreed or strongly agreed with the statement, "If Rwandan leaders would leave the population to themselves, there would be no more ethnic problems."

Conclusion

It is too early to know the long-term impact of the Rwandan government's efforts to shape memory, identity, and culture in Rwanda. If public discourse remains strictly controlled, younger generations may be more thoroughly influenced, particularly if programs such as solidarity camps continue to be implemented.[55] However, if leaders act in ways that seem to contradict their own arguments and interpretations, then it is likely that the effect of their efforts at social engineering will be reduced. If the government continues to act in ways that some see as ethnically discriminatory or exclusionary, people will fail to be convinced that ethnicity no longer exists. If the government continues to call on the people to take responsibility for their actions during the genocide, but fails to take responsibility for its own war crimes and human rights abuses, it is likely that people will continue to mouth the messages of justice and unity in public while privately decrying continuing injustice and inequality. The case of Rwanda indicates that a government can effectively dominate the discourse of memory and reconciliation. It is yet to be seen, however, whether this domination can create a collective memory or bring about reconciliation.

NOTES

1. Interview subjects included: ministers or other officials from the Ministries of Local Government and Administration; Internal Security; Youth, Sports, and Culture; Education; and Finance; from the attorney general; judges on the Supreme Court; the heads of the Electoral, Constitutional Reform, and Legal Reform Commissions; the leaders of the Rwandan Patriotic Front, the Rwandan Democratic Movement, the Social Democratic Party, and the Christian Democratic Party; representatives of the National Unity and Reconciliation and Human Rights Commissions; Catholic, Anglican, Pentecostal, Presbyterian, and Muslim leaders; and leaders of groups for human rights, economic development, genocide survivors, the Twa minority, women, and youth.

2. Although an administrative reform in early 2001 created new local government units known as districts, we chose to work with the units, known as communes, that were in place at the time of the genocide, because the political organization of the districts remained in flux throughout the period of our research and because the genocide was organized by commune. Until 2001, Rwanda was divided into 12 prefectures each divided into communes, sectors, and cells. The 2001 reforms changed the name of the regional units to provinces, with few changes to their territorial limits, while the 154 communes were consolidated into 106 districts.

3. We focused our research in the sectors of Cyarwa-Cyimana, Cyarwa-Sumo, and Matyazo in Ngoma; Rubengera, Gacaca, Nyarugenge, and Kibirizi in Mabanza; and Zoko, Mutete, Muranzi, and Burenga in Buyoga.

4. We conducted four focus groups in Buyoga and Mabanza but five in Butare.

5. Realizing that this assertion is controversial, we do not mean to imply that no efforts have been made at inclusion of various segments of the Rwandan population. However, both because of the death or exile of many people who were in Rwanda in 1994 and because of the continuing hold on power of the RPF, repatriated Tutsi do hold most of the key posts in the government, industry, education, and religious institutions. Cf. International Crisis Group, "Rwanda at the End the Transition: A Necessary Political Liberalisation" (Brussels: International Crisis Group, 2002), which includes an annex of the key figures in Rwandan politics and society.

6. For example, the journal *Cahiers Lumière et Société*, published by the Dominican Center.

7. Déogratias Byanafashe, "La Famille comme Principe de Cohérence de la Société Rwandaise Traditionelle," *Cahiers Lumière et Société* 6 (August 1997): 20. This and all translations from French done by the authors.

8. Republic of Rwanda, Office of the President of the Republic, *The Unity of Rwandans: Before the Colonial Period and Under Colonial Rule; Under the First Republic* (Kigali: Office of the President of the Republic, 1999), 6.

9. *The Unity of Rwandans*, for example, seeks to demonstrate the hand of the church in writing the 1957 "Hutu Manifesto," an important document in the assertion of Hutu social and political rights. Office of the President, *The Unity of Rwandans*, 42–46.

10. Cf. Paul Rutayisire and Bernardin Muzungu, "L'Ethnisme au Coeur de la Guerre," *Cahiers Centre Saint-Dominique* 1 (August 8, 1995): 68–82; Antoine Mugesera, "A l'Origine de la Désintégration de la Nation Rwandaise," *Les Cahiers Evangile et Société* (June 1996): 46–58; and the December 1996 issue of *Les Cahiers Evangile et Société* devoted to "Les Idéologies."

11. Office of the President, *The Unity of Rwandans*, 64.

12. Ibid., 63.

13. Ibid.

14. For statements of the government position on trials, see Gerald Gahima, "Re-establishing the Rule of Law and Encouraging Good Governance," address to 55th Annual DPI/NGO Conference, New York, September 9, 2002; Richard Sezibera, "The Only Way to Bring Justice to Rwanda," *The Washington Post*, April 7, 2002.

15. The Minister of Local Administration, for example, told us that it was decided to change the national symbols "because not all Rwandans found themselves in these symbols," and because they symbolized negative things and encouraged division. Interview with Desiré Nyandwi, in Kigali, June 8, 2002. This and all other interviews conducted by the authors.

16. International Crisis Group, "Rwanda at the End of Transition: A Necessary Political Liberalisation" (Brussels: ICG, November 2002) presents a detailed account not only of the harassment of non-RPF politicians and civil society members but of the degree to which RPF members retain the key positions in government. A similar documentation of the distribution of power is presented each year in the annual *L'Afrique des Grands Lacs*, S. Marysse and Filip Reyntjens, eds. (Paris: l'Harmattan, 1997–2003). While many ministers are either Hutu or non-RPF, they are always backed up by an assistant who is Tutsi RPF.

17. See Chapter 1 on the RPF in Alison Des Forges, *Leave None to Tell the Story: Genocide in Rwanda* (New York: Human Rights Watch, 1999); Gerard Prunier, *The Rwanda Crisis* (New York: Columbia University Press, 1998), Chapter 10; Filip Reyntjens, *La Guerre des Grands Lacs: Alliances Mouvantes et Conflits Extraterritoriaux en Afrique Centrale* (Paris: l'Harmattan, 1999).

18. In a speech in San Francisco, for example, President Paul Kagame strongly rejected the assertion that the International Criminal Tribunal for Rwanda (ICTR) could try members of the RPF, claiming that if there was any evidence of abuses by his troops, the government of Rwanda could deal with them itself. President Paul Kagame, speech at Commonwealth Club, San Francisco, Calif., March 2003.

19. A report critical of Rwanda's human rights record issued recently by Human Rights Watch (HRW) was greeted by the government with vociferous condemnation and accusations that HRW encouraged division. They apparently also pressured the civil society into issuing condemnations of the report.

20. Pierre Nora, ed. *Les Lieux de Mémoire*, vols. I–III (Paris: Gallimard, 1984, 1992).

21. Nancy Wood, *Vectors of Memory: Legacies of Trauma in Postwar Europe* (Oxford and New York: Berg, 1999), provides an excellent review and critique of the work on memory in the aftermath of the Second World War in Europe.

22. On the ideology of the 1994 genocide, see Jean-Pierre Chrétien, ed. *Rwanda: Les Médias du Génocide* (Paris: Karthala, 1995), and Des Forges, *Leave None to Tell the Story*.

23. The idea of Rwanda as a nation-state is advocated, for example, by Gamaliel Mbonimana, "Le Rwanda Etat-Nation au XIXe Siècle." Paper presented at *Seminar on the History of Rwanda*, Butare, December 14–18, 1998.

24. Catharine Newbury, *The Cohesion of Oppression: Citzenship and Ethnicity in Rwanda, 1860–1960* (New York, Columbia University Press, 1988).

25. Jan Vansina, *Le Rwanda Ancien: Le Royaume Nyiginya* (Paris: Karthala, 2001).

26. Timothy Longman, "Documentation and Individual Identity in Africa: Identity Cards and Ethnic Self-Perception in Rwanda." In Jane Caplan and John Torpey, eds. *Documenting Individual Identity: The Development of State Practices in the Modern World* (Princeton: Princeton University Press, 2001).

27. Focus group of youths, conducted by Théonèste Rutagengwa, Cyarwa, Butare, June 15, 2002.
28. Focus group of elders conducted by Théonèste Rutagengwa, Mabanza, Kibuye, August 10, 2002.
29. Interview in Cyarwa-Cyimana, Ville de Butare, Butare, September 7, 2001. Unless otherwise noted, the identities of all interview participants are kept anonymous for their protection.
30. Interview in Cyarwa-Sumo, September 9, 2001.
31. It is interesting to note that, in the Balkans as well, a common assertion was that the violence was brought to communities from the outside. See Anthony Obershall, "The Manipulation of Ethnicity: From Ethnic Cooperation to Violence and War in Yugoslavia," *Ethnic and Racial Studies* 23:6 (2002).
32. This tendency to attribute violence to people from outside is consistent with research that one of the authors conducted in 1995–96 in Butare, Gikongoro, and Kibuye for the book Des Forges, *Leave None to Tell the Story*. Many genocide survivors also agreed with this explanation of external intervention.
33. Focus group interview with elders conducted by Théonèste Rutagengwa, Mabanza, Kibuye, August 10, 2002.
34. For example, a woman in Mabanza said Radio Rwanda broadcast the following incitement: "In Bugesera [a region where massacres occurred in 1992] they have finished. What are you waiting for?" Focus group interview with women in Mabanza, August 10, 2002.
35. Focus group interview with elders conducted by Théonèste Rutagengwa, Mabanza, Kibuye, August 10, 2002.
36. Interview in Matyazo, Butare, August 17, 2002.
37. Focus group of survivors, Mabanza, Kibuye, August 10, 2002.
38. Focus group of survivors, Mbanza, Kibuye, August 10, 2002.
39. Some 96.8 percent of survey respondents agreed or strongly agreed with the statement, "It is important for those who committed crimes during the war to be tried."
40. Focus group of survivors, Mabanza, Kibuye, August 10, 2002.
41. Focus group of survivors, Matyazo, Butare, August 17, 2002.
42. Interview in Cyarwa-Cyimana, August 22, 2001. The woman lost two children to disease in a refugee camp outside Bukavu, Zaire.
43. Focus group of women, Matyazo, Butare, August 17, 2002.
44. Interview in Gacaca, Mabanza, Kibuye, August 23, 2001.
45. One woman in Kibuye, for example, told us, "It would be better to forget. On both sides, there were victims, and so it is better to forget and think about the future." Interview in Mabanza, Kibuye, August 23, 2001.
46. One man, for example, says, "I find that the memorial sites are necessary and that all the ethnicities should think about them in the same manner. I see that at the time of the anniversary of the genocide, all the ethnic groups participate in ceremonies of commemoration. I think that this is a good thing, because we have the chance to pray and to meditate on [the] collective memory of these people who, after all, were savagely killed even though they were innocents." Focus group of elders conducted by Théonèste Rutagengwa, Mabanza, Kibuye, August 10, 2002.

47. Interview in Rubengera, Kibuye, August 23, 2001.
48. The Minister of Local Administration, who was ultimately in charge of changing the symbols, explained to us at length the negative connotations of the old symbols and their exclusionary and injurious implications. Interview with Desiré Nyandwi, in Kigali, June 8, 2002.
49. Focus group of elders conducted by Théonèste Rutagengwa, Mabanza, Kibuye, August 10, 2002.
50. Interview in Rubengera, Mabanza, Kibuye, August 24, 2001.
51. Focus group of elders conducted by Théonèste Rutagengwa, Mabanza, Kibuye, August 10, 2002.
52. Focus group of women, Matyazo, Butare, August 17, 2002.
53. Interview in Cyarwa-Cyimana, Butare, September 9, 2001.
54. Focus group of elders conducted by Théonèste Rutagengwa, Mabanza, Kibuye, August 10, 2002.
55. For example, a Hutu youth leader in Byumba who had attended several solidarity camps was able to present a nearly perfect version of the government account of Rwandan history and the genocide, and he seemed to have no doubt that the version was true. Interview in Buyoga, Byumba, January 24, 2003.

9   Attitudes toward justice and social reconstruction in Bosnia and Herzegovina and Croatia

Miklos Biro, Dean Ajdukovic, Dinka Corkalo, Dino Djipa, Petar Milin, and Harvey M. Weinstein

In this chapter, we examine the factors that may contribute to or prevent the rebuilding of war-torn societies based on two surveys of attitudes and beliefs of the inhabitants of three cities – Vukovar, Mostar, and Prijedor – in Croatia and Bosnia and Herzegovina (BiH) in 2000 and 2001. Prior to the war, these three cities were integrated societies where different nationalities had intermarried and lived together in relative harmony for centuries. Since the end of hostilities in 1995, the cities have remained fairly peaceful, although conflicts between national and civic identity still continue among the three principal national groups. While the war experience of these cities may have been unique in its ferocity, it also is true that the manifestations of enmity that persist can be found in similar towns and villages throughout BiH and Croatia.

The principal goals of our survey were: to investigate some of the underlying attitudes and beliefs of the population of Mostar, Prijedor, and Vukovar toward the (re)building of community; to investigate attitudes toward reconciliation and members of other national groups; and finally, to investigate attitudes toward war crimes, war crimes trials and, specifically, the International Criminal Tribunal for the former Yugoslavia (ICTY).

Background

Psychological and social origins

The 1991–1995 wars in the former Yugoslavia will be remembered for their cruelty, including widespread war crimes, ethnic cleansing, and genocide. From the perspective of social psychology and the practice of social reconstruction, these wars raise two important questions: first, was the horrendous violence a spontaneous expression of "centuries-long hatred among peoples," as claimed by warlords, some writers, and diplomats, or were the wars a result of manipulation by political leaders with nationalist agendas? This disagreement about the origins of the violence then raises an additional question – is reconciliation possible and, if so, how can it be achieved?

The thesis that the war among Yugoslav national groups was a natural sequence of historical conflicts is supported by the assertion that these same national groups (and the Albanians) fought bloody conflicts during the Second World War – violence that also was characterized by monstrous crimes and ethnic cleansing. That these passions calmed down following the Second World War can be attributed largely to the authoritarian government of Josip Tito, which repressed, but did not eliminate, nationalist tensions. As a result, significant rebellious movements emerged even during Tito's rule and the immediate post-Tito era (in Croatia during the 1970s and in Kosovo in the 1980s) demanding more extensive national rights.

However, the rise in nationalist movements does not tell the whole story. Psychological research on ethnic distance[1] conducted in 1989–1990 in the Socialist Federal Republic of Yugoslavia on the eve of the most recent conflict indicates there was actually little "ethnic distance" in the region.[2] Indeed, in Bosnia and Croatia there was almost no ethnic distance among Serbs, Croats, and Bosniaks. These results may reflect the socially and politically desirable answers expected in the Communist era under Tito's program of "Brotherhood and Unity." The high number of ethnically mixed marriages in the region, however, bolsters these findings.[3] According to 1991 census data, as many as 36 percent of marriages in BiH crossed national group lines.[4]

How then do we make sense of the often-extreme xenophobia and nationalist rhetoric that developed in the two decades following Tito's death in 1980? Part of the answer lies in the breakdown of Communist ideology in the former Yugoslavia that left a void in the value system of the society. Since political and ideological transitions are usually characterized by social uncertainty, it was not surprising, as Realistic Conflict Theory[5] suggests, that national groups in the region would look for safety and security within a group of people who shared common concerns. Such similarities were easiest to find in one's own nationality, and consequently nationalism was the most direct pathway toward security. As a result, a revitalized ideology based on ethnocentrism emerged to replace the societal values imposed under Communist rule. Moreover, the distributive economy of the socialist system meant that a greater share in the distribution process required proximity to the ruling elite and/or membership in the dominant social group (party, clan, nationality). When the dominant group, the Communist party, began to disintegrate, ordinary citizens looked for a new group to join. Once they had identified themselves as members, fighting for the dominance of that group became inevitable.

Another part of the answer lies in authoritarianism.[6] Patriarchal tradition, followed by fifty years of Communist rule, stifled the development of ideas that were not in accordance with official ideology. Yugoslav society became increasingly authoritarian. For example, studies in the 1970s using the F scale,[7] a measure of authoritarianism, found scores that were among the highest in the world. In such a society, an authoritarian perspective is accompanied by profound passivity as the rank and file awaits instructions on acceptable thinking and behavior prescribed by the powerful elite. In the 1980s, Communist leaders, fully aware that the system was collapsing, donned neo-nationalist clothing and, commanding complete control of the media, took advantage of a population that was ready to obey authority without reserve or criticism. This kind of authoritarian rigidity in the former Yugoslavia, coupled with a view of the world as either "black or white," contributed to the speed with which division into opposing groups occurred,[8] while authoritarian aggression facilitated the strength and cruelty of the conflict. Threat of conflict and the conflict itself[9] accelerated the partition of people into safely homogenized environments.

To understand the ethnically based disintegration of the country requires that we consider two social-psychological theories – Social Identity Theory[10] and Self-Categorization Theory.[11] As described in the introductory chapter of this volume, these theories conceptualize how specific social situations, often in the face of perceived threat, accelerate both group cohesion and differentiation – attributes that reinforce the perception that "we" are better than "them." The process serves to enhance the positive identity of the members of the group, with a resultant increase in self-regard. This phenomenon has been demonstrated repeatedly over the years in the laboratories of social psychologists and offers some insight into the rapidity with which a relatively well-functioning but vulnerable multi-cultural nation can disintegrate under political manipulation.

Factors that promoted division

Much has been written about the role of the media during the recent wars in the former Yugoslavia.[12] Both print and broadcast media promoted ethnic homogenization in the months leading up to the outbreak of war in June 1991, and then went on to play the role of warmongers. The media not only rekindled the memories of past crimes committed during the Second World War, they also misinformed the public in order to spread fear of the "enemy" nationality.[13]

Along with the media, the Communist-nationalist leadership promoted activities that were designed to turn abstract fear into major threat. In Slobodan Milosevic's trial before the ICTY[14] evidence was presented of numerous actions of the Serbian secret police (most often disguised as "paramilitary formations") aimed at provoking interethnic conflicts. For example, in March 1992, local authorities in Sarajevo arrested an armed group of Serbs supplied with symbols of all three ethnicities. They were distributing flyers warning each of the three ethnic groups of the "danger from the other two" groups, and calling on them to take up arms to defend themselves.[15]

Tone Bringa, a Norwegian anthropologist who studied ethnic customs in central Bosnia in the early 1990s, describes how outside forces, such as the media or nationalist parties, were able to instigate conflict in otherwise harmonious communities:

Even when bombshells fell on their house door, this was still something done by someone unknown, someone they could call *that one* . . . For these locals, war was something created outside. They closed ranks and said: if *they* come here, we will fight them together . . . But, when someone from your family is hurt or wounded, both sorrow and anger pour out on the ones around you. Now this is not someone from outside, now it is *us*.[16]

This process took place in thousands of towns and villages throughout Croatia and Bosnia in the early 1990s. "Any one of us," Bringa says, "could undergo such metamorphosis in just a few weeks, with a little help of mad nationalistic war- and chaos-mongers."

Prospects for reconciliation

The factors that contributed to the onset of a vicious war must be attended to for reconciliation to occur. We do not believe that the war's onset reflected an ingrained hostility toward other ethnic groups; if that were so, then the process of reconciliation would be a formidable task indeed. Rather, the society was vulnerable to political manipulation. Historic remembrance of past conflicts was of significance only because it was backed up by a current danger, the continuous threat from other ethnic groups. We believe that the more proximal the cause of a war, the more reconciliation is a reasonable possibility. With this framework in mind, we designed our survey to look at the interrelationship of these factors with the likelihood of reconciliation.

Methods

The total sample of the survey consisted of 1,624 participants: 404 subjects from Vukovar, 412 from Prijedor, and 808 subjects from Mostar,[17] divided equally among national groups in each city. The survey sample was randomly selected using a three-stage cluster procedure: the first-stage unit was the part of the city inhabited predominantly by one of the nationalities, the second-stage unit was households (using the "Random Walk Technique"), and the third-stage unit was members of the households (whose birthday was closest to the date of the interview).

The questionnaire consisted of sixty-eight items and contained three scales (Ethnic Distance Scale, Stereotype Scale, and Authoritarian Scale) and questions about attitudes toward nationalism and xenophobia, other national groups, reconciliation, the ICTY and war crimes, as well as questions about prior experience with members of other national groups, traumatic experiences during the war, and demographic data.

Trained interviewers, using a standardized interview procedure, conducted the survey. The interviewers were of the same nationality as the subjects. The surveys were carried out in June 2000 in Vukovar, in October 2000 in Mostar, and in September 2001 in Prijedor. A resurvey of the same sample with a slightly modified questionnaire was done in Vukovar (June 2002) and Prijedor (September 2002), and on a different sample in Mostar (June 2002).

Survey findings

War experiences

The people in our sample had experienced a number of traumatic events. With the exception of the Serbs in Prijedor, more than 50 percent of our participants suffered extreme trauma during the war. More than one-third of our subjects (both Croats and Serbs) in Vukovar and Bosniaks in Prijedor lost their homes, and 15 percent of our sample lost a member of their family.

Attitudes and beliefs

Ethnocentrism and ethnic prejudice

Social psychologists have found that ethnocentrism (and consequently, negative stereotypes about out-groups), once established, is difficult to change.[18] And there is no doubt that the conflict itself, especially one with

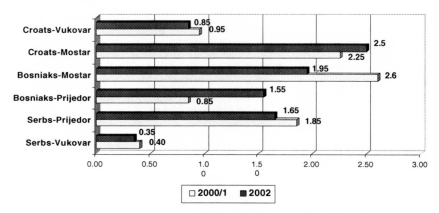

Figure 9.1 Mean scores on the Ethnic Distance Scale for "neutral nationalities"

such cruelty, was fertile soil for strengthening nationalistic and xenophobic ideas and creating barriers toward the "opposing" nationality.

The changes in ethnic distance among warring nationalities of the former Yugoslavia[19] are a good example of the consequences of war on interethnic relationships. After the war erupted, ethnic distance among Serbs Croats, and Bosniaks dramatically increased. By the end of the war it began to decrease, slowly but constantly. Unfortunately, it remains significantly higher than pre-war. By the late 1990s, in answer to the question from Bogardus' Social Distance Scale[20]: "Would you accept a member of . . . nationality to be your son- or daughter-in-law?", only 21 percent of Croats from Croatia would accept such a relationship with Serbs, and 23 per cent with Bosniaks.[21] Bosniaks from BiH would accept such a "blood" relationship with Serbs in 20.5 percent and with Croats in 25.1 percent.[22] This readiness was somewhat higher for Serbs in Serbia – 49 percent would accept a familial relationship with Croats, and 36 percent with Bosniaks,[23] but it was much lower among Serbs in BiH – only 13.9 percent would accept such a relationship with Bosniaks and 15.9 percent with Croats.[24]

As one possible measure of ethnocentrism, we took the average score on the Ethnic Distance Scale (readiness to accept different nationalities as: citizens of "my" state, neighbors, friends, collaborators, or close relatives) for four "neutral" nationalities – Hungarians, Macedonians, Slovenians, and Roma. In all previous studies[25] the score toward "neutral" nations showed high reliability – contrary to the score for nationalities in conflict, which is radically changeable.

As shown in Figure 9.1, ethnocentrism in the larger sense remains a significant problem in Prijedor and Mostar. Bosniaks in Mostar expressed

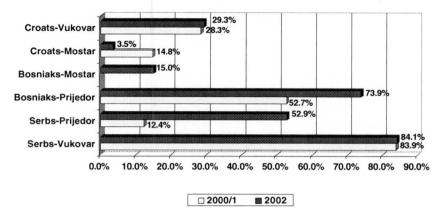

Figure 9.2 Readiness for "blood" relationship with the "opposing" nationality

the highest ethnic distance[26] toward four "neutral" ethnic groups, followed by Croats in Mostar and Serbs in Prijedor. It was, significantly, lowest for Serbs in Vukovar. Bosniaks in Prijedor showed low ethnocentrism in the first investigation but were significantly higher in the resurvey.

As shown in Figure 9.2, Serbs in Vukovar and Bosniaks in Prijedor were most open to a "blood" relationship, or intermarriage, with the "opposing" nationality. While the Serbs in Prijedor showed more openness to intermarriage with Bosniaks, especially in the 2001 resurvey in which a slight majority indicated a willingness to support these relationships, the results in Mostar[27] did not suggest much openness to "the other" among either the Bosniaks or the Croats.

Figure 9.3 represents the results of one illustrative item from the set of questions on nationalistic and xenophobic attitudes.[28] Serbs in Prijedor, Croats in both cities, and Bosniaks in both cities expressed high levels of suspicion about the "other" groups; we interpret this to suggest more nationalistic attitudes. However, on this item, the Bosniaks in Mostar reported significantly more openness to other ethnic groups in the resurvey. On the other hand, Serbs in Vukovar were significantly less nationalistic in the original survey and remained so two years later.

Figures 9.1, 9.2, and 9.3 illustrate different dimensions of the relationships between ethnic groups in the three cities. These data suggest that changes occur in the groups differentially and over time. The Serbs in Vukovar are the most consistent, with the least ethnocentrism, more openness to intermarriage, and while expressing suspicion toward other ethnic groups, they consistently are the lowest. The Bosniaks in Prijedor,

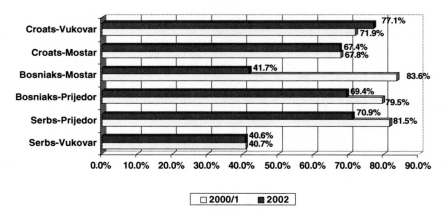

Figure 9.3 Percentage of "Yes" answers to the statement: "One should be cautious with other nations, even when they are our friends"

although quite open to intermarriage, reported higher ethnocentrism in the resurvey and showed no change in their high level of caution toward the opposing groups on the resurvey. The Serbs in Vukovar and the Bosniaks in the "Republika Srpska"[29] appear quite different from the other ethnic groups. How do we explain this?

Both Serbs in Vukovar and Bosniaks in Prijedor are minority nationalities in their surroundings (Vukovar Serbs are a recognized minority in Croatia and Bosniaks have returned to the Serb "entity" of BiH). These minority groups have chosen to live in areas where they likely will always be a minority but which they rightfully consider to be their home. It also may be that these people are less nationalistic and less concerned about the national symbols, habits, and even nationalistic attitudes of the majority group. However, there also is a possibility that, as minorities, they may have been more cautious in their answers: they may have answered what they thought was expected rather than what they believed. The fact that Bosniaks in Prijedor expressed higher ethnocentric attitudes in the resurvey, along with great suspicion of the opposing groups, could be a sign that they felt more secure after one year. But it is also possible that the previous answers did not represent their true beliefs and values. One final explanation for the shift may be that the realities of life in a difficult situation may have led to more cynicism in the Prijedor Bosniaks, despite the initial joy of homecoming. There is another interesting change in Prijedor, where the Serb population reports more openness to intermarriage in the resurvey despite high levels of ethnocentrism and caution. As we shall see, this also may reflect more positive experiences with members of the opposing group.

Table 9.1 *Stereotypes*

Group (nationality)	Positive stereotype	Negative stereotype
Serbs – Vukovar	Croats are clean	Croats don't like other nations
Serbs – Prijedor	Bosniaks are hospitable	Bosniaks are perfidious
Croats – Mostar	Bosniaks are hospitable	Bosniaks are perfidious
Croats – Vukovar	Serbs are hospitable	Serbs are perfidious
Bosniaks – Mostar	Croats are civilized	Croats are dirty
Bosniaks – Prijedor	Serbs are hardworking	Serbs don't like other nations

It also is striking that the situation in Mostar is less optimistic. Ethnocentrism is high, openness to intermarriage is low, and caution toward the other group is high. However, the Bosniaks in Mostar showed much less caution at the time of the resurvey. It is possible that the positive changes in the city brought about by the policies and actions of the Office of the High Representative (OHR) may be helping to reduce suspicion among the group seen as the principal victims of the war in that city. These variations in ethnocentrism, stereotyping, and nationalism among groups illustrate the complexity of reconciliation. We suggest that geography, ethnicity, war experience, exposure to the opposing group, and time all may be important factors in considering how reconciliation between national groups may be supported.

Since we hypothesized that ethnic prejudice and stereotypes could be an obstacle to the process of reconciliation, we used a Stereotype Scale to measure the stereotypes toward the "opposing" nationality. The results showed the general tendency of our subjects to hold stereotypes that could be attributed to the consequences of interethnic war: the most common stereotype among all nationalities is that members of the "opposing" nationality "don't like other nations" and that they are "perfidious."

In Table 9.1 we present the most striking stereotypes of the "opposing" nationality among the national groups.

Authoritarianism

We measured authoritarianism by the adapted and shortened version of the F scale, psychometrically developed on the population of the former Yugoslavia.[30] The thirteen items of the scale cover three clusters of attitudes: authoritarian submissiveness, authoritarian aggressiveness, and conventionalism, similar to Altemeyer's[31] concept of Right-Wing Authoritarianism.

As shown in Figure 9.4, all national groups had extremely high scores on the Authoritarian Scale. In all groups, the mean score is over 7 (out

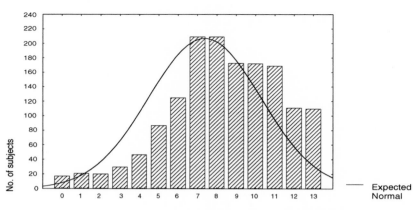

Figure 9.4 Distribution of scores on the Authoritarian Scale

of 13 items), and the distribution of frequencies shows that more than 60 percent of the sample expressed high authoritarianism (score >7).

Experiences with the "opposing" nationality

The survey results suggest that experiences with members of the "opposing" nationality and perceptions of discrimination could affect readiness for reconciliation and the development of a multi-national society.

After the war, positive experiences slowly came to predominate over negative ones. However, with the exception of Serbs in Vukovar, in all other groups positive experiences were still reported by a minority of those who participated in the survey. One of the most optimistic findings of our study was that positive experiences with the members of the "opposing" nationality increased in almost all groups (Figure 9.5).

Another optimistic finding was that renewal of friendships also increased. As shown in Figure 9.6, with the exception of Croats in both cities, in all other groups the majority of people reported unspoiled friendships with members of the "opposing" nationality. However, even here, Vukovar Croats also showed a pattern of increase.

Attitudes toward the ICTY and war crimes

The results shown in Figure 9.7 represent attitudes toward the ICTY. The results are the mean scores between absolute acceptance (5) and absolute non-acceptance (1).

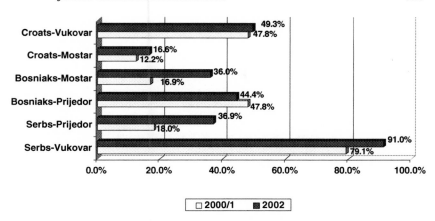

Figure 9.5 Positive experiences with the members of the "opposing" nationality

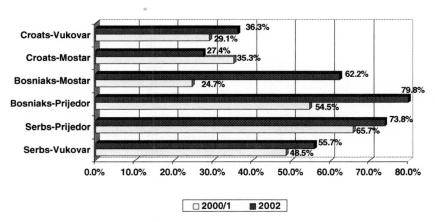

Figure 9.6 Unspoiled friendships with the members of the "opposing" nationality

As Figure 9.7 illustrates, Bosniaks had the most positive attitudes toward the tribunal, while the Serbs in Prijedor and the Croats in Mostar showed the greatest resentment toward the ICTY. From the comments attached to the questionnaires, Croats and Serbs were deeply convinced that the ICTY was biased against them. On the other hand, one of the most common comments (especially among Bosniaks) was that the ICTY sentences were too soft.

One possible explanation of the resentment toward the ICTY among Serbs in Prijedor and Croats in Mostar may lie in the fact that those two

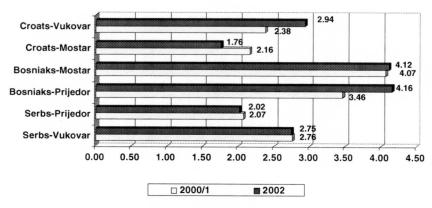

Figure 9.7 Attitudes toward the ICTY

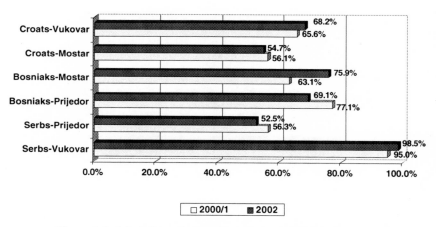

Figure 9.8 Admission of war crimes committed by own nationality

groups are least ready to admit the existence of war crimes committed by members of their own nationality. As shown in Figure 9.8, almost half of Mostar Croats and Prijedor Serbs do not accept the fact of their group's participation in the commission of war crimes.

These data suggest that recognition of and, perhaps, a sense of responsibility for the commission of war crimes vary with national group and the history of the recent war. The Serbs in Vukovar and the Bosniaks seemed most open to that recognition, whereas the Croats in Mostar and the Serbs in Prijedor were highly resistant to accepting that their own side might have committed war crimes. Although any explanation of these differences would be tentative at best, it is possible that the Croats in Mostar and the Serbs in Prijedor are still trying to attain recognition for their status and need to distance themselves from the horrors that occurred in their name. The Bosniaks are recognized as the principal victims of the war and maintain that any war crimes were committed by rogue elements. The Vukovar Serbs lost their primacy and have chosen to remain in Croatia; they must admit to the existence of war criminals on their side if they wish to remain as accepted citizens of the state.

Further, from a theoretical perspective, numerous experiments in social psychology show that, in the process of formation of a "Group Self," an important role is played by the mechanism of categorizing people as "us" and "them."[32] Here, "us" always has positive attributes, in order to make a distinction with "them." The stronger this social identity, the less it allows recognition of individual differences; this does not permit the possibility that a part of "us" can be war criminals, nor does it permit the possibility that a part of "them" can be worthy of our respect or empathy. This mechanism suggests why national groups cannot accept that sanctioning one's own war crimes will enable individualization of guilt and lead to removal of collective guilt.[33] When legal theorists debate the value of war crimes trials, what is not factored into the deliberation is the evidence from social psychology – namely, that group identity often leads to a distorted interpretation of the court record.

Readiness for reconciliation

In contemporary literature, there is no empirically validated definition of the process of reconciliation.[34] According to research in South Africa, the most frequent connotation of the word reconciliation is "forgiveness," followed by "unity."[35] Etymologically, the word reconciliation (*pomirenje*) in the Bosnian, Croatian, and Serbian languages[36] means reconstitution of peace, but in its most common usage it also means forgiveness and re-cooperation.

The ecological paradigm and the model of social reconstruction offered in the introductory chapter to this volume suggest that reconciliation processes may be conceptualized as part of the wider process of social reconstruction or may, in fact, proceed at their own pace independent of the social reconstruction of communities. While this framework suggests reconciliation is largely a process undertaken between individuals, the social aspects of reconciliation should not be underestimated.[37] The media and political elite (especially in authoritarian societies), for example, can greatly affect the way one group perceives the "enemy" group. Moreover, how the media presents "majority opinion" can have a bearing on the process of reconciliation. Immediately after the fall of Milosevic,

Serbian television began to broadcast a serial on Serb crimes in Srebrenica, but after "great pressure from the public" this broadcast was
terminated after the first episode. At the same time, public opinion polls
in Serbia showed that more than 70 percent of the population was aware
of the existence of war crimes committed by their own group.[38] Similarly, after the broadcast of the popular talk show "Latinica" on Croatian
television, which addressed the subject of Croat war crimes, there were
so many calls protesting the program, the station broadcast a short film
on Serb war crimes in Croatia in order to establish "balance" again. It is
obvious that a loud minority can heavily influence the reported sense of
"public attitudes." However, when this minority attitude, with the help
of the media, is presented as the voice of the majority, then to those who
fought on the other side it sends the message that "They *all* hate us."

An example of how the behavior of the political elite can influence reconciliation can be seen in the resistance of Serbian and Croatian authorities to deliver their war criminals to the ICTY. Justifying this by saying
"There is no public opinion support for this," they send their people the
message that "The majority thinks there are no criminals in our nationality" and, at the same time, to the nationality with whom the conflict
existed they send the message that they are unprepared to apologize for
crimes committed; nevertheless, such an apology may be one of the fundamental preconditions for reconciliation. The recent apologies by President Marovic of Serbia and Montenegro and Mesic of Croatia for the
pain and suffering caused by individuals from each national group was a
milestone in this regard.[39]

Institutional solutions and administrative acts also may either help or
hinder reconciliation. For example, government decisions can be interpreted as messages that "the state" of one people sends to the members
of another people. One negative example of this is restrictive visa requirements on the members of a national group; a positive example might be
the introduction of uniform license plates that do not identify geographic
origin and thus facilitate freedom of movement. The point here is that the
elements of reconciliation occur at multiple levels, and in a post-war transitional period there are multiple influences on how readily reconciliation
can be accomplished. As an example of how reconciliation is progressing
in these towns, we present the results on acceptance of members of the
"opposing" nationality in "my" surroundings.

Respondents were asked to indicate "yes" or "no" to whether they
would accept members of the opposing groups in eight different situations. Maximum approval for a subject would be indicated by a score of
8. As shown in Figure 9.9, much openness to the other group is expressed
by Serbs in Vukovar, but significantly less by other groups.

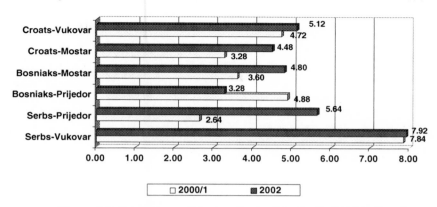

Figure 9.9 Acceptance of the members of the "opposing" nationality

Multi-variate prediction of readiness for reconciliation

To investigate which factors contributed to or prevented the process of reconciliation, we used multi-variate statistical procedures – factor and regression analysis.

Since the concept of reconciliation is so complex, for the purposes of this study we defined reconciliation operationally by three variables:
1. Readiness to accept the presence of members of the "opposing" nationalities in eight different situations (stores, parks, sporting events, sport teams, concerts, parties, schools/offices and non-governmental organizations) as illustrated in Figure 9.9.
2. Readiness to be reconciled with the conflicted nationalities.
3. Readiness to accept interstate cooperation.

Since those variables have high mutual correlation and form a unique factor, in the multi-variate analysis that follows we formed a composite variable, "Readiness for Reconciliation," out of Z scores of the three variables.

Using Principal Component Analysis with the Promax rotation, we have extracted seven factors that explain 54.28 percent of total variance (variables with the high loading on the factors are presented at the left side of Figure 9.10). A second-order Factor Analysis produced three interpretable factors, which explain 57.71 percent of the variance.

Our next step in analyzing the data was to see what complex of variables (factors) predicts readiness for reconciliation. For that purpose, we tested the General Linear Model, using three extracted factors as predictors and the variable "Readiness for Reconciliation" as the criterion (dependent) variable.

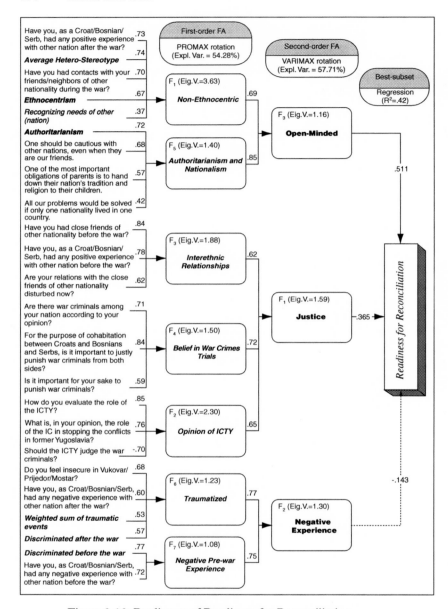

Figure 9.10 Predictors of Readiness for Reconciliation

A Best-Subset Regression Analysis[40] resulted in a highly significant model.

Arrows from factors to criteria in Figure 9.10 represent regression relationships, with statistically significant beta-coefficients.

The model suggests that certain attitudes and values represented by the factors "Non-Ethnocentric" and "Non-Authoritarian and Non-Nationalistic" are the best predictors of Readiness for Reconciliation. Since the factor "Non-Ethnocentric" also contains the variable on preserving the friendships with members of the "opposing" nationality during the war, being non-ethnocentric allows people to distinguish individuals from their nationality and, consequently, to preserve their friendships despite being from "opposing" nationalities (even during the war). The experiences with these friends (ie experiences on a personal level) increase readiness for reconciliation as we have defined it. Intergroup (national) conflict does not affect their interindividual relationships and their perception of the out-group members.

Also, a belief in war crimes trials, combined with a readiness for having friends among the "opposing" nationality and with positive experiences with the members of opposing national groups, is highly related to readiness for reconciliation. Our findings that previous friendships contribute to readiness for reconciliation are in concordance with the results of Pettigrew's studies[41] and his conclusion that those findings support the Contact Hypothesis.[42]

The factor combining negative experiences with the opposing nationality and experiences of war trauma is also a significant predictor, but against reconciliation. It is interesting that regression analysis using the first-order factors has shown that the factor "Traumatized" by itself is not a significant predictor of the variable "Readiness for Reconciliation." It appears that the experience of trauma itself is not sufficient to reject reconciliation.[43] Nevertheless, in combination with the feeling of being discriminated against by the opposing group and/or with a series of negative experiences with that group, trauma becomes an additional obstacle.

Conclusions

Our results suggest that authoritarianism, nationalism, and ethnocentrism may be the most important obstacles to the process of reconciliation among national groups in the former Yugoslavia. This raises the question of how prejudice can be changed so that different national groups will recognize their joint interests, remember the advantages offered by a similar language and find a common "superordinate goal." Education for democracy, tolerance of differences, and respect for human rights are critical steps to take in order to create a foundation for change. This is a slow but critical perspective. The schools, the media, civil society and, ultimately, the politicians have key roles to play in this process.

Is authoritarianism an obstacle for reconciliation? Since people who are prone to authoritarianism will listen to different messages and will obey their political elite when the elite promotes peace, tolerance, and cooperation, obedience to authority could be used to promote democracy, ethnic tolerance, and human rights. Previous studies[44] show that authoritarian personalities tend to support and behave according to rules when they believe that human rights are protected, even when they themselves do not agree with the rules. Ironically, authoritarianism could be used to reduce ethnic tensions and ease reconciliation in these countries. Over time, with rule of law, political openness, and transparency we might expect a lessening of this societal tendency.

The study results also indicate that the war crimes trials in The Hague are viewed through a nationalist lens. Bosniaks, who both see themselves and are seen by the international community as the principal victims of the war, feel positively about the ICTY, while the Serbs and Croats feel negatively about the court and believe that the members of their nationality are unfairly selected for prosecution. However, it should be noted that in the resurvey there was a trend for the Croats in Vukovar to express more positive views about the ICTY, although this did not reach statistical significance. In addition, there was an increase in positive perceptions of the ICTY by the Prijedor Bosniaks.

The overall survey results suggest that the role of the ICTY in promoting reconciliation in Croatia and BiH is problematic. However, a more vigorous public education campaign about the tribunal's impartiality and the facts about its organization and goals could contribute to an increase in positive attitudes toward international war crimes trials and, in general, to the development of a positive image of the ICTY. It goes without saying that international pressure on recalcitrant politicians to cooperate with the ICTY and to send their indicted war criminals to The Hague would have a significant impact on public perceptions as well. Our findings also have implications for the future work of the International Criminal Court as it adjudicates criminal liability across countries and cultures.

We were surprised to find that the level of traumatic experience did not correlate with seeking war crime trials, or with positive attitudes toward the ICTY: "I have nothing out of this belated justice," one of the war victims wrote. "Things lost will not be returned to me, nor will this ease my suffering." Another survivor noted: "The best thing is to let everything be forgotten. The greatest justice for me would be to let me live and die in peace there where I was born." And yet we also heard such comments as: "Punishing criminals would bring us satisfaction." While it is clear that everyone has an opinion about trials, their relationship to trauma is obviously less straightforward.

Since the international community believes that trials are for the victims and that they promote reconciliation, this finding is very provocative. Further, comments such as these suggest that we need to be very careful about how we define the term "justice." For many survivors, justice may not mean trials but a much more personal sense of what they need in order to move on with their lives.

One of the most optimistic findings of our research was that pre-war positive experience and friendships with members of the opposing national group are associated with the continuation of such friendships and an orientation toward reconciliation. It may be that the experience of individual contacts and friendships allows this group to believe in criminal trials partially because they can differentiate between individual war criminals and collective accountability. Besides contemporary elaboration of the Contact Hypothesis[45] that proposes very slow and delicate use of communication between conflicted groups to achieve cooperation, our findings about the contribution of positive experiences and unspoiled friendships in the process of reconciliation may be an example of the importance and possible influence of relationships across national groups. Positive experiences with a member of the opposing nationality, and especially of help from the other side during the war, might be used to promote the "other nationality's positive characteristics" as a basis for promoting the process of reconciliation. As Hewstone[46] has suggested, the main limitations of the positive effects of intergroup contacts are the absence of generalization and promotion of positive attitudes that emerge as the result of contact experience. While we are not suggesting a public relations campaign to change the image of a group, we do believe that these kinds of fact could be incorporated into the teaching of history or the literary and media representations of war to offer a more balanced perspective. Balance in this sense does not mean equal accountability but reflects a picture that considers individual acts untarnished by stereotyped perceptions of the "other."

Our findings of nationalism and ethnic distance suggest that there is still little demonstrated empathy for the needs and the experience of the opposing national groups in the community. For some groups, such as the Bosniaks, we suggest that the distance grows out of a sense of victimhood as a result of war experience and its effects. For others, such as the Croats in Mostar and the Serbs in Prijedor, distancing emerges from nationalism. Each of these root causes may require unique interventions.

Because this study was done in only three communities, albeit those where formerly opposing groups meet and where vestiges of the conflict remain, our findings cannot be generalized to all citizens of the countries of the former Yugoslavia. While they do represent the views of the residents of Vukovar, Mostar, and Prijedor, we must express some caution in interpreting the results. Although not definitive, our findings indicate that diplomacy, trials, or economic investment on their own may be insufficient to bring about reconciliation if they are not integrated into a comprehensive plan that takes into account the social and psychological dynamics of the people directly affected by the conflict.

NOTES

1. Ethnic distance is most often studied using the Social Distance Scale (E. S. Bogardus, "Measuring Social Distance," *Journal of Applied Sociology* 9 (1925): 216–226), the method of studying social distance by checking inclination to accept members of other social group as co-citizens, friends, marital partners, etc.
2. D. Pantić, *Jugoslavija na kriznoj prekretnici* (Beograd: Institut Društvenih Nauka, 1999).
3. R. Petrović, *Etnički mešani brakovi u Jugoslaviji* (Beograd: Institut za sociološka istraživanja Filozofskog fakulteta, 1985); V. P. Gagnon, Jr., "Reaction to the Special Issue of AEER 'War among Yugoslavs'," *The Anthropology of East Europe Review* 12 (1994): 1, 50–51.
4. Contrary to the data on ethnic distance and mixed marriages among Serbs, Croats, and Bosniaks, there are data about great ethnic distance between Albanians and all other Yugoslav peoples (and vice versa), as well as less than 2 per cent of mixed marriages between Serbs and Albanians (mostly registered outside of Kosovo), according to 1991 census data.
5. Realistic Interest approaches, which include Realistic Group Conflict Theory (L. D. Bobo, "Whites' Opposition to Busing: Symbolic Racism or Realistic Group Conflict?," *Journal of Personality and Social Psychology* 45 (1983): 1196–1210), suggest that group membership translates into political cohesion when group members have tangible interests in common.
6. The original concept of the authoritarian personality is first presented in T. W. Adorno, E. Frenkel-Brunswik, D. Levinson, and R. N. Sanford, *The Authoritarian Personality* (New York: Harper and Brothers, 1950). It implies a set of attitudes and behaviors: authoritarian submissiveness (blind obedience toward authorities and cruel dominance toward subordinates), aggressiveness (especially toward out-group members), rigidity (ideological dogmatism, "black and white" perception of the world), and conservatism (conventionalism).
7. N. Rot and N. Havelka, *Nacionalna vezanost i vrednosti srednjoskolške omladine* (Beograd: Institut za psihologiju i Institut drštvenih nauka, 1973).

8. The role of authoritarianism in the process of group homogenization is emphasized in several social-psychological studies, eg J. Duckitt, "Authoritarianism and Group Identification: A New View of an Old Construct," *Political Psychology* 10 (1989): 63–84; S. Perreault and R. Y. Bourhis, "Ethnocentrism, Social Identification, and Discrimination," *Personality and Social Psychology Bulletin* 25 (1999): 92–103.

9. The role of threat in the process of homogenization is demonstrated in several psychological experiments (see, for example, R. A. Levine and D. T. Campbell, *Ethnocentrism: Theories of Conflict, Ethnic Attitudes and Behavior* [New York: Wiley, 1972]).

10. H. Tajfel and J. Turner, "An Integrative Theory of Intergroup Conflict." In W. Austin and S. Worchel, eds. *The Social Psychology of Intergroup Relations* (Monterey, Calif.: Brooks/Cole, 1979), 33–48; H. Tajfel and J. P. Forgas, "Social Categorization: Cognitions, Values and Groups." In C. Stangor, ed. *Stereotypes and Prejudice* (Philadelphia: Psychology Press, 2000), 43–63.

11. J. C. Turner, M. A. Hogg, P. J. Oakes, S. D. Reicher, and M. S. Wetherell, *Rediscovering the Social Group: A Self-Categorization Theory* (Oxford: Blackwell, 1987).

12. See: J. Walsh, "The Butcher of the Balkans," *Time*, January 4, 1993, 1; M. Biro, *Psihologija postkomunizma* (Beograd: Beogradski krug, 1994); M. Glenny, *The Fall of Yugoslavia* (London: Misha Glenny, 1996); and M. Thomson, *Forging War: The Media in Serbia, Croatia, Bosnia and Herzegovina* (Luton: University of Luton Press, 1996).

13. For example, during the prime-time news on Serbian TV, prior to any serious conflict, a report indicated that eight Serbs had been killed in the Croatian town of Pakrac – this was a fabrication and no correction was ever presented. TV news: "TV Dnevnik," February 16, 1991.

14. International Criminal Tribunal for the Prosecution of Persons Responsible for Serious Violations of International Humanitarian Law Committed in the Territory of the former Yugoslavia, placed in The Hague.

15. News in *Oslobodjenje*, March 4, 1992.

16. Interview reprinted by newspaper *Borba*, March 22, 1994.

17. For a description of the pre- and post-war political events in Mostar, see S. Bose, *Bosnia After Dayton: Nationalist Partition and International Intervention* (New York: Oxford University Press, 2002), 95–148.

18. See, for example: S. Fein and J. C. Spencer, "Prejudice as Self-Image Maintenance: Affirming the Self through Derogating Others." In C. Stangor, ed. *Stereotypes and Prejudice* (Philadelphia: Psychology Press, 2000), 172–190.

19. I. Šiber, "War and the Changes in Social Distance Toward the Ethnic Minorities in the Republic of Croatia," *Politička Misao* 34 (1997): 5, 3–26.

20. Bogardus, "Measuring Social Distance."

21. Šiber, "War and the Changes in Social Distance."

22. S. Puhalo, *Etnička distanca građana Republike srpske i Federacije BiH prema narodima bivše SFRJ* (Banja Luka: Friedrich Ebert Stiftung, 2003).

23. M. Biro, V. Mihić, P. Milin, and S. Logar, "Did Socio-Political Changes in Serbia Change the Level of Authoritarianism and Ethnocentrism of Citizens?", *Psihologija* 35 (2002): 1–2, 37–47.

24. Puhalo, *Etnička distanca.*
25. Biro et al, "Socio-Political Changes in Serbia."
26. The results were scored from 0 (full acceptance) to 4 (full rejection).
27. We did not present the data from the first survey for Bosniaks in Mostar because there was too much missing data to accept the data for this variable as valid.
28. We were unable to create a composite score on "Nationalism" because in some items there was an unacceptable amount of missing data, and in others the variance was too small.
29. Serb "entity" of BiH.
30. Rot and Havelka, "Nacionalna vezanost"; D. Popadić, *Socijalnopsihološka struktura pravne socijalizovanosti na adolescentnom uzrastu* (Beograd: Doktorska disertacija na Filozofskom fakultetu, 1992).
31. B. Altemeyer, *Authoritarian Specter* (Cambridge, Mass. and London: Harvard University Press, 1996).
32. Turner et al., *Rediscovering the Social Group.*
33. The tendency to deny the existence of war crimes committed by the members of its own nation is not typical only of the people of the Balkans. After Lieutenant Calley was sentenced for war crimes for his actions in the Vietnam village of My Lai, according to a Gallup poll some 79 percent of American citizens were against that sentence and rejected the idea that there were war crimes caused by American soldiers at all (H. C. Kelman and V. L. Hamilton, *Crimes of Obedience*, New Haven, Yale University Press, 1989).
34. C. Villa-Vicencio, "Reconciliation as Metaphor." In L. Holness and R. K. Wustenberg, eds. *Theology in Dialogue* (Cape Town: David Phillip Publishers, 2002).
35. K. Lombard, *Revisiting Reconciliation: The People's View. Research Report of the "Reconciliation Barometer"* (Rondebosch: Institute for Justice and Reconciliation, 2003).
36. These languages are similar and mutually understood by all three ethnic groups.
37. See, for example, R. Hardin, *One for All: The Logic of Group Conflict* (Princeton: Princeton University Press, 1995).
38. Biro et al., "Socio-Political Changes in Serbia."
39. Transcript from "The Word Today," Australian Broadcasting Corporation, September 11, 2003 on World Wide Web at http://www.abc.net.au/worldtoday/content/2003/s944064.htm
40. J. Neter, W. Wasserman, and M. H. Kutner, *Applied Linear Statistical Models: Regression, Analysis of Variance, and Experimental Designs* (Homewood: Irwin, 1985).
41. T. F. Pettigrew, "The Contact Hypothesis Revisited." In M. Hewstone and R. J. Brown, eds. *Contact and Conflict in Intergroup Encounters* (Oxford: Blackwell, 1998), 169–195.
42. The Contact Hypothesis predicts that contact among individuals from conflicted groups could help distinction between group and the individual, and indirectly help the process of reconciliation. It was originally postulated in G. W. Allport, *The Nature of Prejudice* (Cambridge, Mass.: Addison-Wesley, 1954).

43. Similar results on Holocaust survivors were found by Lina Cherfas in her BA thesis (*Explaining Variation in Aversion to Germans and German-Related Activities among Holocaust Survivors*. Unpublished BA thesis at the Department of Psychology, University of Pennsylvania, 2003).

44. M. Biro, A. Molnar, D. Popadić, "Stavovi građana Srbije prema Pravnoj Državi: Relacija sa Obrazovanjem, Autoritarnošcu i Poznavanjem Ljudskih prava," *Sociologija* 49 (1997): 2, 168–182.

45. See M. Hewstone, "Contact and Categorization: Social-Psychological Interventions to Change Intergroup Relation". In C. Stangor, ed. *Stereotypes and Prejudice* (Philadelphia: Psychology Press, 2000), 394–418.

46. Ibid.

10 Connecting justice to human experience: attitudes toward accountability and reconciliation in Rwanda

Timothy Longman, Phuong Pham, and Harvey M. Weinstein

After the 1994 Rwandan genocide, the government of Rwanda and the international community implemented three judicial responses in an effort to punish those responsible for the violence, help rebuild the country's war-ravaged society, and encourage reconciliation – the International Criminal Tribunal for Rwanda (ICTR), national-level domestic genocide trials, and local-level gacaca courts. The Rwandan government has also established commissions for human rights and for national unity and reconciliation; instituted re-education camps for returned refugees, former prisoners, students, and politicians; established memorials and commemorations to the genocide; and instituted a series of political reforms. While these programs have been adopted in the name of reconciliation and national unity, neither the Rwandan government nor the international community has solicited the views of the Rwandan population regarding the best means of achieving reconciliation and unity.

In implementing policies in a top-down manner, Rwanda is, of course, not alone. Governments and international institutions, such as the United Nations, rarely, if ever, consult affected populations when formulating policies aimed at rebuilding post-war societies. Indeed, while many national leaders and international officials claim to speak on behalf of those most affected by the violence, what people themselves believe is most needed to rebuild and reconcile their war-torn country is usually ignored. In 2002, we set out to gain a clearer idea of how Rwandans understood the concepts of justice and reconciliation and of whether they believed that the judicial initiatives underway in their country would contribute to the process of reconciliation and national unity. To explore these questions, we surveyed Rwandans in four communities. We based the survey on the assumption that a randomly selected group of Rwandans could best assess the requirements for the social reconstruction of their country.

Survey methods

The survey instrument included questions on demographic information, justice and reconciliation, ethnic attitudes, attitudes toward the ICTR, Rwandan national courts, gacaca courts, and exposure to trauma. The survey also included a checklist to assess the symptom prevalence of post-traumatic stress disorder (PTSD).[1] As has been discussed elsewhere in this book, the concept of reconciliation, although widely used, is vague. For the purposes of this survey, we developed an operational definition of reconciliation as the process whereby individuals, social groups, and institutions develop a shared vision and sense of collective future (community); establish mutual ties and obligations across lines of social demarcation (interdependence); accept and actively promote individual rights, rule of law, tolerance of social diversity, and equality of opportunity (social justice); and adopt non-violent alternatives to conflict management (non-violence). We developed a series of twenty-nine self-reported items that we believe reflect the components of the reconciliation process. From factor analysis, we obtained four factors comprising fourteen items that accounted for 58 percent of total variance. We labeled the four factors as hypothesized and estimated the Cronbach alpha ($[\alpha]$), a measure of internal-consistency reliability, as follows: 1) attitudes toward community ($[\alpha] = 0.69$), 2) measure of interdependence ($[\alpha] = 0.46$), 3) attitudes toward social justice ($[\alpha] = 0.75$), and 4) attitudes toward violence ($[\alpha] = 0.88$). In addition, given the centrality of ethnicity to the conflict in Rwanda, we included a separate measure for the degree of comfort that individuals felt regarding members of other ethnic groups. We asked a series of seven questions about the sorts of situation in which individuals were comfortable with the presence of members of another ethnic group. We then aggregated the responses to form a scale that we labeled "ethnic distance" ($[\alpha] = 0.94$).

To measure attitudes toward justice initiatives, we developed a series of items probing opinions about each of the three judicial processes that have been adopted in response to the Rwandan genocide – the ICTR, domestic trials, and gacaca. We constructed a similar series of statements about each judicial mechanism, its policies, and its functioning, to which we asked respondents to express whether they strongly agreed, agreed, were uncertain, disagreed, strongly disagreed, or were uninformed. From factor analysis, we obtained three factors comprising nine items that accounted for 63 percent of variance: 1) attitudes toward the ICTR ($[\alpha] = 0.82$), 2) attitudes toward domestic genocide trials ($[\alpha] = 0.61$), and 3) attitudes toward gacaca ($[\alpha] = 0.51$). Finally, to measure the prevalence of PTSD symptoms, we also included the PTSD Checklist – Civilian

Version (PCL-C), which is a brief, self-reported, seventeen-item instrument corresponding to the symptoms associated with the DSM-IV diagnostic criteria for PTSD.[2]

We trained a team of twenty-six Rwandan interviewers who were all final-year college students or recent college graduates and who were nearly evenly divided in terms of ethnicity and gender. After a week of training, the interviewers conducted survey interviews February 4–23, 2002 in four Rwandan communes, the most important local political unit at the time of the genocide.[3] We selected the communes to represent Rwanda's diversity in terms of region, level of urbanization, experience with the genocide and massacres, and level of involvement with the ICTR. As described in the Introductory chapter to this volume, two of the communes, Ngoma in Butare Prefecture and Mabanza in Kibuye Prefecture, are in the southern and central part of the country, while two others, Mutura in Gisenyi Prefecture and Buyoga in Byumba Prefecture, are in the north, reflecting the historically significant regional divide between north and south in Rwanda. Ngoma (the commune for Butare town, Rwanda's second-largest city) is an urban commune, whereas the other three are rural. In Mutura, close to former President Juvénal Habyarimana's home commune, massacres of Tutsi began in 1991. While Ngoma, Mutura, and Mabanza experienced extensive slaughter of Tutsi during the genocide, the genocide occurred in only three out of the thirteen sectors in Buyoga, since the other sectors were in the demilitarized zone that fell quickly under the control of the Rwandan Patriotic Front (RPF), but numerous massacres of civilians in Buyoga have been attributed to the RPF. Massacres of civilians by the RPF and its supporters were also reported in Ngoma. Thousands of civilians fled from Ngoma, Mutura, and Buyoga into exile in neighboring countries, some for as long as five years. In contrast, Mabanza was under French control for several months, which resulted in a lower incidence of revenge attacks and fewer people fleeing into exile. Finally, no ICTR cases have directly affected Buyoga or Mutura, while Mabanza has been affected by several cases, including those of the Prefect of Kibuye, Clement Kayishema, who was found guilty of genocide and other charges, and the burgomaster (similar to a mayor) of Mabanza, Ignace Bagilishema, who was acquitted. A case involving key figures in Ngoma was on-going at the time of the survey.

We interviewed a minimum of 500 individuals in each commune, for a total of 2,091 interviews (Ngoma n = 544, Mabanza n = 508, Buyoga n = 534, and Mutura n = 505). Subjects for interviews within each of the four selected communes were sampled through a multi-stage cluster sampling method. Due to a high rate of illiteracy, we developed a standardized oral consent format, with the approval of the Committee for the Protection of Human Subjects at the University of California, Berkeley. During the survey, we replaced twenty-three (1 percent) selected households with the next qualifying household after two failed attempts to reach an eligible participant. We were also unable to interview fourteen selected individuals (<1 percent) due to their unavailability, and hence we selected the next eligible household member. Only one household refused participation and had to be replaced by the next eligible household.

Statistical analysis

Means and proportional 95 percent confidence intervals (C.I.) were calculated by EPI Info C-Sample Analysis, which adjusts for design effect. We also imputed the middle score of all missing data for the questions on the two scales measuring attitudes toward reconciliation and judicial responses. We conducted multi-variate logistic regression to find the correlate of PTSD symptoms and attitudes toward judicial responses. Similarly, to examine the relationships between attitude toward judicial process and reconciliation, we ran four separate multi-variate stepwise logistic regressions using as dependent variables the four factors of openness to reconciliation scale (interdependence, community, social justice, and violence). For all four models, the independent variables were: 1) sex; 2) age; 3) education; 4) presence in Rwanda during 1994; 5) frequency of exposure to trauma (events listed on Table 10.2); 6) ethnicity (based on the order of mean openness to reconciliation score of each ethnic group, we coded 1 for Hutu, 2 for Other/Twa, and 3 for Tutsi); 7) ethnic distance; 8) economic frustration defined as the perception of current poverty level compared to 1994 (ie, improved, same, worse; labeled as "SC Poverty") and belief that poverty was the root problem of the 1994 genocide (based on a five-point Likert scale – 1 for strongly agree and 5 for strongly disagree; labeled as "COG poverty"); 9) perception of current access to security compared with before 1994 (improved, same, or worse); 10) PTSD symptoms; and 11) attitudes toward judicial response factors. To adjust for the multiple analyses, we used the Bonferroni adjusted level of significance, which is .007.

Survey results

Slightly more than half of respondents were female (51.5 percent), reflecting the larger portion of women in the population in the aftermath of the war and genocide. Despite the political sensitivity of discussing ethnicity,

Table 10.1 *Socio-demographic profile of respondents, February 2002*

	Ngoma, % (n = 544)	Mabanza, % (n = 508)	Buyoga, % (n = 534)	Mutura, % (n = 505)	Overall, % n = 2091 (95% C.I.)
Sex					
Female	68.2	52.2	43.2	41.7	51.5 (49.3, 53.5)
Age, mean (standard deviation)	37.4 (14.2)	38.1 (14.4)	35.3 (13.9)	35.0 (12.8)	36.4 (35.8, 37.0)
Marital Status					
Single	27.2	17.9	27.0	12.5	21.3 (19.1, 23.4)
Married	56.9	73.2	65.5	76.9	67.9 (64.6, 71.2)
Divorced	1.1	1.8	1.3	1.2	1.3 (0.9, 1.8)
Widowed	14.8	7.1	6.2	9.3	9.4 (7.2, 11.5)
Educational Status					
No School	17.1	27.4	29.6	33.3	26.7 (24.6, 28.8)
Some/Completed Primary	54.9	58.7	61.8	49.4	54.6 (51.7, 60.8)
Some/Completed Secondary	22.5	13.5	8.2	17.3	22.5 (14.7, 16.1)
Some/Completed University or Higher	5.5	0.4	0.4	0	1.6 (0.9, 2.4)
Monthly Income (USD)					
No Income	24.3	28.7	26.2	20.2	24.9 (23.0, 26.7)
< $43.47	42.5	59.4	67.8	68.9	59.4 (57.4, 61.5)
$43.47–$106.52	16.7	9.6	5.4	10.3	10.6 (9.3, 11.9)
>106.53	11.4	2.0	0.6	0.4	3.7 (2.4, 5.1)
No Response or Missing	5.1	0.2	0.0	0.2	1.4 (0.8, 2.1)
Religion					
Protestant	21.2	42.0	35.8	30.3	32.2 (29.7, 33.6)
Catholic	68.6	29.6	58.4	21.8	45.2 (42.7, 47.5)
Adventist	5.0	23.7	2.6	42.3	17.9 (15.1, 20.7)
Muslim	2.8	2.0	0.4	0.6	1.4 (0.9, 2.0)
Other	2.4	2.8	2.8	5.0	3.2 (2.1, 4.3)

Table 10.1 (*cont.*)

	Ngoma, % (n = 544)	Mabanza, % (n = 508)	Buyoga, % (n = 534)	Mutura, % (n = 505)	Overall, % n = 2091 (95% C.I.)
Ethnicity					
Hutu	37.3	70.5	80.0	64.2	62.7 (59.3, 66.2)
Tutsi	48.0	13.6	6.0	24.2	23.1 (20.2, 26.1)
Others/Missing	14.7	15.9	14.0	11.6	14.1 (10.5, 17.6)
Residence in Rwanda before 1994	81.0	97.6	99.8	78.4	89.3 (88.0, 90.6)
Displaced during 1994*	79.1	37.6	87.6	89.8	72.8 (70.9, 74.7)

*Among the respondents who were residing in Rwanda before 1994.

87.3 percent of respondents (1,825 of 2,091) were willing to provide their ethnic identity. Of those who specified their ethnicity, 72.0 percent were Hutu, 26.5 percent Tutsi, and 1.5 percent were Twa, mixed ethnicity, or other (mostly immigrants). We found a statistically significant difference among the four stratified communes on all socio-demographic variables, as well as on attitudinal variables, levels of traumatic exposure, and prevalence of PTSD symptoms ($p < .001$), so we present the results in Table 10.1 by commune.

Prior to the events of 1994, 10.7 percent of respondents lived outside Rwanda, primarily as refugees (Table 10.1). Of those who lived in Rwanda in 1994, 72.8 percent reported being displaced. As demonstrated in Table 10.2, an extremely high portion of respondents reported experiencing traumatic events during the war and genocide: 65.5 percent of respondents reported losing a brother or sister during the events of 1994, 52.2 percent claimed to have lost a cousin, 19.2 percent reported losing their mother, and 21.8 percent their father. We found that, overall, 24.8 percent of the population reported symptoms consistent with the symptoms of PTSD. Risk factors included number of traumatic events, gender, presence in Rwanda in 1994, age, and ethnicity.

Table 10.2 *Exposure to traumatic events in 1994 or its aftermath*

Trauma Events	Ngoma No. (%) n = 536	Mabanza No. (%) n = 503	Buyoga No. (%) n = 534	Mutura No. (%) n = 501	Overall No. (%) [95% CI] N = 2071
Property destroyed or lost	382 (71.3)	304 (60.4)	379 (71.0)	407 (81.2)	1472 (70.9) [68.5, 72.3]
Forced to flee your home	400 (74.6)	242 (48.1)	476 (89.1)	445 (88.8)	1563 (75.4) [73.0, 76.5]
Serious illness	169 (31.5)	194 (38.6)	146 (27.3)	182 (36.3)	691 (33.0) [31.0, 35.1]
Close family member killed	439 (81.9)	315 (62.6)	365 (68.3)	407 (81.2)	1526 (73.0) [71.1, 74.9]
Close family member died from illness	222 (41.4)	240 (47.8)	202 (37.8)	265 (52.9)	926 (44.5) [42.3, 46.5]
Sexual violence involving you or close family member	128 (23.9)	45 (8.9)	30 (5.6)	41 (8.2)	244 (11.7) [10.3, 13.0]
Physical injury	130 (24.2)	96 (19.0)	63 (11.8)	90 (18.0)	379 (18.3) [16.5, 19.8]

Attitudes toward judicial responses

Table 10.3 presents the results of a series of questions regarding the possible purposes of trials for genocide suspects, stratified by ethnicity. Respondents strongly supported using trials to punish the guilty (92.3 percent agreed or strongly agreed) and to reveal the truth about what happened in 1994 (94.0 percent agreed or strongly agreed), but they also strongly supported using trials to separate the innocent from the guilty (89.4 percent), rebuild trust in the community (87.1 percent), and recognize the suffering of survivors (83.2 percent). More reservations were expressed for the idea of trials as a process to provide reparations (70.6 percent agreed or strongly agreed), while using trials to release prisoners was regarded more negatively than positively (34.2 percent agreed or strongly agreed, compared with 48.4 percent who disagreed or strongly disagreed). The results reflected certain important differences between Hutu and Tutsi on several questions. While a majority of Tutsi strongly agreed that trials should punish the guilty, a majority of Hutu merely agreed. Similarly, support for reparations was much stronger among Tutsi, while a much larger percentage of Hutu supported using trials to release prisoners (although slightly more Hutu opposed this purpose than supported it).

Table 10.4 provides the results of a series of questions related to the ICTR, which is based in Arusha, Tanzania. The most striking result

Table 10.3 *Purpose of trials (in percentages)*

	Strongly Agree	Agree	Uncertain	Disagree	Strongly Disagree
To punish those who	39.4	53.9	3.0	3.5	0.2
have done wrong	*50.6*	*43.2*	*2.9*	*3.1*	*0.2*
	40.7	**51.6**	**3.8**	**3.7**	**0.2**
To reveal the truth	34.4	60.1	3.6	1.8	0.1
about what happened	*42.8*	*53.3*	*2.1*	*1.9*	*0.0*
in 1994	**35.9**	**58.1**	**4.0**	**2.0**	**0.0**
To rebuild trust within	35.0	54.1	7.2	3.3	0.3
the community	*33.5*	*48.1*	*11.8*	*5.0*	*1.7*
	33.7	**53.4**	**8.4**	**3.8**	**0.8**
To provide reparations	18.7	51.0	16.1	12.6	1.7
to victims	*31.2*	*45.5*	*10.1*	*9.9*	*3.3*
	21.4	**49.2**	**15.2**	**12.0**	**2.2**
To separate the	39.4	51.8	5.2	2.9	0.7
innocent from the	*35.7*	*53.3*	*5.8*	*4.8*	*0.4*
perpetrators	**37.1**	**52.3**	**6.2**	**3.9**	**0.6**
To release prisoners	9.1	31.1	18.2	33.3	8.3
	4.3	*13.6*	*11.8*	*45.7*	*24.6*
	7.4	**26.8**	**17.3**	**36.4**	**12.0**
To recognize the	20.5	62.1	11.3	4.9	1.2
suffering of survivors	*34.1*	*52.1*	*8.1*	*4.3*	*1.4*
	23.1	**60.1**	**10.9**	**4.7**	**1.2**

Hutu, *Tutsi*, **Total**

was the large portion of respondents who selected "not informed" for each question. Those who chose "not informed" represent a plurality on questions 1, 2, 5, 9, and 10. The problem of insufficient information is illustrated more clearly by the responses to another question: "How well informed do you feel about the Arusha Tribunal?" Only 0.7 percent claimed to be "well informed" and 10.5 percent to be "informed." On the other hand, the majority (55.9 percent) claimed to be "not well informed," and 31.3 percent to be "not informed at all."

Despite the problem of limited information, attitudes toward the ICTR were slightly positive. Figure 10.1 presents the results of the ICTR Attitude Scale derived through statistical analysis, indicating that while the largest portion of respondents had a neutral attitude toward the ICTR, more people had a positive attitude (31.8 percent) than negative (20.9 percent). Ethnicity significantly affected these attitudes, however, with 35.7 percent of Hutu holding positive views and 14.3 percent negative, compared with 21.9 percent of Tutsi who held positive views

Table 10.4 *Attitudes toward the ICTR (in percentages)*

	Strongly Agree	Agree	Uncertain	Disagree	Strongly Disagree	Not informed
1. Overall, the Arusha	2.4	29.2	15.2	7.1	3.5	41.0
Tribunal has	*1.7*	*19.1*	*17.0*	*18.5*	*11.1*	*22.2*
functioned well.	**3.1**	**26.1**	**16.7**	**10.4**	**5.9**	**37.7**
2. The information	2.5	24.4	19.7	8.5	2.5	42.5
available about the	*0.8*	*18.1*	*21.7*	*18.7*	*12.3*	*28.5*
Arusha Tribunal is	**2.0**	**22.5**	**20.9**	**11.3**	**4.7**	**38.6**
reliable.						
3. The Arusha	5.0	34.6	16.1	7.5	3.3	33.5
Tribunal is fair to all	*3.5*	*29.7*	*14.8*	*19.5*	*10.8*	*21.6*
ethnic groups.	**4.4**	**33.4**	**16.3**	**10.5**	**5.2**	**30.1**
4. The International	16.3	30.0	11.5	12.7	6.5	23.1
Criminal Trials should	*39.5*	*37.2*	*6.2*	*4.0*	*1.2*	*11.9*
be held in Rwanda	**21.4**	**32.7**	**16.8**	**10.6**	**4.7**	**19.8**
rather than Arusha.						
5. The Arusha	3.5	28.7	19.6	9.5	2.2	36.5
Tribunal is there above	*8.4*	*36.1*	*20.8*	*10.0*	*2.9*	*21.7*
all to hide the shame	**4.5**	**30.6**	**20.3**	**9.7**	**2.4**	**32.5**
of foreigners.						
6. The Arusha	6.1	33.1	12.3	16.9	4.8	26.9
Tribunal should try	*11.3*	*36.7*	*10.2*	*21.9*	*5.6*	*14.2*
suspects for sex	**7.2**	**33.9**	**12.1**	**18.4**	**5.2**	**23.1**
crimes.						
7. The Arusha	17.3	31.5	11.5	9.4	3.0	27.4
Tribunal should try	*3.5*	*20.0*	*13.6*	*28.2*	*18.4*	*16.1*
members of the RPF	**13.4**	**28.6**	**12.8**	**14.5**	**6.9**	**23.9**
who committed war						
crimes.						
8. The Arusha	5.6	33.6	16.6	8.4	4.4	31.5
Tribunal is promoting	*1.2*	*22.9*	*20.1*	*21.0*	*16.8*	*17.9*
reconciliation in	**4.3**	**31.3**	**27.7**	**11.8**	**7.3**	**27.4**
Rwanda.						
9. The Arusha	3.8	7.8	19.6	24.4	8.4	36.1
Tribunal has been a	*13.7*	*22.9*	*20.7*	*16.2*	*4.2*	*18.5*
waste of money.	**6.1**	**11.8**	**19.7**	**22.7**	**7.0**	**32.7**
10. The Arusha	2.6	16.0	21.9	19.5	5.6	34.4
Tribunal is nothing	*2.9*	*11.7*	*18.2*	*26.4*	*18.6*	*22.2*
but victor's justice.	**2.4**	**15.2**	**21.1**	**21.5**	**8.7**	**31.2**

Hutu, *Tutsi*, **Total**

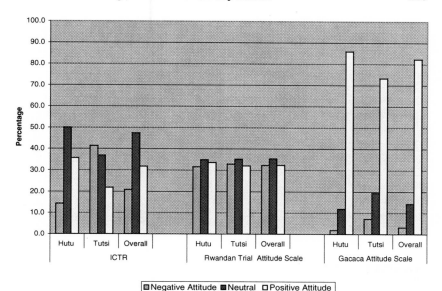

Figure 10.1 Attitudes toward judicial responses by ethnicity, Rwanda 2002

and 35.1 percent negative. Ethnicity was a significant factor on a number of individual questions. The differences were most pronounced on the question of holding international genocide trials in Rwanda rather than in Arusha, Tanzania, and regarding the ICTR as a waste of money, a sentiment which Tutsi more strongly supported, and on the question of whether members of the RPF who committed crimes should be tried, which Hutu supported.

As indicated in Table 10.5, ethnicity was not a significant factor for most questions referring to domestic genocide trials. In fact, ethnicity was only significant on the question about the treatment of prisoners, about which Tutsi were more positive than Hutu. For example, Figure 10.1 presents the results of the Rwandan Trial Attitude Scale, which shows that overall 32.4 percent of respondents had a positive attitude, compared with 32.7 percent with a negative attitude. There were no significant differences in attitudes between the ethnic groups. Table 10.5 also indicates a much higher rate of information regarding the Rwandan trials.

Table 10.6 presents attitudes toward gacaca. Although respondents expressed concern over the qualifications of the judges and the potential for corruption among the judges, overall attitudes toward gacaca were

Table 10.5 *Attitudes toward Rwandan genocide trials (in percentages)*

	Strongly Agree	Agree	Uncertain	Disagree	Strongly Disagree	Not informed
1. Overall, the Rwandan tribunals have functioned well.	10.7	46.4	12.1	11.7	3.4	15.7
	10.3	*46.7*	*16.9*	*11.8*	*3.3*	*11.0*
	10.1	**46.4**	**14.3**	**11.6**	**3.3**	**14.3**
2. Detainees in Rwandan prisons have been treated fairly.	11.8	38.9	16.4	13.8	4.4	14.7
	26.9	*46.5*	*13.6*	*4.3*	*0.2*	*8.5*
	15.2	**40.3**	**16.7**	**11.5**	**3.3**	**13.0**
3. The trial of genocide suspects has taken too long.	25.8	42.3	9.9	13.3	1.8	6.8
	35.5	*45.2*	*6.6*	*2.2*	*1.0*	*2.1*
	27.0	**43.2**	**10.0**	**12.5**	**1.6**	**5.7**
4. The categorization of accused for the genocide is a good policy.	31.1	50.6	4.9	5.6	1.4	6.2
	28.7	*56.8*	*5.2*	*5.2*	*2.7*	*1.4*
	28.9	**52.4**	**6.1**	**5.8**	**1.6**	**5.1**
5. The encouragement of confession is a good policy.	33.2	57.0	3.4	3.1	0.5	2.7
	33.1	*59.5*	*1.9*	*4.1*	*1.2*	*0.2*
	31.7	**58.2**	**3.8**	**3.3**	**0.9**	**2.1**
6. The genocide trials in the Rwandan tribunals are fair to all ethnic groups.	5.8	34.1	21.2	16.7	6.5	15.8
	7.4	*32.3*	*22.3*	*21.5*	*8.1*	*8.5*
	5.9	**32.9**	**22.7**	**17.9**	**6.4**	**14.2**
7. The Rwandan tribunals have adequately addressed sexual violence.	14.9	49.6	13.2	7.2	2.4	12.6
	14.7	*48.6*	*8.7*	*14.3*	*6.6*	*7.2*
	14.4	**49.4**	**12.9**	**9.6**	**3.3**	**10.5**
8. The Rwandan tribunals have adequately addressed reparations.	5.5	37.7	21.2	13.0	2.6	20.0
	5.8	*28.5*	*19.2*	*23.1*	*13.8*	*9.5*
	5.2	**36.0**	**21.4**	**15.3**	**5.2**	**16.9**
9. Encouraging confession encourages prisoners to lie.	4.6	18.6	21.0	31.7	10.4	13.7
	6.8	*29.3*	*22.9*	*26.0*	*8.1*	*6.8*
	5.0	**21.4**	**22.2**	**29.9**	**9.4**	**12.0**
10. The Rwandan tribunals are promoting reconciliation.	12.6	53.7	15.5	8.4	2.2	7.5
	14.0	*50.2*	*16.7*	*9.5*	*2.7*	*6.8*
	12.4	**53.2**	**16.1**	**8.7**	**2.3**	**7.3**

Hutu, *Tutsi*, **Total**

Table 10.6 *Attitudes toward Gacaca (in percentages)*

	Strongly Agree	Agree	Uncertain	Disagree	Strongly Disagree	Not informed
1. The election of	38.4	54.9	2.7	2.1	0.5	1.4
gacaca judges was	*34.7*	*50.6*	*4.3*	*5.4*	*1.7*	*3.3*
conducted fairly in my	**36.7**	**54.1**	**3.5**	**2.8**	**0.8**	**2.2**
community.						
2. Community service	31.9	45.9	6.8	5.7	1.8	7.9
is a good alternative to	*17.8*	*44.4*	*8.3*	*14.5*	*9.5*	*5.6*
imprisonment.	**27.1**	**45.4**	**8.0**	**7.9**	**3.8**	**7.7**
3. Community service	13.0	39.0	15.2	13.9	7.6	11.3
to benefit society is an	*8.1*	*31.2*	*13.6*	*25.0*	*16.7*	*5.4*
adequate form of	**11.6**	**36.7**	**15.6**	**16.5**	**9.5**	**10.1**
reparations.						
4. Sexual crimes	17.8	51.8	6.6	14.2	7.6	2.0
should be included in	*17.1*	*46.1*	*6.4*	*20.5*	*25.5*	*1.2*
the public gacaca	**17.1**	**50.4**	**6.9**	**15.6**	**7.9**	**2.1**
trials.						
5. I am concerned that	12.9	41.6	10.5	22.2	7.3	5.4
the gacaca judges are	*18.4*	*44.2*	*9.9*	*16.3*	*5.4*	*5.8*
not well qualified.	**13.6**	**42.4**	**11.3**	**20.5**	**6.7**	**5.5**
6. I am concerned that	6.5	26.4	16.0	33.0	12.6	5.6
the gacaca judges are	*14.5*	*33.9*	*17.6*	*20.0*	*9.1*	*5.0*
corrupt.	**8.1**	**27.5**	**17.4**	**29.7**	**11.9**	**5.3**
7. Crimes committed	15.5	31.1	14.5	18.1	10.4	10.4
by the Rwandan	*1.9*	*15.3*	*12.4*	*20.8*	*29.1*	*10.5*
Patriotic Army should	**11.0**	**26.8**	**14.7**	**21.4**	**15.2**	**10.9**
be included in gacaca.						
8. I have confidence in	27.1	59.9	8.4	2.6	1.1	1.0
the gacaca process.	*20.5*	*54.1*	*13.8*	*6.6*	*3.5*	*1.4*
	24.6	**58.3**	**10.7**	**3.4**	**1.7**	**1.2**

Hutu, *Tutsi*, **Total**

quite positive, as indicated in Figure 10.1, the Gacaca Attitude Scale. Ethnicity was a significant factor on several questions, with opinions diverging most sharply over whether gacaca should have jurisdiction over crimes allegedly committed by the RPF. Hutu were also more supportive of community service as an alternative to imprisonment. Ethnicity was not significant in the Gacaca Attitude Scale.

Table 10.7 presents the factors associated with attitudes toward the three judicial processes. More education was associated with less support for all three forms of trial. Traumatic experiences were slightly associated

218   *Timothy Longman et al.*

Table 10.7 *Stepwise multiple logistic regression analysis: associates of attitudes to judicial processes*

	Outcome Variables		
	ICTR	Rwandan Trials	Gacaca
Independent Variables	Adjusted OR (95% C.I.)	Adjusted OR (95% C.I.)	Adjusted OR (95% C.I.)
Education	0.91 (0.84, 0.98)	0.72 (0.66, 0.79)	0.82 (0.72, 0.93)
Age	NS	NS	NS
Ethnic	a. 0.58 (0.45, 0.74)	NS	NS
a. Tutsi/Hutu	b. 0.55 (0.40, 0.77)		
b. Tutsi/Other	c. NS		
c. Other/Hutu			
Ethnic Distance	NS	NS	0.86 (0.77, 0.96)
In Rwanda	NS	1.63 (1.15, 1.30)	0.55 (0.33, 0.90)
Trauma Level	1.10 (1.04, 1.17)	0.90 (0.84, 0.96)	0.80 (0.72, 0.89)
PTSD	NS	0.77 (0.61, 0.98)	NS
Poverty Level	a. NS	a. 2.21 (1.76, 2.79)	a. 1.95 (1.29, 2.91)
a. Improved/Worse	b. 1.42 (1.07, 1.90)	b. NS	b. NS
b. Improved/Same		c. NS	c. NS
c. Same/Worse			
SC Security	NS	a. 1.56 (1.22, 2.00)	a. 1.53 (1.04, 2.25)
a. Improved/Worse		b. NS	b. NS
b. Improved/Same		c. NS	c. NS
c. Same/Worse			
Model Goodness of Fit	*GF = 10.83*	*GF = 1.71*	*GF = 9.67*
Chi-Square (GF) Test	*Df = 8*	*Df = 8*	*Df = 8*
	P Value = 0.211	*P Value = 0.9*	*P Value = 0.289*

Odds Ratios are calculated from logistic regression models. Multi-variate logistics regression was used to adjust (OR_{adj}) for age, sex, ethnicity, commune sampled, economic frustration, and trauma exposure level.
NS = Not statistically significant using Bonferroni adjusted significance level of 0.007.

with more support for the ICTR but less support for Rwandan trials and gacaca. Perceptions of deteriorating security conditions and of increased poverty were associated with more negative attitudes toward the two domestic judicial initiatives, whereas those who believed economic conditions had improved were more negative regarding the ICTR. Those who lived outside Rwanda prior to and during the genocide were less likely to be positive toward Rwandan trials than those who lived inside the country and, at the same time, more likely to support gacaca. One explanation of this finding is that those living, for example, in Congo or Uganda had less knowledge of the Rwandan system of justice and were likely to be more suspicious of its fairness or efficacy. At the same time, they might be more likely to trust a community-based, traditional, non-government approach.

Attitudes toward reconciliation

In the survey, we were interested in ascertaining not only Rwandan attitudes toward justice initiatives but also about reconciliation and, specifically, what contribution, if any, justice could make to reconciliation. Table 10.8 shows the responses to the eighteen questions that comprise the four factors in the Openness to Reconciliation Scale – social justice, non-violence, community, and interdependence – derived through principal component analysis. Variables that are associated with these four aspects of reconciliation were determined using a stepwise logistic regression, the results of which are presented in Table 10.9. More education is associated with less support for three of the four reconciliation factors, as is greater experience of trauma. PTSD symptoms as measured by the scale are associated with less support for two of the factors. Perceptions of improved security and an improved situation for poverty are associated with greater openness to reconciliation on two factors.

We were particularly interested in the relationship between justice and reconciliation. In response to the statement, "It is important for those who committed crimes during the war to be tried," 48.1 percent strongly agreed and 48.7 percent agreed, compared with only 1.7 percent who disagreed. At the same time, in response to the statement "It is better to try to forget what happened and move on," 22.3 percent strongly agreed and 40.7 percent agreed, compared with 19.4 percent who disagreed and 9.9 percent who strongly disagreed. We asked respondents how much of a contribution they believed each judicial initiative would make to reconciliation. As Table 10.10 reveals, respondents see foreign trials, such as those carried out in Belgium, followed by the ICTR, making the least contribution to reconciliation in Rwanda. In contrast, 69.2 percent believe that genocide trials in Rwanda will make a significant or very significant contribution to reconciliation in Rwanda, while 84.2 percent believe that gacaca will make a significant or very significant contribution. The stepwise logistic regression, however, finds little relationship between attitudes toward the various trials and openness to reconciliation.

Discussion

The results of the survey lead to a number of interesting and provocative observations. Respondents believe that trials should serve a multiplicity

Table 10.8 *Questions for Reconciliation Scale (in percentages)*

	Strongly agree	Agree	Uncertain	Disagree	Strongly Disagree
I. Social Justice					
When I have a problem, I usually go for help to someone from my own ethnic group.	3.3	13.9	4.0	55.6	23.2
Children should marry members of their own ethnicity.	3.8	7.9	4.4	60.1	23.8
People must learn to live together and depend on each other, no matter what their ethnic group.	44.3	49.9	2.9	1.5	1.4
Our community would be a better place if there were only people of my ethnic group.	1.7	3.6	3.9	59.1	31.8
If my neighbor were in trouble, I would assist him, no matter what his ethnicity.	42.0	53.5	2.1	1.4	1.0
Every ethnic group should have the same opportunity to find work.	34.4	59.6	4.1	1.5	0.4
I prefer to buy things from a shopkeeper of my own ethnicity.	0.9	2.4	3.3	57.8	35.6
Forgiveness is important to reconciliation.	41.5	52.1	4.2	1.5	0.8

II. Non-Violence

Do you think it is appropriate for government authorities to ask civilians to use arms in any of the following circumstances:

	Yes (%)	No (%)
To keep a politician in office at all cost	3.7	94.2
To promote a political party	5.0	92.0
To defend the interests of a single ethnic group	2.6	95.2
To defend the community against enemies	52.9	45.0
To combat crime	51.7	46.2

III. Community

For each of the following social conditions, please state whether you think the condition has improved, is about the same, or is worse today than before the events of 1994 (in percentages):

	Improved (%)	About the Same (%)	Worse (%)
Distrust among neighbors	42.9	13.2	44.0
Conflicts over housing	40.2	15.4	44.3
Conflicts over land	29.5	14.3	56.3

IV. Interdependence

	Yes (%)	No (%)
Have you shared a drink with a member of another ethnicity during the past month?	88.9	10.0
Have you attended a funeral for someone of another ethnicity during the past year?	63.7	34.1
Do you have members of your family who are from another ethnic group?	42.0	55.1

Table 10.9 *Stepwise multiple logistic regression analysis: associates of openness to reconciliation factors*

	Outcome Variables			
	Interdependent	Community	Social Justice	Violence
Independent Variables	*Adjusted* OR (*95% C.I.*)	*Adjusted* OR (*95% C.I.*)	*Adjusted* OR (*95% C.I.*)	*Adjusted* OR (*95% C.I.*)
Education	0.73 (0.68, 0.80)	0.85 (0.78, 0.92)	0.91 (0.84, 0.98)	NS
Ethnic	NS	NS		NS
a. Tutsi/Hutu			a. 1.67 (2.13, 1.28)	
b. Other/Tutsi			b. NS	
c. Other/Hutu			c. 1.73 (1.31, 2.30)	
In Rwanda	NS	1.54 (1.11, 2.15)		NS
Trauma Level	0.86 (0.81, 0.92)	0.92 (0.87, 0.98)	NS	0.92 (0.87, 0.97)
PTSD	0.71 (0.56, 0.90)	0.76* (0.60, 0.97)		
Poverty Level	NS		NS	
a. Improved/Worse		a. 2.42 (1.95, 3.00)		a. NS
b. Improved/Same		b. NS		b. 1.44 (1.08, 1.92)
c. Same/Worse		c. 2.11 (1.59, 2.82)		c. NS
SC Security	NS		NS	
a. Improved/Worse		a. 2.89 (2.17, 3.84)		a. 1.43 (1.13, 1.81)
b. Improved/Same		b. NS		b. 1.74 (1.20, 2.52)
c. Same/Worse		c. 2.24 (1.43, 3.50)		c. NS
Rwandan Trial Attitude	NS		NS	NS
a. Positive/Negative		a. 1.96 (1.52, 2.50)		
b. Positive/Neutral		b. NS		
c. Neutral/Negative		c. 1.39 (1.22, 1.57)		
Gacaca Attitude	NS	NS		NS
a. Positive/Negative			a. NS	
b. Positive/Neutral			b. 1.47 (1.11, 1.95)	
c. Neutral/Negative			c. NS	
Model Goodness of Fit	*GF = 12.25*	*GF = 2.99*	*GF = 5.07*	*GF = 12.06*
Chi-Square	*df = 8*	*df = 8*	*df = 8*	*df = 8*
(GF) Test	*p = 0.14*	*p = 0.93*	*p = 0.75*	*p = 0.15*

Odds Ratios are calculated from logistic regression models. Multi-variate logistics regression was used to adjust (OR_{adj}) for age, sex, ethnicity, commune sampled, economic frustration, and trauma exposure level.

NS = Not statistically significant using Bonferroni adjusted significance level of 0.007.

Table 10.10 *Contributions of trials to reconciliation for each of the following types of trial for genocide suspects, please indicate how much of a contribution to reconciliation in Rwanda you think the trial will make (in percentages)*

	No Contribution	Limited Contribution	Moderate	Significant Contribution	Very Significant	Not Informed
The ICTR	23.0	9.9	17.7	15.5	5.7	28.1
Trials in foreign countries	29.6	10.3	16.8	8.2	2.5	32.5
Rwandan tribunals	3.7	5.3	15.2	37.6	31.6	6.6
Gacaca trials	1.2	1.8	8.3	30.8	53.4	4.5
Military trials	15.6	6.5	16.6	19.8	15.8	25.7

of purposes, not simply punishing those guilty of crimes but also revealing the truth about what happened, freeing the innocent and punishing the guilty, helping to rebuild community, and recognizing the suffering of victims. The survey finds more positive than negative attitudes toward all three major judicial initiatives. Respondents also feel that all the trials will make at least some contribution to reconciliation in Rwanda, as demonstrated in Table 10.10. They feel that domestic genocide trials and gacaca will make a significant contribution to reconciliation. Nevertheless, the regression analysis finds only a very limited relationship between attitudes toward trials and openness to reconciliation.

The survey indicates strong support for gacaca among those surveyed, reinforcing what other surveys have found.[4] While indicating a few reservations about potential corruption and the qualifications of judges, respondents express great confidence in the gacaca process, and they believe that it will make a substantial contribution to reconciliation. These attitudes contrast with the much more muted support for the ICTR and are also much stronger than support for domestic trials. It is important to note that the survey was conducted after gacaca judges had been elected but before trials had actually begun, so people's opinions are not based on having watched gacaca in operation. Nevertheless, the survey does provide some clues to gacaca's popularity. Strong support for the idea that the ICTR should be held in Rwanda and the evidence that people feel ill-informed about the ICTR may indicate that people support gacaca because it is closer to them and therefore more transparent. A substantial portion of people also responded that they were not informed about Rwandan trials. Furthermore, 30.3 percent strongly agreed and 55.2

percent agreed with using gacaca "to demonstrate that Rwandans can solve problems using their own traditions," suggesting that gacaca is considered consistent with Rwandan traditions. The issues of availability of information, transparency, and consistency with local traditions all may affect how populations view trials.

An important conclusion drawn from the regression analysis is that a higher level of education is associated with less support for trials and less openness to reconciliation. This challenges the commonly held belief that education contributes to greater understanding, while ignorance contributes to conflict and division. It is consistent, however, with answers to the survey that implicate the elite in the violence of 1994 and that see the elite as a continuing source of conflict. When respondents were asked what was the primary cause of the violence, 49.4 percent chose "bad governance." Further, in response to the statement, "If Rwandan leaders would leave the population to themselves, there would be no more ethnic problems," 34.9 percent strongly agreed and 41.8 percent agreed.

Trauma also proves to be a factor in shaping attitudes. We found that greater experience of traumatic events is associated with more negative attitudes toward the domestic judicial responses, particularly gacaca, and slightly with more positive attitudes toward the ICTR, while PTSD symptoms are associated with negative attitudes toward Rwandan trials. This raises questions about the relationship of trials to the needs of victims. Trauma was also associated with less openness to reconciliation.

The survey offers a mixed perspective on the relationship between economic issues, such as poverty and housing shortages, and reconciliation. A perception of improved economic conditions is strongly associated with positive attitudes toward Rwandan trials and gacaca, and toward support for community and opposition to violence. At the same time, in response to the statement "Reconciliation will not happen without the alleviation of poverty," 46.1 percent of respondents disagreed and 17.1 percent strongly disagreed. This issue clearly needs to be explored further.

The survey suggests that ethnicity remains important in Rwanda and continues to shape people's perceptions. Ethnicity was significantly related to responses to a number of questions, particularly regarding justice. Hutu were much more likely to believe that the members of the RPF who committed crimes should be tried. In response to the statement, "Both the government and the RPF were behind the events of 1994," 53.8 percent of Hutu agreed or strongly agreed, compared with 19.2 percent who disagreed or strongly disagreed, while only 21.2 percent of Tutsi agreed or strongly agreed, compared with 54.8 percent who disagreed or strongly disagreed. Meanwhile, Tutsi showed much stronger support for reparations as an aspect of the justice process. Although ethnic identity continues to divide Rwanda's population, it is important to note that, with the exception of the social justice scale, it is not a significant factor in determining openness to reconciliation.

This survey represents only a first attempt to understand popular attitudes toward justice and reconciliation. The relatively positive attitudes toward judicial initiatives and the high level of openness to reconciliation on a number of factors should be encouraging signs for those engaged in these processes. However, the relationship between justice and reconciliation is hardly straightforward. More research needs to be conducted to ascertain what conditions are needed within post-war societies for reconciliation to take hold and to understand better the contributions that justice can make to this process. Governments and the international community rarely consult local populations on what they believe is necessary for rebuilding, in part because of the difficulty of conducting research in post-conflict situations and the urgency of the need to implement programs. The survey results suggest that consulting the population can help make post-war policies more effective at promoting social reconstruction and reconciliation. Understanding the importance for Rwandans of transparency and accessibility of information, for example, could have influenced the ICTR to publicize its work more effectively in the country. Without a clear understanding of the beliefs about justice, accountability, and reconciliation among populations affected by mass violence and war, policies risk missing their mark and wasting opportunities to rebuild societies and promote durable peace.

NOTES

Some of these data appear in a recent paper in the *Journal of the American Medical Association*: Phuong N. Pham, Harvey M. Weinstein, and Timothy Longman, "Trauma and PTSD Symptoms in Rwanda: Implications for Attitudes Toward Justice and Reconciliation," *Journal of the American Medical Association* 292 (2004): 602–612.

The authors are much indebted to Urusaro Alice Karekezi and the Center for Conflict Management at the National University of Rwanda for their assistance with this survey.

1. PTSD is defined in the 1994 Diagnostic and Statistical Manual of the American Psychiatric Association as a condition that occurs in response to events that are life-threatening to oneself or others and where one experiences profound fear or helplessness. There are three characteristic sets of symptoms: *re-experiencing* the events, eg through recurrent dreams or intrusive images; *avoidance* of stimuli associated with the events, or numbing of general responsiveness; and symptoms of *increased arousal*, such as insomnia, irritability, and problems with concentration. For the complete definition, see *Diagnostic and Statistical Manual of Mental Disorders* (4th edn.) (Washington, D.C.: American

Psychiatric Association, 1994). The PTSD Checklist has been found to be a valid measure of the presence of PTSD symptoms. See David Forbes, Mark Creamer and Dick Biddle, "The Validity of the PTSD Checklist as a Measure of Symptomatic Change in Combat-Related PTSD," *Behaviour Research and Therapy* 39 (2001): 977–986.

2. While there is legitimate concern raised about scales developed in western populations and then applied in lesser-developed countries, several studies suggest that the syndrome as defined can be found with varying prevalence rates among these populations. De Jong and colleagues utilized survey techniques to study prevalence rates for PTSD in post-conflict countries. They found prevalence rates of 37.4 percent in Algeria, 28.4 percent in Cambodia, 15.8 percent in Ethiopia, and 17.8 percent in Gaza. The authors isolated patterns of risk factors in each of the countries and noted the importance of context in assessing PTSD. In an earlier study in Rwandan and Burundian refugee camps, De Jong and colleagues assessed the prevalence of mental health problems using the GHQ, or General Health Questionnaire. With prevalence rates of 50 percent, they suggest that intervention programs should focus on communities and not on individuals. See Joop de Jong et al., "Lifetime Events and Post-Traumatic Stress Disorder in Four Post-Conflict Settings," *Journal of the American Medical Association* 286 (2001): 555–562, and Joop de Jong et al., "The Prevalence of Mental Health Problems in Rwandan and Burundese refugee camps," *Acta Psychiatrica Scandinavica* 102 (2000): 171–177.

3. In 1994, Rwanda was divided into 11 prefectures. (A twelfth was added post-1994 for returning Tutsi.) Each prefecture was divided into communes, roughly equivalent to counties in the United States. The 154 communes in Rwanda were divided into sectors, and the sectors into cells.

4. Ligue Rwandaise pour la Promotion et la Défense des Droits de l'Homme (LIPRODHOR), *Juridictions gacaca au Rwanda: Résultats de la Recherche sur les Attitudes et Opinions de la Population Rwandaise* (Kigali: LIPRODHOR, 2000); and Stella Ballabola, "Perceptions about the Gacaca Law in Rwanda," *Cahiers du Centre de Gestion des Conflits* 3 (May 2001); Simone Gasibirege and Stella Ballabola, "Perceptions about the Gacaca Law in Rwanda: Evidence from a Multi-Method Study," *Special Publication No. 19* (Baltimore: the Johns Hopkins University School of Public Health, Center for Communication Programs, 2001). The LIPRODHOR study found 93 percent support. The Johns Hopkins study found similar support but also that support dropped off the greater the level of information about gacaca.

11 Public education and social reconstruction in Bosnia and Herzegovina and Croatia

Sarah Warshauer Freedman, Dinka Corkalo, Naomi Levy, Dino Abazovic, Bronwyn Leebaw, Dean Ajdukovic, Dino Djipa, and Harvey M. Weinstein

Throughout history, governments of all political stripes have used history and literature curricula to reinforce national ideologies and identities. The promulgation of official memory through the school system can be an effective form of propaganda. The educational setting can become a conduit for the government or leaders' views, presenting political ideas and beliefs as either "correct" or "incorrect." Textbooks and curricula can be used to justify or deny past state crimes, create revisionist history, present on-going injustices as natural, or perpetuate attitudes that replicate the conditions under which injustices are committed. Where school systems remain segregated and unequal, education can be manipulated to perpetuate inequalities that are a legacy of past conflicts, dispossession, or repression.

If public education can function to inflame hatreds, mobilize for war, and teach acceptance of injustice, it can be used also as a powerful tool for the cultivation of peace, democratic change, and respect for others. This premise has been a prominent focus of the United Nations (UN) Office of the High Representative (OHR) in Bosnia and Herzegovina (BiH), as well as numerous non-governmental organizations (NGOs) throughout the Balkans and in conflict zones around the world. If children living in divided societies can come together in the schools, this contact can be used to help them question the prejudices and stereotypes in their surrounding environment.[1] Where authoritarianism in the classroom fosters blind obedience and militarism, such attitudes might be transformed by educational reforms that promote critical thinking, democratic principles, and the examination of competing views and perspectives. Similarly, if incommensurable conceptions of justice and interpretations of traumatic historical events have fueled conflict and mistrust, so schools might alternatively provide an arena for examining the past in a constructive manner.

Such aspirations notwithstanding, education reform in societies after ethnic conflict poses very serious challenges, and children are often caught in the middle of competing ideologies. To begin with, those in power may resist reforms that promote democratic values. For example, in BiH, the Dayton Accords devolved authority over education to the leadership that was in power during the war. The OHR often struggled to implement educational reforms against the wishes of the elected leaders, who advocated divisive school structures and curricular decisions. In addition, reforms that emphasize democratic approaches may actually fuel intergroup hatreds if they are implemented without the active consultation and participation of the local community. For example, when open debate encourages the expression of alternative and competing viewpoints, parents or local authorities may see this as a provocative attack on the resolution that terminated the conflict. Parental resistance might then encourage antagonistic or even violent confrontations both in and out of the classrooms. This has been particularly true when "outsiders," such as the UN, assume the role of a custodial government in post-war countries and, with the best of intentions, compel educational systems to adopt democratic reforms, with little regard for local traditions and culture. Nowhere has this been more apparent than in Croatia and BiH, where internationals and NGOs have devoted a tremendous amount of attention to *ad hoc* educational programs in conflict resolution, human rights, democracy, and civic education, while paying less attention to local attitudes about the role of schools in the process of social reconstruction.

One of the first steps often undertaken is to remove from curricular materials any stereotypes of ethnicity or descriptions of aggression on the part of any group. In 1998, under pressure from the international community, the Sarajevo Education Working Group carried out a textbook review as part of the process of encouraging refugee returns under the Sarajevo Declaration. Leaked reports indicated bland and inaccurate text that obfuscated the facts of the war. The communities summarily rejected the proposed textbook reform, although there may have been some distortions exaggerated by the media.[2] The push to integrate schools across ethnic lines did not solicit the cooperation of parents and teachers, and led to resistance and sabotage that was reflected in the behavior of the children. Focusing solely on curricular material or on which ethnic group occupies a particular building reflects a unidimensional view of important problems.

In 2000, we launched a series of studies to try to understand what role, if any, public education could play in social reconstruction in Croatia and BiH. We had two questions: what do communities think about the role

Table 11.1 *Survey, interview and focus group subjects*[16]

Town	Language Program	Subject Type	Survey	Interviews	Focus[17] Groups	Total[18]
Mostar	Bosnian	Students	285	2	–	287
		Parents	261	2	–	263
		Teachers	26	6	–	32
	Croatian	Students	274	2	20	296
		Parents	389	1	11	401
		Teachers	40	6	10	56
Vukovar	Croatian	Students	345	2	9	356
		Parents	483	2	9	494
		Teachers	50	6	9	65
	Serbian	Students	373	2	15	390
		Parents	470	1	15	486
		Teachers	45	6	4	55

schools should play in creating a memory of the past through curriculum? And, second, how do they want the schools organized to deliver that curriculum? Our premise was that a better understanding of the aspirations and experiences of those most immediately affected by the education system is a critical component of effective education reform. Over the course of three years, we solicited the views of parents, teachers, students, and administrators in two of the most ethnically divided cities of the former Yugoslavia – Vukovar (Croatia) and Mostar (BiH) – on a wide range of issues, including interethnic relations in schools, the teaching of history, school integration, curricula development, and national identity. Our research team, which consisted of scholars from BiH, Croatia, and the United States, conducted one large-scale survey and one qualitative interview and focus group study in the two cities. The surveys centered on the sixth and eighth grades of elementary school and the second year of secondary school. The interviews and focus groups centered on the second year of secondary school. Table 11.1 provides a breakdown of the sample for the surveys, interviews and focus groups, by national group, and location.

Educational systems in BiH and Croatia

Before presenting the findings of our studies, we offer a brief introduction to the educational systems of BiH and Croatia, beginning with the organization of the school system in post-war BiH and specifically in the

city of Mostar which, prior to the 1991 war, was a multi-ethnic community made up primarily of Bosniaks and Croats with a significant Serb
minority (see the description of Mostar in the introductory chapter to
this volume). Following the signing of the Dayton Accords in December
1995, the newly decentralized educational system in BiH allowed can-
tons to establish their own education ministries and, if desired, to set
standards, and to develop separate curricula and textbooks.[3] This decentralized system did not, however, foster an atmosphere of cooperation
and coordination among the cantonal ministries.

The schools of Mostar are almost entirely segregated. Bosniak children
attend schools on the east side of the city, while Croat children attend
schools on the west side. Although, in theory, the cantonal education
ministry is supposed to supervise the administration of local schools,
in practice, administrators of each ethnic group supervise the schools
on their side. Until 2002, this separation was accomplished by having a
Croat Minister of Education and a Bosniak Deputy Minister who acted as
Minister for the Bosniak schools. The Minister's and Deputy Minister's
offices and parallel administrations were staffed by members of their
respective national groups and were housed in separate locations. Schools
in Mostar also use different curricula. Bosniak schools use the curricula
developed by the Bosniak pedagogical institute in Mostar, which is based
on a framework developed by the Bosnian Federal Education Ministry.
Croat schools use curricula from the state of Croatia, modified by the
Institute of Education in West Mostar, the institution that most closely
parallels the Bosniak Pedagogical Institute. After the first BiH-run elections in fall 2002, the OHR annulled these parallel systems of administration but left the separate curricula in place.

The OHR and the Council of Europe have worked to remove material that is offensive to other national groups from all textbooks in
BiH. In 1999, when new textbooks could not be prepared, it ordered
the blackening-out of offensive material in existing textbooks, an exercise that was fraught with controversy. In many schools, students were
given the task of marking out the offending passages, which only served
to highlight the material. In July 2002, the Organization for Security
and Cooperation in Europe (OSCE) assumed the OHR's former role
in education. By fall of 2003, the OSCE had brokered agreements
with the local ministries that led to the introduction of new, inoffensive textbooks and a common core curriculum. In an important and
symbolic move, the OSCE also mandated the integration of the old
Mostar Gymnasium, the premier institution for secondary education
pre-war. By working at both the curricular and institutional level, significant steps were taken toward an integrated, non-ethnically based school
system.

Unlike in BiH, Croatia has had little international involvement in its education system since the end of the war. It is highly centralized, and all primary and secondary education is regulated by the Ministry of Education and Sport (MoES), which struggles to balance the conflicting agendas of local political leaders, especially in regions experiencing continuing tensions.[4] The MoES is responsible for drafting legislation, defining the curriculum for all schools, approving textbooks, appointing head teachers, approving the number of pupils and school budgets, and settling all expenditures except those met by local authorities. Simultaneously, the MoES must balance the often conflicting imperatives of meeting the needs of state-building and honoring minority rights by educating minority youth in accordance with the standards of the European Union.

Minority schooling is regulated by a set of laws allowing for three different options for minority education. The first option, which is practiced by some Italians and Hungarians, offers separate schooling that is fully in the language of the minority. The second option involves separate courses in "national" subjects for minority students taught in their mother tongue (eg. Serbian) but with the remainder of the instruction in the Croatian language. These students attend the regular Croatian classes for all non-national subjects. The final option for minority education offers courses as an additional school activity. Minority students attend the regular schools in the Croatian language but have additional classes in their mother tongue relevant to their cultural heritage.

The Erdut agreement, signed by the Croatian government and Croatian Serb representatives in 1995, created a different form of separate schooling for Serb children living in the Vukovar region.[5] The agreement was facilitated by the international community with the political purpose of ensuring the protection of Serb minority rights, and was mandated for a period of five years. During this period the Croatian MoES and Serb representatives agreed that Croat and Serb children could go to schools with joint administrations but be taught separately in different languages. This practice frequently has led to Serb and Croat students attending classes in separate shifts or in different locations. Further, the Erdut agreement placed a moratorium on teaching about the recent war in Serb language programs, but that moratorium is now being lifted, and Serbs were to receive new textbooks and begin learning about the war in fall 2003.[6] However, these plans have not materialized.

Attitudes toward controversial issues

In this chapter, we present survey results related to the issues of school integration and history education.[7] We compare the responses of parents, teachers, and students of each national group in each town (Table 11.2). For the interviews and focus groups, we examine all discussion about school integration and teaching about the past.

School integration

The surveys reveal that the youth of all national groups in both Mostar and Vukovar are less in favor of school integration than adults. The only exception is Croat youth in Mostar, who respond neutrally, like their parents. The Bosniak youth, although less enthusiastic than their parents or teachers, are the only young people clearly in favor of school integration. The Croat students in Vukovar are more strongly opposed to integration than any group in either town.

The different national groups in these two towns have set themselves in opposition over the issue of school integration. In Vukovar, Serbs are less opposed to integration than Croats, with the exception of the teachers, and Croat teachers are less opposed than Serb teachers. The teachers' responses could be explained by the fact that many Serb teachers report fears that their jobs will be threatened if the schools are integrated.

In the Mostar surveys, the Bosniak groups all favor integration. While none of the Croat groups oppose integration, their opinions are significantly less positive than those of the Bosniaks. On the whole, the citizens of Mostar tend to think more favorably about school integration than the citizens of Vukovar. Significantly, while the old Mostar Gymnasium is set to be integrated (albeit under external pressure), there is no movement on issues of school integration in Vukovar.

When we looked to the qualitative data, we found that many objections to school integration were grounded in two basic, but related, fears: fear of conflict and of loss of identity. In Vukovar, the fear of renewed conflict permeates much of the discussion, although there is also evidence that Serb adults, and especially Serb leaders, fear a loss of their culture and traditions. In Mostar, the Croats, who are least in favor of school integration, are motivated primarily by the threats to their identity.

Fear of conflict in Vukovar

Although more in favor of integration than Vukovar's Croats, the Serbs expressed reservations. They voiced strong fears that integration of the schools would lead to increased violence. The students seemed more afraid than the adults, which perhaps explains why they were more opposed to integration. As one Serb student put it: "The war may be almost forgotten in other parts of the country, but not here. I think that

Table 11.2 *Survey Results*[19]

Town	National Group	Subject Type	School Integration[20]	History
Vukovar	Croats	Students	1.89	2.91
			(.72)	(1.23)
		Parents	2.43	2.72
			(1.01)	(1.27)
		Teachers	2.83	3.25
			(.80)	(1.06)
		S/P/T F-test	47.31***	5.31**
	Serbs	Students	2.22	3.61
			(.73)	(.78)
		Parents	2.78	3.79
			(.79)	(.62)
		Teachers	2.28	3.84
			(.69)	(.56)
		S/P/T F-test	56.92***	7.78***
	T-tests Croat vs. Serbs	Students	−6.17***	−9.25***
		Parents	−5.92***	−16.54***
		Teachers	3.45**	−3.64***
Mostar	Bosniaks	Students	2.87	3.39
			(.64)	(.92)
		Parents	3.26	3.42
			(.60)	(.94)
		Teachers	3.52	3.15
			(.25)	(1.19)
		S/P/T F-test	31.56***	.9253
	Croats	Students	2.56	3.29
			(.70)	(1.12)
		Parents	2.54	3.60
			(.79)	(.85)
		Teachers	3.14	3.75
			(.51)	(.63)
		S/P/T F-test	11.56***	9.79***
	T-tests Bosniaks vs. Croats	Students	5.35***	1.13
		Parents	12.02***	−2.52*
		Teachers	3.03**	−2.65**

Table entries are mean scores with standard deviations in parentheses.
* $p < .05$
** $p < .01$
*** $p < .001$

there would be a lot of conflicts [in integrated schools and classrooms]. I mean, there are conflicts even now when schools are divided." He explained that he did not feel safe around Croat youth because he could not trust responsible adults to intervene to stop youth violence. He described how he watched a teacher stand by when his younger brother got into a fight with a Croat student. Serb students blamed politicians, the media, and others in the community for inflaming an already tense cross-national situation. They felt powerless to make changes themselves and thought change would take a substantial amount of time.

These fears are not entirely unfounded. The majority of Croat youth in the surveys and focus groups said clearly and unequivocally that they wanted their schools and classes to remain segregated. They voiced a strong dislike of Serbs and a desire not to be forced to associate with them. One student commented: "As far as I'm concerned, . . . let them go elsewhere. I don't care." Croat boys in one focus group voiced even more negative attitudes than individual Croat students did in their interviews.[8] It is clear from the field notes and transcripts that this was a difficult group, because the boys often seemed not to take the task seriously and may have been purposefully provocative. Also, peer pressure to express negative feelings about Serb youth was palpable. For example, one of the boys said: "Children should be taught from the beginning to hate Serbs . . . We saw in the war what they are like. These are not people at all [others laugh]. Well yes, like animals for what they have done." One way of interpreting these data is that the boys were deliberately provoking the group leader and did not mean what they said. Another reading based on the findings from the surveys and individual interviews recognizes that they were being provocative, but that the emotions expressed in the focus group, though extreme, easily could have had some basis in reality.[9] Croat adults also confirmed that a great deal of hostility toward Serbs still prevailed among Croat youth. "Most [Croat] pupils hate Serbs," a Croat teacher said. Another explained: "Children are strictly separating and distancing themselves from one another here. It seems as if those differences are irreconcilable . . . The wounds are still very, very fresh."

Like their Serb counterparts, Croat students feared that integrated schools would lead to increased conflict. A Croat student, who said he avoided Serbs whenever possible, had this to say: "[Segregated schools] work for me, and I think that it should stay like that, because if we go to the same schools, there might be national conflicts. There are already conflicts in the streets, and if we were together in the schools, it would probably be even worse." While Serbs fear the hatred of their Croat neighbors in the present, the Croats base their fear on memories of what happened in Vukovar during the war.[10] Croats feel that they cannot trust

Serb residents because many of them participated in war crimes during the armed takeover of the town. "Before the war, our parents were normal with the Serbs," said a Croat student. "Nobody was insisting on 'Serb–Croat' relations. They all sang together and did things together. But, as the war started, they cheated us . . . and we simply started to kill each other." In this story, the student sees no motivation for the Serbs' perceived betrayal; rather, the killing simply happened. And it happened suddenly. The possibility of sudden and unmotivated violence leaves the storyteller feeling profoundly unsafe.[11]

In spite of the students' fears of one another, there seemed to be some openness to the possibility of changing opinions. For the Croats, the openings are more evident in individual interviews than in the focus groups, suggesting that it is social pressure more than individual opinions that pose stumbling-blocks. One student said that he preferred segregated schools, but he would accept a change in policy: "If I must, I would adjust." He even suggested, "Maybe we should try [integrated schools]." The Serbs were even more optimistic, as one student explained:

I believe that if children went to school together, after some time, everyone would meet everyone else, and they would become friends. There wouldn't be any problems in the long run.

Both sides in Vukovar think the other wants the schools to remain segregated, and each makes assumptions about the reasoning of the other group. One of the reasons for Serb resistance to integration cited frequently by Croats was everyday Serbs' unwillingness to accept Vukovar as part of Croatia and a corresponding reluctance to identify with the state of Croatia. One mother explained that even though Serbs have lived in Vukovar for many years, they should be treated as an immigrant group that must become part of a new country to survive.

Some, like this Croat teacher, expressed even more strongly their assumption that Serbs did not want to identify with the state of Croatia:

Since this is the Croatian state, please listen to the lectures in the Croatian language . . . And if you want to go, then please go. No one will stop you! . . . If you don't want to [study in the Croatian language], then please cross [the border] – it is not far away.

These assumptions on the part of Croats about Serb students' views may be based on the public positions of Serb political leaders, given the lack of daily contact across groups. However, our data suggest that ordinary Serbs' views do not uniformly support the views of their leaders. This finding suggests the possibility of an opening where accurate information might influence misguided belief. While the Serbs say they want to maintain their cultural and linguistic rights, they see this as compatible with a desire to identify with the state of Croatia. In addition, Serb youth express more interest in identifying with the Croatian state than their parents do. In what might be surprising to their Croat neighbors, Serb students discussed the importance of learning the Croatian language and Croatian history, and the fact that they had chosen to live in Croatia, not Serbia. Serb girls in a focus group repeated the sentiments of some of their Croat neighbors, but substitute "I" and "we" for "they." One girl said: "If I don't want to learn . . . according to their program, we can simply go. Why should we live here if it doesn't suit us? We can always go to Serbia." Other students made such remarks as, "We are, after all, citizens of this state, and I can, as much as I want, wish the best for Serbia, but I still live here."

Fear of losing one's national identity in Mostar

While the survey revealed very little opposition to school integration in Mostar, it did show that Bosniaks were more positive about it than Croats. The interviews and focus groups also demonstrated that integration is divisive. While most Croats we spoke to in Mostar said they did not object to students of different nationalities attending school together, they were quick to assert that members of each group had a right to learn in their mother tongue. The qualitative data reveal that the willingness of Croats to accept integrated schools is predicated on the assumption that Croat students would have the option to attend schools taught in their language. One administrator said, "Anyone can come to the school who wants to, but they must respect the school rules. If it's a school using the Croatian language, they must respect the Croatian language." He went on to say that "the school must be national." The interviews and focus groups reveal that language is a significant stumbling-block to integration, and often is used by the Croats as a proxy for opposing school integration in Mostar.

Underlying the language issue is the fear on the part of Croats in Mostar that if they cave in to pressures to assimilate, they will lose their national identity. "It is true we feel pressure to assimilate," said a Croat teacher. "And we fear that the Croatian language will suffer or be lost in the process. So we have every right to request schooling in the Croatian language." Another teacher exclaimed, "Language is a part of the being, part of the identity of a people!"

In their focus group, Croat girls said they thought segregation was absurd but feared that integration would inevitably lead to curricular biases against Croats. "I think it's stupid the way we all have different textbooks," said one of the participants. "We all learn different things, but we're all living in the same state." However, she feared that new books produced in BiH would be biased against Croats:

Songs would be banned, Croatian patriotic songs about the Croatian homeland, about our people. They'd be banned. Why? We need to celebrate who we are. And for sure we'd have to read and learn some of theirs over there, but they wouldn't learn ours.

This student then said: "I personally wouldn't learn Bosnian or Serbian." Another agreed: "Nor would I." A third chimed in: "I'd only learn Croatian. It's my language. I know we live in BiH, and that we're together, but what's mine is mine." Although segregation seems absurd to them, these girls favor it because they cannot envision a workable integrated school system.

Like Croats in Mostar, Bosniaks often revealed internal contradictions in their thinking. Many Bosniaks said they favored Croats having a right to their language and culture and at the same time maintained that the Croatian and Bosnian languages were not very different; thus, language issues should not pose a problem in regard to school integration. Although they did not seem to see Croats' language rights as a threat to state-building in BiH, they said they wanted a united BiH. They did not want a divided country that allowed a separate Serb Republic or any other kind of separatism. One teacher put it this way: "We must build a single state, a single monolithic society, a uniform society." This teacher saw some measure of Croat assimilation and identification with the state of BiH as integral to that process.

The Bosniaks talked with enthusiasm about both the promise and the inevitability of school integration. One student said: "I think everyone is looking forward to the day when we'll all go to school together." Bosniak parents seemed to feel similarly, recalling the days of their youth with nostalgia and associating its integrated ways with a more civilized, modern, European way of life. One of the teachers offered a striking metaphor of interdependence:

Like the tree that we seed on the other side, it doesn't choose between Bosniaks' and Croats' water, but simply grows. So the student shouldn't just take the knowledge that is related to his nationality.

The Bosniaks were so serious in their desires for integration that many voiced concrete and sometimes carefully thought-out plans for how to integrate the schools. One of the students had attended an event held by a Norwegian NGO on the topic of school integration and from that experience developed a vision for linking students from both sides of the river. One of the parents was attempting to secure funds to begin a private, integrated, technology-rich international school for students from all national groups. One of the school administrators discussed his plan for phasing in integrated schools, first with students in the same school but separate classes, then with half of the teachers from each side teaching students from the other side, then putting the students together for extracurricular activities, and finally moving to fully integrated classes taught by a fully integrated teaching staff.

Teaching history

Survey respondents in both Vukovar and Mostar agreed that history should be taught in ways that are not offensive to any ethnic group. However, there were significant differences between groups about how strongly they agreed (Table 11.2). In every community, except the Bosniaks in Mostar, teachers were the most positive. In Vukovar, Serbs agreed more strongly than Croats. In Mostar, Croat adults agreed more strongly than Bosniak adults, while there was no significant difference between students.

According to the interviews and focus groups, two fears underlie opinions about teaching history. One is the fear that the past will be forgotten. The other is the fear that the way schools officially promote remembering will be inconsistent with the beliefs of some groups and will cause more problems. Vukovar Serbs insisted that history contains multiple truths, depending on one's experiences and point of view. They feared that if a Croatian version of history were introduced into the schools, Serbs would be vilified. This fear explains why surveys revealed that Serbs preferred inoffensive versions of the past. But what they really wanted was to forget the past. Meanwhile, the Croats tended to be more conflicted about remembering and forgetting. Although they recognized that Serbs have their version of the past, most considered the Serb version to be wrong. They seemed less concerned than their Serb neighbors about the importance of an inoffensive version of history, mainly because they were confident that the Croatian version would be the one taught.

In Mostar, the Bosniaks wanted their truth told; they did not want it forgotten. The Croats, on the other hand, expressed concern that their perspective might not be included in new versions of the history curriculum. Although they did not want to forget the past, they worried about how a single curriculum could harmonize the views of the different groups. Most thought it could be done, but some disagreed.

Fears of forgetting and remembering in Vukovar

Most Serbs in Vukovar resisted any mention of the recent war in the history curriculum, since they feared they would become scapegoats. A Serb teacher explained: "It is well known that winners always write history [laughter]. So I'm afraid that . . . [whatever curriculum is developed] would insist too much on blame and guilt."

The Serbs talked a great deal about wanting to forget the past. Some things, a teacher insisted, "should be forgotten as soon as possible." In response to a question asking whether children should be taught about the recent war, another said:

The best thing to do, if only it was possible, would be to erase [everything about the past] so that all people, from the youngest to the oldest ones, can forget all about it. Grant God that we start living a normal life again.

The Serbs also called for adopting a future-oriented position. The adults, especially, feared that talking about the past would create more "splits" within their already divided city.

The Serbs did not think there was a clear truth about who was a victim and who was an aggressor. A student explained that every side has its own explanation and that what really happened is unknowable:

Every side has their own explanation as to why the war started. One side claims this, the other that, and it's up to you who you will believe. I don't know. We cannot know why, how, or who fired the first shot.

A Serb mother, while trying to allow for a middle ground between the different truths, eventually doubted the possibility of compromise:

You know what, everybody has his or her truth. And they are all truths for the one who interprets the truth. However, the truth is somewhere in the middle. I do not know. Now that, too, is debatable. Very debatable.

Another mother noted the limitations of objectivity:

I think that our brains are not that universal to understand what is actually most correct . . . I don't know what universal truth is. So how could anyone else know?

Serbs, fearing that the Croat version of the war might be forced on their children, expressed anxiety that the new textbooks scheduled for 2003 would have an anti-Serb slant and would blame the war on the Serbs. Indeed, many Serbs felt that Croats blamed them personally for what happened – a burden they were unwilling to assume. A student explained his lack of interest in learning about the recent war and his desire to blame others in the community:

We shouldn't talk about [the recent war in school]. We should forget everything that was . . . Why should we pay for the mistakes that, I don't know, our politicians, people in high places, have made?

The Croats voiced multiple opinions about remembering the past but were more in favor than the Serbs of teaching the history of the war. They were unconcerned whether what was taught was offensive to Serbs. While most Croats recognized that there were different versions of what happened, many teachers and every parent we interviewed said that "the truth," meaning their truth, should be taught. One teacher, when asked what should be taught, said:

The truth and nothing but the truth. [The Serbs] should learn what it was like. They should learn that Croatia was a victim that suffered and lost the most, that it was attacked by the aggressor, the then Serbia, with the help of the then Yugoslav army which was disintegrating.

Some Croat teachers disagreed, saying that the war should not be taught in school, because what happened was too complicated for young people to understand, and that young people should not be burdened. They also noted that many young people already knew about the war, both from first-hand experience and from what they learned at home and in the community. All of the Croat students with whom we spoke said that the war should be addressed in schools, and many discussed their resentment of the adults' unwillingness to talk about past events.[12]

Fears of forgetting and remembering in Mostar

The Bosniaks in Mostar, like the Croats in Vukovar, tended to think of themselves as the primary victims of the war. This view led them to stress the importance of keeping the memory of what happened alive, as they feared the past would be forgotten. One teacher went as far as to say that he would teach about the war, even if it were illegal to do so:

I will tell you, I am free enough to talk about this to my children, regardless of whether I am legally bound to remain silent about history. If I am legally obligated not to talk, I will not stay quiet, because history is universal, and everyone should be aware of these facts. The law shouldn't prevent professors from teaching their pupils about truth and values.

Most of the Bosniak students stressed the importance of learning about the war. As one explained:

I think the people should know all that and remember it, so future generations don't forget . . . It should never be forgotten. It's always in the subconscious and children should know about it too.

In talking about what parents want their children to be taught about the war, one teacher said:

Children know who the aggressor on BiH was, who the perpetrators are, [and] what the reasons are for that, why the crimes were committed, why their dearest suffered so much, their close relatives hurt. Parents simply want that memory not to be erased, because it is the same crime, perhaps even bigger, to forget as it is to commit the crime.

Although they recognized the fact that other perspectives exist, many Bosniaks spoke about wanting their truth told. Teachers feared that changes in textbooks could contradict the Bosniak point of view. They mentioned the fact that the word "aggression" had been blackened out as part of the removal of offensive material. One teacher asked, "What other expression [could] replace it?" Such talk is consistent with the findings in the survey, in which nearly a quarter of the Bosniak teachers were unconcerned about offending others when teaching history.

Many teachers were apprehensive about whether multiple truths could be reconciled. They thought their version was the most correct, and they found validation from the international community. One history teacher invoked the work of the International Criminal Tribunal for the former Yugoslavia as proof:

If the International Tribunal in The Hague said that there was aggression on my country, then I cannot say to my pupil, "Wait a minute. I don't know if it was like that, or if it was not." . . . All in all, we should tell the truth to children.

Like the Bosniaks, Mostar's Croats also wanted the history of the war taught. However, they tended to believe that they should be entitled to teach a Croatian version of events. They were less likely than the Bosniaks to think of their perspective as the single, objective truth. Ironically, in Mostar, nearly everybody with whom we spoke, regardless of national affiliation, noted that there are multiple versions of past events, and that objectivity is elusive.

Some Croats felt that each national group should be entitled to teach its own version of the recent war. One school administrator said that the international community's efforts to create "unitarianism [*sic*] in history" were detrimental to BiH's ability to "survive . . . as a democratic, pluralistic, equal state of all three constituent peoples." A Croat teacher felt that any effort at harmonization would be impossible because it would necessarily discriminate against one of the groups:

All three sides claim that they are the winner. So now, history should tell the truth, and here would be needed three truths. And these three truths no one can unite, meaning that it would always mean that someone would claim that [his truth] is endangered.

Most, however, while noting the difficulty in doing so, thought that harmonizing the various perspectives within one, unified curriculum was important. Many said that the task of reconciling the different versions should fall to those who could attain some measure of objectivity, although they differed on who that might be. The majority felt that, with the passage of time, historical objectivity could be achieved. A history teacher said, "We need a little time to go by before we historians know that the truth could be written about [the past war]." Others thought that it would be unnecessary to wait for such objectivity, that experts, whether historians or politicians, should be able to harmonize the curriculum. One Croat teacher appealed to a higher authority, saying: "It's hard now to satisfy everyone . . . I think that there must be some higher authority that will say what is needed and how."

Croat students tended to think differently from their teachers and parents about the recent past; they expressed feelings of wanting to learn about the war, with less concern about offending other groups. One student noted that the extent to which the war is currently mentioned is not satisfactory, saying that teachers present facts and figures without "really talking about it to us." Another student recommended that students research the war as a school project. In envisioning this project, she said: "It should be considered from all three points of view, and the Internet should be used, to see how other countries saw this war."

Tensions about school integration and the teaching of history

School integration and the teaching of history have presented school administrators in Mostar and Vukovar with two dilemmas. Underlying each of these dilemmas are tensions between equally desirable but conflicting goals – supporting ethnic culture and language, and developing a common identity. While these tensions are not easily resolved, we propose that a more thorough understanding of these dilemmas as they manifest themselves in each city can generate critical insights that will be useful in evaluating the promise and pitfalls of post-war educational reforms.

School integration and conflicts in social identity

At times of ethnic conflict, the only security often lies in a strong sense of belonging to one's own group. In the midst of chaos, identification with the group offers an illusion that survival is possible. For many, in the face of threat, circling the wagons becomes the only choice. When the conflict ends, the barriers that have been erected are not easily demolished. A tension exists, then, between a state's need to inculcate a state identity among its citizenry so as to foster peaceful coexistence and the importance of upholding cultural rights that will enable national groups to preserve their identities. Tensions arise because minorities and national groups fear that the promotion of a unified state identity will involve forced assimilation and the subsequent denial of their histories, literatures, languages, and cultural practices. Given the close relationship between social identity and culture, the schools can become a battleground in which the possibility of a common civic identity is challenged. While it may be important to establish and protect separate group rights, over-protection resulting in segregated schools and separate languages might lead to hostile separatism that can hinder the development of a common state identity and undermine the legitimacy of shared institutions. Efforts to integrate schools must address these fears and the conflicting imperatives that underlie them.

In BiH, where there are three constituent peoples, this tension between state and national group identity challenges efforts to protect the rights of all citizens. National groups, such as the Croats in Mostar or the Serbs in the Republika Srpska may identify more powerfully with (respectively) Croatia and Serbia, the states that embody their group origin. Indeed, current stalemates in the process of forming a multi-national state have even led some to question the very viability of the state of BiH.[13] In Croatia, this tension poses a severe challenge for efforts to develop a state identity that is inclusive of minority national groups that live within its borders, particularly of Serbs. The problem for Croatia is that education policies for national minorities make no distinction between the groups. It is hard, indeed, for the Serbs, who may constitute some 200,000 people, to be equated with the Hungarians, who constitute some 15,000. Furthermore, the Serb population has recently fought and lost a war. It can perceive this equation as a denial of its heritage and experience and, thus, as a threat. How to assure minority rights and respond to the specific needs of a vanquished group poses a unique challenge for Croatia, and the stakes are high.

The morass of social identity politics is further confounded by the processes of normal child development. In Eriksonian terms (see Weinstein and Stover, Introduction, in this volume), the challenge of adolescence lies in forming a secure individual identity in the context of peer relationships. The school setting can be a battleground, a forum for teasing, bullying, forming fast friendships, sexuality, codes of dress, experimentation, and moral development. In these critical years, school experiences mold how young people see themselves and how they see others. If ethnic group identification is the most important dimension of who a person is, and if stereotyping becomes the modus operandi for defining people, then the future of the country will assuredly exclude tolerance and integration, and a new generation of bigots will emerge. However, it is similarly dangerous to suppress ethnic group identification altogether. For schools and for the state, the dilemma is how to promote the development of multiple identities. School integration, then, involves far more than mixing people together across ethnic lines. Post-conflict societies will not achieve any form of reconciliation unless the schools as systems of influence on individual and social development are included in the processes of societal change.

History, education, and memory

In a recent book, *The Politics of Memory: Transitional Justice in Democratizing Societies*,[14] Alexandra Barahona de Brito and colleagues write: "Memory is a struggle over power and who gets to decide the future." Citizens of the former Federal Socialist Republic of Yugoslavia were brought up with an official history that blurred the events of the Second World War – in particular, the actions of Tito's Partizans.[15] There is a profound mistrust of historical documentation as evidence. Historiography more likely reflected choices about the best light to place on events or how to use the culture, traditions, and experiences of specific groups to create the myth of "Brotherhood and Unity." Yet the opportunity exists for schools to provide a forum to combat falsification or amnesia. In the classroom, suffering can be acknowledged and the origins and consequences of past events can be debated and analyzed. Schools must confront the dilemma of deciding which is the lesser of two evils. On the one hand, when there is no consensus on the circumstances or causes of past conflicts, dwelling on the past can be divisive and open to manipulation. On the other hand, attempts to leave the past behind, without any public acknowledgment of responsibility, can be equally problematic. If past crimes are not examined and acknowledged, people may become more vulnerable to manipulative rhetoric and more prone to suspicions and fears.

The greatest challenge facing public education in Croatia and BiH today is the development of unified history curricula that will be appropriate for children of all national groups. These curricula must deal with the facts surrounding the recent wars and with the history of ethnic relations in each country. This task is made even more difficult by the multiple and incongruous perspectives held by the different groups living within each state. While it might be possible to design history curricula taught through multiple perspectives that elicit active student participation, the Communist legacy in the field of education is strong both in Croatia and BiH. As such, there is another barrier to change: the predominant pedagogy in both countries is didactic and authoritarian, with little room given to discussion. Students commonly expect to learn a singular, unitary "truth" from their teachers. Challenge, debate, and analysis are discouraged and could be seen as provocative. If there can be only one "official" truth regarding past events, the particular memories of each sub-group will be either denied or repressed. When one side's heroes are considered another side's war criminals, a unitary telling of history that is inoffensive to all groups necessarily will be incomplete.

Conclusions

In spite of their differences, there are important similarities between the Serbs and Croats of Vukovar and the Bosniaks and Croats of Mostar. These similarities provide a foundation that can contribute to reconstructing the societies of these towns. In Vukovar, members of both groups have lingering fears of the other brought on by the war, leading to profound distrust. They fear violence among the youth if the schools are integrated; they care about the education of the youth; they care about preserving their language and culture but also want to be responsible citizens of Croatia; they blame politicians for maintaining and encouraging segregated schools; and finally, members of both groups feel powerless to make change.

In Mostar, members of both groups favor integrated schools and classrooms; they believe that the other group has a right to its own language and culture; and they want to be part of modern Europe, with its prospects for economic advancement. Most importantly, members of neither group feel overtly hostile toward members of the other group.

Based on these findings, we offer the following suggestions.

Vukovar

To make progress with respect to social reconstruction and resolving dilemmas about the school in Vukovar, the Serbs and Croats through public debate and their elected representatives need to reach a consensus on what the concept of minority rights entails. Croats believe Serbs deserve minority rights, but the data suggest that they think these rights can be satisfied by simply allowing the Serbs to live in Croatia and to preserve their culture on their own without interference from the state. Serbs want their culture to be recognized and in some cases supported by the state. Such a consensus is integral to finding a common ground on the structure of public education.

Further, in order for integration to succeed, a series of confidence- and trust-building exercises at the local level must be organized to help the

Serb and Croat populations learn to work together. These are needed for parents, teachers, and students, and should consider the different experiences of each group. These exercises might be led by NGOs (domestic or international) or by specially trained teachers from each ethnic group. Additionally, any plan for integration needs to include ensuring the safety of students. Our interviews suggest strongly that violence remains just below the surface and that students feel unsafe. Adults must take responsibility for the safety of the youth.

A curriculum could be developed to support students in recognizing the importance of tolerance and human rights, and their own barriers to achieving those goals in Vukovar. Such a curriculum would need to include democratic content as well as democratic ways of teaching, such as holding debates in the classroom and the community. The implementation of such a curriculum has implications for teacher education as well as for student learning. Finally, the effects of any new history curriculum that is introduced will need to be closely monitored. It will be important to see how the teachers, students, and parents respond to new textbooks, and to examine what actually is taught and learned.

Mostar

Schools and classrooms in Mostar should be integrated in a timely fashion. Our findings reveal that while the Bosniaks are ready for integration, Croat youth are neutral on the issue of school integration, but their peer culture fosters an anti-integration stance. It would be helpful to build on the neutral or positive orientation of the youth before the peer culture pushes these predispositions in a negative direction.

As part of plans for school and classroom integration, work must be done with the Croat community to help its members feel secure about fostering a Croat national identity outside of school as well as in integrated schools and classrooms. One approach to helping the Croat community feel more secure might involve consultation with educational linguists about options for maintaining a home language in an integrated school system, for example through examining successful programs used in other multi-lingual countries that could serve as models for Mostar schools. Further, increased opportunities for contact are needed that are designed specifically to help break down negative stereotypes. Given the geographic separation for most Bosniaks and Croats, the two groups have few opportunities to interact.

Finally, a curriculum for teaching history could be developed in ways that teach students to explore multiple perspectives and to interpret historical sources. Such a curriculum would need to include attention to critical thinking and democratic methods of teaching. It also would have implications for teacher education.

Schools in these two cities have become lightning rods for the political and ethnic conflicts that permeate the larger society. As critical settings for socializing the youth during an important developmental period, the conflicts have intense consequences. Finding solutions assumes special urgency.

NOTES

We would like to thank the staff of Centar Za Mir for their assistance with data collection in Vukovar. We especially thank Branka Kaselj for organizing the project and Snjezana Kovacevic for supervising the work. We also thank the Human Rights Center in Mostar for their support in collecting data in Mostar.

1. Gordon Allport, *The Nature of Prejudice* (Cambridge, Mass.: Perseus Publishing, 1988). According to Allport, the "contact hypothesis" operates if there are common goals, intergroup cooperation, institutional support, and equality of status.
2. See Ann Low-Beer, "Politics, School Textbooks and Cultural Identity: The Struggle in Bosnia and Hercegovina," *Paradigm* 2:3 (2001) for a good discussion of the educational structure in all of BiH.
3. Ibid.
4. Vedrana Spajic-Vrkas, "Visions, Provisions and Reality: Political Changes and Education for Democratic Citizenship in Croatia," *Cambridge Journal of Education* 33:1 (2003): 33–51.
5. See Global IDP Database, "UNTAES Agreements for the Danube Region Provide the Protection of the Serb Minority" (2000). Available on the World Wide Web at http://www.db.idpproject.org/Sites/IdpProjectDb/idpSurvey.nsf/ 1c963eb504904cde41256782007493b8/6083d813ce17671ec 1256993003597f1?OpenDocument
6. Drago Hedl, "Croatia: Painful History Lessons," *Balkan Crisis Report* 432 (May 23, 2003). London: Institute for War and Peace Reporting. Available on World Wide Web at http://www.iwpr.net/index.pl?archive/bcr3/bcr3 200305 432 2 eng.txt.
7. When the survey results were analyzed, factor analyses yielded a number of scales about varied issues related to schooling. Those results will be published separately.
8. Despite repeated attempts, we were unable to recruit Croat girls to participate in a focus group.
9. In the surveys, the Croat boys hold the most negative attitudes toward school integration of any group (1.78). Another survey item asked students whether they agreed or disagreed with the statement, "It is not important to me what the national background of my friends is." The Croat boys were the only group that, on average, disagreed with the statement.

10. See Stover, Chapter 5 this book.
11. See Ajdukovic and Corkalo, Chapter 14 this book, for a fuller explanation of issues of trust and betrayal.
12. For a fuller discussion of this tension between the youth and adults in Vukovar, see Sarah W. Freedman and Dino Abazovic, "Growing up during the Balkan Wars of the 1990s." In C. Daiute, Z. Beykont, G. Higson-Smith, and L. Nucci (eds.), *Global Perspectives on Youth Conflict and Development* (New York: Oxford University Press, in press).
13. Michael Ignatieff, *Empire Lite: Nation-Building in Bosnia, Kosovo, Afghanistan* (Toronto: Penguin Canada, 2003).
14. Alexandra Barahona de Brito, Carmen Gonzalez-Enriquez, and Paloma Aguilar, *The Politics of Memory: Transitional Justice in Democratizing Societies* (Oxford: Oxford University Press, 2001), 38.
15. In a June 2000 interview, a former Yugoslav Communist Party official in Mostar told one of the authors: "There were attempts of pushing away, pushing aside some events. I was not only the witness but also the actor, the protagonist of some of these activities. We did not allow these events to be turned into myths, for the sake of reconciliation and life itself."
16. The teachers were mostly those who teach the "national" group of subjects (particularly national language and literature, history, geography, music and art) and/or religion, ethics, or democracy and human rights. The principals, their deputies, and pedagogues who were in charge of curriculum were also part of the teacher sample.
17. At the time of the writing of this chapter, the teachers in the Bosnian language schools were on strike. These data had not yet been collected.
18. It is likely that subjects were included in more than one sample.
19. The history scores are based upon a single item, whereas the school integration scores are based upon a scale computed by averaging scores from eight items dealing with school integration. All survey items indicate the level with which a subject agreed or disagreed with a given statement, and were scored between 1 (strongly disagree) and 4 (strongly agree). Thus a score of 2.5 represents the neutral point. Survey items are available upon request.
20. The school integration scale reported here is different from those produced in the separate factor analyses of each town's data, as these analyses produced scales that did not include identical items. Rather than use two different scales with empirical bases, we chose to construct a single scale with a theoretical basis to increase comparability between the two towns' data.

12   Confronting the past in Rwandan schools

Sarah Warshauer Freedman, Déo Kambanda, Beth Lewis Samuelson, Innocent Mugisha, Immaculée Mukashema, Evode Mukama, Jean Mutabaruka, Harvey M. Weinstein, and Timothy Longman

> Rwandans need to talk about their experiences, not just an imagined history, but what actually happened to them. That means they have to tell the truth.
>
> Rwandan professional, May, 2002

Shortly after the Tutsi-led Rwandan Patriotic Front (RPF) took power in July, 1994, the Rwandan Ministry of Education (MINEDUC) placed a moratorium on teaching Rwandan history in the country's schools until consensus could be reached on how history should be taught. Almost a decade later, this emergency measure remains in effect. There is much disagreement among government officials, intellectuals, and Rwandan citizens about the significance of the events leading up to and occurring during the war and genocide. So there is little agreement about what historical account to teach. In making their case, government officials pointed to the fact that hundreds of highly educated Rwandans, including doctors, lawyers, teachers, and clergy had directly or indirectly participated in the genocide. According to the government, these professionals had been educated in post-independence schools that had taught a virulent form of ethnic hatred toward Tutsi.[1] "The propagandists," as Alison Des Forges wrote in her book on the genocide, "built upon the lessons Rwandans had learned in school."[2]

The difficulty and importance of making decisions about teaching history cannot be overemphasized. Further, the ways in which memory, history, myths, and symbols are used can lead people to develop identities that either promote intergroup conflict or help to draw diverse groups together. Just as distorted collective memories have been used to construct identities around division and differentiation, social identities might be constructed around commonalities in a way that encourages cooperation and cross-ethnic affiliation.

In recent years, the Rwandan government, while not rescinding the moratorium on teaching national history, has come to recognize that if schools can be used to promote ethnic divisions they can also be used to foster national unity. The MINEDUC, along with several non-governmental organizations (NGOs), has initiated a number of projects to revive the teaching of history in Rwandan schools. These projects have included the development of a provisional curriculum on human rights,[3] national symposia on the teaching of history,[4] manuals, and teacher education for civics curriculum.[5] Despite these initiatives, no new history textbooks or teaching materials had been published in Rwanda by early 2004. Nor had Rwandan officials and policy-makers solicited the views and opinions of local people regarding their schools.[6]

In Rwanda, as in many countries, most attempts to approach curricular change are initiated from the top down. We wondered whether a better understanding of the hopes and fears of those most immediately affected by education would provide greater insight into the complexity of educational reform, and aid in the formulation of more democratic means with which to pursue a reform agenda. In 2000–2002, we set out to fill this research gap by interviewing 376 Rwandans, including teachers, school administrators, students, and parents, about the role of education in the teaching of past history, ethnicity, and reconciliation.[7] During the first phase of our study, we spoke with eighty-four people at six secondary schools, three general secondary schools, and three special schools for training elementary school teachers. The schools selected for study are located in three of the regions of Rwanda that we have described earlier in this volume: Save, Byumba, and Kibuye. Save, located in the southern part of the country near the university town of Butare, has been a region with a high Tutsi population, known for its cultural and educational institutions. During the early weeks of the genocide this region remained relatively peaceful, and many Tutsi from other parts of the country sought shelter there until armed militias arrived, killing thousands of residents. Byumba, in the north-east near the Ugandan border, has a predominantly Hutu population. This region experienced little genocidal violence because the invading RPF forces took control of the area early on in the war. Kibuye, situated by Lake Kivu in the west, experienced some of the worst violence. The area is now majority Hutu because most Tutsi residents lost their lives or fled.

In each school, we interviewed the school director, the head of curriculum, and students of different socio-economic statuses with different experiences during the 1994 violence, parents who represent a similar diversity, and teachers whose courses dealt with social values, including such topics as the Kinyarwanda language and literature; French or English language and literature; religion; and/or political education. We asked about the roles the schools currently play in contributing to national unity, about the roles the schools should play, about the successes and challenges faced in fulfilling these roles, and about the curriculum.

In the second phase of the study, we talked to 272 people in forty-two focus groups, seven in each of the three towns and an additional seven in each of three other provinces selected by the Rwandan team as somewhat different in experience and geographic diversity. The focus groups included five groups for students, one for parents, and one for teachers. The student groups of mixed Hutu and Tutsi ethnicity included one group each for males, females, and students who had left the country as refugees during the genocide. A fourth student group consisted mostly of Tutsi students who had survived the genocide and were recipients of FARG (Fonds d'Assistance pour les Rescapés du Génocide) scholarships. The fifth student group was for repatriated students who had left Rwanda immediately after the genocide and its aftermath and had recently returned to Rwanda. These students were recipients of MINALOC (Ministry of Administration and Local Government) scholarships and were mostly Hutu.

One of our earliest findings was how local constituencies, often out of the public eye, are themselves finding creative solutions for teaching about tolerance, human rights, and the recent past. In one community in Rwanda, for example, two schools have collaborated to develop extracurricular human rights clubs in which students study major documents, write stories and essays, and create artwork celebrating human rights. The leaders of these clubs have helped nine other secondary schools establish similar human rights clubs. As this initiative demonstrates, and in confirmation of what we have suspected, often those most immediately affected by education are the best positioned to advise educators about the complexity of educational reform. The views of local people can also be instructive to governments that wish to develop a reform agenda in an open, inclusive, and democratic manner.

Rwandan schools and school policies

During the genocide and massacres of 1994, the educational infrastructure in Rwanda was virtually destroyed. School buildings were demolished, stores of supplies decimated, and most devastating, approximately 75 percent of the teachers were killed during the violence or are in jail for allegedly participating in the genocide.[8] Tens of thousands of pupils were also killed or fled the country. Others witnessed killings, sometimes of their entire families, and remain too traumatized to study. Still others are incarcerated alongside adult offenders.[9]

Soon after the hostilities ceased, the international community began to assist in restoring Rwanda's educational system. A rebuilding campaign, funded primarily by the World Bank, provided schools with many essential needs, including safe and well-built classrooms. UNICEF and UNESCO provided basic teaching materials in Emergency Teaching Kits. By 2000, when we began our study, most of the schools had been rebuilt, but as our focus group participants described, serious infrastructure problems remained. Many schools had electricity, but only 20 percent of the primary schools had running water, and others had insufficient natural lighting and few books. Some schools had only a blackboard.

Today, Rwanda has three categories of schools: government-run public schools, private but publicly subsidized schools, and private schools. Purely government-run public schools are relatively rare. According to data collected in 1997, public schools serve 15.6 percent of the secondary school population. Privately subsidized schools (*libre-subsidé*) comprise the next largest group, with 30 percent of all secondary schools, and these serve 47.6 percent of the student population. They receive government funding to pay teachers, purchase teaching materials, and board students, but the management and administration of the school is carried out by a mission or a private group, such as a parent organization or a local non-profit group. Private schools are the largest group in number (51 percent) and are almost entirely supported by private funds. In 1997, they served 36.8 percent of students.[10] Many are owned by the Catholic Church, which began the national school system and has heavily invested in the educational system. While the Rwandan Government has its Ministry of Education, the Catholic Church also has a department of education that employs a large staff.

In spite of private and parochial assistance, access to education is far from universal. According to 1997 statistics, although a relatively high percentage of the student population begins primary school, approximately 70 percent drop out by age 12 or 13. In 1997, 47.3 percent of the population was illiterate.[11] No more than 19 percent of those who completed primary school in 1997 went on to secondary school.[12] There are places in the National University for fewer than 1 percent of secondary school graduates, although several private universities have been created since 1994.[13] A prominent goal of the MINEDUC, with assistance from UNESCO and UNICEF, is to increase access to schooling for the general population through the program "Education for All." Statistics show that rates of primary school attendance are increasing, from 65 percent in 1999 to 75 percent in 2000.[14]

Such progress notwithstanding, a severe teaching shortage still plagues Rwanda's educational system. By 1997, the percentage of qualified primary school teachers had fallen from 57 percent in 1992 to 32.5 percent, and the percentage of qualified secondary school teachers had plummeted from 63 percent to 33 percent.[15] To add to the teaching shortage, in 2000 the government summarily fired many uncertified teachers, who were later replaced by teachers from surrounding countries.[16]

Rwanda's schools are also seriously overcrowded, largely because student enrollment figures have risen significantly, while the number of qualified teachers has dropped well below acceptable figures since 1994. By 1997, the student–teacher ratio in primary schools averaged 57:1, while the ratios in secondary schools, which serve only 15 to 19 percent of students who finish primary school, were at 22:1.[17] Many teachers have expressed concerns about the lack of trained teachers, but with few results. Meanwhile, private and semi-private schools have helped alleviate some of the problems of overcrowding.

The cost of schooling is also a barrier for many Rwandan families who live in extreme poverty.[18] In a country where the gross domestic product (GDP) is US $260, many children are needed at home to tend the fields, mind the livestock, and generally help support the household. Many families cannot afford school fees and the cost of uniforms. The government has responded with education support funds; however, some students expressed concerns about the potential for discriminatory policies in allocating funds. Moreover, since 1994 many orphans have become the head of their household. Without adults to support them, they face particularly difficult financial obstacles. These problems are exacerbated by the fact that secondary schools and universities are often located so far from students' homes that students have the extra burden of paying room and board. While the government pays the fees for university studies at the National University of Rwanda (NUR), this is not the case at the private universities. These schools require tuition in addition to room and board, placing college studies beyond the reach of all but the few who gain admission to the national university or whose families have discretionary income.

Conditions in the education sector profoundly affect the progress that can be made on creating a history curriculum and teaching about unity and reconciliation. Experts cite lack of funding as a major impediment to developing curriculum. Insufficient funding for teacher education slows efforts to train teachers to use existing materials. Although many Rwandans told us that they understood the importance of teaching for peaceful coexistence, they also emphasized that schools should be addressing more immediate needs, such as increased assistance for students unable to pay their school fees and helping students develop skills that would lead to more jobs upon graduation. As a result, reforms aimed at developing a curriculum on Rwandan history and promoting reconciliation are in jeopardy of being sidelined in favor of programs that offer more tangible benefits, including computer equipment and training, improved physical facilities, and science laboratory equipment.

Teaching for unity and reconciliation

At first glance, the study participants seemed to agree on most issues. They expressed a desire for national unity and reconciliation where all Rwandans would feel that they are one people. Regardless of their ethnicity, focus group participants who were asked to define unity described it as mutual understanding and cohabitation, lack of mistrust, sharing a common Rwandan language and culture, and lack of segregation. No differences were observed between parents, teachers, and students.

Many participants felt that education, particularly the teaching of history and ethnicity, was an important means of achieving this goal. A school director who refused to state his ethnicity said: "The problem of ethnicity will be solved by a good education – education that doesn't separate people, which doesn't favor one group and disfavor another." Most participants said that education should include the teaching of tolerance and human rights. A focus group participant described the importance of teaching unity in this way: "Yes, ethnicity should be taught in schools, because it would help students see themselves as brothers and sisters and as Rwandans who should live in harmony, with love for one another." Many focus group participants suggested that the teaching of ethnicity should move beyond the commonly discussed categories of Twa, Tutsi, and Hutu and include older and encompassing categories with which Rwandans identify, such as clans, of which there are eighteen throughout Rwanda. Participants frequently mentioned the country's clan structure when asked what they thought about the term "ethnicity." Students sometimes said they did not know what the term meant, or that they had learned that it no longer existed. One participant noted:

I went to solidarity camps. We learned about the origins of the so-called ethnic groups: Hutu, Twa, Tutsi. We were told that these don't really have a historical background; they were brought by Europeans (colonists) in order to rule us. Instead we had the so-called [clan names]: Abasinga, Abanyiginya, Abasigaba . . . which are the real ethnic groups Rwandans have.

Participants also maintained that education for unity and reconciliation should focus on distributing scarce resources and alleviating poverty.

"Personally," a parent said, "I would wish to have the youth discuss . . . the problems our country is facing, so that they can be able to initiate solving these problems . . . In order for this to be possible, such people should have the basic needs of food, shelter, and clothing to enable them to carry out their work." These responses indicate an awareness of and a promotion of social justice, and a basic agreement with the philosophy espoused by the current government.

In addition to this consensus over the importance of teaching about unity, most participants concurred in their assessment of ways that the government, schools, and the international community were fulfilling this goal. They felt that their schools were actively engaged in promoting reconciliation but described two problems: a lack of systematic curricula on the topic and teachers' lack of preparedness to teach these subjects, a gap in teacher education programs. Some individual teachers were covering a range of subjects, including justice, gacaca, human rights, ethnicity, democracy, current events, and history. Such topics were also being discussed in professional seminars, workshops, and conferences.

According to the participants, schools were also promoting reconciliation in their efforts to help students cope with the effects of the violence-related trauma, including unpredictable crying, fearfulness, depression, hallucinations, and insomnia. As one teacher explained: "The scars are still open, and they are not healed yet." Schools help students by assigning teachers to keep children with such problems close to them for counseling. When this approach fails, they refer students to specialists in trauma counseling. Some focus group participants worried, however, that the efforts to deal with trauma were generally ineffective and sometimes even punitive. Teachers do not possess the knowledge to adequately respond, leading a student to express concern that so-called inappropriate comments by a troubled student may lead to dismissal rather than assistance. One student, who was a genocide survivor, explained:

If a child suffers from post-genocide trauma and he seeks some advice from the teacher, the latter won't explain to him how to deal with his problem; and then the student will have to take a disciplinary leave of absence, supposedly because he made inappropriate comments!

The Rwandan government also supports many efforts to promote unity and reconciliation outside the schools, including solidarity camps and other government-organized workshops. Participants reported that campers are taught about unity, reconciliation, Rwandan history, economic development, human rights, and self-defense. Some gave detailed accounts of the lessons they learned:

We learned that before colonization, Rwandans lived on good terms. Clichés of Hutu farmers and of Tutsi stockbreeders did not exist. The man who owned a lot of cattle, whatever the ethnic group he belonged to, was a Tutsi, and the one who was poor, even if he had been a Tutsi, became a Hutu.

Other efforts include youth programs and conferences run by the National Commission for Unity and Reconciliation, as well as programs organized by national and international NGOs. Although there was some ambivalence about the role of the international community in rebuilding the country, most still felt that international governments and NGOs could assist by providing instructional materials and funding.

A further effort by the MINEDUC to promote reconciliation in the schools has met with widespread approval. Participants pointed to a perceived improvement in merit-based admissions policies as a positive indication that admission to secondary schools and the NUR is now fair and no longer based on political affiliation, ethnic identity, or regional quotas. Participants were pleased with the transparency of the current admissions process, and spoke favorably of the national examination council responsible for developing and administering national examinations and making the results public. A Tutsi student observed that: "I can say that education has progressed, because ethnic discrimination no longer exists as it did long ago when a Tutsi child could not go to secondary school because his spot was given to a Hutu child. But now, this is no longer the case." A Tutsi parent noted:

One of the major changes in schools is the transparency in the running of the schools, especially in the admission of students. These days your child can be confident enough, on the basis of the previous performance, to tell a parent to start buying secondary materials even before the examination results are released. This implies that if a student is capable of passing national examinations, the admission into secondary schools is assured. Today, admission in schools is based purely on merit, unlike in the past, when it was not transparent but based on one's ethnicity or which part of the country you originated from.

A Hutu teacher who had participated in scoring the exams said: "It is done in transparency, and the best students absolutely pass. There is no partiality."

Tensions over curricular content: history and ethnicity

Despite general agreement about the importance of promoting unity and reconciliation, and despite the current efforts in the schools, several tensions surrounding the proposed history curriculum emerged in our interviews. These tensions suggest that basic understandings of the means and rationales for promoting unity vary widely among Rwandans. These tensions also pose a threat to the ultimate success of efforts to promote unity.

When asked to discuss their views about what should be included in a new history curriculum, many participants responded with some discomfort. Much of the anxiety stemmed from continuing conflicts over how to deal with the topic of ethnicity. Despite general agreement about the importance of promoting unity and reconciliation, ethnicity was still very much at the forefront of people's thinking, whether their origin was Hutu or Tutsi. Teaching history and issues of ethnicity are closely linked in the minds of Rwandans.

Discussions of ethnicity in Rwanda are extraordinarily complex, since official government policy denies its existence in the country. This policy, promulgated by a powerful central government, may explain why several participants refused to acknowledge their ethnicity. It is also possible that these participants truly believe that ethnicity is an evil concept that must be dispensed with.[19] However, participants in a number of the focus groups were more inclined to talk about ethnicity than interviewees.[20] Like-minded peers may have enabled that discussion to occur. The comments below from the returnee focus groups gives an example of how much ethnicity is on everyone's minds, and how complicated this issue is for Rwandans:

- "It's not spoken and not expressed in people's identity cards, but I know it is still in their heads, and they express it through sentiments." (Female Tutsi student)
- "Ethnic issues cannot be abolished. They will always be there. The problem is using them in a wrong manner. So the problem would not be ethnicity, but how these groups live together." (Female Tutsi student)
- "The issue has changed form; it is like a volcano that is waiting to erupt in future, so Rwandans might be living together and after some time problems might arise." (Male student who refused to state ethnicity)

When students discussed ethnicity in ethnically homogeneous peer groups, such as those for repatriated Hutu students on government scholarships, they spoke in depth and revealed sentiments that others generally avoided. These Hutu students were frank about the possibility that ethnic discrimination still exists in Rwandan society, as a young woman in one of these groups said:

If you go and visit a family, you will be welcome; but as soon as you leave, people might say, "He is a pathetic Hutu, his family massacred the Tutsi." Whereas if it were someone else, they would say, "You know that he is one of ours!"

Another example is when you are seeking employment. There are places where you can't even get in someone's office, but when someone else shows up, he is welcome and he is hired. Even if you bribe them a great deal, you cannot be hired.

The exchange continued when a male student spoke up: "Another example is where I live . . . To get a taxi, Tutsi make you pay a fare many times higher than the fare others have to pay, or they will make fun of you." Another young man said: "At the bus station, someone gets off, watches the people who already took a seat in the taxi and says, 'I am not taking this cab. This is a cab for Tutsi' [if he or she is a Hutu] or 'This is a cab for Hutu' [if he or she is a Tutsi]."

Although some students who survived the genocide, mostly Tutsi, mentioned issues of discrimination, the mostly Hutu in other groups were far more likely to bring them up. This suggests that the Hutu scholarship students were more likely than the Tutsi scholarship students to be aware of and affected by inconsistencies between official policy, which legislates equal treatment of all groups, and everyday life for people of different ethnicities.

No respondent in either interviews or focus groups said that the topic of ethnicity and its consequences is taught officially in schools. Some noted that it is discussed in political education classes and in extracurricular activities such as human rights clubs. As one student put it, "Some do talk about ethnicity, while others do not. It all depends on the teacher and the topic under discussion at that time." In general, however, the people to whom we talked hoped that if the issue of ethnicity were dealt with in the schools, it would be handled in a way that would serve to advance the cause of unity and reconciliation.

Study participants seemed conflicted about whether schools should recognize that differences in ethnicity exist. While thirty-nine interviewees (48 percent) felt that differences should be recognized, and fifty-five (67 percent) felt that differences should be ignored, 25 percent of these respondents expressed both views in the course of their interviews. Another 7 percent did not voice their views on ethnicity at all.[21] These differences did not appear to be related to the ethnicity of the respondent. While most have clear opinions and while a small minority remained silent, a sizeable percentage seemed to hold internally conflicting views of ethnicity. For example, one of the teachers we interviewed said: "Ethnicity is a good issue, for everyone has his/her origin . . . It is something that makes a person known, that makes him or her the same as or different from others." But at another point in the interview this same teacher explained: "While teaching gospel, we tell students that they are all God's children, that all ethnicities are the same." The teacher has encapsulated the dilemma of recognizing the need for social identity while at the same time acknowledging its exclusionary limitations that might lead to social inequalities or even violence.

Most focus group participants agreed on the importance of teaching about ethnicity in the school curriculum, but also felt strongly that the curriculum should examine the origins of ethnicity in Rwanda, how the concept of ethnicity had been manipulated in the past, the effects of such manipulation, and how Rwandan youth can avoid the same mistakes. Some participants felt that recognizing and teaching about ethnicity was essential. A Tutsi student presented this point of view:

> I think that we must teach them . . . If Rwandan history is taught and ethnic groups are not mentioned, something would be missing . . . But if we don't explain it, children would always wonder why Hutu killed Tutsi. And also, they would know whether they are Hutu or Tutsi. Maybe they would think about avenging their own people. Ethnic groups should be explained so that we can reveal lies within the truth.

Those who agreed with this position emphasized the early origins of ethnic divisions in Rwanda. Similarly, a female teacher who refused to state her ethnicity felt that it was important to discuss ethnicity in order to move toward unity and reconciliation: "I would propose that each teacher begin his class by talking first about unity and reconciliation. And he cannot talk about unity and reconciliation without talking about ethnic groups." A Hutu parent put it this way:

> The question on ethnicity will be solved if children are taught about it. Children should stop harboring ethnic tendencies. Parents should tell their children that "I am a Rwandese; I have no problem with that Tutsi." A Tutsi should also say, "I have no problem with that Hutu." Let us put our efforts together and build our country.

A Hutu teacher said discussing the origins of ethnicity in Rwanda would help solve society's problems:

> The truth is, keeping quiet over an existing problem does not provide a solution to it. Being a Twa, Tutsi or Hutu is no problem. It's ok, but above all [you should] know that you are a Munyarwanda, a citizen of Rwanda. Let us not be fearful to talk about our ethnicities.

Despite agreement over the central role of ethnic conflicts in past violence, the interviewees and focus group participants held diverging opinions on the history of ethnic groups in Rwanda. Viewpoints varied somewhat by the ethnicity of the participants, and sometimes also by the ethnicity of the interviewer. Some participants expressed more than one opinion. According to one perspective, the three ethnic groups in Rwanda exist now and have existed from long ago. Thirty-nine interviewees (approximately 46 percent) gave responses that suggest they hold this belief. Hutu were more likely to endorse this position when they were interviewed by a fellow Hutu. The comments of a Hutu teacher reflect this view: "Ethnic groups have existed. Nobody can say that ethnic groups have not existed. They have existed, probably as we have learned in history. Except that, as it is said, to define a certain ethnic group is not simple." Another Hutu teacher suggested:

Let us talk about them in a different way. [We should] not say that such an ethnic group came to rule over the other, but rather [discuss] the origin of these ethnic groups. I do not even find the importance of erasing someone's ethnicity from his or her identity card. Let us talk freely about ethnicity, but not the way it used to be talked about in the past.

Although Tutsi were less likely to express this view (39 percent of the thirty-one Tutsi interviewees), a Tutsi student echoed the general view: "About ethnicity, we normally know that there exist three ethnicities: Hutu, Tutsi and Twa. I think all should not have tension between them but should instead have solidarity without any lying." When asked if she thought students should learn about ethnicity in school, another Tutsi student responded: "It would be good to teach about the different tribes, but not to emphasize that one is better than the other." Adherents to these views often emphasized that when Rwandan history is taught, it should help people understand their ethnic identities but should not be used to promote discrimination or disunity.

According to a second perspective, expressed by fifty-five interviewees (approximately 65 percent), ethnic groups in Rwanda do not exist, because the Hutu, Twa, and Tutsi don't fulfill all the necessary criteria of common definitions of ethnicity. All three groups speak the same language, Kinyarwanda, and all three share the same culture and live together in mixed communities throughout the country. Hutu interviewees were in the majority in this opinion. Most Hutu, 71 percent of all interviewed, spoke in favor of the official policy on ethnicity more frequently than they spoke in favor of recognizing differences and teaching about ethnicity, regardless of the ethnicity of their interviewer. Tutsi interviewees were also more likely to support the official policy, with 58 percent of them speaking in favor of it. Those who expressed this opinion favored forgetting about the history of ethnic groups and emphasizing a common Rwandan identity. They also feared that recognizing differences would encourage future conflicts. When asked if she would support lessons on ethnicity, a Tutsi student said:

When we consider physical aspects that distinguish a Hutu from a Tutsi or from a Twa, we make a kind of segregation between people. In this context, three parts are made, and Tutsi take their side, Hutu their side, and so do the Twa. That is why [ethnicity] shouldn't be taught and should even be removed and replaced by only the term "Rwandese."

Although this student proclaims the existence, even salience, of ethnicity, she argues that it should be ignored in the schools. Among the mostly Tutsi students supported by FARG scholarships, many expressed fears about ethnicity and similarly adhered to the position that all traces of ethnicity should be ignored. "If ethnic groups were taught, unity would disappear," said one student. "Students' ethnicity would be reflected in all that they own. No, we must not do it." Hutu students supported by MINALOC grants voiced this position too, as represented by this student from Byumba: "I believe that it should not be taught. Because in order to teach it, you have to give examples and say, for instance, this one is a Hutu, that one a Tutsi, when this is the very thing that we must avoid and fight."

Framers of a Rwandan history curriculum will have to decide how to deal with issues of ethnicity and how to present this complex topic to young people. A Rwandan history necessarily involves confronting facts about past ethnic conflicts, perhaps in ways that search for universal themes in situations of ethnic conflict around the world. Although ethnicity cannot be ignored, it must be treated carefully, so that lessons will be learned about the roots of conflict and the importance of equal treatment for all.

Tensions surrounding teaching methods

Tensions over how best to teach history also threaten to undermine continued progress toward a history of Rwanda that will promote unity. Our data revealed conflicting views over which teaching methods are appropriate for incorporation into the history curriculum. The responses of interviewees and focus group participants were quite similar, with a majority supporting a methodology that encourages open discussion and debate.

Approximately 20 percent (N = 15) of the interview respondents suggested an approach to teaching history that encourages critical analysis and debate. People who supported this approach tended to be Hutu. These interviewees argued that history should be taught in a way that would allow participants to discuss and sift through the pros and cons of the facts under study. A Hutu teacher felt that history should be taught:

We have students whose parents were killed during the genocide; we also have students whose parents are in prison due to genocide charges, but they must all meet in class and study together. Indeed, they generally all get along well. Very often, however, these students have been given a distorted history of the genocide and of the past from older people that may affect their relationship with their classmates, since the distortions prevent them from analyzing issues clearly.

A student who refused to state her ethnicity advocated debates about the history of Rwanda, noting that encouraging "different interpretations of events" would encourage students to see that history is not a simple, cut-and-dried topic and would perhaps prompt them to take greater interest in the subject. Another teacher, a Tutsi, and one of the few Tutsi who supported this view, pointed out that good teaching should invite students to think for themselves: "We teach our pupils where justice prevailed and where it did not in the history of our country so that they are able to judge for themselves how the history of our country came to be what it is." The leader of an extracurricular human rights club reported using a debate format so that students could discuss and express their opinions. This teacher felt that the methods used in history class – memorizing facts and dates – can promote misunderstanding.

In another example of encouraging critical thinking, a teacher of political education noted that the syllabus for political education suggests that teachers use group discussion in class. Students discuss a teacher-selected theme in small groups, and then present their topics to the class. During the subsequent debates, all students can give suggestions and ask questions. The teacher intervenes as moderator and facilitator. However, the syllabus also asks teachers to contact political leaders to obtain official positions on current issues.

A government education official supported a central role for debates in the history curriculum, stating that "the problem with our school system is that it has not encouraged free thought; it has not encouraged communication." He emphasized that students need to learn how to talk and listen to each other, and tolerate people with opposing views. In addition to this role in teaching history, he felt that in-class debates would be necessary for the development of a solid history curriculum. He also highlighted the need for consensus reached through open communication: "What is important to me is that the Rwandan people can come together . . . sit together, and decide what part of history they should teach their children."

Another 38 percent of those we interviewed (thirty-two interviewees total) felt that encouraging contentious discussion might invite disagreements and new conflicts. Of this group, approximately half were Tutsi and half were Hutu. A teacher commented that talking about history could make some participants feel uncomfortable, bitter, or angry with an ethnic group, since differing interpretations of events can lead to conflict. She also noted that politicians could use controversy to further their own plans, and expressed skepticism that the government could produce a history that would solve these problems.

For ten adherents of this perspective (12 percent of all interviewees or 31 percent of this group), the solution is to avoid teaching controversial topics and provide students with simple facts about Rwanda's past. Again, the ethnic breakdown was roughly divided equally (Tutsi – four; Hutu – five). One Hutu student expressed this viewpoint in the following way: "History deals with events. When you become a leader, you tell people the truth of all this." A Hutu parent expressed similar views:

I think students . . . must be told the truth about the events which occurred, because there are some of them who do not understand why. There are some who do not know why such things happened. So, firstly, we must tell the truth about genocide and how it took place. You have to explain it, how it occurred, and why it took place here. Truth first!

A Tutsi student in a focus group did not favor debates because she placed implicit faith in the views of the government as transmitted by the teachers: "They should teach history practically while elaborating how the events happened, identifying the culprits (who did it) and their justifications . . . The teacher . . . will give the reasons, which will have come from the Ministry of Education."

Implications for educational policy

Fairness and equal access to educational opportunities are crucial for promoting peace and social unity in Rwanda. The Rwandans to whom we talked seemed overwhelmingly satisfied that the current system is fairer than it was before 1994, and that for the elite population that reaches secondary school, there is good access to education for students from all ethnic groups. It is important to note that, since we talked only to secondary students, their teachers, and their parents, our conclusions about how Rwandans as a whole feel about access to education are limited. We did not hear from the approximately 80 percent of the population that never reaches secondary school. Future research is needed to see how those who do not have access to secondary education feel about issues of educational access.

Most participants felt that teaching about Rwanda's past is essential to ensure a safe and prosperous future for Rwanda. And further, while almost everyone linked teaching about history to issues of ethnicity, there was disagreement about what to teach and how to teach it. It is likely that this disagreement arises because those in power have used the history of Rwanda and its ethnic groups to manipulate public opinion and to bestow privilege by acknowledging certain groups at the expense of others. History is tied intimately to one's social identity, and many Rwandans see the distant and the more recent past through different lenses. This applies especially to people from different ethnic groups and to those who lived in Rwanda during 1994. In spite of their differences, Rwandans are searching for ways to use their history to move toward a more peaceful and unified future. They want to understand how different ethnic groups came to Rwanda, how they contributed to the building of the nation, and what was positive about past relations between groups. They also want to interpret the genocide and war of 1994 in ways that will allow them to build the nation. It remains difficult for many to focus on positive memories. It is also true that some official versions of the past do not ring true for all Rwandans.[22] All of these issues will need to be confronted as Rwandans make decisions about a history curriculum for the schools.

On the basis of our observations, we make several suggestions that reflect three areas to which attention might be directed – curricular content, classroom instruction, and teacher training. First, we suggest a national dialogue on history content that involves parents, students, and teachers and not solely academics or politicians. Parents possess great potential to make substantive contributions to the development of curricula. Possibilities for building this capacity should be explored further in future work on curriculum development. For instance, the role of parent boards and parent training programs might be expanded to make it possible for parents to contribute in ways that are helpful to the government and to the schools.

Second, we suggest that a national curriculum for history should ideally include participatory and democratic teaching methods that invite discussion and debate, so students can learn to think critically about competing views of history and ethnicity. An effective curriculum might invite students to examine available facts and draw informed conclusions from them. However, in instituting such a curriculum, it will be necessary to confront the fears surrounding this approach as well as the fears associated with teaching history, particularly in handling issues of ethnicity.

Third, a national curriculum for history should not be released without providing extensive preparation for teachers in its use. In-service and distance learning training to help teachers learn to use the curriculum comfortably should be made available. It will be important to help teachers not only with the substance of the curriculum but also with using participatory and democratic techniques of teaching in the classroom.

Finally, this is an opportunity to encourage and support the creativity that teachers can bring to unity and reconciliation. Several promising models for teaching history and ethnicity are currently being used informally in Rwanda in out-of-school settings. These models might be studied closely for effective practices that could be incorporated into a national curriculum. The designers of those models might make important contributions to future curriculum development and to the future of the country.

NOTES

1. Alison Des Forges, *Leave None to Tell the Story*: Genocide in Rwanda (New York: Human Rights Watch, 1999), 65–95.
2. Ibid., 72.
3. Republic of Rwanda, *Workshop Seminar on Reviewing and Harmonizing the Curricula for General Secondary Education (First Phase, Kigali, from 17 April to 22 May 1996)* (Kigali: Ministry of Primary and Secondary Education. Department of Studies and Pedagogical Research. With the assistance of the World Bank and the Government of Canada, 1996).
4. Université Nationale du Rwanda, Département d'Histoire. *Rapport General du Seminaire sur l'Histoire du Rwanda (Butare, 14–18 Déc 1998)* (Butare: Université Nationale du Rwanda, 1998).
5. Diyoseki ya Kabgayi, Catholic Relief Services, *Integanyamansomo y'ingando z'urubyiruko* (Kigali: Bureau of Population, Refugees and Migration, 1999).
6. Sarah Warshauer Freedman, *Preliminary Research on Issues of Justice and Reconciliation in Primary and Secondary Education in Rwanda* (Human Rights Center, University of California, Berkeley, 2001); Beth Lewis Samuelson, *Report on Data Collection Trip for Research on Isssues of Justice and Reconciliation in Primary and Secondary Education in Rwanda* (Human Rights Center, University of California, Berkeley, 2001).
7. The research project was jointly designed and conducted by researchers from the Human Rights Center at the University of California, Berkeley and the National University of Rwanda.
8. The most complete data on civil servants is found in Republic of Rwanda, *Study of the Education Sector in Rwanda* (rev. edn.) (Kigali: Ministry of Education, with support from UNICEF and UNDP, 1998), 13. This provides aggregate data on sectors of the government. We are assuming that the estimates for all public-sector employees apply equally to teachers.
9. "Rebuilding a Shattered System," *The Times Educational Supplement*, August 18, 1995.
10. Ibid.
11. Ibid., i.
12. Ibid., 76.
13. Ibid., 89.

14. Republic of Rwanda, "Workshop Seminar on Reviewing and Harmonizing the Curricula."
15. Republic of Rwanda, "Study of the Education Sector in Rwanda."
16. Even when teachers are considered to have appropriate qualifications, primary school teachers have only a secondary school education, with the last three years of secondary school the principal source of preparation for primary teaching.
17. Republic of Rwanda, "Study of the Education Sector in Rwanda."
18. For the Rwandan report on the Education for All effort, see Republic of Rwanda, *Education pour Tous, Bilan a l'An 2000* (Kigali: MINEDUC, 2000).
19. Some 14 percent of the interviewees and 30 percent of the focus group participants refused to state their ethnicity.
20. The fact that fewer focus group members identified their own ethnicity may be due to the fact that we asked them to provide the information on a written form. Our intention was to insure their privacy; however, in Rwanda, since identity cards and other written documents recording ethnicity have been outlawed, we now realize that participants may have hesitated because of the written nature of the request.
21. We counted the responses of interviewees to some questions which all answered. These statistics do not include focus group participants, because the nature of the conversations made it impossible to determine everyone's opinion on every issue.
22. See Longman and Rutagengwa, Chapter 8 this volume.

Part III

Survivors and justice

Justice and reconciliation often are touted as necessary steps for the rebuilding of a post-war society. But what do these abstract terms mean to individual survivors who find different ways of thinking about or remembering their experience? These reflections occur within and between people. Can survivors of ethnic conflict find common ground and work together to reunite their divided communities? And are there strategies that can help this process along?

The authors in Part 3 explore the long-term effects of war and how they become manifest in individuals and social groups. In Chapter 13, Pamela Blotner traces the work of several western artists who have used art to confront their own personal experiences of war. Based on interviews with Bosnian and Croat artists, she finds that many Balkan artists have focused their work on the importance of place, whether it be home, community, or nationhood. The age of the artists when they lived through the violence, Blotner suggests, determines whether these artists chose to reclaim or avoid place in their work.

In Chapter 14, Dean Ajdukovic and Dinka Corkalo, in an intensive study of survivors on both sides of the 1991 war in Vukovar, describe how the betrayal of neighbors has affected the process of reconciliation. Whether this is an accurate perception or not, any movement toward social reconstruction is sabotaged by the loss of trust that develops when neighbors are seen as betraying their friends. Re-establishing trust between erstwhile friends is more likely to take hold, they suggest, when both sides are willing to acknowledge and apologize for past crimes committed in their names and the victims (or their representatives) accept it. The authors conclude that trust, apology, and forgiveness facilitate the ability of a community to cope with the violence that engulfed them.

In Chapter 15, Jodi Halpern and Harvey Weinstein ask whether the dehumanization that occurs in ethnic war can be reversed. In this inquiry they look at the social-psychological process of empathy and ask how it can be used to rehumanize former enemies. They find that sustained empathy can develop only when the political and social environment allows, supports, and promotes it. The authors suggest that empathy after war is not solely an individual choice: a positive social context is critical.

13   Art out of the rubble

Pamela Blotner

By any stretch of the imagination, Alma Suljevic, 40-something with bleached blond hair and sporting orange lipstick, didn't look like a former soldier who had served in the Bosnian Army. "I didn't really want to join," she told me as we drank coffee in the lounge of the Sarajevo Artist Center. "But what else could I do? They were shelling my city and my neighborhood." During the war, Alma worked in a medical clinic that provided care to soldiers and civilians traumatized by the war. One day a young girl, felled by a sniper's bullet, was brought to the clinic, where she died in Alma's arms. It is a moment seared into her memory and one that has deeply affected her art. "Before the war, my art wasn't political," she tells me. "But now, what else could it be? I feel I have to say something."

Alma, like many other Bosnian artists, uses her art to reclaim spaces stolen by the war. One of her most acclaimed installations, "Annulling Truth," decries the fact that, even today, millions of land mines still litter the fields and mountains of Bosnia. The installation consists of several large maps of local minefields on which she has scrawled her traumatic memories of the war. Alma invites viewers to walk on the maps and talk about their reactions to the installation. If they wish, they can purchase an 8-by-10-inch color lithograph called "Certificat," or "certificate," depicting two hands cradling a PM1 anti-personnel mine. She donates sales from the lithograph to a demining team working on the outskirts of the city. At the bottom of the print Alma writes the name of the buyer, the amount of the donation, and the size of land that the donation will clear of mines.

"As artists we are a part of our environment, of our neighborhood, and of our city or village," she explained. "This is what I am trying to convey with my land mine installation. I don't want my work to be like 'Guernica.' People look at that painting and say, 'Oh, that's a great work by Picasso.' But they don't really think about the people who died in that Fascist attack. I don't want anyone to see my work and say, 'Oh, that's a piece by Alma Suljevic.' I want them to remember what happened to *our* city, and to *our* people. And I want them to do something about it."

Alma raises several questions regarding the role of artists and their art after war and mass atrocity. Is, for example, Alma's land mine installation mostly about her own tormented experiences of war? Or does it transcend the personal to help the residents of Sarajevo understand the conflict and what they must do, individually and collectively, to restore normalcy in their shattered city? In other words, can art contribute to the social reconstruction of a war-torn society?

In this chapter I address that question through the eyes of thirty Bosnian, Croat, and Serb artists and arts professionals that I interviewed during the summers of 2000–2001, some five years after the end of the war in the former Yugoslavia.[1] I look at their views in the context of the work of several western artists, who, throughout history, have used their art to respond to both their individual experiences and their societies' collective experience of mass violence. I suggest that artists gravitate toward certain themes in post-war settings based on the nature of the war, their age and past aesthetic, and their own experiences. Finally, I argue that artists, if given adequate resources, can play a significant role in post-war societies by helping their fellow citizens recognize that they should neither forget the past nor despair for the future.

Artists and their societies

Visual artists serve four fundamental roles in society. First, they record visual images of events so that they will be preserved for historical reference. Before the advent of still photography in 1839, for instance, artists provided the only form of visual documentation of important events in human history. Second, artists give tangible form to the unknown, to what cannot be seen with the eyes or has not yet occurred. Throughout history, artistic interpretation has been an essential aspect of most religions, from representations of deities and spirits and their lives to the creation of ceremonial objects and houses of worship. Third, artists give tangible form to human feelings and emotions. Art provides us with feelings that can be pleasurable or contradictory and disturbing. It fills the human need to communicate and to share intimate and collective experiences in an immediate and visceral manner. Finally, artists provide us with new and innovative ways of seeing the world.

Recording history

Throughout most of human history, artists have been the only visual chroniclers of war and its aftermath. This tradition stretches from the elegiac images of warriors in ancient art to medieval battle paintings to the "comic book novels" of the recent armed conflicts in the former Yugoslavia.

"War art" appeared in classical western art in various forms, including decorative household items, murals, friezes, paintings, and sculptures. Its purpose, with a few exceptions, was to chronicle battles and celebrate the glory of the warrior. Famous examples of this genre include the anonymous friezes of dying soldiers that span the Temple of Aphaia North in the Peloponnesian Islands; the Bayeux Tapestry, an enormous embroidered cloth history glorifying the Norman conquest of England in 1066; and the sprawling battle vistas painted during the Renaissance by Albert Altendorfer and Piero Della Francesca. The benefactors of such art were almost exclusively political, military, and religious elites who had a stake in the glorification of their armed exploits.[2]

By the early Renaissance, art about war began to develop different foci. The persistence of warfare and the resultant expansion of armies had given rise to the middle classes who, in turn, generated more spending power among common people. For the first time, artists were able to sell their art to a growing clientele. This trend was greatly assisted by the invention of the printing press in the mid-fifteenth century, which allowed artists to produce their images en masse and thus make them affordable and accessible to a wider audience. This new market gave artists the opportunity to choose their own subjects and express their own attitudes outside the normal constraints of patronage. Artists began to individualize and humanize images of the "common soldier," recording his preparations at home, his emotional departure to battle, and his life in camp and on the front line.

Giving form to the unknown and unseen

More often than not, war art has been made far away from where the actual events took place and well after the conflict has ended. For example, most of the art from the American Revolution (1775–1783), including Gilbert Stuart's famous painting of George Washington crossing the Delaware, was created years after the end of the revolt. One exception to this rule was the work of the Spanish painter, Francisco Goya. When Napoleon's troops marched into Goya's hometown of Madrid on May 2, 1808, much of the populace, mostly unarmed, resisted the invaders, but by day's end they were soundly defeated. The next day, at the city gate, Goya watched as French soldiers summarily executed the leaders of the resistance. Six years later, after Spain's liberation, the artist presented the Spanish government with his final rendering of the executions, entitled "The Third of May, 1808." The painting, along with Goya's later aquatint series, "Disasters of War," which included the first depiction of rape in wartime, remain some of the most poignant visual renderings of the horrors of war.

Few artists followed in Goya's footsteps. While American combat artist Winslow Homer and his protégés focused on the daily lives of individual soldiers going off to war, creating a sympathetic but dispassionate visual record of the American Civil War (1861–1865), their paintings eschewed the carnage that the soldiers themselves were describing in their diaries and letters home. It would take a photographer like Matthew Brady to bring home to Americans the hidden brutality of the Civil War. In 1862, Brady and a group of photographers under his supervision shocked Americans with their New York exhibit, "The Dead of Antietam." It was the first glimpse that most Americans had ever had of the savagery of war. "If [Brady] has not brought bodies and laid them in our door-yards," wrote a *New York Times* reviewer on October 20, 1862, "he has done something very like it."[3] Brady's images, however, had little deterrent effect on America's readiness to go to war.

Another artist who gave form to the unseen horrors of war was the German painter and social activist Kathe Kollwitz, whose famous print cycle "The Peasant War" is a riveting and unforgettable account of the atrocities visited upon peasant workers during the Industrial Revolution. The uprising Kollwitz depicts actually took place in the sixteenth century, but the artist used that event as an allegorical device to protest against and dramatize the conditions of the contemporary poor and the working class before the rise of National Socialism. When Kollwitz's youngest son, Peter, died fighting in Flanders in the First World War (1914–1918), she made a series of sculptures in his honor, one of which still resides in the collective Soldier's Cemetery in Roggevelde, Belgium, where it serves as a monument to all the fallen. An activist at heart, Kollwitz deliberately chose to create most of her art in print form, so that her images could be widely circulated and purchased. Harassed by the Nazi regime, Kollwitz lost her home to bombing in 1943.

Giving form to feelings and emotions

The First World War, by all accounts, inspired more artistic response than any other war in history. In the years leading up to 1914 a lively art scene influenced by the Italian Futurist and Expressionist movements had already taken hold in Europe and the United States. Indeed, these movements would produce a veritable *Who's Who?* of twentieth-century art – including notables Henri Gaudier-Brzeska, Marc Chagall, Paul Klee, John Singer Sargent, Stanley Spencer, Gustav Klimt, Max Beckmann,

Amadeo Modigliani, Otto Dix, Vasily Kandinsky, and Egon Schiele, many of whom would themselves take up arms in the war.[4]

Initially, many First World War artists were caught up in the swagger of war. "Having grown up in an age of security," wrote the German Expressionist painter Otto Dix, "we all had a nostalgia for the unusual great perils. The war thus seized hold of us like strong liquor. It was under a hail of flowers that we left, drunk on roses and blood. Without a doubt, the war offered us grandeur, strength, and gravity."[5] But, once on the battlefield, Dix and his fellow artists soon confronted the unprecedented ferocity of trench warfare. For many, the experience would incite them to spread the truth about the war's carnage. "I am no longer an artist," wrote the English painter Paul Nash soon after being posted to the Western Front by his government's War Propaganda Bureau. "I am a messenger who will bring back word from the men who are fighting to those who want the war to go on forever. Feeble, inarticulate will be my message, but it will have a bitter truth and may it burn their lousy souls."[6] For other artists, the disgust at what they had witnessed on the front line would leave an indelible mark on their art. Dix, for example, made a series of paintings excoriating the German government for its shabby treatment of wounded and crippled soldiers. In 1924, he joined with other artists who had fought in the war to put on a traveling exhibition of paintings called "No More War!" Dix also produced a book of etchings, *The War*, later described by one critic as "perhaps the most powerful as well as the most anti-war statement in modern art."[7]

After the war, Dix and many of his contemporaries joined the Dada Movement founded in 1915 by Marcel Duchamp, Jean Arp, and Tristan Tzara. The Dadaists used their art both to palliate and to challenge the mindless destruction of the First World War. They held that if traditional art and culture had been created largely by the kind of people who had made possible the horrors of that war, then that culture must be swept aside and replaced by something new. Aware of latent feelings of rage and disempowerment throughout Germany, they focused their artistic slings and arrows on those responsible for the war. The rotten corpses and mangled soldiers they painted came to symbolize a decadent Germany made rich and corrupt by war profiteering.

By the mid-1920s Dadaism was being subsumed by a new, more ordered and less virulent movement called Surrealism, founded in 1924 by André Breton, a French poet and physician who had fought in the war. After the war, Breton, a neuropsychologist, had treated his patients with the psychoanalytic techniques of Sigmund Freud and had been impressed by the disturbed images they were able, both consciously and subconsciously, to produce. These results, combined with dream experiments and automatic writing, helped him develop Surrealism as a vehicle for making art and a way of living one's life. According to art historian Peter Selz, Surrealism, which became the primary avant-garde movement in Europe between the two world wars, emphasized a personal psychology rather than a phenomenological world. "The implication being," Selz writes, "that such a psychological insult was experienced in war so that the only way many could process or deal with it was to turn to expressions of their own personal psychology in a surreal way."[8] René Magritte, a former Belgian soldier, captured the Surrealistic desire to respond to traumatic memory in his painting "Of This Men Knew Nothing" (1923). It depicts a pair of ragged combat boots whose tips seem to be transforming themselves into the toes of the man who had worn them. Like Magritte, many surrealistic artists used their artwork, at least in part, to cope with their own experience of war trauma. These soldiers-artists, who had been psychologically devastated by their utter helplessness in trench warfare, found a community, an audience, and, most importantly, a voice.

While the First World War profoundly affected many of the artists who had fought in its trenches, there is no evidence that their art deterred future wars or even played a significant role in the social reconstruction of post-war Europe. Anti-war art, at best, challenged the bellicose rhetoric of emerging nationalist leaders in Europe who wanted nothing more than for their subjects to forget the horrors of the past. As Fascism reared its ugly head, even Pablo Picasso's famous painting "Guernica" (1937), made in response to the bombing of his hometown in the Basque region of Spain just prior to the Second World War (1939–1945), could do little to stop it.

Although artists remained active during the Second World War, few works exist that reflect the kind of introspective response to combat by artists that we saw in the First World War.[9] Most probably this was because from all sides, at least at its inception, the war was considered moral and honorable, and its leaders heroic. During the war, artists from all sides served the war effort in a variety of ways, most notably as publicists and combat artists. On the Allied front (as in Germany and Japan), artists such as Norman Rockwell and David Stone Martin made posters touting patriotism and self-sacrifice for the war effort. Some poster art was also extremely racist, such as a series of American posters depicting the Japanese as monkeys.[10] Others, like the British poster entitled "Man-eater," which depicted Hitler feasting on the bones of Eastern European countries, were incendiary. Meanwhile, dozens of British and American artists served their countries as combat artists. Their mission, in the words of the American newscaster Walter Cronkite, was "to capture the mood of the war and those who waged it."[11]

Not all artists, of course, aligned themselves with the war effort. Although far fewer than in the First World War, several artists used their art to protest against the war. The American sculptor David Smith produced a series of cast bronze sculptures called "Medals for Dishonor" (1939–1946) which illustrated events and situations he equated with war crimes. One of these, "Medals for Dishonor: Sinking Hospital Ships," protested against attacks of medical transport vessels, acts which had been outlawed by the 1907 Hague Convention.[12] But, by and large, European and American artists, especially in the post-Second World War years, were less concerned with the past and more focused on the reshaping of Europe and the increased influence of the United States in the world. This aesthetic would shape the visual culture of much of the world – as well as generations of artists – for years to come.

It has been argued that never before had artists been able to affect their culture with the impact and immediacy that they had during and after the Vietnam War (1954–1975). As art historian Lucy Lippard has pointed out, the Vietnam conflict was really two wars: one fought on South-east Asian soil and the other waged in the hearts and minds of the American people.[13] When US covert involvement in Vietnam became public knowledge in the late 1960s, dissent was immediate and vociferous. There was enormous opposition to the drafting of thousands of young men to fight in what many considered an illegal war against innocent people of color. Television brought vivid and immediate images of distant combat and casualties to millions of Americans.

Just as artists had once used the printing press to produce works that were widely available, they now co-opted photography as a powerful art form, linking the media's power to inform and shock with their own deeper conceptual message, often blurring the lines between photo documentation and art. One of the most powerful examples of this genre was a photo-silkscreen made in 1970 by three artists using a photograph by the combat photographer Ron L. Haeberle. The title of the piece, "Q: And Babies? A: And Babies," is printed at the top and bottom of Haeberle's color photograph of corpses lying across what appears to be a dirt path through a crop field. The title quotation was taken from congressional testimony given by former army helicopter pilot Hugh Thompson in the investigation of the My Lai massacre, in which US troops gunned down unarmed Vietnamese villagers.

As the ferocity of the Vietnam War gained momentum in the late 1960s, a growing number of American artists – young and old alike – took their art to the streets. Martha Rossler, working in California, used photo-collage to great effect in her series "Bringing the War Home: House Beautiful" (1969–1971). By inserting combat photos into banal make-up and household images modeled after the pages of women's magazines of the day, Rossler raised question about "cover-up and make-up, race and gender, power and powerlessness, and ignorance and bliss."[14] Sculptor Duane Hansen staged his "Vietnam Scene" (1969), a life-size, three-dimensional representation of dead GIs, in a Manhattan gallery, turning the exhibition space into a battlefield. Leon Golub, who called himself "simply a reporter," garnered international attention through his "Vietnam" series, with their unabashed look at war and masculinity. Several former soldiers, like the American painter Ben Sakaguchi and the Vietnamese collage artist Chi Lee, produced works about the horrors of battle they had experienced.

Such progress notwithstanding, American art in the post-Vietnam years did little to help reunite American society. Nor did it provide solace to Vietnam veterans who had returned home to a nation that seemed to shun them. It would take time, and not art, however, to help unite a deeply divided nation.

Since the war in Vietnam, photographs of war and atrocity taken in subsequent armed conflicts have increasingly blurred the lines separating art, documentation, and photojournalism. Among those whose work has set a precedent in recent years are Jean-Marie Simon, whose 1988 book of photo essays, *Guatemala: Eternal Spring, Eternal Tyranny*, exposed viewers to the lives of Guatemala's indigenous population and the atrocities they suffered during that country's civil war. Other photographers such as James Nachtwey, Sabastiao Salgado, and Gilles Peress have grappled with modern war and the devastation it has wrought on entire communities. Consistent in all of these photographers is their commitment to "bearing witness" to human suffering; they spend long periods of time among the people they photograph and rely heavily on their subjective response to their surroundings and events.

In recent years, a new medium, the so-called "graphic or comic book novel," has emerged as a new documentary tool that combines art and journalism to make complex political and historical conflicts understandable to a mass audience. In the late 1960s, for example, American underground comics used biting social criticism of the Nixon administration to unite young Americans to protest against the Vietnam War. Today, art galleries around the world are giving "comic art" a second look as a legitimate and influential form of artistic expression.

One of the best-known graphic novelists, Art Spiegelman, made his start in underground comics. His two books on the Holocaust, *Maus: A Survivor's Tale, Part I, My Father Bleeds History* (1986) and *Maus: A Survivor's Tale, Part II, Here My Troubles Began* (1991), are considered classics in the genre. In recent years, artist and journalist Joe Sacco has created comic books to take on serious subjects including the war in Bosnia and the Israeli occupation of Palestine. His book *Safe Area Gorazde: The War in Eastern Bosnia 1992–95* is a moving account of his four-month stay in the UN-designated safe haven. How Spiegelman and Sacco's books have influenced public responses to war and atrocity is impossible to gauge scientifically, but if sales are any indication, their work is, at least, widely seen and contemplated.

Bosnian and Croatian artists

I turn now to my interviews with thirty Bosnian, Croatian, and Serb artists and arts professionals to understand the role, if any, that artists and their work have played (or could potentially play) in the social reconstruction of their post-war countries.[15] To begin with, I found that the age of the artists largely determined their choice of medium: the older artists tended to work in traditional forms of painting and sculpture, while their middle-aged counterparts used traditional materials alongside video and performance, and their younger colleagues worked almost exclusively with video, film, and performance art. Many of the artists, with the exception of the younger generation, shared a preoccupation with the "loss of place" due to the war and the need to reclaim it in their work both visually and literally. This is not surprising given the fact that hundreds of thousands of people of all national groups were forcibly expelled from their homes and communities during the war. By war's end, returning to one's home and community was first and foremost in the minds of many of the region's refugees and internally displaced.

Place has been defined in two overlapping ways. The first meaning describes the geographical site or location – the physical space. The second examines the human interactions that occur within the physical site. Both aspects – the physical geography and the human interactions – invest places with meaning. People become attached to places where they live. "Home is often the site of great attachment, a place of security, and the point to which people set their personal compass," writes Craig Pollack.[16] While attachment to home or community facilitates feelings of comfort and belonging, large-scale trauma, including war and massive displacement, can invest these places with ambivalence. With the loss of home, people can feel powerless and directionless, unable to make sense of the world.

Place has always been present in Balkan art – as it has with most artistic traditions – from the Medieval Bogomil tombstone carvings to the Primitivist paintings of such artists as Ilija Bosilj to Socialist Realism, the official art of the Communist Block countries that emphasized idealizations of the workplace and the worker who toiled there. Place also figured predominately in the rhetoric of the nationalists who emerged after Tito's death in 1980. Calling for the creation of independent ethnic states, they encouraged artists to emphasize ethnic traditions and customs in their work so as to create a sense of "national place." Nada Beros, a Zagreb-based art critic and curator at the Museum of Contemporary Art, observed this process unfold during the war in Croatia. "[The Tudjman regime wanted artists] to abide by the traditional, native values in art and culture, as if they were a condition of national survival. On the one hand, collective memory was insisted upon but, on the other hand, collective amnesia was warmly welcomed when it [came] to the recent 'Communist' past."[17] Several of the artists I interviewed suggested that their countries were experiencing a kind of artistic "identity crisis" brought on by the quick transition from the "official" aesthetic of the Tito regime to a war-induced climate of "national propaganda."

Many of the artists, regardless of their age or nationality, shared similar views about art and its place in society. Nearly all of them cited corruption and the lack of community as threatening artistic expression in the former Yugoslavia, and they repeatedly emphasized their connection with the European art world. However, their views varied considerably regarding the war and how it had affected their art. Age was the predominant factor determining these differences, but nationality, economic status, and place of residence, particularly during the war, were also important.

Typical of their generation, artists who were born before 1950 were educated primarily in Belgrade, Zagreb, and Sarajevo and, in a few cases, western Europe. This age group, more than any other, was nostalgic about life before the war. They spoke of their university years, the relative tranquility of the Tito era, and the strong attachments they had formed to their communities.

Two artists from the central Bosnian town of Mostar – Vladimir Puljic, a Croat, and Jusuf (Jusa) Niksic, a Muslim – illustrate the similarities in experience and outlook of the older artists. Puljic and Niksic, who are old friends, hold a deep affection for Mostar, which has long been a haven for artists and writers. During the war, Niksic's studio, located on the Bosnian Muslim side of the river, was demolished first by bombing and then by a fire, destroying over eighty of his paintings. Meanwhile, Puljic spent most of the war in Rome, and his studio on the Croat side of the river was left undisturbed. "Thanks to the war," says Niksic, "I am now, for the third time, beginning my life. But thanks to God, I am strong, I am healthy, and I am still painting . . . Mostar is my kingdom." Niksic lives on the money he makes from teaching out of his home and from his paintings, particularly those he makes of "Stari Most," the sixteenth-century bridge that was destroyed by Bosnian Croat troops during the war.

Niksic and Puljic said the present reconstruction of the Stari Most, led by Italian engineers, was the most hopeful thing they could contemplate. They would like nothing more than to see their city rebuilt as it was before the war. As artists, they have chosen to focus on Mostar's past beauty.

It would be easy to dismiss their lack of interest in the war as a form of denial, but it may also be the result of this generation's belief in the eventual restoration of order and the ascendancy of human decency. Like Niksic and Puljic, Vladimir Dzanko, a 68-year-old painter who spent the war years directing a small gallery in the Croatian city of Osijek, believes artists in the wake of the war should look beyond the destructive aspects of the violence and create images that "give something beautiful and noble to the world." During the war, Dzanko joined a group of artists that made paintings and graphic postcards decrying the violence that was taking place around them. To bolster the morale of the Croatian people, the artists would circulate their work, often carrying it by hand, from town to town so it could be displayed in the windows of their homes and studios. Salim Obralic, a 57-year-old Bosniak professor at the Sarajevo Art Academy, said that he had made reactionary sculptures during the war, but that his recent works were inspired by something "finer" – namely, traditional Sarajevo old-town handicrafts made of silver, gold, and copper. This reclamation of time-honored skills is a statement in itself.

The second group of artists were all born before 1965. This "middle generation" tended to use their art to reflect upon war and the terrible physical and emotional suffering it had caused.[18] Emerging or mid-career professionals when hostilities began, some of these artists had fought in the war, and, unlike the older colleagues, many of them are women. One of them is the Zagreb-based artist Sanja Ivekovic, whose performance and video art addresses the cultural manipulation of women, the political power of the media over the individual, and the dangers of the sort of extreme nationalism that gripped Croatia during the war. Ivekovic has made at least three pieces about the war in Croatia and Bosnia. In 1992, she responded to the mass rape of Bosniak women by the Serbs with the video installation called "Frozen Images," in which images of a naked woman curled on her side are projected onto a smoking bed of dry ice. Another piece, entitled "Resnik," deals with the plight of war refugees in Croatia and Bosnia. Ivekovic has influenced a generation of younger artists, mostly women, with her political art. "One of the primary reasons I make art," she says, "is to educate people, especially young people, who might not otherwise learn about the censorship and prejudice that has existed in the past and still exists."

Ivekovic's art and that of many of her "middle generation" colleagues exhibits a preoccupation with space and territory, which they re-divide and reclaim, virtually and actually. An example of this "place-based" art is Alma Suljevic's land mine piece entitled "Annulling Truth." By "selling" allotments of mined land to viewers and then giving the donations to a demining team, the artist is enabling the residents of Sarajevo to reclaim public lands that had become circumscribed by the war.

Milica Tomic, a Serb video and performance artist born in 1960 who now lives in Germany, is also concerned about violence and its relationship to place, nationality, and identity. Her 1998 video "I am Milica Tomic," which directly addresses the war in the former Yugoslavia, is presented as autobiographical but is ultimately about national indoctrination. Her piece "Portrait of My Mother," created in 1999, features Tomic with her mother Marija Milutivonic, who is also an artist. The video begins with film footage of Belgrade and the suburb in which Milutivonic lives, and ends with Tomic confronting her about her denial of the Serbian repression and murders of ethnic Kosovo Albanians. Other pieces, many of which feature Tomic walking from her old apartment to various points in Belgrade, examine her support of the NATO bombing of Serb forces in Kosovo in the spring of 1999. Another expatriate, Braco Dimitriejevic, who was born in 1948 in Sarajevo and educated in London, has made his artistic reputation in Paris creating what he calls "invisible links" between people, places, objects, and artworks.

This spatial and territorial genre finds further expression in the work of two Sarajevo art students, Anela Sabic and Suzana Ceric. One day in March 1997, the two young Bosnian women arranged to have the police stop traffic on Marshal Tito Boulevard, the city's main street and promenade, which during the siege had been nicknamed "Sniper Alley." For the next two hours, the two artists walked up and down the boulevard. When viewers asked them what they were doing, they simply replied, "Nothing. Just walking."

Sabic and Cenic, however, are the exception rather than the rule among younger artists, who mostly eschew war-related themes in their work. Zelimir Koscevic, Chief Curator of the Museum of Contemporary Art in Zagreb, believes their lack of interest in making art about the war stems from the fact that Zagreb saw no actual ground combat. Dunja Blazevic, who directs the Sarajevo Center for Contemporary Art, believes that young Bosnian artists, like their Croatian counterparts, have been severely handicapped by the absence of so many of the middle generation of artists who left the region during the war and by the post-war breakdown of museum, gallery, and educational systems.

According to Izeta Grdzevic, the director of Obala Art Center, a cultural mainstay in Sarajevo for the visual and performing arts during the war, young artists in the former Yugoslavia have been heavily seduced by the "irony" of western art and their own intellectual diaspora. "Our culture," she said, "is now very much influenced by trends in American culture and art, especially from New York and Los Angeles. It bothers me that so many of our young artists seem to feel no kind of real need for true understanding, for taking one idea and exploring it intensely. Many of them work like designers looking for solutions to tasks. They don't reflect on real experience. Instead, they prefer to simply entertain themselves." One young woman, Grdzevic recalled, had proposed to fill the Obala gallery with hay as a conceptual response to the influx of refugees in Sarajevo. Grdzevic was shocked: "This girl must never have gone to any real refugee camps. I mean, why would she propose such a thing! . . . So many of these young artists live and work within a kind of closed circle, they have come to see refugees as a social problem, and not as people."

The young Bosnian and Croatian artists I interviewed had a fascination and familiarity with modern technology and communications, which, in turn, exposed them to global art theories and aesthetics. Increasingly, these young artists were drawn to less traditional media, including video, film, installation, and performance. Many learned their craft at a time when scores of westerners, including NATO troops, foreign journalists, and aid workers, were working in the region and had become influenced by this new, alluring subculture. Since the end of the war, a growing number of young artists have moved to Slovenia, the most "westernized" of the former Yugoslav states, where both a stable economy and a lively art scene provide artists with greater opportunities.

Like the invention of the printing press in the mid-fifteenth century, the Internet has provided these young artists with a tool for exposing their art and ideas to a broader audience. Many have created their own websites, which they constantly update with new work, little of which deals with the past war. By comparison, young Bosnian and Croatian expatriates living in Europe and North America are producing a great deal of visual art about the war. Perhaps, like James Joyce, they have found that geographical and chronological distance has provided them with a means of processing and responding to a momentous event like war.[19]

Bosnian expatriates Nebojsa Seric Soba and Maja Bajevic, both in their 40s and residing in Amsterdam and Paris respectively, use their art to explore how identities are formed through the appropriation of place.[20] One of Bajevic's most evocative pieces is her performance series entitled "Women at Work." In the piece "Dressed Up," first presented in Sarajevo's Center for Contemporary Arts in 1999, Bajevic makes a dress from fabric imprinted with a large map of the former Yugoslavia. When the dress is sewn, she strips to her underwear and dons the map/dress and exits the room, leaving only her sewing machine, a television set, and discarded scraps of fabric. In his 1999 photographic work, "Heroes," Seric Soba, who fought in the Bosnian Army during the war, poses in two life-size photographs. In one he is dressed in a helmet and army fatigues, with his right leg bent and balanced on the dirt wall of a trench. In the other he is standing on a pier dressed in casual clothing with a sun-dappled marina in the background. His hands rest on his hips and, like the companion photograph, he wears a tense expression, as though he is looking for distant signs. In his 1998 installation, entitled "Under All Those Flags," Seric Soba hoisted hundreds of plastic transparent flags, devoid of symbolic or collective significance, on lamp-posts along the banks of the Miljacka River in Sarajevo, alluding to national flags that are raised on official occasions. The flags disappeared overnight on the orders of the municipal authorities, making it the first artwork to be censored in post-war Bosnia. His appropriation of space was potentially dangerous because it showed the emptiness of the national or other representations in whose name a bloody war had been waged.[21]

One of the many young artists who have left Sarajevo to live in Slovenia is Srdjan Vuletic. At the time of our interview, many of his fellow film-makers and collaborators, including Jasmila Zbanic, Enes Zlatar, Damir Niksic, and Dzenid Jaganjac,[22] had either joined him or were planning to do so. A 29-year-old Bosnian Serb, Vuletic is one of the few artists of his generation whose work examines war and suffering. During the war, he worked for the Sarajevo hospital and the Bosnian Army as a documentary film-maker, and he now directs his own film company, Refresh Productions. Vuletic believes new video and computer technologies are helping young artists get their message across to a wider public, while older artists who have not joined the "techno wave" are losing out. "The older generation may make art that costs about the same as newer media works," he said, "but, in the end, their work is more expensive to transport and install, and so gets less exposure."

Another "new media" artist, Darko Fritz, a Croat, is committed, like Vuletic, to the idea of a global art aesthetic, but he sees politically informed art, especially relating to the recent war, as suspicious at best. He believes many artists have exploited their war experiences to build their own careers, and even those with purer motives have created work that panders to western expectations, such as Milica Tomic, whose works he finds prurient and overdramatic. "It's all about perception from the westerners' point of view," he said. "Kind of dividing us from central or eastern Europe and western Europe, and of course, the US itself. It's dangerous to try and transplant obviously specific art and side-effects of art. I'm worried about work that is kind of designed for the westerners' point of view. A lot of war art by Bosnian and Serbian artists – and some of them are great – are great examples of 'transplant' art. But it is a very thin line and such art can become extremely kitsch."

Fortunately for Fritz and other young artists concerned with taking their place in the global art world, former Yugoslav curators and other arts professionals have been aiding and abetting them in this goal. In 1998, Zelamir Koscevik opened his traveling exhibition, "Cartographers," at the Museum of Contemporary Art in Zagreb. All 135 works (by 69 artists, 16 of whom were from the former Yugoslavia) took their imagery from maps, globes, or geographic projections. In his preface to the exhibition catalog, Koscevik noted that artists have long been fascinated with cartography and its depiction of both known and unknown terrain. "The works exhibited in this show," he wrote in the preface, "only begin to illustrate the full extent of this obviously overlooked artistic phenomenon of the twentieth century." He is right, of course. But it is also tempting to speculate that these former Yugoslav artists and curators, whether consciously or subconsciously, made and exhibited cartographically inspired works as a way of trying to understand the geographical break-up of their own country. Indeed, in two of the nine essays following this preface, writers made a more "site-specific" argument for this artistic interest in creating new geographies.

Conclusion

Bosnian and Croatian artists, like their post-war counterparts throughout human history, have become the visual archivists of their nation's post-war psyche. As with their historical counterparts, they have given form to feelings often in new genres, and have offered new ways to see the world. However, they have not acted as historians during or after the wars. Whether intentionally or not, they have taken alternative pathways. In Bosnia and Croatia, where war and ethnic cleansing caused such widespread displacement and destruction of property, it is not surprising that many artists have focused their work in varying ways on the reclamation of place, whether it be home, community, or nationhood. By and large, older artists have sought to preserve the beauty and symbolism (and perhaps nostalgia) of past places, such as the Stari Most or the national library in Sarajevo, which was destroyed by a Bosnian Serb mortar attack at the outset of the war. Many middle generation artists, and especially those who, like Otto Dix and René Magritte, actually bore arms in combat, have used their art, at least in part, to probe and protest against wartime atrocities. Such explorations have helped many of these artists understand their own responses to the suffering around them. Then there are the activist artists like Alma Suljevic, Anela Sabic, and Suzana Ceric who have used their art to help communities recognize that it is within their power to reclaim stolen or once dangerous spaces. Meanwhile, many young artists, unlike their older colleagues, have for the most part chosen not to deal with war-related themes. Having come of age during the war, they have a view of place often accompanied by feelings of insecurity and powerlessness in the face of overwhelming force. Understandably, they see the ease and immediacy of video, film, and cyberspace as vehicles for taking them to a place away from the past.

There is no easy explanation for what makes a work of art great, but one factor that most people agree upon is the test of time: a painting, sculpture, photograph, or print that continues to interest and move generation after generation, despite fashion, must be truly remarkable. But whether even great art can help societies make sense of the horrible consequences of war remains an unanswered question. By the same token, it may be too soon to draw definitive conclusions about the effect that contemporary art – whether it is great art or not – is having on the people of Bosnia and Croatia as they rebuild their shattered lives.

We see the world through the stories we tell and the images we create. To paraphrase William Faulkner: art is humanity's way of understanding its history. In the aftermath of war and mass atrocity, it is paramount that we understand our history so as to try to nurture what is positive and prevent what is destructive. In this regard, artists can help postwar societies preserve and restore the good while reminding them of the pernicious attributes that led to war and ethnic hatred. At the same time, they must constantly push their societies' mental horizons beyond their own borders, toward a future of new ideas and visions.

NOTES

1. During 2000 and 2001 I interviewed thirty artists in Bosnia and Croatia. We discussed their activities during the recent war, the role that art has traditionally played in Yugoslav society, and their hopes and aspirations as artists for the future of the new states of the former federation.
2. John Berger, *Ways of Seeing* (London: British Broadcasting Corporation and Penguin Books, 1977), Chapter 1.
3. See Robert Leggat, "A History of Photography: From its Beginnings Until the 1920s," available on World Wide Web at http://www.rleggat.com/photohistory.

4. There was also an enormous literary response to the First World War. Erich
   Maria Remarque's *All Quiet on the Western Front* may be the most famous
   anti-war novel of all time. Poets who wrote memorably about their combat
   experiences include, among many others, Wilfred Owen, Siegfried Sassoon,
   and Robert Graves.
5. Richard Cork, *A Bitter Truth: Avant-Garde and the Great War* (New Haven:
   Yale University Press, 1994), 94–95.
6. See "Beginning in 1915, Both the Allied and Central Powers Governments . . . ," on World Wide Web at www.ablongman.com/levacktour/pages/
   twentyfour_2.pdf. See also "Who's Who: Paul Nash," *First World War.com*,
   available on World Wide Web at http://www.firstworldwar.com/bio/nash.htm.
7. Cork, *A Bitter Truth*, 254.
8. Kristine Stiles and Peter Selz, eds. *Theories and Development of Contemporary
   Art: A Sourcebook of Artist's Writings* (Berkeley: University of California Press,
   1966), 168–169.
9. The art made during and after the Holocaust is highly significant but, for the
   purposes of this chapter, treated as a separate entity from war art.
10. See John W. Dower, *War Without Mercy: Race and Power in the Pacific War*
    (New York: Pantheon, 1986).
11. See, for example, Howard Brodie, *Drawing Fire: A Combat Artist at War* (Los
    Altos, California: Portola Press, 1996).
12. See W. Michael Reisman and Chris T. Antoniou, *The Laws of War: A Compre-
    hensive Collection of Primary Documents on International Laws Governing Armed
    Conflict* (New York: Random House, 1994), 160–162.
13. Lucy R. Lippard, *A Different War* (Seattle, Wash.: The Real Comet Press,
    1990), 10–11.
14. Lippard, *A Different War*, 43.
15. The artists represented the three major nationalities of the region: Bosniak,
    Serb, and Croat.
16. See M. T. Fullilove, "Psychiatric Implications of Displacement: Contribu-
    tions from the Psychology of Place," *American Journal of Psychiatry* 153
    (1996): 1516–1523. For a discussion of the psychology of place among
    rural Croat and Bosnian Muslim women, see Tone Bringa, *Being Muslim
    the Bosnian Way* (Princeton, New Jersey: Princeton University Press, 1995).
    For a discussion on place, trauma, and burial in the aftermath of the Sre-
    brenica massacre, see C. E. Pollack, "Burial at Srebrenica: Linking Place
    and Trauma," *Social Science and Medicine* 56 (2003): 793–801.
17. Nada Beros, "Croatia: What Remains," *Artpress* 232 (February 1998): 63–
    66.
18. According to the study participants, a significant number of "middle gener-
    ation" artists – those in their 30s to early 50s – left the former Yugoslavia
    during the war.
19. Weinstein et al. have described the differences in self-efficacy between
    Bosniak refugees in the United States and those who remain displaced
    in Bosnia, and suggest that distance from the conflict offers an opportu-
    nity to move forward in new ways. See Harvey M. Weinstein, Julienne
    Lipson, Rhonda Sarnoff, and Eleanor Gladstone, "Rethinking Displace-
    ment: Bosnians Uprooted in Bosnia and California." In Julienne G. Lipson

and Lucia Ann McSpadden, eds. *Negotiating Power and Place at the Margins: Selected Papers on Refugees and Immigrants*, vol. VII (Arlington, Va.: American Anthropological Association, 1999): 53–74.

20. Nebojsa Seric Soba's website is located on World Wide Web at http://www.scca.ba/artistfiles/soba/ok/ and Maja Bajevic's is at http://www.scca.ba/artistfiles/maja/works01.htm.

21. Dunja Blazevic, "Ils Arrivent: le Sarajevo de l'Après-Guerre," *Artpress* 245 (April 1999): 37–44.

22. See "Made in Sarajevo: In Search of Lost Time," on World Wide Web at http://www.miroslav-kraljevic.hr/1/sarajevo/sarajevo-sl.html.

14 Trust and betrayal in war

Dean Ajdukovic and Dinka Corkalo

Today, eleven years after the end of the war, Vukovar remains a ravaged and ethnically divided city. Indeed, when Croats and Serbs talk about the 1991 war within their own ethnic group, they invariably ask: "How could we have trusted them?" That such deep feelings of distrust and suspicion can exist in Vukovar, a city that once boasted one of the highest interethnic marriage rates in the former Yugoslavia, seems hard to fathom. So what happened? What caused neighbor to turn against neighbor? How could feelings of betrayal and distrust spread through a once harmonious community like a virulent cancer? And will it ever be possible for the residents of Vukovar to overcome a basic lack of trust and reconcile their differences?

In 2002, we set out to find answers to these questions through an interview study of forty-eight Croat and Serb residents of the city. We approached potential participants through two local recruiters who solicited participation on the basis of recommendations from one person to another, a recruiting process known as "snowball sampling." Participants had to meet the following criteria: first, they must have lived in Vukovar for at least fifteen years prior to the outbreak of war in 1991. Second, during this time, they must have had close friends from the other ethnic group. Third, this relationship must have been severed or seriously threatened since 1991. The final sample consisted of an equal number of Serbs and Croats, from three age categories and three levels of education.

People who have been traumatized by war often live with the belief that the world is an unjust and unpredictable place. Their underlying trauma can be further compounded by feelings of betrayal if they see their neighbors from other ethnic groups as indirectly or directly responsible for their suffering. For many, even seeing former neighbors, friends, or colleagues in the street or the workplace can become a daily challenge. With this in mind, we set out to examine how loss of trust or feelings of betrayal among the participants influenced openness to social reconstruction and readiness for reconciliation after the war and the return of Vukovar to

Croatian authority. Since the participants were asked to explore issues of betrayal between friends and to talk about times that had been extremely difficult, they were cautioned that strong emotions might surface, such as sadness or grief, and told that assistance was available if they should require it. Indeed, some sessions became emotionally charged. Even so, the majority of participants said that they felt safe while telling their story and emotionally relieved afterwards for being able to share it with someone.

In addition to examining the process by which close, interethnic friendships had unraveled in Vukovar since the 1991 war, we wanted to recommend community-based interventions to promote social reconstruction and reconciliation in this highly fractured community. We define social reconstruction in this chapter as a process that seeks to reinstate the norms of social functioning in a community to the level that existed before their breakdown and through which the social fabric of the community is repaired.[1] In other words, social reconstruction is about normalizing everyday social life in a community and building a sense of belonging to a community. Fletcher and Weinstein suggest that social reconstruction in a post-war society consists of four elements: justice, democracy, economic prosperity and transformation, and reconciliation.[2] Thus, interventions to promote social repair must emphasize one or all of these elements.

In an ethnically divided city like Vukovar, where everyday life is colored by bitterness and feelings of betrayal and distrust, we wondered how programs aimed at social reconstruction could be promoted. One possibility would be to initiate conflict resolution projects that would bring together antagonistic ethnic groups to discuss past personal experiences and losses, and to share sympathy and apologies for past transgressions. Another approach would be to bring together opposing groups to focus on a specific community task, such as repairing a school, and thus rebuilding personal relationships. Given what we saw as the underlying problem – the betrayal of trust – we hoped to better understand what mix of strategies would be most beneficial.

Pre-war friendships: a strong community fabric

We began our interviews by asking participants to describe their pre-war relations with close friends from the other ethnic group. Interestingly, many of the participants needed first to describe their general social relations with the other ethnic group. What emerged very clearly was the story of a closely knit community, with strong feelings of attachment to friends and neighbors of all ethnicities. Typically, people either did not know the ethnic background of their friends, peers, or neighbors, or else they simply did not care. Lack of knowledge about the ethnic background of peers was more characteristic of the younger generation who were between 12 and 20 years old in 1991. They were unconcerned about the ethnicity of their peers and tended to make friends within their own neighborhood or school, or through long-standing family relations. The older generation said that they knew the ethnic background of their friends, mostly because they used to celebrate both Catholic and Orthodox religious events together. They usually had half a dozen or so close friends, comprised of an equal number of Croats and Serbs. Vojo,[3] a 50-year-old textile worker and a Serb, described how he and a Croat classmate had become close friends:

This was a friendship that began in elementary school, and went on through adolescence, his marriage, and the birth of our children. When we were about 15 years old we started playing music together. I played the drums and he played the guitar. We went to serve in the army on the same day. When he met his future wife, at a New Year's party, I was there too. When she gave birth to their first daughter, I saw the child only a few days later.

Zdravko, a 29-year-old teacher and a Croat, spoke about his childhood friendship with a Serb boy named Slobodan:

He was a year older than me. We became friends when we were small kids, as we lived across the street from one another. We spent almost all the time together, either in his home or mine. Our parents knew each other, but they did not visit too often; they were in good neighborly relations. As we grew older, Slobodan and I would go to cafés and discotheques, always together.

Most participants said they considered their friend from the other group "a best friend." Typically they spent a lot of their free time together; sometimes they worked and traveled to their jobs together. Often, they went to the same secondary school, and shared the same desk for years. They made daily visits to each other's homes, and often slept there. Like Zdravko and his Serb friend, they went to the same cafés, discotheques, and sporting events. They shared similar interests in music and literature. Often, their parents were either good friends or neighbors who visited each other regularly and "drank coffee together every day."

Middle-aged and older participants said their friendships lasted decades. Personal relationships usually developed into close family relationships. Men went fishing together and belonged to the same fishing or sports club. Women helped each other with household work and in the garden. Friends helped each other build their homes. During times of crisis, their best friend was always the first to help. They attended baptismal and marriage ceremonies together and joined one another to celebrate Catholic and Orthodox Christmas and Easter. "We didn't just spend time together, we lived one life," a Croat participant said of her family's relationship with her best friend's family. "I could never have thought that we wouldn't help each other out under any circumstances."

Circumstances leading to separation: denial and erosion of trust

In the late 1980s, profound changes in the political environment began to take place across the former Yugoslavia. For the first time since the Second World War, a multi-party election system was in place, and there were hopes that democratization would follow. But, at the same time, newly emerging political parties began promoting heavily nationalistic platforms. Proclaiming themselves protectors of their own people, these politicians used fear to promote hatred against other national groups. The strategy worked as more and more people who had never emphasized their ethnic background began identifying more strongly with their own ethnic group. In the 1990 elections, nationalist parties triumphed throughout the federation, setting the stage for interethnic violence and eventually war.

Study participants told us that "deep unease" began to settle over Vukovar following the 1990 elections that had brought hard-line nationalists to power. For many city residents it was an outcome they could neither comprehend nor do anything about. Older residents said the new politicians were opportunists of dubious moral character. Despite the growing ethnic tensions in Vukovar, many participants said they still wanted to maintain their close and intimate friendships with members of other ethnic groups.

Trouble in this part of the country first broke out in the vicinity of Vukovar on May 1, 1991, when Serb paramilitaries detained two Croat policemen who had tried to run their vehicle through a barricade in Borovo Selo, a predominately Serb suburb of Vukovar. The following day, the police sent a busload of reinforcements to rescue the two men. But the Serbs, hiding in houses and buildings at the entrance to the town, ambushed the bus, killing twelve policemen and injuring several others. The mutilated bodies of the policemen were shown on prime-time TV news. Stories about mutilated bodies spread all over Croatia and heated up the already brewing atmosphere. Our participants reported that the media played an increasingly negative role in presenting one-sided and distorted views of events, driving a wedge between old friends and acquaintances.

During the months leading up to the outbreak of war in August 1991, Vukovar residents experienced feelings of helplessness, fear, lack of comprehension of what was happening, and unease about the future. "I was so afraid during the nights," a 50-year-old Serb worker told us. "There was shooting around my house. I was afraid that armed men might break into our home, and our son was small." A 48-year-old school teacher, also a Serb, said that Croatian police and the military were searching Serb homes at night, and many prominent Serbs were taken away and never seen again. At the same time, unknown assailants were blowing up Serb homes and shops. Yet few of our Croat participants admitted that their Serb friends had any reason to feel threatened at that time.

Our youngest respondents were in their early teens when the war broke out. Typically they said that they were too young to understand fully what was happening around them and reported that this did not affect their friendships. They said that, at the time, older people were becoming increasingly attached to their own ethnic group, but they did not notice such a change in their friends. Mirela, who was 14 at the time, said that she and her best friend Ksenija, a Serb girl of the same age, never even talked about the tensions between Croats and Serbs. In the meantime, growing ethnic tensions were affecting the relationships of Vukovar residents in their late teens. An 18-year-old Croat girl said the 1990 elections marked a turning point in interethnic relationships among teenagers her age: "[My high school] class simply divided, and the differences emerged. I do not know exactly how it happened, but we divided. Some of us went to vote and others did not, and this was the first obvious difference. Soon after, upon meeting one another in the street, they would just say hello, without much conversation." At the time, she was dating a Serb boy named Branko. After the elections, they began spending less and less time together, especially in public places.

As ethnic relations deteriorated in Vukovar, many residents realized something was terribly wrong in their community and among their closest friends. Even so, they never discussed these perceptions with their friends from the other ethnic group; they felt that discussing such issues would only make matters worse. This was the last opportunity to forestall the deteriorating chain of events, as the lack of discussion opened up a large space for cognitive distortions about dimensions of difference. This process of societal self-destruction is well described by breakdown theory,[4] which holds that when people confront previously unimaginable events that are distressing and see their community rapidly changing, they begin to believe that the existing norms and value structures are inappropriate. They wonder if they, too, should not also change and adjust. Under these circumstances, social institutions and relationships no longer function in a familiar way. Difficulties in relationships that did not exist before now arise and people become uncertain and frightened. They begin asking themselves: who really are my neighbors? How could my close friends have changed so much? They grow distrustful of people who now belong to the "other" group. They are doubtful about the intentions of the opposing group and turn to their own for psychological safety. What were once unimportant differences, such as ethnic background, are now the salient concern and widely used to explain almost everything. In difficult times, preference for contacts with people who belong to the same group grows stronger, while relationships with people who belong to other groups decay and the negative attributes assigned to them as a group grow. If leaders and the media emphasize the need for group homogenization and exaggerate differences between them, groups with conflicting interests start perceiving each other as enemies.

While some interethnic friendships died gradually, for many the crucial moment was when their friend left town without any explanation or saying goodbye. This was seen as a deep breach of trust. Evica, a Croat health worker, described how betrayed she felt when her Serb friends failed to warn her about the impending assault on the city by Serb forces: "I always believed that if anything happened to me and my husband, our children would have them to turn to. They betrayed not only me and my husband but also our children. They never asked if our children needed anything. Other friends have asked about our needs, and I cannot thank them enough." When asked why their friends behaved as they did, Evica concluded: "This was not a real friendship at all. Perhaps it was a sincere friendship years ago when we were children. Even then, maybe it wasn't so sincere, since the family of my husband was rather wealthy and they were poor."

Several Croat participants described instances where their Serb friends told them about their concerns for the future. Nonetheless, the Croats typically reinterpreted these admissions by their friends as their having inside, privileged information "from their own side," further enhancing the Croat view that their Serb friends were part of the conspiracy. Katarina, a 52-year-old Croat saleswoman, said that her best friend, a Serb, confided in her that she was going to leave because she feared the "Ustashe would go from house to house," slaughtering Serbs. She warned Katarina that she and her family should also leave. Katarina's friend then left Vukovar. "Perhaps she had been secretly informed about what was going to happen," Katarina said. "Who knows, maybe she had been to secret meetings?"

Some Croat participants recognized that their Serb friends had left in secrecy because they felt threatened by the Croats. A 57-year-old Croat ship captain named Antun said he had a close friend who could not accept the independence of Croatia. His friend suddenly left one night for Belgrade, telling no one. "He just left, without a word," Antun said.

"Later on he told me that he had been in danger. I also heard from our people that he really had been in danger, so that it was perhaps better that he left." Fearful for the safety of her family, Smilja, a Serb pre-school teacher, and her husband left Vukovar without talking to their best friends, who were Croats. In mid-August 1991, a day after they went picnicking with their friends, she and her husband left the city. She did not tell her friends they were leaving because she felt that she could not trust them, as they had a friend in the Croatian military. Smilja added that she had seen a change in the behavior of the couple toward her – the wife had stopped speaking directly to her. Smilja was sure that she herself had not changed at that time. Interestingly, they confided their intention to leave Vukovar to another couple with whom they were less close (a mixed Serb-Hungarian couple without children).

Separation: betrayal and fear

Interethnic friendships reached their low point during the chaotic and life-threatening period following the occupation of Vukovar by Yugoslav Army and Serb paramilitary forces. "It was a period of pure survival, a lawless period, with a lot of drunken people shooting in the streets," said a 32-year-old Serb named Zoran. It was also a period when some of the worst atrocities were committed in the city and surrounding countryside. Hundreds of Croats were executed. Others were detained and transported to prison camps, while many more were expelled to Croatian-held parts of the country. Croats living in Vukovar feared for their lives. At the same time, they hoped that their Serb friends would help them, vouch for them, if needed, or just show recognition of their agonizing situation. According to the participants, most interethnic friendships ended at this time, leaving feelings of betrayal and bitterness in their wake.

Take the case of Djuro, a retired Croat journalist who could not understand how a childhood friend, a Serb, could have changed in only a matter of days. Djuro's friend had assured him a few days before the full attack on Vukovar that no one could spoil their friendship. But, a few days later, Djuro saw the same friend in an army officer's uniform. During Djuro's subsequent imprisonment, he hoped that this friend would help him, but assistance was not forthcoming. Instead, his friend made jokes about killing Croats with an officer of the notorious paramilitary Beli Orlovi unit. Djuro rationalized his friend's change in behavior as something alien, like an infection. He could not accept the fact that his best friend had changed so drastically.

At times of great stress, we all may misinterpret the actions or comments of others. Uncertainty leads us to assert some measure of control by providing our own explanations for why people behave as they do. Djuro's comments reveal the importance of the symbolic meaning of gestures, sentences, and acts that may or may not have had the meaning that was later inferred by the participants. When such statements are directly threatening to powerless people, such as Djuro was in the prison camp, people see these behaviors as signs that their friends have become enemies even though they themselves have not changed. At the same time, those under threat expect their old friends to assist them as they had always done. When this did not happen (often because those friends too were in danger from members of their own group), disappointment, hurt, and then anger ensued. Together with the suffering that followed, these interactions between friends determined the future of the relationship – the closer the friendship had been, the greater the feelings of betrayal and the harder it would be to rebuild the relationship.

Repairing friendships: is it possible?

Not only the war, pain, suffering, and different personal histories distanced the people of Vukovar. The passing of time, diverging interests, social positions, and different interpretations of recent history in terms of who-did-what-to-whom-first also exacerbated the estrangement. Given the multiplicity of forces driving the people apart, the key question for a community like Vukovar is: can the social fabric be repaired?

Social reconstruction in a multi-ethnic community is a complex social and political process that operates at the interpersonal and intergroup level, and, finally, at the level of the society itself, where political processes external to the community may be influential. Here we address community dynamics. Vukovar is composed of many communities, among which the distinction between the Croat and Serb communities is the most obvious. Today, belonging to a distinct ethnic community is the most important identity indicator in the city. As such, crossing the line to socialize with another ethnic group is not encouraged. Such relations are permissible in official and commercial transactions, but generally not tolerated in the private sphere. Thus, intergroup ethnic behavior is the social norm, while one-on-one interpersonal behavior is a violation of the norm. Social relations in Vukovar have become dictated by strong group identities. The theoretical basis for these behaviors is well explained by social identity theorists as described by Weinstein and Stover in the Introduction to this volume and by Biro and colleagues in Chapter 9.

Is it possible to repair friendships broken under such difficult circumstances? And if so, how does that relate to community-building? The answers to these questions are not simple. For some, repairing friendships is impossible; for some it is irrelevant; while for others it is very important. The latter group might be open to a community intervention that would contribute to social reconstruction by bringing social functioning at least to the level that it was before disruption.[5] There is no doubt that feelings of having been betrayed at a crucial point in life by important others, and consequent distrust in the present, color the lives of many people. It is also beyond question that people who used to be close friends have changed. But also there are those who wish to repair their broken friendships, who still dream about their friends, who become very emotional when talking about them, and who, with support, could take the risk of reaching out.

Often these people are simply too anxious to approach their old friend for fear of rejection and thus lose the remaining idealization of the past. But if programs were in place to encourage them and provide a psychologically safe space, then perhaps these friendships could regain legitimacy in the Vukovar social arena and serve as models of social reconstruction at the interpersonal level.

Take, for example, the case of Gordana, who was pleased when she heard from her cousin in 1996 that her Croat friend Antonija had been asking about her. Once, explained the cousin, Antonija visited Vukovar but did not have the time to visit Gordana. Three years later, Gordana went for a trip to the coastal city of Porec where Antonija was living. She wanted to visit her friend, and even went into a telephone booth to call her, but could not bring herself to do so. Gordana knew her friend worked in a bank, so she never entered one for fear that she might run into her friend by accident. Gordana thought that Antonija might ignore her, thus rejecting her friendship for good. She spoke with great distress about a pre-war colleague whom she met two years earlier who had turned his head away from her. After that, Gordana decided that she would not approach any former friends and acquaintances. In her opinion, the renewal of contact among friends actually depended on who was going to make the symbolic gesture of recognition. When asked directly, Gordana said that she would very much like to see Antonija again but wondered whether her cousin had been exaggerating the interest that Antonija had reportedly expressed. She was clear that she would be pleased if someone could arrange (or even mediate) a meeting. Gordana's humiliating experience with the former friend who turned away from her led Gordana to generalize to all members of the other group, even to her friend that she missed very much and who perhaps had showed a willingness to rebuild their relationship.

The symbolic gesture of avoiding eye contact and then turning the head away sends a very strong message that hurts people greatly. Petar, a 37-year-old Serb driver, explained: "Some [Croats who have returned to Vukovar] turn their heads away when they see us. This happened to me once, and I was very hurt. These first encounters were very difficult and dramatic for both sides." Veljko, a Serb teacher, kept asking himself why his Croat friends held him responsible for actions during the war for which only a fraction of the Serb people were responsible. How could this be, after knowing him so well for so many years and after what they suffered together in the bomb shelter? He was puzzled that other Croats, with whom he was less close, contacted him, but not a couple whom he still loved. He kept pondering what the true face of his friends was: was it the one he knew for so long? Or was it the one in the present? He spent hours critically reviewing whether he had said anything that could have hurt this couple, but he had not arrived at an answer. He concluded: "I do not want to do anything more regarding them. I am trying to get rid of the need for them."

Obviously, it would be very important if Veljko could hear the views of his former friends. Perhaps they would say something like Marijan, a Croat in his late 20s, said about his former Serb friend. Marijan was angry because his friend had stood by as the Serbs were taking Croats away. For him, this friendship was finished and he wished no contact under any conditions. Such intergroup behavior and generalization to all members of the other ethnic group was evident in a number of intervie-wees. However, others made a point of distinguishing between the former friend and "all others." Zdenka, an unemployed Croat in her late 40s, explained that she would very much like to see her friend Dragica but was afraid that she would become very emotional:

Whenever I think about her, I cry. I'm afraid to show how important she is to me, and how sorry I am because I don't know how she feels toward me. Perhaps she does not care about me . . . When somebody asks me about her, I say that I do not care any more, but this is not true. Many people say the same about their former friends. But I ask myself now that perhaps they are not telling the truth, maybe they are afraid or are uneasy to admit that they still care and that these friends are important to them.

Most Croat participants said they were deeply hurt and offended that their former Serb friends were unable or unwilling to recognize the extent to which they and their families had suffered during the war. None of the Croats said that they expected their Serb friends to ask for forgiveness, although several Serb participants thought that such a plea from them was expected. However, the Croat participants longed for some kind of acknowledgment of or an apology for the anguish and persecution that so many Croats had been exposed to during the war and subsequent

occupation of the city by Yugoslav troops. Djuro, the retired Croat journalist, said he wanted his childhood friend, Aleksandar, a Serb, who had
served as a rather tough guard in the Serb prison where Djuro was incarcerated, to apologize to him. Djuro hoped that Aleksandar might make
some "fine, small gesture" on the occasion of the upcoming forty-fifth
anniversary of their graduation from the Vukovar high school. Such a
gesture, Djuro said, would be extremely important to him. He also was
dreaming that, at this event, someone among the Serb schoolmates would
say on behalf of the others that they were sorry for what happened to
Croats in Vukovar.

Many Croat participants had no desire to re-initiate friendships with
their past Serb friends. For example, Katica, a Croat women in her early
30s who returned to Vukovar in 1996, said she could never forget what
some of her Serb friends had done to her and her family. During the
war, her fiancé was killed and her father was badly wounded, while an
uncle was killed at the Ovcara farm massacre (see Stover and Shigekane,
Chapter 4 in this volume). While Katica was detained in the Velepromet[6]
detention facility, she saw one of her best Serb friends, Branko, working
there as a guard. During her detention, he failed to recognize or help her
in any way, although she was sure he could have done something. "I'm not
interested in his reasons for behaving the way he did," she said. "What is
done, is done. This cannot be repaired. We have nothing in common, we
can't have common friends, we can't spend time together any more . . . I
have suffered too much in the war to try to improve relations with the
Serbs." When asked if she could ever forgive Branko, she replied: "How
can I forgive, if no one is asking for forgiveness?"

Evidence of social pressure from both ethnic groups not to cross invisible but strong ethnic boundaries emerged in a number of interviews.
Goran, a Croat engineer who rarely sees his Serb friend with whom he
has re-established contact, said that they occasionally visit each other in
their homes, but they never go out together:

My social circle is now exclusively Croat. There are guys whose parents got killed,
and they view these things [i.e. relations with Serbs] differently . . . They are
uncomfortable meeting Serbs. My friend also has his social circle made up only
of Serbs . . . He told me that he does not feel comfortable in a Croat café because
he has to watch every word he says, not to use a wrong word, that he could not
relax because of this, and thought that someone might provoke him . . . I had the
same feeling when I went to a Serb café with him once.

Katarina, the Croat salesperson, said that she was afraid that Croats
would criticize her if they saw her talking to her Serb friend in public.
Milan, a Serb technician in his early 30s, attributed this to the efforts on

both sides to avoid offending one another. He said: "The Croats do not like folk music (meaning Serbian music), while we can't imagine having a good time without it. If I invited a Croat and played this music, he might feel offended or provoked. They play some other kind of music, those nationalistic songs, and if I came into their group, of course I would feel uncomfortable." However, Zlatko, a 27-year-old Serb who is unemployed, did not agree that social pressure works the same in both ethnic groups. He said that he avoided any discussion with his best Croat friend, Dane, about what had happened "because of respect for him, as I know that he has lived through many traumas." He referred to many former relationships as "forbidden friendships," because the in-group pressure among the Croats was stronger than among the Serbs. Interestingly, he was the only Serb participant to acknowledge how important it was for Croats to receive information about their missing family members. He talked about meeting a Croat friend whose grandmother was missing:

When I met him, I knew exactly what question was in his head. I told him that I really didn't know what had happened to her and that she was a person that we all liked . . . On the Croat side, they are definitely sure that we all know something about the missing. This is absolute nonsense. We here, we also were afraid of the Chetniks, volunteers, paramilitaries. At the beginning I was so afraid of them that I used to take a side street when I saw them coming down the street. I think that there are very few people in Vukovar who really know the truth about these crimes. I would very much like if the Croats understood this . . . I also feel the burden of this guilt, although I had nothing to do with these events. I feel in a way guilty that I was here, because of my nationality, because of this hell. I bear the guilt of other people and this troubles me a great deal. I can't get rid of this feeling of guilt.

Conclusion

Vukovar remains a highly polarized community. According to our interviews, Croats in the city feel betrayed by their former Serb friends and continue to avoid any rapprochement with them for fear that they may be rebuffed a second time. Croats feel betrayed because they believe their Serb friends had information in the months leading up to the war about what was going to happen to the Croats in Vukovar but failed to warn them, thus endangering their lives and the lives of their families. In the meantime, Serbs are adamant that they never possessed such information and therefore could not have withheld it from their Croat friends. They also maintain that their decision to leave Vukovar abruptly was made under chaotic and uncertain circumstances. Further, they feel little acknowledgment from their Croat neighbors that prior to the 1991 attack by the Yugoslav Army and Serb paramilitaries the local Serbs had experienced months of provocations and fear as Croat nationalists vilified them.

Distrust and betrayal have paralyzed ethnic relations in Vukovar. On one side are the Croats, who are bitter and disappointed that their Serb friends failed to show them any sympathy when they were forced into exile. Above all, they cannot understand why their former Serb friends, and especially those who remained living in Vukovar after the war, act as if nothing happened to the city's Croat population, even though they, as individual Serbs, may not have been responsible for the violence. The Croats want their Serb friends to acknowledge their suffering, to show some remorse for the past crimes committed in their name, and to help them reveal the truth about their missing family members. On the other side are the Serbs, who are disappointed that their former Croat friends could even think that they would betray them. They are surprised that their former friends do not understand that the violence directed against Croats during the war had nothing to do with them. They maintain that they personally harmed no one and could not possibly know the fate of the missing. They see no reason to show remorse or apologize for crimes they never committed, much less seek forgiveness. Unfortunately, one of the few issues on which both Croats and Serbs agree is one that hardly bodes well for the prospects of reconciliation in the city: namely, that those who suffered great personal losses are entitled to show strong resentment to the other ethnic group. Unfortunately, this resentment is bolstered by pressure from their own group not to cross ethnic boundaries.

Such sentiments notwithstanding, the prospects for eventually re-uniting former friends may not be as gloomy as they might seem at first blush. To begin with, the war in Vukovar caused friendships to break up in a variety of ways. Over the years, some former friends, though few in number, maintained their friendships, while others actively sought out one another after the hostilities had ended. Others, still cautious, maintained contact, although on a superficial level. Some wanted nothing to do with their former friends. One of the important findings from this study is that there is a critical moment of opportunity in a post-war setting when friends from opposing sides meet again. Typically, the key moment in re-establishing contact or failing to do so hinged on who would reach out first, and thus expose themselves to the humiliating risk of being rejected. In such cases, non-verbal communication, especially avoidance of eye contact, seemed to play a key role in determining whether a relationship would be ended or given another opportunity. The poignant symbolism of this meeting cannot be underestimated. Under these circumstances, those who have experienced what they see as abandonment must take a giant step, with no guarantee of a welcoming response.

What, then, are the conditions that would facilitate the rebuilding of past friendships, and, ultimately, help repair the social fabric of Vukovar? A way forward would be to create a community-based program that targeted those former friends who were willing, at a minimum, to meet and talk. Such a program could help former friends, and possibly groups of old friends and acquaintances, by providing them with a safe environment where the risk of emotional rejection would be minimal. Key to the success of the program would be the extent to which both sides would be willing to acknowledge and apologize for past crimes committed in their name, even if the scale of such abuses vary greatly. That is, Serbs would have to acknowledge that Serb military commanders and civilian leaders committed widespread and systematic crimes against Croats, while Croats would have to recognize that their leaders in the pre-war years also committed crimes, if far less in scale. Our study indicates that individuals and communities can best cope with their violent past only if and when the perpetrators (or their symbolic representatives) admit their wrongdoings and ask for forgiveness, and the victims (or their representatives) accept it. In this regard, Nadler[7] emphasizes that trust is a precondition for both offering and accepting apology. Namely, the perpetrator must have confidence that the victim will respond with forgiveness and readiness to open a new chapter in their relationships. The victim must have confidence that the perpetrator who asks for forgiveness is sincere, and not manipulative. The ultimate aim of such exchanges should be for both sides to agree upon a set of *shared* values and beliefs that places respect for human rights and dignity above all else.

Effectuating such an exchange is, of course, fraught with challenges, especially after a multi-ethnic conflict where all sides, if in varying degrees, were responsible for war crimes. The dilemma in Vukovar and throughout the former Yugoslavia is that Croats and Serbs, including our study participants, have developed different narratives of victimhood. We suggest that a basic sense of trust is more likely when an armed conflict ends with a shared agreement that clearly delineates victims from perpetrators. In such situations there is no need to prove who the victim is, and the perpetrator can expect that his confession of guilt will be returned with forgiveness. However, more commonly, the scenario is murkier; when different interpretations about the roles of victims and perpetrators exist, as in Vukovar, relations between the groups will invariably remain conflicted.

Since the current Serb and Croat leaders in Vukovar are unlikely to acknowledge the suffering inflicted by their ethnic group, we must find ways of gradually building trust by developing shared empathy and an awareness of responsibility at the individual and, where possible, at the group level. Such an approach, a kind of "instrumental reconciliation," involves initiating a series of steps in which former enemies cooperate with one another to accomplish a shared goal. Whether this can lead to a full socio-emotional reconciliation among community members remains to be tested. Even so, it should not be passed over because of a lack of political will. As this is the more common outcome of intrastate war between ethnic groups, it is essential that we look for ways to address the collective shame that is a residual of crimes committed across ethnic lines.

Any program developed in Vukovar to help re-unite former friends and acquaintances will need to emphasize the need for participants to recognize and respect the losses suffered by members of the other group. Experience indicates that intervention programs that encourage joint dialogue about past events of collective violence, the consequences of traumatic experience and mechanisms of recovery, and shared personal experiences can contribute to positive change.[8] Such changes are key for social reconstruction because they may diminish traumatic symptoms, increase cooperation with other groups, and encourage readiness to accept sympathy and apology. Our own experience[9] showed that positive results in building connections between members of antagonistic ethnic groups can be achieved through a program which includes several components: education about psychological processes related to loss and trauma, recognizing alternatives for constructive conflict resolution, sharing experiences about losses, and planning for social action. Along these lines, an intervention program aimed at facilitating dialogue between former friends and other community members could go a long way toward helping Vukovar on the path to recovery.

NOTES

1. Dean Ajdukovic, "Socijalna rekonstrukcija zajednice" (Community social reconstruction). In Dean Ajdukovic, ed. *Socijalna rekonstrukcija zajednice: psiholoski procesi, rjesavanje sukoba i socijalna akcija* (Community social reconstruction: psychological processes, conflict management and social action) (Zagreb: Society for Psychological Assistance, 2003), 11–39.
2. Laurel E. Fletcher and Harvey H. Weinstein, "Violence and Social Repair: Rethinking the Contribution of Justice to Reconciliation," *Human Rights Quarterly* 24: 3 (2002): 573–639.
3. Names of the interviewees and those mentioned by them have been changed to preserve the confidentiality guaranteed during the interviews.
4. Bert Useem, "Breakdown Theories of Collective Action," *Annual Review of Sociology* 24 (1998): 215–238.
5. Ajdukovic, "Community social reconstruction."

6. Velepromet was a large storage area turned into a transit detention point where the Croats were first detained by the Yugoslav army and paramilitaries before being transported to camps in Serbia or to an execution point such as the nearby Ovcara farm.

7. Arie Nadler, "Post-Resolution Processes: Instrumental and Socio-Emotional Routes to Reconciliation." In Gavriel Salomon and Baruch Nevo, eds. *Peace Education: The Concept, Principles, and Practices Around the World* (New Jersey: Lawrence Erlbaum Associates, 2002), 127–141.

8. Ervin Staub, "From Healing Past Wounds to the Development of Inclusive Caring: Contents and Processes of Peace Education." In Gavriel Salomon and Baruch Nevo, eds. *Peace Education: The Concept, Principles, and Practices Around the World* (New Jersey: Lawrence Erlbaum Associates, 2002), 73–86.

9. Dean Ajdukovic, Marina Ajdukovic, and Dinka Corkalo developed the project "Conflict Management and Community Social Reconstruction," in which an intervention program was tested with informal community leaders. Implemented by the Society for Psychological Assistance in 2002, the program integrated a community mental health approach, conflict management, social action, and education on coping with loss in order to facilitate social reconstruction.

15 Empathy and rehumanization after mass violence

Jodi Halpern and Harvey M. Weinstein

Milosevic did not kill – our neighbors were killing.

Male Croat, Vukovar, 2000

We are all pretending to be nice and to love each other. But be it known that I hate them and that they hate me. It will be like that forever, but we are now pretending.

Female Bosniak, Mostar, 2000

As interethnic conflicts have swept the world since the fall of the Berlin Wall, states torn apart by ethnic cleansing or genocide have been forced to confront the implications of communal violence where neighbor has turned against neighbor, and friend against friend. Those victimized by ethnic war must face the daunting challenge of restoring the health and well-being of their communities in an environment of physical and social destruction. For countries emerging from such periods of turmoil, the daunting task is to repair the social fabric of their societies. Perhaps the word "repair" is incorrect, because the task at hand is not to return to the status quo but to construct a new state framework based on rule of law, protection of minority rights, and a vision of a shared future. Given the tragic consequences of ethnic hatred and genocide, the goal of reconstruction is daunting. Much of the literature on peace-building or stabilization focuses at the level of the state and its efforts to rebuild institutions, bring about legal and electoral reform, maintain security, foster economic development, and help displaced persons return to their homes.[1,2,3] Despite research showing the unique harms inflicted by interethnic violence, little attention has been paid to the fact that people who once saw each other as the enemy must learn to live together again on a daily basis – in shops, the market, in schools, playgrounds, concerts, and coffeehouses.[4] In response, much of the focus of governmental and non-governmental agencies has been on institution-building. Aside from some attempts at conflict resolution usually derived from western-based perspectives and promulgated by international non-governmental organizations (NGOs), we know surprisingly little about how neighbors who have tortured neighbors, looted their homes or fired them from jobs can learn to live together again.

It is the interpersonal ruins, rather than the ruined buildings and institutions, that pose the greatest challenge for rebuilding society. Robert Putnam, a political scientist, suggests that social capital is critical to the development of community and that social capital is based on building networks of social relationships.[5,6] As with physical capital and human capital, social capital can enhance the ability of societies to flourish. Important in this task is his concept of "bridging social capital," a process of reaching beyond one's own group to build interconnectedness and interdependence. Such social relationships, however, must be accompanied by interactions and encounters at the individual level that allow for the discussion and/or acknowledgment of past events, however painful, and thus lead to some level of openness and trust.

In the wake of mass violence, societies are trying to re-establish trust and to foster acknowledgment of the past by turning to legal mechanisms and other forms of reckoning.[7] During this era of intense intrastate violence, we have witnessed a revitalization of international criminal law and the development of a new form of truth-telling – the truth commission – directed at establishing a historical record of past events. The implicit assumption held by many supporters of tribunals is that criminal trials are an important component of reconciliation. The fact that hundreds of millions of dollars have been devoted to these trials indicates a consensus in the international community that a juridical response is critical to the rebuilding of post-war societies.[8,9] While we agree that trials have a significant role to play, we have argued elsewhere that they are only one part of a much larger process of social repair.[10] Further, we suggest that an ecological model that supports interventions at multiple levels, from state actors to communities and neighborhoods, will have the greatest likelihood of success.

Truth-seeking processes in South Africa and elsewhere have emphasized that reconciliation must be accompanied by the religious ideal of transcending conflict through forgiveness and mercy.[11,12,13,14] Conflict resolution theorist and practitioner, John Paul Lederach conceptualizes reconciliation as a social space that requires relationship, encounter, and a discourse that reflects a shift in paradigm from the state-level focus traditionally found in political science.[15] He views this space as representing the confluence of four elements – truth, mercy, justice, and peace – and suggests that interventions at multiple levels of leadership and within multiple systems are critical to achieving reconciliation.

The problem with emphasizing transcendent forgiveness and mercy is two-fold. First, not everyone who is committed to rebuilding social relationships necessarily believes that this necessitates forgiveness.

Second, and more importantly, "forgiveness" is past- rather than future-oriented, and still does not provide a psychological basis for how people can overcome systematic dehumanization to see their neighbors once again as people.

Most work on social reconstruction in post-war societies focuses on the rule of law, state-building, community development, and conflict resolution. Further, the study of collective memory, state myths and symbols, and conceptions of social identity offer important theoretical conceptions of the factors that contribute to the break-up of states and suggest issues that must be attended to in order to restore social stability in a post-war society. However, we would argue that social reconstruction must also attend to interactions between neighbors and friends; since interethnic violence is frequently intimate and relational, repair also must function on that level. Beyond the literature on forgiveness, psychosocial treatment and community development, few authors have addressed the critical dimension of what must happen between people to lead to genuine *rehumanization*.[16,17] In this chapter, we argue that the perceptual shifts that take place when one becomes interested in another's distinct subjective perspective are central to rehumanization.

Yet discussions of reconciliation in the aftermath of mass violence rarely address the rebuilding of relationships – a fundamental precondition for reconciliation to occur. Central to this process is the question of what is involved in rehumanizing the other. One place to start to address this is in the literature on dehumanization. Social psychologists Herbert Kelman and Lee Hamilton, in their important study of the My Lai massacre, suggest that there are three critical factors that allow individuals to commit war crimes.[18] These are dehumanization, routinization, and authorization. Their work suggests that under certain systemic conditions, a cascade of social processes may rapidly overtake individuals so that they act in ways that lie outside the realm of expected moral behavior.

These ideas emerge from decades of study by social psychologists who have articulated theories of intergroup phenomena that result in the categorization of in- and out-group membership. These processes subsumed under social identity theory suggest that we all categorize ourselves within some social framework, ie where do I, as an individual, belong?[19,20] A corollary of this phenomenon is in-group favoritism and out-group exclusion. If, as Anthony Oberschall writes, polarization and escalation occur, then the groups diverge, differences become magnified, and, along with a host of other social factors, vulnerability to violence emerges.[21] In situations of heightened tension, negative stereotyping becomes pervasive; as Bar-Tal notes, "the opposing group is delegitimized."[22] The delegitimization, of course, may be used to support the violence.

Under certain conditions, stereotypes, defined as a set of consensual beliefs, may contribute to actions that are destructive to those stereotyped. The individuality of the stereotyped group members is then lost.[23] Under conditions of social breakdown, there may be a shift of identity from the individual to the collective self, and individual actions become heavily determined by group influence – those in the out-group become dehumanized and come to represent merely categories. The dilemma in reconciliation is how to reverse this process of dehumanization and to return their humanity to those where categorization has removed all individual attributes.

We hypothesize that one of the fundamental components of reconciliation between former enemies is the development of empathy, which we describe as a fundamentally individualizing view of another. In advancing this thesis, we are not suggesting that all that is required to address the wrongs that perpetrators have visited upon victims is empathy, but we do suggest that if the desired outcome is reconciliation, as opposed to coexistence or cohabitation, an empathic connection must occur.

One question this raises is whether emphasizing empathy, an individualizing perspective, represents a bias toward western individualism. Our response to this is two-fold. On the one hand, reconciliation in any society requires re-establishing a basis for each person seeing another as an individual, as a human being, and this process requires empathy. For example, interest in another as a person in his or her own right is captured in the traditional African value of "ubuntu," literally "I am because you are." This comes from the Xhosa saying "a person is a person through persons."[24] In practice, ubuntu refers to face-to-face understanding between two human beings.

On the other hand, not all cultures focus on the particular version of empathy developed here, which emphasizes curiosity about another's mental life. This emphasis on subjectivity is, in our view, appropriate in studying the people of the countries of the former Yugoslavia. Interview and focus group data from our projects suggest that prior to the war, people had relationships based on this kind of empathy. Relationships were individualized, mostly without group attributions. Yet today we see a marked absence of empathy after the war, a finding of great significance. Nevertheless, we are aware that in other societies, close individual relationships might be rooted in less mentalistic processes.

Empathy and reconciliation

Reconciliation must begin at the level of the individual – neighbor to neighbor, then house to house, and finally, community to community.

Reconciliation requires the rehumanization of the "other," and for that to occur, the "other" must be vested with qualities that are familiar and accepted. Finding commonality through identification with a former enemy is a first step.[25] Reflecting on the process of reconciliation between Germans and Poles in the aftermath of the Second World War, Gesine Schwan writes:

> If reconciliation is not merely an intellectual but also an emotional process (contritia cordis), then a major role in making reconciliation between peoples possible, in generating a capacity for reconciliation, will be played by the education of attitudes, or what used to be known by the old-fashioned term "cultivation of the heart." Naturally the intellect and judgment also participate in remembrance, but the emotional dimension of empathy, which enables us to incorporate other people's perceptions, to see the experience with their eyes, plays a key role.[26]

Schwan suggests that empathy, and not just sympathy, plays a major role in genuine reconciliation. The distinction between empathy and sympathy is important. Sympathy is about experiencing shared emotion, while empathy involves imagining and seeking to understand the unique perspective of another person.[27] Both sympathy and empathy involve experiencing emotional resonance, or attuned feelings in the presence of another. However, while this is sufficient for sympathy, it is not for empathy.

Empathy is an imaginative inquiry that presupposes a sense of the other as a distinct individual. Schwan claims that empathy is particularly important for reconciliation, but does not provide a theoretical basis for this claim. Halpern's conceptualization of empathy provides the beginning of such an account.[28] Specifically, the major function of empathy is to individualize and particularize and thereby to challenge the major aspects of dehumanization. First, empathy differs from sympathy in seeking the individual perspective of another, rather than generalizing or stereotyping what that perspective might be. Descriptions of the dehumanization involved in violence recount how people stereotype and distance themselves from their enemies. Second, empathy involves being genuinely curious about another person. In contrast, war involves closing one's mind toward the other's experiences, and presuming that one can already predict the other's behavior ("They'll never change"). Third, empathy involves emotional as well as cognitive openness, and tolerating the ambivalence this might arouse.

Social anthropologist Tone Bringa has described the complex but warm and cordial relationships among people of all national groups that were the norm in the countries of the former Yugoslavia for at least fifty years before the war.[29] Mirko Tepavac[30] and Elizabeth Neuffer[31] describe neighborhood life as genuinely multi-ethnic and multi-cultural. Journalist Slavenka Drakulic mourns, "Not only was I educated to believe that the whole territory of ex-Yugoslavia was my homeland, but because we could travel freely abroad . . . I almost believed that borders, as well as nationalities, existed only in people's heads."[32]

However, much has changed in the countries of the former Yugoslavia since the war. While people from different ethnic groups are working and living as neighbors again, there appears to be a paucity of empathy. Indeed, our data from ninety key informant interviews and twenty-four focus groups in selected cities contain not a single expression of empathy. Nowhere does someone from a particular ethnic group demonstrate curiosity and emotional openness toward the distinct perspective of someone from another ethnic group. This suggests that there are very large barriers to establishing empathy after mass violence. Given such difficulties, if people are coexisting peacefully at the present time, and frequently cooperate in the workplace, why not be satisfied with coexistence?

In our view, coexistence without empathy is both superficial and fragile, for mistrust, resentment, and even hatred linger just below its surface. As one of our informants told us, "We can live together, we just can't sleep." In the interviews, we looked for interactions where we would expect and yet did not find empathy. We found many instances of on-going fear, mistrust, stereotypes, feelings of betrayal, ethnic group pressure, on-going ethnic discrimination and occasional violence.[33] Despite the "contact hypothesis"[34] and other theories that posit that simple coexistence under certain conditions is rehumanizing, we learned that even after six years many people in these communities remain suspicious and resent their co-workers and neighbors of other ethnic groups. Two informants had this to say:

The two colleagues that I used to work with – neither said hello to me nor have asked me how I was or do I need anything. They have not shown even a bit of good will. They have betrayed me as human beings. And now I should be glad to see them? They are not asking for forgiveness that I am actually offering – the point is they are just not asking for it at all.

My best man was a Serb. He lives here but I have no contact with him. There are many things that I cannot forgive him. He did not warn me, although he knew everything. He socialized with such Serbs that he knew everything, and my children and I could have got killed.

Those informants who were somewhat empathic to members of other ethnic groups said they understood the social pressure their former neighbors or colleagues were under, given the generally accepted interdiction against socializing between ethnic groups. A few also recognized that they shared the experience of a common tragedy: "Some of them are normal people who went through hell. They, too, had their own hell." Yet, while this statement reflects compassion, it is addressed toward a generic, rather than a particular, "other." These interviews are disheartening. Despite six years of apparent rebuilding of social ties, many people in the countries of the former Yugoslavia find it difficult to connect with each other.

While some scholars and diplomats suggest that coexistence should be sufficient for the present, we believe that the lack of overt conflict may only hide schisms that could potentially lead to future rupture. In order to elucidate further our initial hypothesis that empathy relates to rehumanization, we studied examples of social relationships from other locations of mass trauma and the data gathered by our colleagues to see if we could find even partial or transient moments of empathy. Our hope is that this preliminary investigation will facilitate empirical inquiry into the barriers preventing empathic relations. In the next section, we introduce three descriptions of empathy and rehumanization. In the first, the focus is on individual initiative. The second illustrates the importance of social context, and the last demonstrates how critical the passage of time is for the development of social processes. These examples will suggest that in communities that have emerged from violent interethnic conflict, societal change is necessary for individual change to take hold.

Rehumanization

Humanizing the perpetrator

In 1995, after a long process of consultations, conferences, and public discussion, the South African government established its Truth and Reconciliation Commission (TRC), with Archbishop Desmond Tutu as the chair. As Priscilla Hayner, a scholar of transitional justice notes, the TRC was the most carefully thought-out and meticulously planned truth commission that has emerged as an alternative or as a complement to trials.[35] While its strengths and weaknesses have been extensively debated, the TRC's emphasis on the humanity of both victims and perpetrators, and its focus on restorative justice make it a unique contribution to the field of transitional justice.[36] Its most unusual step was to offer a truth-for-justice opportunity. The TRC was empowered to offer individual amnesty to perpetrators who committed politically motivated crimes between March 1960 and May 1994, so long as they made a public confession. In a very perceptive and provocative paper, psychologist Pumla Gobodo-Madikezela describes an encounter between an assassin for the *apartheid* government of South Africa, Eugene de Kock, and two African women whose husbands he murdered.[37] Eugene de Kock, who earned the name "Prime Evil," headed a secret police unit based at Vlakplaas farm near Pretoria that functioned as a death squad. Gobodo-Madikezela describes a meeting with de Kock in which he expresses remorse for his crimes and seeks forgiveness from the widows. She describes this meeting as a critical post-trauma instance of mutual empathy between the women and de Kock. She labels what she observes in the interaction as empathy partially based on her own felt responses, which she believes exemplify empathy for a perpetrator. The underlying thesis of the paper, then, is that empathic engagement converts the stereotype; the fear becomes subsumed by humanness; the devil becomes a human being who committed evil acts. Here is her description:

Sitting directly across from me in the small prison consulting room where I saw him, he shifted his eyes uncomfortably. His feet shuffled, and I could hear the clatter of the leg chains that bound him to the chair, which was bolted to the floor. His mouth quivered and there were tears in his eyes. As he started to speak, his hand trembled and he became visibly distressed. With a breaking voice he said: "I wish I could do much more than 'I'm sorry.' I wish there was a way of bringing their bodies back alive. I wish I could say, 'Here are your husbands'," he said, gesturing with shaking, outstretched arms and bending them in a holding position. "But unfortunately . . . I have to live with it." At that moment de Kock invited my empathy.

Gobodo-Madikezela describes de Kock as perceiving and being moved by the women's pain, and says that to do this is to recognize the women as human beings. In so doing, he differs from those who seek forgiveness without genuinely appreciating the humanity and suffering of the being in front of them. She takes de Kock's affective reaction to the women's loss to be an indicator of his empathy, and this triggers her own empathy for him. He appears genuinely moved by the women's suffering, hence the wish to be able to bring their husbands back. Although the wish is only a wish (a wish does not commit one to action in any sense), it is presumably motivated by a felt sense of the women's suffering, and not just his need to be exonerated. Being moved by another's suffering is an essential first step in empathic recognition.

A further aspect of empathy is to be genuinely interested in the particular perspective and needs of another individual. De Kock responds to the wives' need to know exactly what happened to their husbands by giving them a detailed account, something no one else had done. This suggests that de Kock recognized their particular needs rather than offering only generic sympathy. Interestingly, it is less clear whether the women empathize with de Kock, despite the fact that they are clearly moved by him. Here is Pearl Faku's (the wife of one of the victims) description of what Gobodo-Madikezela calls empathy:

I was profoundly touched by him, especially when he said he wished he could bring our husbands back. I didn't even look at him when he was speaking to us . . . Yet I felt the genuineness in his apology. I couldn't control my tears. I could hear him, but I was overwhelmed by emotion, and I was just nodding, as a way of saying 'Yes, I forgive you.' I hope that when he sees our tears, he knows that they are not only tears for our husbands, but tears for him as well . . . I would like to hold him by the hand, and show him that there is a future, and that he can still change.

Gobodo-Madikezela writes that "the image of the widow reaching out to her husband's murderer is an extraordinary expression – and *act* – of empathy, shedding tears not only for her loss but also, it seems, for the loss of de Kock's moral soul – wishing to hold his hand to lead him into a future where 'he can still change' and rejoin the world of moral humanity."

In our view, what Gobodo-Madikezela describes is a tentative step toward rehumanization. While the women resonate with de Kock's suffering and display clearly their sympathy for him, their emotions cannot be described as wholly empathic. They are caught up in an idealized moment, in which they seem to share the same views and feelings as de Kock. Emotional resonance is a core aspect of both sympathy and empathy. In sympathy, this resonance is used to form an identification with the other, so that it seems that the two are having a shared emotional experience. In empathy, resonance helps guide an imaginative inquiry into the individual experience of a distinct, complex, other person. What Faku describes is her experience of emotional identification with de Kock.

It is unclear whether Faku could see de Kock as an individual in a broader sense. What Faku imagines is not how it feels to be de Kock, but what she and de Kock have in common – intense pain over the death of her husband (and of course they don't feel the same about this loss either). The limitation of sympathy is that such moments of identification are necessarily static and cannot provide the basis of an on-going relationship. A critical step in rehumanizing is to see another person as a non-idealized other who has distinct emotions and views.

What is missing is the ability of his victims to see de Kock in all his complexity. Presumably, recognizing those aspects of his personality that relate to narcissism and control would evoke anger or hatred in the women. To tolerate such feelings while continuing to resonate with de Kock's feelings of remorse would require tolerating intense emotional ambivalence. While it may be too much to expect victims to tolerate the intense emotional ambivalence evoked by a perpetrator like de Kock, the issue of what empathy demands is a central one for reconciliation. If reconciliation is the goal, on-going relationships with former enemies must move beyond sympathy and idealization. Rather, the challenge is to recognize another as a distinct, three-dimensional human being, with faults and negative attributes that surely will evoke upsetting emotions, but without being catapulted into rejecting and dehumanizing him again. This is the work of empathy.

Why is this so important for reconciliation? One obvious reason is that relating to another on an on-going basis involves disagreements, and therefore tolerating differences is part of a resilient relationship. Further, cooperation and political or joint action among individuals depend on the idea of respecting each other's distinct perspectives. Reconciliation does not occur merely in imagined solidarity, but rather shows itself in the degree to which people actually can act as distinct individuals, with mutual regard, in the real world.

The emotional resonance and sympathy that occurs between de Kock and Faku goes a long way toward rehumanization. First, to recognize another as a sufferer is to recognize that person as an emotional being. Second, to be capable of remorse is to experience oneself as morally human, so for de Kock to feel remorse is to reclaim his moral potential, and when the women recognize him as remorseful they are recognizing his status in the moral universe. Third, to feel sympathy for another who wronged you is to get over a dominant mood of resentment.

Yet sympathy is not enough for reconciliation to occur – it is limited to the moment of emotional resonance and does not offer a foundation on which trust and relational interdependence may be constructed. Social reconstruction then depends upon the degree to which people act in concert to rebuild societal structures, and that process requires respect for and the synthesis of divergent views.

Humanizing the enemy in war

The next case study is in some sense a mirror image of the previous one. Here two former enemies are forced into a situation where, in order to survive, they must cooperate in the sense just defined: they must find a way to act together while recognizing that they do not share each other's perspective. This example comes from the film *No Man's Land* – a film about Serb and Bosniak soldiers made by Bosnian film-maker Danis Tanovic in 2001. The film opens as Tchiki, a Bosniak, and Nino, a Serb, find themselves trapped in a trench in the middle of a battle. A third man, Tsera, also a Bosniak, is lying on a land mine that will explode if he moves. Both sides are shooting at them, and the UN forces, portrayed by the film-maker as bumbling and incompetent, endanger rather than help them.

The two enemies, Tchiki and Nino, must cooperate in order to secure assistance and to survive. They must keep anything from moving the man on the bomb until it can be deactivated. After initial angry words about who started the war, they quickly set such conversations aside, and respond to the need to work together. They say, "Who cares who started the war? We're in the same shit now."

As the two men try to cooperate to save their lives, the narrative moves toward partial "empathy" and then backward, in a dance of approach and avoidance. Initially, the two Bosniaks talk to each other, and not to Nino, the Serb. The men from opposing sides do not even know each other's names. The first personal moment comes when Nino gives his backpack to Tsera (the Bosniak who is lying on the bomb) to rest his head on. Nino then walks over to Tchiki to introduce himself to him and Tchiki rejects his outstretched hand. However, shortly after this, Tchiki apologizes to Nino for the rejection and they introduce themselves. Nino then expresses curiosity about Tchiki as an individual, asking him how he knows Tsera. This leads them to start talking about their real lives, and it quickly emerges that they both had an affair with the same woman, Sanja. They become bonded in a show of masculine solidarity, a shared identity, and attune emotionally at this moment, lighting up with pleasure together thinking about her, and recognizing together the sad fact that she was forced to leave the country.

However, this moment is short-lived. A UN armored personnel carrier appears at the trench and its blue-helmeted commander offers to take Nino and Tchiki with him, leaving Tsera behind lying on the land mine. Tchiki would never abandon his friend, but Nino starts to leave. Tchiki shoots at Nino to keep him from leaving, fearing that the Serbs will bomb him and Tsera if the Serb soldier escapes. This traps Nino, who now feels threatened by Tchiki. He waits and, when he sees an opportunity, he grabs Tchiki's knife and stabs him in the leg in an attempt to escape. Tchiki then vows to kill him, saying in a hurt voice, "He betrayed me with my own knife." These words are significant: Tchiki now does not see Nino as any Serb, but as a particular man he had begun to trust and who betrayed him. While he no longer is the stereotype, he is still the "enemy." He ultimately shoots Nino, saying, as one would to a friend who betrayed the friendship, "You tried to kill me with my own knife – is that how you thank me?" The film's dialogue echoes the words of betrayal and pain that many of our informants in Bosnia and Herzegovina and in Croatia expressed when they talked about their former friends and neighbors from another ethnic group:

Some of them used that trust and have shown another face which I hadn't known until then.

Well, the worst thing actually is that I never could imagine that like, you know, your ex-, your former friend could attack you; you know, to wear guns and everything, you know, to kill you . . .

While Tchiki and Nino have not been friends, they had begun to relate on a more personal level, making the betrayal all the more potent.

The film ends with the message that individuals are powerless to be reconciled in the face of social forces that continue to polarize them. The moments of connection between Tchiki and Nino are extremely short-lived. Yet the fact that they occur at all is interesting. A premise of the film is that being literally trapped together in a place that is no place, an utterly barren "no man's land," somehow makes this connection possible. The idea that the removal of social forces facilitates interethnic connection points out how on-going social factors create barriers to reconciliation. In the project's key informant interviews, people frequently raised a concern that if they became friends with former enemies, their own people would ostracize them. It is apparent and must be remembered that empathy is socially situated. While some individuals may be able to go against the tide and establish relationships across ethnic or other social barriers, for most, the social, political, and cultural environment must be supportive of that process. In the film, the isolation of the trench at a moment suspended in time allows for some rapprochement to occur.

Despite the tragic ending of the film, the possibility of sustained empathy is supported by the fact that the film-maker is himself a Bosniak, yet he depicts the Serb, Nino, in fully human terms. The Bosniak film-maker imagines and is moved by the particular perspective of a Serbian soldier, while retaining an awareness of the distinct perspective he and his comrades might have. The very creation of the film shows that the cognitive elements of empathy, and not just sympathy (as depicted in de Kock's case), are recoverable in the aftermath of mass violence.

Rehumanization over time

What is strikingly absent in the two previous cases is the development of a relationship over time. This is a crucial absence, since the ultimate outcome of reconciliation must be the ability to live together over the years. In contrast to the one-time encounter between de Kock and the two women and the short-lived meeting of the two men in *No Man's Land* stands the five-year relationship between two women, Dobrinka, a Serb, and Marija, a Croat, from the former Yugoslavia, who lost sons during the war. They met in 1997 and have been working together on projects related to finding the thousands of people who went missing during the Balkan wars. Initially, so much enmity existed between the new states and entities that there was little cooperation between them in finding the missing, especially those who were buried in mass graves. Interstate and interentity cooperation was essential to finding these graves, exhuming them, and identifying the remains, if possible. As the two women both describe, they hated each other during their initial meetings in 1997. Dobrinka said it was "revolting, how badly people behaved." Yet, five years later, she said:

[Marija and I] have come to a point of interpersonal tolerance. We can now get together and have conversations without hatred; we have really done a lot together. We participated until last year in joint conferences, in which there were also disagreements about everything – but we finally realized that we are at base the same – we are the same because of our common tragedy, the loss of someone dear, and most essential is to find those who are lost.

Marija gives a more complex answer than Dobrinka. On the one hand, she states generalized feelings of forgiveness toward Dobrinka and all the other Serb mothers who have lost children. She seems more comfortable speaking about the Serbs in idealized, static, and group terms – she says, "We have already forgiven *them*." She describes putting flowers on the graves of unidentified bodies, together with the Serbian mothers, saying it does not matter which bodies were people from which ethnic groups. Compassion for the dead is clearly a step toward rehumanization, but it does not require developing an on-going relationship.

On the other hand, when asked about her feelings toward a specific individual – Dobrinka – her answer is more nuanced. Marija describes the changes in their relationship just as Dobrinka does. She remembers the initial meetings as terrible, full of conflict, and also points to the progress the two have made in working together. She expresses her own skepticism about whether she is really able to be friends with Dobrinka, describing how they can "give support" but not have "the feeling to sit and eat together." She does not idealize Dobrinka, and in fact implies she does not like her personality very much. At one point she says that she has "nothing nice to say" about Dobrinka. Yet a colleague reported that when Marija witnessed Dobrinka being criticized by others after speaking up in a meeting, she urgently went to her and hugged her, expressing her heartfelt respect for Dobrinka's words.

Marija and Dobrinka relate more fully than de Kock and Faku do. First, their relationship is not idealized – it allows for conflict and ambivalence. Marija can say she has "nothing nice to say" in one moment and hug

Dobrinka in another. Second, their relationship changes over time. This is not necessarily only for the better. Dobrinka, for example, describes how she is developing resentment for Marija because, as a Croat, Marija has economic entitlements that she, a Serb, lacks. These resentments, however, are not overgeneralized into a dehumanized view of the other. Both women find it hard to believe that in 1997 they viewed the other as inhuman. Rather, the "other" is normalized as a human being like any other. They share some things in common, and yet there are differences as well.

Third, the two are able to share real-world goals and values, not just wishes. De Kock's wish to bring back the husbands operates entirely in the realm of fantasy and idealization. It is not related to his agency, to what he is actually willing to build his life around, given serious choices. In contrast, Dobrinka and Marija make difficult choices in concert – they share a commitment to finding the missing over seeking justice. While accountability is important to them, their clear priority is to find those who disappeared. To hold values reciprocally is the basis of genuine respect for each other as moral agents. To put this slightly differently, Dobrinka and Marija do not see each other opportunistically, as people to be manipulated to meet their own needs. They genuinely see each other as holding the same values regarding their shared activity, and are committed to acting in concert on this basis.

Empathy: a normative ideal after mass violence

These cases suggest that individual effort is insufficient to re-establish empathy in the aftermath of mass violence. What individuals can achieve in rarified moments bracketing the social world (meetings with de Kock the prisoner, encounters in a *No Man's Land*) are moments of emotional resonance. As the de Kock–Faku example shows, resonating with another person emotionally breaks the spell of dehumanization. To be genuinely moved by another's suffering is to see the other *as* human. A first step in rehumanizing another is to see him or her *as* another human being. Similarly, identification is mentioned often in discussions of reconciliation, overlapping with examples of sympathy. Identification, in our view, is similar to sympathy in precipitating the process of rehumanization, yet in limiting itself to a strategically partial view of the other. As Laurel Fletcher and Harvey Weinstein have described it, identification is "an other-oriented feeling that is congruent with the perceived welfare of the subject . . ." It is an unconscious process in which "we identify with people in situations where some aspect of the (subject) resonates with an unrecognized aspect of the (individual's) psychological make-up."[38] Consider the moment in *No Man's Land* when Tchiki and Nino identify with each other's feelings about Sanja. As they relate warmly to their shared experiences as lovers of this woman, they clearly are viewing each other *as* human beings, not as a generic enemy. Yet this moment does not carry them forward to empathize with the other's distinct experiences during the war. However heartfelt, this moment presumes and builds nothing regarding their openness to, or tolerance for, the other's complex and differing views. Identification does not guide one in the future-oriented task of living and working with others, with whom disagreement is inevitable. Sympathetic feelings, in and of themselves, involve an idealizing, or at least a strategically incomplete, view of the other.

In contrast, the goal of empathy is to see the world *from* the complex perspective of another person. This is pertinent to reconciliation. After war, it may be easy for a Bosniak and a Serb to recognize that the other is angry or afraid, and even to sympathize with such feelings, given that each has his or her own anger and fear. However, it is considerably more difficult to view the world in the unique way the other person does, to see why a person once seen as a perpetrator feels victimized by certain policies, or feels entitled to have defended himself. To change perspectives implies that one can reframe an attitude born from terror and violence and convert that fixed view into something that accepts the frailty, the humanness, of the other.

Without empathy, it is impossible to accept the other's view of past events. To do so requires accepting that people hold different beliefs about a sequence of events, and that agreement on the "truth" may never occur. After war and ethnic cleansing, truth is always contested, even when the facts are revealed in a court of law. Without seeing the events through the enemies' eyes, there is little to help one tolerate disagreement, and reconciliation may never be achieved.

One might take issue with our emphasis on curiosity and cultivating a realistic view of the other. After all, the sympathy between Faku and de Kock and the identification between Tchiki and Nino do have important social value. But it must be recognized that these rarified moments occur far removed from the social world and historical reality. Indeed, social forces that are barriers to reconciliation are suspended or bracketed during idealized moments of sympathy and simple identification – de Kock is a prisoner, immobilized and presumably with no future power to harm, while the two men in *No Man's Land* are momentarily free of the social forces that make it so threatening to build ties with former enemies. One of the most frequent comments in our interviews with key informants was how people fear social ostracism if they are reconciled with other ethnic groups. Presumably it is only because they are removed from such pressures that Tchiki and Nino are able to identify.

Interestingly, despite the absence of full-blown curiosity in our interviews, we did find examples of people who were able to view each other in
more complex ways, and tolerate the accompanying emotional ambivalence. Dobrinka and Marija, for example, identified with each other as
mothers who had lost sons. This shared, real-world experience appears
to be the fabric that holds everything together in their day-to-day transactions. Marija and Dobrinka not only see each other's shortcomings,
but they even dislike each other. Yet they also care deeply for the other's
feelings, coming to comfort each other during difficult times. As noted
earlier, tolerating ambivalence, as opposed to temporarily idealizing (and
later devaluing) another person, is a critical part of genuine empathy.

While the relationship between Dobrinka and Marija and the making of
the film *No Man's Land* show that empathy is possible, it can be achieved
only if the actual practices and social conditions, such as regaining trust,
voicing disagreement, and securely developing relationships that facilitate empathy, are also present over time. In the countries of the former
Yugoslavia, specific barriers to this include bias in the media, corruption
in government, distrust in the rule of law, schools divided by ethnicity, special-interest groups that are either overly attended to or ignored,
unemployment, and political passivity that is a legacy of the Communist
era. Changing these societal conditions is critical to enable a shift from
coexistence to reconciliation and social reconstruction.

The emergence of civil society in post-war countries helps create social
conditions whereby people reach across "enemy" lines in pursuit of
common objectives. Hence, the empathic relationship that Marija and
Dobrinka have developed since 1997 was facilitated by the fact that,
as mothers searching for their missing sons, they worked within NGOs
developed to pursue this goal. It is critical that interventions focusing
on empathy must be integrated with people's realistic on-going social
circumstances. They must be introduced and supported with sufficient
time for real development and change to take place in a region. Social
conditions that allow people to appreciate each other in three dimensions
in their real social situations are essential. For this to occur, a state must
exist where the rule of law is the norm, human rights are embraced, and
security for all groups is protected.

The film *No Man's Land* reminds us that reconciliation is not the work
of individuals alone, but also depends upon the social circumstances
in which individuals find themselves. While reconciliation must occur
between individuals, the process can only occur within the context of a
society that not only gives permission for people of opposing groups to
interact but indeed promotes their collaboration in pursuit of a common
goal – building a humane society based on principles of justice and equity.

Ultimately, then, reconciliation will not occur without both individual and social change. While the international community has emphasized development and rule of law in post-war societies, we argue that while those interventions are important, they are also limited in their ability to promote and sustain social reconstruction and reconciliation. Hand in hand with macro-level interventions must be the development of grassroots programs that facilitate interpersonal interaction, and research that examines the social conditions that help people to maintain curiosity and emotional openness toward each other's distinct perspectives.

In the aftermath of mass trauma, it is extraordinarily threatening and painful to imagine the perspective of another whose people so hurt one's own. We propose that empathy serves as a kind of normative ideal for a rehumanized view of the other. Each aspect corresponds to something that war robs people of – individualization rather than stereotyping, curiosity about others rather than being too knowing, and tolerance of ambivalence rather than organizing experience through feelings of resentment, anger, or fear. Moreover, empathy is not achieved in an intense moment of sympathy, but in living together and genuinely attending to another's perspective over time. This kind of understanding seems to be the basis of genuine social cooperation.

More direct empirical study of post-war communities is needed to understand what fosters or hinders empathy over a sustained period of time. While discerning the value of empathy in concrete health and societal terms will be challenging, the alternative, to equate emotional reconciliation with sympathy, and accompanying attitudes like forgiveness, idealizes personal relationships and promotes the goal of transcending social influences. This not only diminishes interpersonal relations, it lets society off the hook and is likely to have devastating consequences for the health and well-being of communities.

NOTES

The authors wish to acknowledge the contributions of Emily Shaw, who interviewed two women who had lost family members in Croatia, and Felicia Lester, who assisted with the literature review and data analysis. An earlier version of this chapter was published as a paper in Jodi Halpern and Harvey M. Weinstein, "Rehumanizing the other: Empathy and Reconciliation," *Human Rights Quarterly* 26:3 (2004), © The Johns Hopkins University Press; reprinted with permission of the Johns Hopkins University Press.
1. Payan Akhavan, "Justice in The Hague: Peace in the Former Yugoslavia? A Commentary on the United Nations War Crimes Tribunal," *Human Rights Quarterly* 20 (1998): 737–816.

2. Michael Pugh, *Regeneration of War-Torn Societies* (New York: St. Martin's Press, Inc., 2000).

3. International Crisis Group, *The Continuing Challenge of Refugee Return in Bosnia and Herzegovina* (Sarajevo and Brussels: Balkans Report No. 137, 2002).

4. Colin Knox and Padraic Quirk, eds. *Peace Building in Northern Ireland, Israel, and South Africa: Transition, Transformation and Reconciliation* (London and New York: St. Martin's Press Ltd, 2001).

5. Robert Putnam, *Making Democracy Work: Civic Traditions in Modern Italy* (Princeton: Princeton University Press, 1993).

6. Robert Putnam, *Bowling Alone: The Collapse and Revival of the American Community* (New York: Simon and Shuster, 2000).

7. Neil Kritz, "Coming to Terms with Atrocities: A Review of Accountability Mechanisms for Mass Violations of Human Rights", *Law and Contemporary Problems* 59: 4 (1996): 127–152.

8. "The ICTY at a Glance," website of the International Criminal Tribunal for the former Yugoslavia, available on World Wide Web at http://www.un.org/icty/glance/index.htm (last modified May 2, 2003). These institutional domestic and international responses have become equated with a process of reconciliation. The website of the ICTY lists as one of its objectives "to contribute to the restoration of peace by promoting reconciliation in the former Yugoslavia."

9. UN Security Council, 3453rd mtg., at 1, U.N. Doc. S/RES/955 (1994). United Nations Security Council Resolution 955 (1994), which established the International Criminal Tribunal for Rwanda, incorporates the concept of reconciliation in laying out the goals of the court.

10. Laurel E. Fletcher and Harvey M. Weinstein, "Violence and Social Repair: Rethinking the Contribution of Justice to Reconciliation," *Human Rights Quarterly* 24 (2002): 573–639.

11. Pumla Gobodo-Madizekela, "Remorse, Forgiveness, and Rehumanization: Stories from South Africa," *Journal of Humanistic Psychology* 42 (2002): 7–32.

12. Debra Kaminer, Dan J. Stein, Irene Mbangh, and Nompumelelo Zungu–Dirwayi, "Forgiveness: Toward an Integration of Theoretical Models," *Psychiatry* 63 (2000):344–357.

13. Desmond Tutu, *No Future Without Forgiveness* (New York: Doubleday, 1999).

14. Charles Villa-Vincencio and Wilhelm Verwoerd, *Looking Back, Reaching Forward: Reflections on the Truth and Reconciliation Commission of South Africa* (London: Zed Books, 2000).

15. John Paul Lederach, *Building Peace: Sustainable Reconciliation in Divided Societies* (Washington, D.C.: United States Institute of Peace Press, 1997).

16. Inger Agger, "Psychosocial Assistance During Ethno-political Warfare in the Former Yugoslavia." In D. Chiron and M. E. P. Seligman, eds. *Ethnopolitical Warfare: Causes, Consequences, and Possible Solutions* (Washington, D.C.: American Psychological Association, 2001), 305–318.

17. Krishna Kumar, *Rebuilding Societies After Civil War: Critical Roles for International Assistance* (Boulder: Lynne Rienner, Publishers, 1997).

18. Herbert Kelman and V. Lee Hamilton, *Crimes of Obedience: Toward a Social Psychology of Authority and Responsibility* (New Haven:Yale University Press, 1989).

19. Miles Hewstone and Ed Cairns, "Social Psychology and Intergroup Conflict." In D. Chiron and M. E. P. Seligman, eds. *Ethnopolitical Warfare: Causes, Consequences, and Possible Solutions* (Washington, D.C.: American Psychological Association, 2001), 319–342.

20. John Turner and Riina Onorato, "Social Identity, Personality, and the Self-Concept: A Self-Categorization Perspective." In T. Tyler, R. M. Kramer, and O. John, eds. *The Psychology of the Social Self* (Mahwah, N.J.: Lawrence Erlbaum Associates, Publishers, 1999), 11–46.

21. Anthony Oberschall, "From Ethnic Cooperation to Violence and War in Yugoslavia." In D. Chiron and M. E. P. Seligman, eds. *Ethnopolitical Warfare*, 119–150.

22. Daniel Bar-Tal, "The Nature of Reconciliation." In *A Conference on Truth, Justice, and Reconciliation: Proceedings* (Stockholm: Stockholm International Forum, 2002), 19.

23. Robert Gardner, "Stereotypes as Consensual Beliefs." In Mark Zanna and James Olson, eds. *The Psychology of Prejudice: The Ontario Symposium* Vol. VII (Hillsdale, N.J.: Lawrence Erlbaum Associates, Inc., 1994), 1.

24. Jennifer Llewellyn and Robert Howse, "Restorative Justice – A Conceptual Framework, 2002," Law Commission of Ottawa available on World Wide Web at http://www.lcc.gc.ca/en/themes/sr/rj/howse/howse_main.asp.

25. Fletcher and Weinstein, "Violence and Social Repair."

26. Gesine Schwan, "The role of education in German–Polish reconciliation." In *A Conference on Truth, Justice, and Reconciliation: Proceedings* (Stockholm: Stockholm International forum, 2002), 180.

27. Jodi Halpern, *From Detached Concern to Empathy: Humanizing Medical Practice* (New York: Oxford University Press, 2001).

28. Ibid.

29. Tone Bringa, *Being Muslim the Bosnian Way: Identity and Community in a Central Bosnian Village* (Princeton, N.J.: Princeton University Press, 1995).

30. Mirko Tepavac, "Tito: 1945–1980." In Jasminka Udovicki and James Ridgeway, eds. *Burn This House: The Making and Unmaking of Yugoslavia* (Durham: Duke University Press,1997), 64–79.

31. Elizabeth Neuffer, *The Key to my Neighbor's House: Seeking Justice in Bosnia and Rwanda* (New York: Picador, 2001).

32. Slavenka Drakulic, *The Balkan Express: Fragments From The Other Side of War* (New York and London: W. W. Norton & Company, 1993).

33. Miklos Biro et al., "Social Values, Attitudes, and Reconciliation in the Post-War Communities of the former Yugoslavia." Paper presented at the *6th International Conference for Health and Human Rights*, Cavtat, Croatia, June 2001. Phong Pham et al, "Trauma Experience, PTSD, and Their Relationship with Attitudes Toward Justice and Reconciliation Among Different Ethnic Groups in Rwanda." Paper presented at the *Annual Meeting of the American Public Heath Association*, November 2002. Harvey Weinstein, "Convening

Speech." Presented at the *6th International Conference for Health and Human Rights*, Cavtat, Croatia, June 2001.

34. Gordon Allport, *The Nature of Prejudice* (Cambridge, Mass.: Addison-Wesley Publishing Company, 1954).
35. Priscilla Hayner, *Unspeakable Truths: Confronting State Terror and Atrocity* (New York and London: Routledge, 2001).
36. Ibid.
37. Pumla Gobodo-Madizekela, "Remorse, Forgiveness and Rehumanization."
38. Laurel E. Fletcher and Harvey Weinstein, "When Students Lose Perspective: Clinical Supervision and the Limits of Empathy," *Clinical Law Review* 9:1 (2002): 135–156.

Conclusion: a common objective, a universe of alternatives

Eric Stover and Harvey M. Weinstein

> Don't tell us
> how to love, don't tell us
> how to grieve, or what
> to grieve for, or how loss
> shouldn't sit down like a gray
> bundle of dust in the deepest
> pockets of our energy, don't laugh at our belief
> that money isn't
> everything, don't tell us
> how to behave in
> anger, in longing, in loss, in home-
> sickness, don't tell us,
> dear friends.
>
> Mary Oliver[1]

This book set out to explore how communities rebuild themselves after war and mass atrocity, and what contributions, if any, criminal trials make to that process. So, what have we learned?

First, our studies suggest that there is no direct link between criminal trials (international, national, and local/traditional) and reconciliation, although it is possible this could change over time. In fact, we found criminal trials – and especially those of local perpetrators – often divided small multi-ethnic communities by causing further suspicion and fear. Survivors rarely, if ever, connected retributive justice with reconciliation. Reconciliation, in their eyes, was mostly a personal matter to be settled between individuals. When speaking about reconciliation, survivors often spoke of post-war encounters with past friends or colleagues from other ethnic groups, and only occasionally did they speak of reconciliation in the larger, collective sense of involving all members of an ethnic group.

Second, for survivors of ethnic war and genocide the idea of "justice" encompasses more than criminal trials and the *ex cathedra* pronouncements of foreign judges in The Hague and Arusha. It means returning stolen property; locating and identifying the bodies of the missing; capturing and trying *all* war criminals, from the garden-variety killers in

323

their communities all the way up to the nationalist ideologues who had poisoned their neighbors with ethnic hatred; securing reparations and apologies; leading lives devoid of fear; securing meaningful jobs; providing their children with good schools and teachers; and helping those traumatized by atrocities to recover.

Third, there is no direct link between exposure to trauma and a desire for trials of suspected war criminals. It is colored by previous relationships with members of the opposing group, the types of trial that are contemplated, and other social factors. Similarly, the association between trauma and openness to reconciliation is also affected by such factors as prior relationships. This finding calls into question claims that trials have some kind of "therapeutic value" and can provide a sense of "closure" to those most traumatized by war and mass atrocity. Indeed, such people may find it too painful to follow the progress of trials. Or, as we found in Rwanda, may not even be aware that trials are taking place at all.

Fourth, social reconstruction after ethnic conflict is a slow process that occurs at multiple levels – individual, community, and state – and is heavily influenced by social identity, fear, collective memory, governmental policies, security and protection, and past experience with the international community. A corollary finding suggests that reconciliation will only begin to take hold in divided communities once the societal context allows for and promotes social interaction between ethnic groups. In this context, individuals may be ready to be reconciled but feel inhibited from doing so because of pressures from their own ethnic group not to associate beyond their "kith and kin." Our findings suggest that support for rekindling old friendships is an important first step that may eventually shift the balance for the wider community from active avoidance of "the other" to engagement. Influential opinion-makers such as the media are critical in shaping individual and group receptivity to social reconstruction and reconciliation. Similarly, outsiders such as international aid agencies and humanitarian organizations can facilitate this process, so long as their interventions are based on the expressed needs of community members. Fifth, attention to public education and the teaching of history and literature are critical. If future genocidal wars are to be prevented, the young must learn critical thinking about the causes of the recent wars and the nature of stereotyping, tolerance, and human rights. Often considered as an afterthought or looked at in a piecemeal fashion, school reform must be considered an integral part of social rebuilding in order to prevent denial and ethnic stereotyping by future generations. Education of people about the events that led to the violence is a critical factor in confronting any myth of "collective innocence."

Finally, greater attention needs to be paid to the economic and social well-being of post-war communities. Our informants told us that jobs, food, adequate and secure housing, good schooling for their children, and peace and security were their major priorities. This finding suggests that creating incentives as basic as starting a food cooperative or a community health clinic can help survivors and their divided communities put aside their ethnocentrism and work toward larger civic goals.

No overarching theory can explain why individuals and communities descend into mass violence, or divine how they will reconcile their differences. At best, we can create ecological models of social reconstruction informed by multiple theories and by the views and opinions of those most affected by war and atrocity. Such models must be flexible and be able to draw on several different forms of ethnic conflict but still address the particulars of each conflict. The model we present below should provide helpful guidelines for designing social reconstruction projects in varied post-war settings, but it should not be viewed as prescriptive. Nor do we mean to suggest that a one-size-fits-all approach to social reconstruction will cure the manifold problems faced by post-war communities. Indeed, in the face of enormous and unspeakable human loss and suffering, all our endeavors must always be tempered by pragmatism and humility.

An ecological model of social reconstruction

In the August 2002 issue of *Human Rights Quarterly*,[2] Laurel Fletcher and Harvey Weinstein presented an ecological model of social reconstruction for post-war countries that have experienced extreme forms of interethnic violence, including genocide and ethnic cleansing. Drawing on research by developmental and community psychologists, Fletcher and Weinstein suggest that social change in post-war countries must be mindful of the interrelationships and dependencies that exist between and among individuals, institutions, and community and societal groupings.

Anchored to this ecological model, social reconstruction should consist of programs that promote justice, democracy, economic prosperity and transformation, and reconciliation.[3] Critical to the development of these programs is the recognition that change in one part of a system causes reactions throughout the entire system. Consequently, those who initiate systemic change in post-war societies, whether it be the introduction of criminal trials of suspected war criminals or the development of a new history curriculum for high school students, must anticipate how each new intervention or policy will affect other parts of the system.

Social reconstruction is comprised of several intrinsic features and conditions. First, to work effectively (and democratically), social reconstruction must be informed, where appropriate, by population-based data that reflect the opinions, attitudes, and needs of all sectors of a society. Unfortunately, as we found in Rwanda and the former Yugoslavia, most international aid agencies and their national counterparts forgo collecting and analyzing population data prior to launching social reconstruction projects because they lack the appropriate expertise, or consider data collection too time-consuming, or fear it will cause friction among former belligerents. As a result, millions of dollars were wasted in these countries on ill-conceived projects that failed to meet the basic needs of those most affected by the violence.

Second, social reconstruction commences at varying times for different sectors of society. An individual's receptivity to social change, for example, may vary or be wholly absent depending on his or her experiences of war, exposure to trauma, and economic status, as well as whether he or she was a perpetrator, accomplice, victim, or bystander. Similarly, some segments of communities, hardwired to their nationalist ideologies, may never be receptive to change, while others may begin to go down the path to cross-ethnic engagement once a small factory or new school is opened in their neighborhood. Social change can never be forced, which is often a problem when the international community is involved. Too often, the foreign governments and aid agencies want quick solutions in post-war countries and are unwilling to invest in slow-paced developmental projects, such as education and economic development, that generate no immediate outcomes. Finally, efforts to impose fixed ideologies of democracy or capitalism can backfire if introduced at the wrong time or in cultures that have different value structures or forms of governance.

Third, social reconstruction will be most effective when implemented by an authority that is viewed as legitimate by its target audience. In this sense, social repair brings with it the baggage of history. Even though it is years since the fighting ended, many Rwandans, Serbs, Croats, and Bosniaks still view the international community, and particularly the United Nations (UN), with suspicion either because it failed to intervene to stop the war and carnage or because it supported – through UN declarations and public statements – the opposing side. Governments in post-war countries can also manipulate their citizenry to either accept or reject international criminal courts or international projects aimed at social reconstruction, as can nationalist parties and leaders that hold sway over segments of the population.

Fourth, social reconstruction will be influenced by the legacies of past regimes. Post-war countries emerging from Communism will have to deal with passivity, obedience to and dependence on authority, in-group favoritism, powerlessness based on membership of the Party, corruption, and the exposure of long-held myths. Likewise, post-colonial countries must deal with the legacy of colonial attitudes and discriminatory laws that often favored some groups over others, created a sense of powerlessness, and stifled opportunities for individual or group advancement. These historical and social facts influence the way in which societies perceive and grapple with social change.

Fifth, social reconstruction must work synergistically, with no single component aspiring to address all the needs of a post-war society.[4] This means that while a successor state or other steward attends to basic security, it must also find ways to return refugees and the internally displaced to their homes, restore freedom of expression, build a consensus about or at least a way of discussing the historical record, punish perpetrators, honor the memory of the missing and the dead, create economic opportunities, educate youth about the rights and responsibilities of an open and democratic society, and create or support community-based programs that foster cross-ethnic engagement.

Sixth, social reconstruction must engage all levels of society – the individual, community, society, and state – though, undoubtedly, at different periods of time and in different ways. At the individual level, psychological interventions can help those most affected by the war cope with trauma. At the level of community, there is a need to re-establish pre-war social and economic networks, as well as create new relationships within and outside of one's own ethnic group, with the primary aim of restoring trust. At the societal level, common civic and economic goals need to be established that reach beyond the self-interest of ethnic groups. Finally, the rule of law must be established at the state level to protect the rights of *all* individuals and to demonstrate that known rules, and not force, will be used to judge the actions of individual citizens.

Any ecological model of social reconstruction must be contextualized to adapt to each unique post-war setting and the availability of resources. As Hans-Jörg Geiger, who directed the federal office opening access to the files of the East German secret police, puts it: "Every system, every time has its own special situation – even as far as the reasons for human rights violations are concerned . . . it's more important to look for the correct way to reckon with each past separately rather than to develop a theoretical system."[5] However, what the ecological model does is to emphasize the interrelatedness of all steps, no matter where in the system the intervention occurs or when the particular step is taken. Each decision, each policy, has consequences, both expected and untoward. The challenge is to monitor and respond to these while seeing the whole picture.

Our studies suggest that social reconstruction in the aftermath of collective violence must consist of the following components: (1) security; (2) freedom of movement; (3) the rule of law; (4) access to accurate and unbiased information; (5) justice; (6) education for democracy; (7) economic development; and (8) cross-ethnic engagement.

Security

In the aftermath of war, successor governments and other stewards of power face the task of restoring peace and stability. Yet establishing security after armed conflict is not always a straightforward and predictable process. While this dilemma was apparent in the Balkans and in Rwanda, nowhere in recent times has it been more evident than in post-war Iraq, where US forces entered and occupied the country in 2003 without a clear plan for restoring peace and security. As a result, Iraq has been racked by severe instability, resulting in excessive civilian casualties and widespread looting of hospitals, museums, schools, power plants, nuclear facilities, government buildings, and other infrastructure. Instability has delayed other facets of social reconstruction, including the restoration of basic services and the rebuilding of the country's health and judicial systems, and, ultimately, tarnished the legitimacy of the US occupation in the eyes of many Iraqis.[6] Without the physical and institutional reconstruction that underlies the rebuilding of a country, efforts at social repair will always be undermined; social and physical reconstruction are inherently interrelated and must proceed apace.

Freedom of movement

The free movement of people, goods, and information in post-war countries is critical. First, it allows refugees and the internally displaced to return to their homes and begin to take control over their lives and reconnect with former neighbors and colleagues. In some cases, refugee return will need to be delayed until the environment is safe from land mines and other unexploded munitions and until procedures are in place for resolving property disputes. Refugees may themselves fear returning home if suspected war criminals still walk the streets and hold positions of authority. Such obstacles demonstrate why it is important to adopt an ecological model of social reconstruction that promotes multiple interventions, including criminal trials.

Second, the return of refugees to their homes can have salutary psychological benefits. "The greatest justice for me," a refugee told one of our researchers, "would be to let me live and die in peace there where I was born." Home, as this refugee suggests, can be a site of great attachment, a place of security, and the point to which we set our personal compass. But war and mass displacement can also turn homes into sites of ambivalence. Some refugees find the shock of returning to their war-blasted homes – and to the memories they once held – too great to bear. Others have forged new lives for themselves and their children, and may not wish to return. Still others, mired in the nullity of a refugee camp or the isolation of a foreign land, feel powerless and directionless without their homes. In the wake of mass violence, refugees often are compelled to return to their home communities to search for family members who have disappeared. Whatever the necessity or motivation, refugee return after an ethnic war, though difficult and at times harrowing, can be a formative step toward social repair and reconciliation.

Finally, the free movement of people, goods, and information can bring economic benefits to post-war countries. Refugee return can shift the financial burden from supporting refugee camps, which are largely non-productive, to state-building. Similarly, the free movement of goods and information can stimulate commerce and economic development.

The rule of law

Like security, the rule of law is the glue that holds the process of social reconstruction together. Without it, social programs can turn despotic, favoring certain individuals and groups over others. To be effective, the rule of law must be institutionalized at every level of society. Court systems must be rebuilt, legal reforms passed, prosecutors, judges, and law enforcement officers trained, and rules of procedure and evidence adopted. Often, this process requires international interventions, including training programs and resources which, if not handled sensitively, can undermine good intentions.

The rule of law consists of three components. The first is the development and administration of a fair system of justice where individuals can be heard both in accusation and in defense. The second is the intent to treat each individual in light of particular, demonstrated evidence. And the third is the commitment to redress for past harms within the framework of pre-existing norms. The rule of law, writes Martha Minow, a professor of law at Harvard Law School, means, "no one is above or outside the law, and no one should be legally condemned or sanctioned outside legal procedures. The rule of law creates a community in which each member is both fenced in and protected by the law and its institutions."[7]

Re-establishing the rule of law, however, can be problematic, especially when undertaken by outsiders who lack a sound knowledge of local legal traditions, customs, and politics in a post-war country. Fletcher and Weinstein describe in Chapter 1 of this volume how a large-scale international effort to reform Bosnia's judicial system in 1999 offended many of the very people they were trying to help. Many Bosnian judges and prosecutors they interviewed were "angry and confused over the criticisms by international lawyers who did not appear to understand the legal tradition of civil law countries or, if they did, were perceived as showing disrespect for the judicial system to which Bosnian legal professionals were devoted."[8] Prior to the war, these judges and prosecutors were people of stature – community leaders with means and position. Having lost their homes, family members, and friends, they had little else to cling to but their professional identities. Thus, they perceived criticism of the Bosnian judicial system as attacks on their own professional integrity and competence.

Fletcher and Weinstein believe many of these ill-feelings could have been avoided had the internationals undertaking these educational interventions taken the time to ascertain the views of Bosnian legal professionals regarding the professional capacity and problems of their judicial system. Such an approach would not only have better informed the internationalists about the Bosnian judicial system, it would have also actively engaged Bosnian legal professionals in the process of institutional change. The lesson learned here is that foreign ideas, even if theoretically sound, must be bought into and owned by those they will affect. Otherwise, they will be resisted and possibly rejected.

Post-war countries must create judicial systems that treat victims and witnesses of mass atrocity with dignity and respect. In Chapter 5 of this volume, Stover notes that victims of crime must be regarded as *active and engaged participants in* – not merely *auxiliaries to* – the criminal justice system. This means creating a "rights-based approach" that provides victims and witnesses with adequate protective measures; keeps them informed of developments in their cases, including details about the progress of the case and the offender's status; and treats them with dignity at all times. As Stover's study suggests, those victims who are respected fare better in court, and are more inclined to encourage others to testify. And, as rights-bearing agents, they are in a better position to regain control over their lives and influence the events that impinge on them as they pass through the criminal justice system.

Access to accurate and unbiased information

For social reconstruction to take hold in post-war societies, people must have access to accurate and unbiased information. This conclusion is reflected in all our studies in Rwanda and the former Yugoslavia. But what constitutes "accurate and unbiased information," especially in the face of the post-modernist argument that such a term is highly suspicious, insofar as most information, and especially that generated in the aftermath of war and mass atrocity, is by its very nature biased and often inaccurate?

While we accept the ambiguity of the term, we propose that the ecological model can potentially establish norms and standards for determining what constitutes accurate information, while it creates a climate where ideas can be freely debated.

Yet creating an environment of open debate and discussion in a post-war society is an enormous challenge. To begin with, war, and especially ethnic war, is antithetical to truth. As we have seen, both the power and wartime tactics of Slobodan Milosevic in Serbia, Franjo Tudjman in Croatia, and the extremist Hutu in Rwanda were intrinsically tied to their censorship of the press and total control of radio and television. To generate fear and war hysteria, Serbian and Croatian television stations showed footage of war atrocities by the other side that was likely to have been taken from their side, or even from films about the Second World War. All sides used attacks (and mutual recriminations of blame) on cultural monuments, on civilians in breadlines, on wedding and funeral parties, on busloads of orphans, and on international troops to mobilize sympathies and hostility at home and abroad.[9]

Similarly, over a four-month period in 1994, Hutu extremists used a radio station and several newspapers to mobilize Hutu against the Tutsi, who were massacred at churches, schools, hospitals, and roadblocks. In a judgment against three Hutu defendants, issued by the Arusha Tribunal in December 2003, the court detailed how one of the accused had turned the hugely popular RTLM station into a messenger of death. "What RTLM did," the court quoted a trial witness as saying, "was to spread petrol throughout the country little by little, so that one day it would be able to set fire to the whole country." The judges found that one newspaper owned by another defendant relentlessly denigrated the Tutsi by suggesting on its cover that the machete was the best way to deal with them.[10]

Ethnic and nationalist extremists often find it in their interest to perpetuate the same distortions, lies, and myth-making in times of peace that gained them power during war. Likewise, their followers often cling to these mendacities because they too have profited from war or because they fear that confronting the truth about the crimes committed by their own ethnic group will shatter their sense of victimhood. Whatever the reason, the perpetuation of a distorted past leads to denial which, in turn, inhibits the ability of individuals and communities to recognize and to take responsibility for the crimes committed in their name.

Memories of wartime atrocities, like all memories, are embedded in the psyche of individuals and, through the process of retelling and memorialization, are deposited – often, in distorted ways – into the collective memory of a community. In Chapters 9 and 10 in this volume, Biro and Longman and their colleagues report that when so-called "impartial" or "objective" outsiders, such as an international criminal tribunal, try to recast these localized memories to fit a larger truth, they will be ignored or viewed with suspicion by many – if not most – local residents.[11] The Yugoslav Tribunal has convened four trials focusing on the village of Ahmici in central Bosnia, where Bosnian Croat troops killed over one hundred Muslim civilians on April 16, 1993. Despite over a dozen Bosnian Croat defendants, ranging from foot soldiers to high-ranking military and civilian leaders, and a factual record numbering tens of thousands of pages of trial transcripts and numerous guilty verdicts, the information generated by these trials has not transformed the way in which Croats in the village interpret what happened on that fateful day over ten years ago. Ahmici remains a divided village, where Croat and Muslim neighbors remember and mourn their dead separately.[12]

Factual information alone cannot erase localized memories of war and atrocity, but when it works in conjunction with other components of social reconstruction, including educational reform and development of the arts and humanities, it can, over generations, undermine the narcissism of collective victimhood found in many post-war communities. An accretion of accurate information about the past can limit the number of distortions and lies that can be told in public, and thus create a "collective acknowledgment" among ethnic groups that, despite their rhetoric, some facts will always be contested and challenged. In this context, educational reform is essential and must encompass two dimensions – curricular change and change in teaching methods. The first implies that students should learn to examine historical sources and debate the findings critically; the second suggests a shift in teaching strategies toward a more democratic classroom where student opinions are shared and listened to. Finally, in Chapter 13 in this volume Blotner reminds us that art is humanity's way of understanding its history, and we must remember history so as to try to nurture that which is positive and prevent that which is destructive.

Justice

The pursuit of justice and accountability in their various forms, including criminal and civil trials, truth commissions, lustration programs, and reparations, plays a fundamental and necessary role in the social reconstruction of post-war countries. Yet it is an illusion to suppose that international criminal tribunals, located hundreds of miles away from where the massacres took place, can forge a common version of the history of these conflicts that would be accepted by all sides. Even if the tribunals establish a factual record of what happened, they cannot contribute to national reconciliation if those most affected by the violence are unable or unwilling to recognize and internalize this record.

The reality is that the logic of law can never make sense of the logic of mass atrocity, or how survivors and perpetrators will interpret it.[13] This is especially true in post-conflict situations where survivors believe that the international community could have intervened to stop the violence but failed to do so. As our studies show, strictly legal interpretations of wartime atrocities, especially when they involve widespread and horrific crimes such as genocide and ethnic cleansing, rarely satisfy those who have been most affected by the violence. For many survivors, tribunal justice, with its complex and lengthy procedures and often low sentences, fails to palliate the injustice of losing family members and neighbors and of witnessing the destruction of their communities. Meanwhile, those who have been labeled perpetrators through the attribution of collective guilt often feel that they have been singled out for retribution based on their ethnicity, without any recognition of their own losses and suffering.

In Chapters 9 and 10 in this volume, Biro and Longman and their colleagues describe the complex relationship between survivors, their perceptions of criminal justice, and their openness to reconciliation. In Bosnia and Herzegovina and in Croatia, two principal factors influence a survivor's belief in the worth of trials. First, those survivors who had close pre-war friendships with members of the opposing group generally viewed trials more favorably. It may be that these individuals could more readily distinguish between individual and collective responsibility for past crimes because their prior relationships reminded them that not all Croats, or Serbs, or Bosniaks were necessarily wrongdoers, and that only those responsible for crimes should be punished. Second, recognition of the fact that members of one's own ethnic group committed war crimes led to more favorable attitudes toward trials. On the other hand, individuals who had experienced war trauma and had negative pre-war relationships with the opposing group were less open to reconciliation. In Rwanda, the experience of trauma and symptoms of post-traumatic stress disorder show different kinds of relationships with reconciliation, and these vary with the type and location of trials. While many see trials as important, they see many possible outcomes, and these beliefs are influenced by ethnicity. Importantly, one analysis finds few relationships between attitudes toward the various trials and openness to reconciliation. These quantitative studies illustrate the need for tempering assumptions or generalizations about the effect that trials may have on the process of reconciliation. Further, these relationships suggest that we must consider carefully the most appropriate judicial options, and recognize that any particular route will generate both positive and negative reactions depending upon ethnic group and war experience; each judicial choice affects the possibility of its contributing to reconciliation.

Finally, while our informants from Rwanda and the former Yugoslavia generally supported trials as a means of punishing the guilty, they viewed the *ad hoc* international tribunals as distant institutions that had little to do with their lives. Most Rwandans in our sample knew nothing or very little about the international tribunal in Arusha. Eighty-seven percent of 2,091 Rwandans we surveyed in 2002 were either "not well informed" or "not informed at all" about the work of the international tribunal in Arusha. Similarly, in our survey of 1,624 residents of Croatia and of Bosnia and Herzegovina, a significant number of Serbs and Croats expressed strong resentment toward the Hague Tribunal largely because they were convinced that the court was biased against their national group. In their 1999 study of Bosnian judges and prosecutors, conducted three years after the end of the war, Fletcher and Weinstein found that most of their interview subjects, no matter their national group, did not "accept the record of the war" established by the Hague Tribunal and saw the court's prosecutions "as proof of the [tribunal's] failure to understand and accurately reflect the experience of their national group."[14] Rather than conform to the views of the tribunal's verdicts, the jurists pointed "to divergences between the 'truth' as they 'know' it and as reflected in the [tribunal's] record." Embracing the "collective victimhood" of their ethnic groups, these jurists were unwilling and unable to accept the Hague Tribunal's "objective" pronouncements of individual wrongdoing so long as it involved members of their own group.

It is often argued that justice, like the pursuit of rights, is a universal, a historic practice that exists above politics. But such positivist notions fail to recognize that courts, like all institutions, exist because of, not in spite of, politics. People and entire communities can interpret a tribunal's decisions, procedures (modes and manner of investigation, selection of cases, timing of trials, types and severity of punishment), and even its very existence in a variety of ways. In their study of the Yugoslav Tribunal's investigation of mass graves in Kosovo and near the Bosnian town of Sarajevo (Chapter 4 in this volume), Stover and Shigekane found that these communities had grown distrustful of the tribunal because it was unable and unwilling to conduct large-scale forensic efforts to identify the remains of *all* of the deceased.

Similarly, in Rwanda, following two controversial incidents at the international tribunal in Arusha in 2001, several survivor organizations called on their members to stop participating as prosecution witnesses in trials before the court. In the first incident, the survivor organizations condemned the tribunal after a stunning revelation that the court had unknowingly employed a Hutu defense investigator who was a high-level genocide suspect. In the second incident, the survivor organizations accused a panel of judges of unprofessional conduct after laughing during the cross-examination of a Tutsi rape victim. Although these incidents drew little international attention, they became front-page news in Rwanda and continued to be scrutinized by the local media for more than a year.[15]

Criminal trials in the wake of mass atrocity are inevitably limited and symbolic: a few war criminals stand for a much larger group of guilty. Nor do trials address the responsibility of those who, swept along by group emotion or solidarity, participated at the margins – looting, taunting, or profiting from the misfortune of their neighbors – or of those who did nothing to stop or mitigate the violence, the so-called "innocent bystanders." Thus, what is billed as individual justice actually becomes a *de facto* form of collective innocence that exonerates the far larger number of individuals who were indirectly responsible for the physical, social, and psychological destruction of their communities.

For justice to play a meaningful role in post-war reconstruction it must be comprised of several elements. First, to the extent possible, it should be a consultative process that incorporates the views and opinions of those most affected by the violence. Whenever possible, the consultative process should begin early, either during the conflict or soon after the end of hostilities. Second, whatever mechanism of justice is pursued, there should be clarity about its goals and processes. Those who establish such mechanisms must be careful, especially in the initial establishment phase, not to project unrealistic expectations of what justice can accomplish. Third, whenever possible, the pursuit of justice should involve both international and local mechanisms. International bodies should provide financial support for the establishment of community outreach and educational programs. One aim of such programs should be to prevent the manipulation and distortion of justice by nationalist extremists. Fourth, mechanisms must be established to address the indirect complicity of bystanders in genocide and ethnic cleansing so as to dispel the myth of collective innocence and avoid the possibility of future cycles of violence. If this acknowledgment does not occur, history may be rewritten, as we saw in the former Yugoslavia after the Second World War – a development that helped lay the foundation for the tragic events of the 1990s.[16] Finally, the pursuit of post-war accountability must also encompass social justice. As noted throughout this volume, many of the people we interviewed chafed at a definition of justice that focused solely on the punishment of suspected war criminals. Instead, they said that justice had to include an array of social and economic rights for the persecuted, including the right to live where they wanted and to move about freely and without fear; the right to have the bodies of loved ones returned for proper burial; the right to have meaningful and secure jobs; the right to send their children to decent schools; and the right to receive adequate treatment for psychological trauma.

Education for democracy

No one, of course, knows how to deter genocide or mass violence. But there are ways in which we can prevent it from taking root in a society. It is important to consider the historical role of education in fostering both nationalism and democracy. As Anthony Smith[17] has emphasized, the nation is not invented out of thin air, but rather draws from pre-existing religious and ethnic sentiments to inculcate a spirit of self-sacrifice and a mass standardization of outlook, largely through the education of the young in literature, history, and geography. The emergence of mass public education is widely recognized as central to the development of modern nations and nationalism.

One of the primary ways that education facilitates nation-building is by constructing an "official memory" of past events. While this can be subverted to meet the needs of a repressive regime, it can also be used positively to teach critical thinking about past events. One of the best means to do so is through the teaching of democracy and tolerance. One of the leaders in this field is the US-based organization, Facing History and Ourselves, which develops curricular materials and teacher-training sessions for high schools and middle schools around the United States, and increasingly with similar programs in other countries, to build teachers' capacities to teach about the conditions that led to the Holocaust and more recent genocides and about the human potential for responding to early signs of intergroup violence and abuse.[18] The organization's founder, Margot Strom, writes that educational programs should teach "that history is largely the result of human decisions, that prevention is possible, and that education must have a moral component if it is to make a difference."[19]

It is also important, however, to recall that efforts to construct official memory through mass education have not always been effective. Wolfgang Hoepken argues that Tito's effort to construct a collective memory of the Second World War in Yugoslav schools generated a gap between the "hushed history" remembered privately at home or among one's ethnic group and the "official history" espoused in public fora. According to Hoepken, the imposition of this official memory left "niches where 'subversive' memories could take root, which under circumstances of political disintegration and economic and social crisis became vulnerable to manipulation."[20]

In Chapters 11 and 12 in this volume, Freedman and her colleagues, in their studies of public education and social reconstruction in post-war Rwanda and the former Yugoslavia, confirm Strom's notion that the teaching of history should move beyond blame and denial. Rather than substituting one propaganda for another, they argue that education after war and mass atrocity should: (1) help young people think critically and independently about a contested past; (2) allow for open and free debate about facts and their interpretations; (3) teach civic and cultural values, including respect for human rights and dignity, tolerance of diversity, and the need for forgiveness; (4) help students come to terms with both their social (ethnic, religious, cultural, racial) and civic (citizenship) identities; (5) provide young people with a multi-disciplinary perspective on the world derived from literature, philosophy, ethics, art, history, and the physical and social sciences; (6) be developed through a process of consultation with parents, teachers, and students; and (7) be given priority, along with security, justice, refugee return, human rights, and economic development in negotiating peace accords and treaties.

Equal access to education opportunities is crucial for promoting social unity in post-war countries. Yet, as we found in Rwanda and the former Yugoslavia, numerous barriers in certain regions of these countries are preventing children from attending school or receiving the best education possible. In Rwanda, only one out of five children ever goes beyond secondary school. This means they are losing the opportunity not only of learning new life skills but also of being exposed to a larger universe of ideas. Meanwhile, most Croat and Serb children in the Croatian city of Vukovar and Bosniak and Croat children in the Bosnian city of Mostar attend schools or classrooms separated by ethnicity. Without social contact with children of other ethnic groups, these children run the risk of never moving beyond their wartime prejudices. Segregated schools and classrooms also place a heavy burden on members of other national minorities, as well as children of mixed marriage, who must choose whether to attend Croat, Bosniak, or Serb classes. While we recognize the dilemma for countries that attempt to balance minority rights with the need to inculcate a civic identity, in our view school segregation based on ethnicity or race is anathema to social reconstruction and reconciliation in post-war countries, and should be avoided.

Economic development

Ethnic war usually results in extensive damage to a country's economic infrastructure. Witness Bosnia and Herzegovina, where land mines and unexploded ordnance left many parts of the country uninhabitable, and where fighting damaged or destroyed a third of all homes and completely decimated the country's industrial, agricultural, and telecommunications sectors, causing the gross domestic product (GDP) to plummet from US $2,429 per capita in 1990 to US $500 per capita in 1995.[21] The per capita GDP in Croatia, formerly the second-richest of the former Yugoslav republics, dropped from US $5,438 in 1990 to US $4,402 in 1996.[22] These figures only hint at the war's devastating effect on small business owners, tradesmen, and farmers, who often become obscured by such figures.

Our informants in the Balkans returned again and again to the loss of employment as a significant barrier to social reconstruction. Idle men not only feel powerless to provide for their families, particularly in a patriarchal society, but also may turn to alcohol or domestic violence, or become depressed as the empty days stretch ahead. Both men and women suggested that reconciliation would only proceed apace when people were again in the workplace, interacting with each other in commercial transactions. As Ajdukovic and Corkalo point out in Chapter 14 in this volume, the restoration of interethnic relationships after war and mass atrocity usually develops in stages – first in an impersonal, task-oriented manner, then perhaps with coffee together while at work, leading ultimately to socialization in the home. Secure jobs in a multi-ethnic workplace can help move people from one stage to the next.

In Rwanda, a profoundly impoverished land to begin with, our studies showed that perceptions of improved economic conditions were strongly associated with positive attitudes toward Rwandan trials and gacaca, support for community, and opposition to violence. At the same time, as Longman and his colleagues report in Chapter 10 in this volume, 46.1 percent of their Rwandan respondents disagreed and 17.1 percent strongly disagreed with the statement: "Reconciliation will not happen without the alleviation of poverty." This suggests that while economic advancement appears to be related to the rebuilding of Rwandan society, the parameters of that relationship have yet to be determined. Our conclusion is that the well-being of a country after ethnic violence is strongly influenced by the ability of people to live productive lives and provide for their families; how this process relates to reconciliation is a fruitful area for further research.

Cross-ethnic engagement

Social repair requires that people reach across ethnic lines to seek engagement. In Rwanda, this is essential, since former enemies live together; in the Balkans, a relatively segregated society has emerged in many countries. Allport's "contact hypothesis," referred to in the Introduction and Chapter 9 of this volume, suggests that, under certain conditions, engagement with "the other" is the only way to move beyond an in-group/out-group mentality. So far, this effort in the former Yugoslavia has been confined to the work of NGOs, which use conflict resolution mechanisms to increase interaction between ethnic groups. This is a good start, but success may be limited to defined settings and time periods in which the processes are undertaken. The larger social context must be targeted simultaneously for sustainable change to occur. If people leave these encounters and return to their home communities where cross-ethnic engagement is not tolerated, then the process of social repair will be stymied. Given the loss of trust and the sense of betrayal described in Chapter 14, mechanisms of repair must work at multiple levels.

Similarly, efforts to rehumanize perceptions of former enemies through empathy-building can take place only through consistent contact and the reawakening of memories shared by old friends from different ethnic groups. Piecemeal attempts to do this are doomed to failure – contact is so important that strategies to encourage relationships must be moved from the category of "psychosocial" interventions, which are recognized but not often given the due they deserve, to that of "development," an objective more supported by international funding. If the goal of the international community is social reconstruction, and reconciliation in particular, then time and money must be invested in studying and developing these mechanisms. Until we recognize the limitations of legal mechanisms and the need to promote self-efficacy post-conflict, we will be missing significant opportunities to facilitate social repair.

Future research

This book is a first attempt to examine, in a systematic way, the interplay of post-war justice and social reconstruction in societies that have experienced severe and widespread collective violence. Hopefully, doors have been opened and many comfortable, and perhaps well-meaning, assumptions about the "miracle-working" powers of justice and reconciliation have been exorcised. That said, our findings are by no means sacrosanct and should be widely tested to see whether they are valid in similar settings and whether commonalities exist, and if not, why not. This, in turn, can help us to develop and deepen a vocabulary for assessing and developing more effective responses to societal-level atrocities.

More specifically, we need to develop empirical tools for defining and measuring reconciliation and how it unfolds at the individual, community, and societal level. Does civil society aid or impede reconciliation? Are traditional, locally based accountability mechanisms, such as truth commissions and gacaca trials, or "hybrid courts" comprised of foreign and national judges and prosecutors, better able to promote reconciliation than international trials?

More needs to be learned about how trauma and economic growth affect attitudes about justice and reconciliation. What can be done to help large segments of a population cope with trauma and overcome despondency? Are individual models of trauma, such as post-traumatic stress disorder, the most useful in rebuilding societies? How effective are microcredit projects and social action funds as instruments of social repair? And what does it take to pull divided communities out of the vicious circle of betrayal and denial? Implicit in these questions is the recognition of the importance of using the tools of many disciplines – demography, epidemiology, anthropology, political science, psychology, economics and others to test assumptions and to generate data that will assist policy-makers in reaching decisions that can have substantive effects.

In the meantime, we should apply the lessons we have learned. Creative ways need to be found of providing reparations for survivors. International and national courts need to establish outreach programs that inform the public about their work and develop more efficient protection and support measures for victims and witnesses. The International Committee of the Red Cross or another international organization needs to take on the task of training local forensic teams and overseeing the humanitarian exhumation of mass graves. Programs that build on prior social relationships can be initiated to overcome ethnic distance. Education reform must be made a high priority when providing international aid to post-war countries. And on-going study and evaluation should accompany all these efforts. Above all, the world community must do everything in its power to prevent future genocides. This requires moving upstream to prevent human calamities before they unfold in all their ugliness. It means staying the course and continuing to help post-war countries like Rwanda and Bosnia and Herzegovina build civil societies and democratic institutions that can reach through the morass of distortions, myths, and lies of the past and pull their divided communities out of the slipstream of denial. It demands the vision, as Ariel Dorfman writes so eloquently in the Preface to this volume, to create "a world where people die peacefully in their beds when their time has come, surrounded by the friends of yesterday and the neighbors of tomorrow."

NOTES

1. Mary Oliver, "On Losing a House." In "Reimaging Place," *Michigan Quarterly Review* 40:1(winter 2001): 96.
2. Laurel E. Fletcher and Harvey M. Weinstein, "Violence and Social Repair: Rethinking the Contribution of Justice to Reconciliation," *Human Rights Quarterly* 24 (2002): 622.
3. Ibid., 623.
4. Ibid., 625.
5. See Hans-Jörg Geiger, "Consequences of Past Human Rights Violations: The Significance of the Stasi Files for Dealing with the East German Past." In Menard R. Rwelamira and Gerhard Werle, eds. *Confronting Past Injustices: Approaches to Amnesty, Punishment, Reparations and Restitution in South Africa and Germany* (Durban, South Africa: Butterworth, 1996), 41.
6. See Human Rights Watch, *Off Target: The Conduct of the War and Civilian Casualties in Iraq*, December 2003.
7. Martha Minow, *Between Vengeance and Forgiveness: Facing History after Genocide and Mass Violence* (Boston: Beacon Press, 1998), 25.
8. See the Human Rights Center, University of California, Berkeley, the International Human Rights Law Clinic, University of California, Berkeley, and the Human Rights Center, University of Sarajevo, "Justice, Accountability, and Social Reconstruction: An Interview Study of Bosnian Judges and Prosecutors," *Berkeley Journal of International Law* 18:1 (2000): 142.
9. Susan L. Woodward, *Balkan Tragedy: Chaos and Dissolution After the Cold War* (Washington, D.C.: 1995), 230–236.
10. See Sharon LaFraniere, "Court Convicts 3 in 1994 Genocide Across Rwanda," *New York Times*, December 4, 2003.
11. See, for example, Michael Ignatieff, "Articles of Faith," *Index on Censorship* 5 (1996): 114.
12. Another contemporary example is the town of Jedwabne, Poland. On July 10, 1941, shortly after the Nazis occupied the town, hundreds of Jews from Jedwabne and the surrounding hamlets were assembled in the town square, where some were brutally killed while others were beaten and, finally, forced into a barn. Kerosene was then poured on the barn and it was set alight, burning more than 400 people. The story was nearly forgotten until 1999, when the historian Jan Gross assembled evidence that Jedwabne's pogrom was not, as local legend had it, the work of Polish townsmen acting on orders from occupying Nazi soldiers. Instead, documents and eyewitness accounts showed the Catholic Poles organized and carried out the massacre of their Jewish neighbors. Despite these findings, many of the town's Catholic residents, who claim Jedwabne's Jews had helped the Red Army deport Catholics to the East during the brief Soviet occupation of Jedwabne, deny that their forefathers were responsible for the massacre. See Jan T. Gross, *Neighbors: The Destruction of the Jewish Community in Jedwabne, Poland* (Princeton, N.J.:

Princeton University Press, 2001), and Peter S. Green, "Polish Town Still Tries to Forget Its Dark Past," *New York Times*, February 8, 2003.

13. See Lawrence L. Langer, *Admitting the Holocaust* (New York: Oxford University Press, 1995) and Hannah Arendt, *Eichmann in Jerusalem: A Report on the Banality of Evil* (Harmondsworth: Penguin Books, 1964).

14. Also, see Laurel E. Fletcher and Harvey M. Weinstein, "Violence and Social Repair."

15. See Victor Peskin, "Rwandan Ghosts," *Legal Affairs* (September/October 2002): 21–25.

16. Several scholars have noted the role that denial of past crimes played in the emergence of extreme nationalism and war in the former Yugoslavia following Tito's death in 1980. See, for example, Susan L. Woodward, *Balkan Tragedy: Chaos and Dissolution After the Cold War* (Washington, D.C.: the Brookings Institution, 1995), and Laura Silber and Allan Little, *Yugoslavia: Death of a Nation* (London: Penguin Books, 1997).

17. Anthony D. Smith, *Myths and Memories of the Nation* (Oxford: Oxford University Press, 1999), 154.

18. See Martha Minow, *Between Vengeance and Forgiveness*, 7.

19. Ibid.

20. Wolfgang Hoepken, "War, Memory, and Education in a Fragmented Society: The Case of Yugoslavia," *East European Politics and Societies* 13 (1999): 191.

21. See *Bosnia and Herzegovina: 1996–1998 Lessons and Accomplishments: Review of the Priority Reconstruction and Recovery Program and Looking Towards Sustainable Development.* Report prepared for the May 1999 Donors Conference hosted by the European Commission and the World Bank.

22. *Croatia at a Glance*, the World Bank Group, on World Wide Web at http://www.worldbank.org/data.

Index

CPSIA information can be obtained at www.ICGtesting.com
Printed in the USA
267685BV00003B/19/A